T0301615

Newspapers and newsmakers

The Dublin nationalist press in the mid-nineteenth century

Newspapers and newsmakers

The Dublin nationalist press in the mid-nineteenth century

Ann Andrews

LIVERPOOL UNIVERSITY PRESS

First published 2014 by
Liverpool University Press
4 Cambridge Street
Liverpool
L69 7ZU

British Library Cataloguing-in-Publication data
A British Library CIP record is available

ISBN 978-1-78138-142-7

Typeset in Adobe Garamond by Carnegie Book Production, Lancaster
Printed and bound by CPI Group (UK) Ltd, Croydon, CR0 4YY

Contents

List of Tables

Abbreviations

CSORP	Chief Secretary's Office Registered Papers
CUA	Catholic University of America
GAA	Gaelic Athletic Association
HCP	House of Commons Papers
IDA	Irish Democratic Association
IHS	Irish Historical Studies
IRB	Irish Republican Brotherhood
LA	Leading Article
NAI	National Archives of Ireland
NLI	National Library of Ireland
RA	Repeal Association
RIA	Royal Irish Academy
TCD	Trinity College Dublin
TNA	The National Archives, Kew
UIL	United Irish League

Acknowledgements

This book originated from a doctoral thesis completed in 2008. I wish to thank Dr John Stuart for his helpful comments on my thesis, while encouragement and support from Peter Beck, Emeritus Professor of International History at Kingston University, was invaluable. I was privileged to have the advice of D. George Boyce, the foremost historian of Irish nationalism, who was the main examiner of my PhD. Inspiration for my thesis particularly came from Emeritus Professor Penelope J. Corfield while I was working for a Masters degree at Royal Holloway, University of London. However, I am mostly indebted to Dr Sally Warwick-Haller, the main supervisor of my doctoral thesis, whose meticulous guidance was priceless. Many libraries in London are owed my thanks, particularly the British Library Newspaper Library, formerly at Colindale, where I spent many a Saturday for what seemed like years on end.* The British Library at St Pancras proved highly useful for my research, as did The University of London Library at Senate House and Kingston University Library. The National Archives at Kew in London also proved helpful. In Dublin, I am especially grateful to the National Archives of Ireland, the National Library of Ireland, the Manuscript Room at Trinity College and, not least, the Royal Irish Academy. Naturally, my family deserve much thanks for their support throughout my research.

* The British Library newspaper collection is now located at Boston Spa, Yorkshire, for original copies, and St Pancras for microfilm and digital copies.

Irish newspapers can now be sought online via membership of academic institutions or through commercial websites.

Introduction

DESPITE THE VAST AMOUNT of published works on nineteenth-century Irish history, its nationalist press is a comparatively little-researched area. In an attempt to remedy this omission, this book offers an insight into the impact of the Dublin nationalist press on the development of Irish nationalism between 1842 and 1867. Those responsible for what was written in these newspapers were actively involved in the Irish nationalist movement and were often the leading *dramatis personae* in the unfolding development of Irish nationalism: they not only compiled, reported and analysed news, but created it. This book focuses on nationalist newspapers in Dublin, where most of the nationalist leaders were located. It particularly highlights both the complex and paradoxical nature of Irish nationalism and the indissoluble conflict between peaceful and militant ideologies. Journalists who worked for the Dublin nationalist press in the mid-nineteenth century believed that their cause was just; many thought that it was spiritually elevated, that its pursuit was worth suffering for, and even at times worth dying for. This thinking formed part of the concept of romantic nationalism that was conveyed in their newspapers through powerful and emotive rhetoric. A period of the utmost importance in modern Irish history for the development of Irish nationalism, the mid-nineteenth century saw the creation of a new national identity, mass mobilizations, a challenge to the ruling Protestant elite, three rebellions, and the Great Famine that, apart from its horrors, accelerated social and economic changes in Irish society. It was indeed a time of upheaval, uncertainty, experiment, and much debate when, importantly, ideological foundations were laid that were to impact upon the destiny of the Irish nation.

While newspapers are invaluable as primary sources to support the research and writing of Irish history, it is surprising how few in-depth investigations have explored the relationship between newspapers and nationalism in the nineteenth century. A broad survey of newspapers in the late eighteenth and nineteenth century was conducted in 1911 by T.H.S. Escott, which includes a chapter on Irish political journalism.[1] Little was written on Ireland in Arthur Aspinall's 1949 work, *Politics and the Press 1780–1850*, which is berated in a review by Brian Inglis for virtually omitting newspapers opposed to the government.[2] A study with a similar time span, which concerns the relationship between the press and the government, is Brian Inglis's *The Freedom of the Press in Ireland 1784–1841* (1954).[3] His article two years earlier, however, 'O'Connell and the Irish press 1800–42,' is far more relevant, showing how the Irish nationalist leader Daniel O'Connell tried to use the press to advance his cause.[4] In an essay published in 1957, Inglis discusses the Irish press in the first half of the nineteenth century, and includes a brief assessment of one of the most renowned nationalist newspapers, *The Nation*.[5] An earlier period of the Irish press, from the late seventeenth century to around the middle of the eighteenth century, was the subject of a general study by Robert Munter, published in 1967.[6] Hugh Oram also begins his history of Irish newspapers in the seventeenth century but continues up to the 1980s, which makes his interesting work very broad in content, but unfortunately lacking in sources.[7] The formidable Irish leader Charles Stewart Parnell was the subject of an analysis by James Loughlin, which focussed on his relationship with the press and is included as a chapter in Boyce and O'Day's *Parnell in Perspective* (1991).[8] Felix Larkin also addresses this subject in 'Parnell, politics and the press in Ireland,

---

[1] T.H.S. Escott, 'The Journalist in Ireland', in *Masters of English Journalism. A Study of Personal Forces* (London: T. Fisher-Unwin, 1911).

[2] Arthur Aspinall, *Politics and the Press 1780–1850* (London: Home & Val Thal, 1949); Brian Inglis, 'Review of Arthur Aspinall, *Politics and the Press*', *Irish Historical Studies* (*IHS*), vol. 6 (24), Sept. 1949, pp. 301–3.

[3] Brian Inglis, *The Freedom of the Press in Ireland 1784–1841* (London: Faber & Faber, 1954).

[4] Brian Inglis, 'O'Connell and the Irish Press 1800–42', *IHS*, vol. 8 (29), March 1952, pp. 1–27.

[5] Brian Inglis, 'The Press', in R.B. McDowell (ed.), *Social Life in Ireland, 1800–1845* (Dublin: Colm O'Lochlainn, The Sign of the Three Candles Press, 1957).

[6] Robert Munter, *History of the Irish Newspaper, 1685–1760* (Cambridge: Cambridge University Press, 1967).

[7] Hugh Oram, *The Newspaper Book. A History of Newspapers in Ireland, 1649–1983, vol. I* (Dublin: MO Books, 1983).

[8] James Loughlin, 'Constructing the political spectacle: Parnell, the press and national leadership, 1879–86', in D. George Boyce and Alan O'Day (eds.), *Parnell in Perspective* (London: Routledge, 1991).

1875–1924,' a chapter in McCartney and Travers's *Parnell Reconsidered* (2013).[9] Anne Kane's essay in 2003 argues that reading nationalist newspapers and attending Parnell's 1879–82 Land War meetings contributed to the building of an Irish national identity, a phenomenon that has its antecedents in the huge Repeal Association meetings and the 1840s Dublin Repeal press.[10] The following year an article by Michael Foley offered a brief survey of the Irish press in the nineteenth century.[11] The most comprehensive publication to date of the nineteenth-century Irish nationalist press is Marie-Louise Legg's *Newspapers and Nationalism: The Irish Provincial Press 1850–92* (1999), which explores the role of local newspapers and their association with nationalist politics, showing how the provincial press began to acquire prominence in the development of Irish nationalism.[12]

In the context of their biographies of Irish nationalists John O'Leary (1967), Charles Kickham (1985) and James Stephens (2007), Marcus Bourke, R.V. Comerford and Marta Ramón respectively have provided some discussion of the Fenian newspaper, *The Irish People*.[13] Furthermore, two biographies of the revered Thomas Davis by John N. Molony (1995) and Helen F. Mulvey (2003) offer insights into his contributions to *The Nation*.[14] In a short chapter in *Irish journalism before independence: More a disease than a profession* (2011), entitled 'Loyalty and Repeal: The *Nation*, 1842–46,' M.L. Brillman analyses the paper and its stand in relation to Daniel O'Connell's political decisions.[15]

---

[9] Felix Larkin, 'Parnell, politics and the press in Ireland, 1875–1924' in Donal McCartney and Pauric Travers (eds.), *Parnell Reconsidered* (Dublin: University College Dublin Press, 2013).

[10] Anne Kane, 'The ritualization of newspaper reading and political consciousness: The role of newspapers in the Irish land war', in L.W. McBride (ed.), *Reading Irish Histories. Texts, contexts, and memory in modern Ireland* (Dublin: Four Courts Press, 2003).

[11] Michael Foley, 'Colonialism and Journalism in Ireland', *Journalism Studies*, vol. 5 (3), Aug. 2004, pp. 373–85.

[12] Marie-Louise Legg, *Newspapers and Nationalism: the Irish Provincial Press 1850–92* (Dublin: Four Courts Press, 1999).

[13] Marcus Bourke, *John O'Leary: A Study in Irish Separatism* (Tralee: Anvil Books, 1967); R.V. Comerford, *Charles J. Kickham. A Study in Irish nationalism and literature* (Dublin: Wolfhound Press, 1979); Marta Ramón, *A Provisional Dictator: James Stephens and the Fenian Movement* (Dublin: University College Dublin Press, 2007).

[14] John N. Molony, *A soul came into Ireland: Thomas Davis 1814–1845* (Dublin: Geography Publications, 1995); Helen F. Mulvey, *Thomas Davis and Ireland: A Biographical Study* (Washington, D.C.: The Catholic University of America Press, 2003).

[15] M.L. Brillman, 'Loyalty and Repeal: the *Nation*, 1842–46', in Kevin Rafter (ed.), *Irish journalism before independence: More a disease than a profession* (Manchester: Manchester University Press, 2011).

As for unpublished theses, Mary Leo's most useful 1976 study, 'The influence of the Fenians and their press on public opinion in Ireland, 1863–70,' surveys general themes in *The Irish People* (1863–65) and *The Irishman* (1858–85), while 'James Stephens and the *Irish People* in the evolution of Irish nationalist politics in the nineteenth century' by Patrick Michael Cullen (1997), provides a coherent analysis of the political thinking of the Fenian leader in the context of the main theories of nationalism.[16] Growing interest in the Irish nationalist press is evidenced by Patrick F. Tally's doctoral study in 2003.[17] Spanning much of the nineteenth century, his well-researched narrative concentrates on the expansion of the Dublin nationalist weekly newspaper industry. Tally particularly focuses upon these newspapers as commercial enterprises; for instance, making extensive use of statistical data, his dissertation provides detailed information on the price of papers, their frequency of publication, and government stamp returns. A doctoral work by William George O'Brien, 'Imagining Catholic Ireland: The nationalist press and the creation of national identity, 1843–1870' (2007) focuses on one of the themes of the present book, while also covering a similar time-span.[18] These two latter theses are highly welcome additions to what was a somewhat neglected area of Irish history, suggesting an increasing recognition of the importance of newspapers to the development of Irish nationalism.

There are two works of particular note directly related to the link between the press and Irish literary nationalism. In 1972 Malcolm Brown skilfully demonstrated the relationship between literature and politics in books and newspapers.[19] Mary Helen Thuente's valuable investigation, *The Harp Re-strung*, published in 1994, aimed to bring recognition to the importance of the United Irish press in the Irish nationalist literary tradition.[20] A chapter is specifically devoted to the 'United Irish Newspapers' of the 1790s and analyses the important relationship between politics and

---

[16] Mary Leo, 'The influence of the Fenians and their press on public opinion in Ireland, 1863–70' (MLit., Trinity College Dublin, 1976); Patrick Michael Cullen, 'James Stephens and the *Irish People* in the evolution of Irish nationalist politics in the nineteenth century', (MPhil, University College Cork, 1997).

[17] Patrick F. Tally, 'The Growth of the Dublin Weekly Press and the Development of Irish Nationalism, 1810–79', (PhD, University of Wisconsin-Madison, 2003).

[18] W.G. O'Brien, 'Imagining Catholic Ireland: The nationalist press and the creation of national identity, 1843–1870 (PhD, University of Limerick, 2007).

[19] Malcolm Brown, *The Politics of Irish Literature: From Thomas Davis to W.B. Yeats* (London: Allen & Unwin, 1972).

[20] Mary Helen Thuente, *The Harp Re-strung. The United Irishmen and the Rise of Literary Nationalism* (Syracuse: Syracuse University Press, 1994).

literature developed by the United Irish press. Another chapter, 'Young Ireland Poetry,' shows how the United Irishmen inspired the writers of the revered nineteenth-century nationalist newspaper, *The Nation*, who were highly successful in continuing their tradition.

In the 1840s Irish nationalists inherited an historical legacy of conquests and confiscations of property owned by Catholics; while the Penal Laws (designed to restrict the power and influence of Catholics in Irish society after the seventeenth-century religious wars) were mostly gone by then, the law of land tenure imposed on the peasantry by Anglo-Irish ruling-class landlords was believed by many Irish nationalists to be the cause of endemic poverty and social unrest in Ireland. Although an Irish Parliament had existed in the eighteenth century, it was subordinate to the British government. When a campaign by the Protestant Ascendancy achieved legislative independence in 1782, the Irish executive remained staffed by politicians who reported to the cabinet in London, one of the problems that eventually led to the 1798 rebellion by the United Irishmen, who had sought French military assistance.[21] After the rebellion was crushed, direct rule was imposed by Westminster in the form of the 1800 Act of Union. This legislation maintained the Anglican Protestants as a ruling elite over the majority Catholic population, but it was challenged in the successful Catholic Emancipation movement (1823–29). While these Protestants believed that it was in their interests to remain a constituent part of the United Kingdom, many Irish Catholics believed that a severance from the Union was the only way to secure a just and prosperous future for the people of Ireland.

Many theorists perceive nationalism as a modern construct that emerged in the eighteenth or nineteenth century whereby nations believed that, having their own national identities, they should fight for their right to be independent nation states. While an Irish national identity had its antecedents from the seventh century onwards, by the mid-nineteenth century the Young Irelanders, a group of Irish nationalists, believed that Ireland's national identity had been slowly eroded by the connection with England, and that a new national identity should be forged that represented all of Ireland's inhabitants, whatever their race, creed or class. The Young Irelanders, and Thomas Davis in particular, believed that the framing of a new national identity could be achieved by the encouragement of

[21] The administration at Dublin Castle, the seat of government in Ireland, included the posts of Lord Lieutenant (also known as Viceroy) and Chief Secretary; French military contingents to Ireland were led by Theobald Wolfe Tone (1763–98), one of the founders of the Society of United Irishmen in 1791.

contemporary culture, especially literature, combined with the recreation of a forgotten Irish national identity from the past.

In his critical analysis of the core literature of nationalism, Jonathan Hearn offers a useful definition: 'Nationalism is the making of combined claims, on behalf of a population, to *identity*, to *jurisdiction* and to *territory*.'[22] Many mid-nineteenth-century Irish nationalist journalists saw themselves as leading and articulating the collective will of the Irish people. These newspaper writers asserted the presence of an Irish national identity that was separate from Britain, and urged the need for its protection against a growing tide of Anglicization, especially since the Great Famine. They expressed the right and the need of the Irish people to make laws for themselves, to be independent of what they perceived as a highly unjust and illegitimate British government. Many nationalist journalists further argued that the land of Ireland should not be owned by the Protestant Ascendancy; it belonged to the people of Ireland and should be restored to them. These three strands of Irish nationalism could be summed up as 'Ireland for the Irish,' a motif that was often used in nationalist journalism during the nineteenth century and thereafter.

The cause of Irish nationalism was the campaign to achieve the above claims, with or without physical force. Both constitutional and revolutionary nationalists working for the Dublin nationalist press in the mid-nineteenth century appropriated aspects of the ideology of the late eighteenth-century United Irishman, Theobald Wolfe Tone, who is widely recognized as the founder of modern Irish republicanism. Revolutionary nationalism in modern Irish history began with the United Irishmen and their rebellion in 1798. Characterized by physical force, conspiracy and republicanism, and often identified by historians as advanced nationalism, its legacy had a lasting influence on later Irish nationalists. Constitutional nationalism meant working through non-violent means to redress Irish grievances, while ideally achieving some form of independence from Great Britain. In the mid-nineteenth century, Irish nationalist newspapers became highly important for articulating the nationalist message and mobilizing public opinion in support of both the constitutionalists and the physical force nationalists.

In *Imagined Communities* Benedict Anderson associates the rise of print capitalism with the growth of nationalism.[23] Certainly newsprint had a key

---

[22] Jonathan Hearn, *Rethinking Nationalism. A Critical Introduction* (Basingstoke & New York: Palgrave Macmillan, 2006), p. 11.

[23] Benedict Anderson, *Imagined Communities: Reflections on the Origin and Spread of Nationalism*, 3rd ed., (London & New York: Verso, 2006).

role in promoting Irish nationalism. Jeremy Black notes in *The English Press 1621–1861* that, 'The press was central to politicization, the strengthening, sustaining and widening, if not of a specific political consciousness, then at least of national political awareness,' and he cites the role of leading articles as an example of this process of politicization.[24] In mid-nineteenth-century Ireland, the Dublin nationalist press proved a powerful tool in fomenting a political nationalist consciousness, disseminating nationalist rhetoric and mobilizing public opinion, mainly through its leading articles. Forging a separatist ideology that was communicated through the medium of the press was an effective way of awakening nationalist consciousness. The Dublin nationalist press was not just a myriad of reflected images of society, but a vehicle for the spreading of knowledge, and for the presentation and debate of nationalist issues and policies. Newspapers were important for the articulation of the concept of Irish nationalism and a vital medium for its communication, not only with society in Ireland, but also with Great Britain and America and their large Irish immigrant communities.

Newspapers in Dublin had their origins in the seventeenth century and early eighteenth century, when they emerged as news sheets that were published intermittently. At first written by hand, and starting as one sheet of paper, newspapers grew to a large sheet that could be folded to provide four pages. Initially, occasional publications appeared from the middle of the seventeenth century in Ireland; from 25 December 1703 Richard Pue's *Impartial Occurrences*, issued three times a week, seems to be the first Irish newspaper to be published on a regular basis.[25] Numerous newspapers were printed in the eighteenth century, but they endured an extremely low survival rate; one of the very few successes was the twice-weekly *Dublin Gazette*, which started in 1705 and ran under this title until 27 January 1922. Its longevity was no doubt partly due to its close links with the government, who supplied it with official material for publication. Over time *The Dublin Gazette* came under the control of the government, and from 31 January 1922 it became the official organ of the Irish Free State and was retitled *Iris Oifigiúil*.[26] Provincial newspapers were also published in the eighteenth century, mainly in the larger urban communities of Cork and Belfast; for instance, while *The Corke Journal* ran from December 1753

[24] Jeremy Black, *The English Press 1621–1861* (Stroud: Sutton Publishing Ltd., 2001), pp. 132, 152.

[25] This newspaper was retitled *Pue's Occurrences* in 1712 and lasted until the 1790s.

[26] Joseph W. Hammond, '"The Dublin Gazette", 1705–1922', *Dublin Historical Record*, vol. 13 (3/4), 1953, pp. 108–17.

to 1772, *The Belfast News-Letter*, begun in 1737, still survives today under the title *News Letter*.

These early newspapers were produced by those who were already engaged in other commercial occupations, usually printing or bookselling. Publishing newspapers became a profitable commercial venture, mainly due to the revenue from advertisements that appeared in them. Subscribers, who bought directly from the publisher, tended to be those in official or government occupations or individuals connected with commerce. Besides collecting news from local sources, such as court proceedings, newspapers could include resolutions of political meetings, notices of charities and theatrical performances, as well as items to sell, such as wine and books. Initially opposed by the government, Parliamentary debates were allowed to be printed in newspapers, which also carried British and foreign news that was copied from the London press. Coffee houses, opening in the latter part of the seventeenth century, and popular throughout the eighteenth century, were often used as meeting places for various clubs, and abounded with gossip that publishers could use as copy for their newspapers. Some newspaper publishers were also coffee house owners, and the two could be located nearby or even share the same premises; for example, Richard Pue was the proprietor of Dick's Coffee House. As a way of controlling what was deemed to be a threat from publishers, the government imposed taxes on newspapers; libel laws were another deterrent that could be used by the government, enforced more strictly in Ireland than in Great Britain. Those newspapers that were uncritical of the government were given rewards, such as being commissioned to print official proclamations and notices.

With the expansion of their readership, newspaper publishers saw an opportunity to influence public opinion. The political reformer Charles Lucas launched *The Censor, or Citizen's Journal*, the first newspaper that came into conflict with the government; Lucas was forced to flee the country for a number of years in 1749 to escape imprisonment. During the closing decades of the eighteenth century a growing political radicalism was articulated in the Irish press. For instance, prior to coming under the influence of Dublin Castle in 1784 for eighteen years, *The Freeman's Journal*, founded on 10 September 1763, represented the views of the leading patriots of the Protestant Ascendancy such as Henry Grattan, who campaigned for parliamentary independence.[27] As a way of stirring up public opinion, *The Freeman's Journal* critically reported on the conflict between England and the North American colonies and reprinted Thomas Paine's *Common*

[27] Some patriots, such as Henry Grattan, also sought Catholic reform.

Sense.[28] For the ruling elite, the most dangerous newspapers of the Irish press came in the 1790s with the radical publications issued by the Society of the United Irishmen. They were threatening not just because of their lively critique of the way Ireland was governed; their desire for complete separation from England offered the people of Ireland a new ideological base from which an Irish nation could be recreated.

Up to the last decade of the eighteenth-century Irish newspapers were mostly written for an English-speaking Protestant upper- and middle-class public, the Protestant Ascendancy, even if at times it criticized the government. By the early nineteenth century this pattern had altered, particularly with the emergence of Daniel O'Connell, a Catholic barrister. He was a formidable leader of the Irish Catholics who ideally sought a repeal of the 1800 Act of Union but would, in the meantime, settle for limited political reform. Highly skilled in mobilizing popular opinion and manipulating the press, O'Connell campaigned for Catholic Emancipation, achieved in 1829, whereby prestigious official positions in society that were previously barred from Catholics were now open to them. With the passing of this Act, O'Connell took up a seat as a Member of Parliament. During his political career O'Connell was supported by several Dublin liberal newspapers, such as *The Morning Register* (1824–43) and *The Pilot* (1828–49). With Daniel O'Connell at the helm of the Irish nationalist movement at this time, nationalist rhetoric in newsprint evolved from the United Irishmen's radical newspapers in the latter part of the eighteenth century into a distinctive form where Catholic Ireland was now represented by a constitutional nationalist press.

Irish nationalists recognized that a newspaper had the potential to be a powerful force for their cause. Newspapers were certainly deemed as essential to a nationalist organization, where the political arguments of the leading articles could be complemented by the reports and news of the organization's activities. A key mission of these newspapers was to achieve maximum mobilization of opinion. Words and phrases steeped in meaning were used with regularity; for example 'Repeal' was the byword for political freedom from Britain and the cure for all of Ireland's social and economic ills. Political policies were formulated from debates in the press, often influenced by the unfolding nature of contemporary events. The way journalists engaged the public in the nationalist cause and aligned themselves with their readers impacted upon the role and effectiveness of the nationalist press. With powerful rhetoric newspapers could imbue a sense

---

[28] Paine's pamphlet, advocating independence for the American colonies, was originally published in January 1776.

of belonging and cohesion that would strengthen a nationalist organization. While employing rational argument to convince people to join its cause, much of the language used by the nationalist press was adorned with highly emotive rhetoric intended to stir deep feelings, for example, when reporting the great outdoor spectacles of the Repeal Association's meetings, especially when Daniel O'Connell, the esteemed leader of the Irish Catholics, was present. An important aspect of the nationalist press was its democratizing effect, whereby those who lacked the vote could have a voice by contributing letters to newspaper offices of nationalist leaders and sometimes having them printed. The compelling need of the Dublin political activists to harness the potential that newspapers offered demonstrated their immense belief in the power of the press as an integral mover in their cause, where they saw themselves in the vanguard of advocating a separate Irish political and cultural identity in the struggle for severance from Britain. These individuals shaped nationalist policies, not only by their writings, but also their actions: the effect they had on their contemporaries, their relationships with each other and the political influence they exerted impacted on the present and the future of the Irish nationalist cause.

The Dublin nationalist press was inextricably associated with politics, not only directly through its journalism, but also indirectly by its literary contributions. This strategy of fusing literature with political ideology in newspapers originated with the United Irishmen's press in the late 1790s and continued into the next century, where it was further developed by the Dublin nationalist press in the middle decades. Although Mary Helen Thuente argues that the United Irishmen were the originators of Irish cultural nationalism, unlike the Young Irelanders, they did not embrace culture as part of their nationalist vision, but essentially used it as another way of promoting their political aspirations.[29] While the United Irishmen's republicanism emanated from a response to Enlightenment ideology based on the American and French revolutions, their rhetoric was expressed in terms of romantic nationalism. The nationalist message in newspapers was disseminated through the medium of conventional journalistic practices such as leading articles, and also through literature. Stories and verse were not present in the nationalist press merely for entertainment or leisure purposes; rather, they performed an integral role by engaging readers in the vision and the pursuit of the Irish nationalist cause.

During the 1830s and 1840s a great interest arose in the history and culture of Ireland when a number of writers became involved in cultural nationalism. The Ulster Gaelic Society, for example, established in 1830,

---

[29] Thuente, *The Harp Re-strung*.

expressed interest in the Irish language. Societies such as the Irish Archaeological Society, founded in 1840, which researched Gaelic manuscripts, formed a base for the development of literature. *The Dublin University Magazine* was one of the main literary and political journals in Ireland and represented Protestant Unionists. It began publication in 1833 and Samuel Ferguson became a significant contributor. Ferguson belonged to a group of cultural scholars and writers in the early to mid-nineteenth century, who light-heartedly called themselves Orange Young Ireland, but who had been overshadowed by the Young Ireland phenomenon associated with *The Nation* newspaper. While Young Irelander Thomas Davis's cultural writings were politically motivated, Ferguson's were not. Both sought a cultural identity for Ireland through their writings. Ferguson, however, was not to achieve recognition for the quality of his work until the advent of the Irish literary revival at the end of the nineteenth century. In the 1840s the Young Irelanders developed and articulated the notion that literature should be used as a way to advance Irish political nationalism. They also believed that literary quality was less of a priority than nationalist content and reader accessibility, which was contrary to the view of those writers, most notably W.B. Yeats, who were involved in the literary revival of the 1890s. In producing their own nationalist literature, newspapers had a major role in fostering a popular Irish nationalist literary tradition. Findings from the study of folklore by eighteenth-century antiquarians were popularized by poets such as Thomas Moore, who was an inspiration both to the United Irishmen and the Young Irelanders. His major work, *Irish Melodies* (1808–34), words set to traditional Irish airs, was important for the development of nineteenth-century Irish nationalism, and by the 1830s Moore was seen as Ireland's national poet. Folklore was pivotal to the transformation of cultural nationalism into political nationalism. Verse based on folklore was an important feature of *The Nation*, the most influential newspaper of the mid-nineteenth century for the development of Irish nationalism.

One of the main purposes of this book is to show that what was written in the Dublin nationalist newspapers in the mid-nineteenth century not only dramatically impacted on the development of Irish nationalism at that time, but was also conspicuous for laying ideological foundations that were taken up by Irish nationalists in the future. So, rather than offering a definitive history of every Dublin nationalist newspaper from 1842 to 1867, this book mainly concentrates on selective aspects of newspapers that have had an ideological impact on the development of Irish nationalism during this period. The first chapter focuses on the positive and unifying power of the Dublin nationalist press, where the advent of *The Nation* in particular had a key role in making 1843 a highly successful year in Irish nationalist history. Daniel O'Connell's Loyal National Repeal Association, in seeking to repeal the 1800 Act of Union, will be shown to greatly profit not only from how the Dublin nationalist press exploited the seeming negativity of the British government towards Ireland, but more importantly from the extensive and colourful coverage of Repeal activities. Chapter 2, in contrast, demonstrates the destructive power of the Dublin nationalist press from 1844 to the summer of 1848. During this time, with the strain of the Great Famine severely impacting on Irish society, two highly damaging splits occurred in the Irish nationalist movement with opposing sides drawn into newspaper battles. In the first split O'Connell and his close followers were aligned against *The Nation*'s Young Irelanders. Emerging from the latter group was the Irish Confederation, represented in the press by *The Nation*, but it too experienced a break-up, and in its wake followed the publication of a barrage of rebel papers as the Famine intensified, leading to an attempted rebellion and the collapse of the Irish nationalist movement in 1848. Chapter 3 is concerned with the resilience of the nationalist cause despite its temporary downfall, arguing that the Dublin nationalist press, with its ideological renascence, helped to inject new life into Irish nationalism. While this action manifested itself in support for peaceful nationalist issues, after 1848 the idea of physical force revolution to achieve separation from Great Britain would not go away. This was reflected by another attempted rebellion in 1849 and the appearance of new Dublin newspapers that opposed constitutional nationalism, two of which, the 1849–50 *Irishman* and the 1855–56 *Tribune*, have, thus far, received scant attention from historians. Chapter 4 concentrates upon the republican and revolutionary ideology of the Dublin nationalist press, focusing essentially on *The Irish People* newspaper. The period between its foundation in 1863 and its suppression in 1865 coincided with an expansion of the physical force group that it represented, the Irish Republican Brotherhood (IRB), along with its counterpart in America, the Fenian Brotherhood. Members of both organizations were known as Fenians, whose survival after an unsuccessful rebellion in Ireland two years later was to have a long-lasting impact on the future of Irish nationalism.[30]

The power the Dublin nationalist press wielded over the Irish nationalist cause in the mid-nineteenth century is a major theme of this book. Importantly, while those who controlled these newspapers made a positive contribution to the development of Irish nationalism, nationalist newsprint could be a battleground for divergent ideologies and strategies, especially with commercial rivalry between newspapers; this caused much dissension

[30] Throughout this book members of the IRB will mostly be referred to as Fenians.

within the nationalist movement manifesting itself in the destructive nature of the Dublin nationalist press. Conflicting ideologies among Irish nationalists were especially noticeable in the struggle between peaceful and militant strategies. The paradox of the unifying nature of the Dublin nationalist press and conversely its polar opposite, its destructive nature, is explored, where groups and individuals exerted their will over the cause of Irish nationalism. The idea of Ireland as an independent nation, and a panacea for Ireland's ills, especially during and after the Great Famine, also constitute enduring themes throughout this book.

Finally, a key theme in this work portrays the need of newspaper writers to safeguard Irish national identity through attempts to resist the continual Anglicization of the country. An overriding concept used by the writers of the Dublin nationalist press in the struggle for independence in the mid-nineteenth century was the wish to portray the English hierarchy as a common enemy with an identity that was different from that of the Irish people. One way to implement this idea was through political journalism, especially in leading articles. A second method was to show that the Irish people possessed a distinct nationality from their English rulers through the creation and recreation of an Irish cultural and literary tradition, which could justify their independence. The literary columns formed an integral part of a nationalist newspaper and could include items such as historical essays, poetry and book reviews. They not only reflected the political aspirations of Irish nationalists by being the means through which an Irish literary tradition could be transmitted, but they could also serve as another way of persuading readers to join the nationalist cause. Whether through political journalism or its literary columns, the need to show Irish separateness from Britain was a foremost strategy of the Dublin nationalist press.

An event that was to have a defining effect on the development of Irish nationalism was the Great Famine from 1845 to 1852. The Famine was initially caused by a fungal disease that damaged the potato crop which formed a substantial part of the staple diet of around a third of Ireland's population. It has been estimated that during the Famine over a million people died of hunger and disease, and well over a further million emigrated. Even before the Famine the structure of rural Ireland was precarious, with most of its lower-class inhabitants living in poverty. Many landowners were absentee landlords who employed agents to administer their estates; rents were high, and while tenant farmers had no security of tenure and could be evicted at any time, they were not compensated for seeking improvements to lands or buildings on leaving their rented property. The Famine brought social and economic upheaval and produced many changes in Irish society, though these were essentially a speeding up of trends that were already present. Labourers were the worst affected by the Famine, followed by the cottiers, and then the smaller farmers holding up to fifteen acres, who were more vulnerable than ever to eviction.[31] The number of medium-sized and large farms rose, and in many places livestock farming increasingly replaced tillage farming, a trend that continued into the 1860s. Hunger, disease and loss of livelihood for the most vulnerable led to massive emigration overseas, to Britain and America, which was to impact greatly on the development of Irish nationalism. The dispossessed were also drawn from rural areas into urban areas, and this helped the dissemination of Irish nationalist newspaper rhetoric. Those who died or emigrated were mostly from the poorest areas of Ireland, and this had a significant effect on the Gaelic language, which had already been in decline before the Famine. In the National School system, introduced in 1831, English, not Irish, was taught for the next four decades. William Smith O'Brien, one of the most important Irish nationalists of the mid-nineteenth century, complained that the teaching of children in these schools 'wholly ignores the history of Ireland, and carefully excludes from the circle of their studies everything that can remind them that they are Irish.'[32] With the changing rural economy and the decline of the Irish language, Ireland became more Anglicized. Irish characteristics were disappearing. This suggests an anomaly in the aspirations of the Dublin nationalist press. How could independence from Great Britain be justified when the Irish national identity, more than ever since the Famine, was being eroded by Anglicization? While the Dublin nationalist journalists attempted to address this question by continuing to promote an Irish cultural identity and to draw distinctions between the characteristics of Britain and Ireland, they concentrated their campaign more on the way Ireland was governed, a theme that, because of the Famine, would be pursued with more justification and determination than ever before.

The Dublin nationalist press was intended to appeal to every class in Irish society, and there were opportunities for this to be achieved. Literacy levels seem to have been high in mid-nineteenth-century Ireland, suggested, for example, by Niall Ó Ciosáin in his study published in 1997.[33] Most of the population in Ireland spoke Irish in 1750, but from the late eighteenth century the number of English speakers accelerated. Literacy was essentially

---

[31] Cottiers worked as labourers on someone else's land in exchange for a plot to grow their own food.

[32] 'The Irish Language', *The Irishman*, 21 Aug. 1858.

[33] Niall Ó Ciosáin, *Print and Popular Culture in Ireland, 1750–1850* (Basingstoke: Macmillan; New York: St Martin's Press, 1997).

achieved in English, even for those who spoke Irish, and the advance of literacy was synonymous with the increase in those speaking English. According to the 1841 census data, forty-seven per cent of the population of Ireland over the age of five was literate. Although more indicative than definitive, one particular study suggests that in the middle of the nineteenth century, adult literacy in Ireland can be assessed as being on a similar level to England and France, and all three were considered average in Europe.[34] Anecdotal evidence can add some credence to this research on literacy standards in Ireland. For example, in early 1850 a correspondent to the nationalist newspaper *The Irishman* noted 'the astonishing thirst for national reading, which has, within the last two years, sprung up among mechanics and the labouring classes.'[35] In the 1870s, A.M. Sullivan, a proprietor of *The Nation* for twenty-one years from 1855, observed: 'There is now scarcely a farmhouse or working man's home in all the land in which the boy or girl of fifteen, or the young man or woman of twenty-five, cannot read the newspaper "for the old people," and transact their correspondence.'[36]

For those who were literate but unable to afford the high cost of newspapers, the display of nationalist newspapers in reading rooms widened their availability. During the 1840s reading rooms greatly expanded and became synonymous with Irish nationalism, although they were more likely to be located in urban areas. In addition to the Temperance Movement's reading rooms, numerous Repeal Association reading rooms were opened, followed later by those of the Irish Confederates. Despite the closure of the Repeal and Confederate reading rooms in 1848, others survived. In the 1850s prospective members of the IRB used the reading rooms of the Phoenix Literary Society, and in the 1860s another nationalist group, the National Brotherhood of St Patrick, also had its own reading rooms.[37] Irish nationalism and reading rooms went hand in hand and this link was an important characteristic of popular nationalism in the mid-nineteenth century and beyond.

However, the literate were not the only ones who had access to newsprint. The cultural activity of reading aloud meant that the contents of nationalist newspapers had the potential to reach a much wider public. During the late eighteenth century and continuing into the nineteenth, the

---

[34] Ó Ciosáin, *Print and Popular Culture in Ireland*, pp. 32–3, 154.

[35] *The Irishman*, 19 Jan. 1850.

[36] A.M. Sullivan, *New Ireland: Political Sketches and Personal Reminiscences, vol. I*, 4th ed. (London: Sampson Low, Marston, Searle & Rivington, 1878), p. 35.

[37] Those belonging to the National Brotherhood of St Patrick had similar political views to the Fenians although it was an open society and not secret like the IRB.

practice of reading aloud was a common social activity and a highly valuable asset to the dissemination of nationalist rhetoric. There are numerous instances of this practice. The act of reading aloud after Mass was shown in an Irish painting by Henry MacManus in the 1840s called *Reading 'The Nation.'* Even if the lower classes had gained some proficiency in literacy, the language of newsprint was often complex and those unable to read for themselves or afford to purchase newspapers could nevertheless be made aware of their contents. Furthermore, readers could pass on information orally, relating the contents of a newspaper to someone without necessarily reading it out.

Discovering the number of people who had access to the contents of nationalist newspapers in the mid-nineteenth century has proven problematic: apart from newspapers that were deposited in reading rooms and the existence of the strong tradition of reading aloud, usually involving groups, many copies were shared or passed around from hand to hand, often in public houses. Furthermore, it was common practice in Dublin for newsvendors to hire out newspapers. Circulation in terms of issues sold was therefore scarcely representative of the actual number of people who, one way or another, had access to newspapers' columns. Although up to 1855 newspaper stamp returns could suggest the circulation of a newspaper in terms of copies sold, the amount of stamps purchased did not necessarily correlate to sales; for example, publishers could buy more stamps than they were likely to use in a bid to impress advertisers with their apparent circulation figures. After 1855, when the stamp duty was abolished, except for those that were posted free through the Post Office, it was even more difficult to determine a newspaper's sales figures. Parliamentary stamp returns, however, could be taken alongside the testimony of Irish nationalists and their newspapers, and though none of these sources were necessarily reliable, they could collectively be taken into account to indicate a paper's circulation.

In the mid-nineteenth century improved communications systems greatly assisted the expansion of access to nationalist writing. During the 1840s newspapers were expensive, but from 1855 to 1861, when taxes on newspapers were abolished in Ireland, their lower cost was a contributory factor to their increasing accessibility. Distribution methods had improved by the mid-nineteenth century. Transport by rail started in Ireland in December 1834 and, after a slow beginning, accelerated in the 1840s so that by the 1850s much of the rail infrastructure was complete. During the same period, postal services continued their expansion. Both of these developments naturally facilitated a greater dispersion of newspapers. Nationalist newspapers could be purchased from news agents, individuals recruited by a nationalist organization to sell its own paper. A common method of distribution was through subscriptions, ordered directly from the newspaper office or through a news agent.

Mary Helen Thuente has observed that in the early decades of the nineteenth century numerous periodicals produced in Ireland combined literature and politics, apparently inspired by the United Irishmen's press. For example, the *Irish Monthly Magazine of Politics and Literature* was published in Dublin from 1832 to 1834. *The Citizen* (1839–41) and the *Dublin Monthly Magazine* (1842) were precursors of *The Nation* in that they not only published prose and poetry about the United Irishmen, but some of their poets later contributed to *The Nation*.[38] Although the literary nationalism of the United Irishmen was kept alive by these publications, it was *The Nation*, the Dublin weekly newspaper begun on 15 October 1842, that heralded one of the most important developments in the history of Irish nationalism. While other newspapers supported Irish nationalist issues to varying degrees, *The Nation* of the 1840s was specifically created with the intention of actively imbuing the Irish people with Irish nationalist thoughts and feelings, both for political and aesthetic reasons. The United Irishmen bequeathed to the Young Ireland movement not only a political legacy through its press but also a literary tradition.

The Irish nationalist press, particularly in Dublin where most of the nationalist leaders were located, was the most important medium for the dissemination of nationalist ideology. Like their predecessors in the United Irishmen's press, *The Nation* provided knowledge and education to further the cause of Irish nationalism. Furthermore, romantic nationalism, begun in Ireland by the newspapers of the United Irishmen in the late eighteenth century, was infused into Irish society as the literary columns of *The Nation* complemented and enhanced the paper's political agenda. This newspaper was an important political voice in the Irish nationalist movement of the 1840s and was critical to the ascent and success of Young Ireland. *The Nation* had a crucial role in creating and defining nationalist ideology, and was the centre and focus of Irish nationalism in the 1840s, a model that other newspapers aspired to in the mid-nineteenth century.

---

[38] Thuente, *The Harp Re-strung*, pp. 197–9.

CHAPTER I

The Nation and the Dublin Repeal Press

'We are sir, singularly fortunate in our Repeal press, and I sincerely believe that no country was ever better served than Ireland now is by the newspapers which advocate our cause,' Daniel O'Connell at a Repeal Association meeting, 22 March 1843.[1]

IT WAS EXTRAORDINARY how much support there was for the nationalist cause in Irish society during 1843. In that year, it was not just the immense number of people involved in its activities that was impressive but also the intensity, the inclusiveness, and the unity that existed both amongst and between its leaders and their followers. Although much of this support came from lower-class Catholics, it also included an array of persons of wealth and station, such as landowners, and members of the municipal corporations and the judiciary; and while the Catholic Church had a high profile in the Irish nationalist movement during this time, Protestants were also encouraged to join the cause.

The Irish nationalist movement in the early 1840s was dominated by the Loyal National Repeal Association. The political aim of the Repeal Association was to overturn the 1800 Act of Union and establish an independent Ireland, while remaining loyal to the monarchy. Naturally, communication was essential to acquire and sustain enthusiasm for a political organization. In later nationalist movements, such as the Parnell era, mass communication in Ireland was steadily advancing, but in the 1840s it was still in its infancy. And yet, from the autumn of 1842, and especially during much of the following year, the Repeal campaign proved so successful that it was forcibly compromised by the British government.

[1] *The Nation*, 25 March 1843.

The first notable movement for the repeal of the Union was founded by Daniel O'Connell following his success in 1829 of achieving Catholic Emancipation. Building on this victory, O'Connell established his Repeal Association in the 1830s. However, in 1835 this campaign was abandoned in favour of the Lichfield House Compact, an alliance between Repeal MPs and a new Whig ministry that promised O'Connell reform for Ireland. An attempt at reviving the Repeal Association came five years later, but recruitment was sluggish, until the appearance of *The Nation* in mid-October 1842. The success of this newspaper, which supported the Repeal Association, coincided with a remarkable expansion in recruitment to this organization, accompanied by a distinctive solidarity within the Repeal leadership. But this favourable state was checked the following October when the Tory Prime Minister, Robert Peel, with military backing, banned a large Repeal demonstration at Clontarf before arresting O'Connell and other Repeal leaders, including members of the Dublin nationalist press. Unlike Catholic Emancipation, the Repeal Association was far more ambitious in its aim, threatening the integrity of the United Kingdom. The British government's action testified to the power of the Repeal Association's press campaign and its impact on Irish society. Especially influential was *The Nation*, at that time the most important advocate in newsprint of the Repeal cause.

The founding of *The Nation*

Although *The Nation* was a newspaper with its own agenda of cultural and political nationalism, it was initially founded to join the existing coterie of liberal newspapers in Dublin that supported the Loyal National Repeal Association and its leader, Daniel O'Connell. One month following *The Nation*'s first issue, a leading article announced: 'The principal measure to which we have resolved to concentrate our energies is the restoration of the Parliament of Ireland. It is the warm desire to advocate this all-essential, vital measure, that has called our journal into existence.'[2] However, having said this, in the course of its duty and loyalty to the Repeal Association, *The Nation* was in a position to promote its own theory of Irish nationalism.

It was Thomas Davis's concept of nationality that was preached in *The Nation*. A Protestant from Co. Cork, Davis had been influenced by the tradition of the United Irishmen, a legacy inherited by a group of Protestants and Catholics belonging to Dublin's Trinity College and the

[2] 2nd Leading Article (LA), *Nation*, 19 Nov. 1842.

College Historical Society.[3] It is likely that Davis was also influenced by the liberal and romantic nationalism that was currently in fashion across Europe. Davis had a great love for Ireland and drew much inspiration from the Gaelic past.[4] He was revered by his peers and his ideology survived long after his untimely death in 1845, a few weeks short of his thirty-first birthday.[5] His close colleague Charles Gavan Duffy, a Catholic from Monaghan and *The Nation*'s proprietor and editor, was to say of Davis in 1890, 'He influenced profoundly the mind of his own generation.'[6] He also inspired later generations; Patrick Pearse, for instance, who played an important role in the 1916 Rising, believed that Davis infused Irish nationalism with a spiritual quality.[7] As the chief writer of *The Nation* and its unofficial co-editor, Davis hoped to use education as the means to instil a sense of Irish nationalism into the people of Ireland. He was assisted by a group of young men, middle-class Catholics and Protestants, many of whom, like Davis, had also attended Trinity College. Along with Davis, they became known as the Young Irelanders.[8]

---

[3] Davis's views on Irish nationality and the foundation of *The Nation* can be found in Charles Gavan Duffy, *Young Ireland: A Fragment of Irish History, 1840–1850* (New York: D. Appleton, 1881), pp. 526–9. The manuscript of Davis's original statement can be located in 'Thomas Davis. The Origin of *The Nation*', 30 April 1844, National Library of Ireland (NLI), MS 3199.

[4] A useful secondary source that analyses Davis's thinking about Ireland is: T.W. Moody, 'Thomas Davis and the Irish nation', *Hermathena. A Dublin University Review*, 103, Autumn 1966, pp. 5–31.

[5] In her biography of Thomas Davis, Helen Mulvey cites his birth as 24 October 1814, the date on his tombstone: Mulvey, *Thomas Davis and Ireland*, p. 21. Charles Gavan Duffy, Davis's first biographer, noted, it seems erroneously, that it was 14 October 1814: Charles Gavan Duffy, *Thomas Davis: The Memoirs of an Irish Patriot, 1840–1846* (London: Kegan Paul, Trench, Trübner & Co. Ltd., 1890), p. 2.

[6] Duffy, *Thomas Davis*, p. 86. Charles Gavan Duffy (1816–1903) was a highly important figure in Irish nationalist journalism in the mid-nineteenth century. He wrote numerous histories of the politics of this period, which, though subjective, are highly valuable to the historian.

[7] Pádraic H. Pearse, 'The Spiritual Nation', 13 Feb. 1916, in *Collected Works of Pádraic H. Pearse: Political Writings and Speeches, vol. V*, (Dublin/Cork/Belfast: The Phoenix Publishing Co. Ltd., [1920–25]), p. 303.

[8] It seems that the first reference to the term 'Young Ireland' came in 1843, made by D.O. Madden [also known as Maddyn], who compared *The Nation*'s writers with Young England, a group aspiring 'after the speculative and ideal': D.O. Madden, *Ireland and its Rulers; since 1829. Part the First* (London: T.C. Newby, 1843), p. 304. Madden refers to Young Ireland again the following year stating, 'Young Germany dreams – Young France quarrels – Young England says prayers – Young America swindles – and Young Ireland sings': Madden, *Ireland and its Rulers; since 1829. Part the Third* (London: T.C. Newby, 1844), p. 236.

These young men possessed a passionate belief in Irish nationalism and used *The Nation* to convey this belief.

The pursuit and promotion of Irish nationality was an important impetus for the creators of *The Nation*. Their concept of Irish nationalism, the inclusion of all classes and creeds, was an ideal inherited from Theobald Wolfe Tone and the United Irishmen who sought parliamentary reform in the 1790s. This vision formed the basis of what the Young Irelanders believed to be the criterion of Irish nationality: those who resided in Ireland, irrespective of race and creed, belonged to the Irish nation. *The Nation*'s 1842 prospectus aspired to 'a Nationality which may embrace Protestant, Catholic, and Dissenter, – Milesian and Cromwellian, – the Irishman of a hundred generations and the stranger who is within our gates.'[9] In other words, the criterion of national identity for inclusion in the Irish nation was, simply, residency in Ireland, rather than being determined by an inherited homogeneous culture. This theory conforms to the view of Philip Spencer and Howard Wollman, who, in *Nationalism: A Critical Introduction*, state that national identities were 'shaped and formed much more on the basis of nationalist imaginings than by any inherent or fixed features of a reified culture.'[10] The concept of what constituted Irish nationality and who should belong to the Irish nation, originally devised by Theobald Wolfe Tone, was broadened by Thomas Davis, who declared in *The Nation*'s prospectus that

> Nationality is their first great object – a Nationality which will not only raise our people from their poverty, by securing to them the blessings of a DOMESTIC LEGISLATION, but inflame and purify them with a lofty and heroic love of country, – a Nationality of the spirit as well as the letter – a Nationality which may come to be stamped upon our manners, our literature, and our deeds.[11]

---

[9] Duffy, *Young Ireland*, p. 80.

[10] Philip Spencer and Howard Wollman, *Nationalism. A Critical Introduction* (London: Sage Publications, 2002), p. 3.

[11] Duffy, *Young Ireland*, p. 80. See also p. 527, where Davis claims that he alone wrote the prospectus for *The Nation*; the original statement can be found in 'Thomas Davis. The Origin of *The Nation*', 30 April 1844, NLI, MS 3199. However, John Blake Dillon, Davis's friend, offered some advice when Davis sent him a draft of the prospectus: 'I do not altogether approve of the one you wrote. It contains many good passages, but as a whole I think it would not answer the purpose for which it was intended … you might wish to improve it': Letter from John Blake Dillon to Thomas Davis, [n.d.], Charles Gavan Duffy Papers (2), Royal Irish Academy (RIA), MS 12 P 15, Box I (3).

Davis promoted a nationalism not just in terms of who should belong to the Irish nation, but one that embraced a way of living and a pursuit of culture which he hoped could be appreciated and shared by everyone in Ireland.

For Daniel O'Connell, Irish nationalism meant seeking Repeal in order to improve the welfare of the mainly Catholic population. He believed that the most expedient way of achieving this was to unify all the classes and creeds of Ireland into one movement. Conveniently, *The Nation*'s concept of nationality, in terms of the inclusivity of class and creed, coincided with the practical objectives of the Repeal cause. Class was important to the Repeal Association, not only in respect of increasing recruitment, but also in terms of the influence the middle and upper classes could bring to bear on the Repeal movement. *The Nation*'s journalism was conducive to the Association's need to expand the nationalist movement numerically, its theory of inclusivity often reiterated in its columns. An article in November 1842, for instance, true to *The Nation*'s prospectus, stated that

> when we come to deal with politics, we must sink the distinction of blood as well of sect. The Milesian, the Dane, the Norman, the Welshman, the Scotchman, and the Saxon, naturalised here, must combine, regardless of their blood ... This is as much needed as the mixture of Protestant and Catholic.[12]

As supporters of Daniel O'Connell's Loyal National Repeal Association were essentially lower-class Catholics, the Repeal movement needed to widen its scope, drawing the disparate elements of Irish society into as united a whole as possible in its attempt to overturn the Act of Union. *The Nation*'s appearance, therefore, was an encouragement to the inclusivity that O'Connell badly needed to broaden the appeal of the Repeal cause in terms of class and creed.

While the other Dublin Repeal papers mainly supported Catholic issues and interests, *The Nation* assumed a non-denominational position and, to a certain extent, helped to redress the balance of a predominantly Catholic Dublin Repeal press, for its writers' intention was to inculcate non-sectarianism into public opinion. The necessity of bringing Catholics and Protestants together to share a future for the combined good of the people of both creeds, and for the future benefit of Ireland as an independent nation state, was sought by many nationalist newspaper writers in the mid-nineteenth century, an ideal spearheaded by the 1840s *Nation*.

[12] 'Continental Literature', *Nation*, 26 Nov. 1842.

In fulfilling its commitment to the Repeal Association, many of *The Nation*'s weekly pages were filled with Repeal information, and the policies and the thinking of the Association's leadership were generally endorsed by the writers of *The Nation* during its first year. A quantitative assessment of *The Nation*'s value to the Repeal Association can be cited in terms of readership. On its first day, Saturday 15 October 1842, 12,000 copies of *The Nation* were printed, to be sold at 6d; its second issue reported that 'there was not one [copy] left at four o'clock on the day of publication, as the whole town will bear witness – that odd copies in the hands of the newsmen are selling at 2s each.'[13] Even though the eagerness of the public was not sustained directly after the first issue, *The Nation* became the highest circulated newspaper in Ireland, not just in terms of copies sold, as evidenced by stamp returns during 1842–43 (see Table I), for Charles Gavan Duffy has estimated that with its distribution from hand to hand 'till it was worn to fragments', and its extensive availability in reading rooms, readership could have surpassed a quarter of a million.[14] The geographical circulation of *The Nation* was widespread, as suggested by the numerous agents in all four provinces.[15] Further evidence of its presence in the provinces came, for instance, from the future IRB journalist, Charles Kickham, who recalled that in the village of Mullinahone, Co. Tipperary, about 100 copies of *The Nation* were sold each week.[16] Even particularly poor rural areas subscribed to *The Nation*. Another of the paper's writers, Catholic John Blake Dillon, informed Duffy one week that he was 'astonished' to find twenty-three *Nations* arriving in Ballaghaderreen (his home in Co. Roscommon), which barely had more than twenty-three houses, and where there was 'not perhaps in Ireland a village more beggarly.'[17] *The Nation*'s success can also be assessed qualitatively by its remarkable effect on countless people, and perhaps this can

[13] 'Answers to Correspondents', *Nation*, 22 Oct. 1842. According to Hugh Oram, many readers hired *The Nation* at a penny an hour as it was too expensive to buy. Oram, *The Newspaper Book*, p. 58.

[14] Duffy, *Thomas Davis*, p. 97; Duffy, *Young Ireland*, pp. 387–8.

[15] Eighty agents were listed in the first issue for Ireland, where it was also noted that there were agents in Liverpool and Manchester: *Nation*, 15 Oct. 1842.

[16] Charles Kickham, 'Notes on Young Ireland', *The Irishman*, 18 June 1881 and 24 Sept. 1881, in Comerford, *Charles J. Kickham*, p. 19.

[17] Letter from Dillon to Duffy, [n.d. but likely to be near the end of 1842], Charles Gavan Duffy Papers, NLI, MS 5756/32–3. John Blake Dillon (1814–66) was a barrister, and although a constitutional nationalist, he was involved in the 1848 attempted rebellion; following exile in America, he returned to Ireland in 1856, becoming an MP for Tipperary in 1865.

Table I Average circulation of stamps per issue of main Dublin papers from the fourth quarter 1842 to the fourth quarter 1843

	4/1842	1/1843	2/1843	3/1843	4/1843
Saunder's News Letter [Daily]	2,308	2,308	2,308	2,385	2,462
Freeman's Journal [Daily]	769	923	1,141	1,263	1,410
Evening Mail [Tri-weekly]	2,769	3,077	2,769	2,769	2,923
Evening Post [Tri-weekly]	1,538	1,231	1,436	1,372	1,949
Evening Freeman [Tri-weekly]	256	192	258	333	449
Evening Packet [Tri-weekly]	1,615	1,641	1,615	1,615	1,936
Evening Pilot [Tri-weekly]	581	628	705	859	1,147
Dublin Monitor [Tri-weekly]	513	526	515	513	513
Dublin Statesman [Bi-weekly]	577	635	625	462	481
Dublin Gazette [Bi-weekly]	96	96	–	115	115
Weekly Register	1,346	1,385	1,269	2,077	2,038
Weekly Freeman	2,962	3,000	4,192	6,000	7,231
Weekly Warder	2,231	1,962	2,538	2,500	3,154
World [Weekly]	1,154	1,065	904	904	887
Nation [Weekly]	4,583	4,885	6,308	9,500	10,730

Note: *Morning Register* [Daily] was 321 in 4/1842 but discontinued after 7 Jan. 1843.
Source: Based on 'Return of Number of Stamps issued to Newspapers and Amount of Advertisement Duty, 1842', House of Commons Papers (HCP), 1843 (98), XXX.513, 'Return of Number of Stamps … January–April 1843', HCP, 1843 (282) XXX.559, 'Return of Number of Stamps … April–June 1843', HCP, 1843 (611) XXX.571, and 'Return of Stamps … July–December 1843', HCP, 1844 (55) XXXII.419.

best be summarized by a correspondent in Paris whose letter was printed four weeks after *The Nation* began:

> I rejoice for Ireland, that she has at length found men who have resolved, through the instrumentality of the press, to restore her to her pristine grandeur – to make her a nation … What heart alive to patriotic emotions does not beat high at the reflection, that a new spirit has sprung up which wishes to show itself by enflaming

> Irishmen of every class and creed with a love of fatherland, and making them all conspire to the attaining of that noble end, nationality.[18]

Evidence of *The Nation*'s quality can also be provided, for example, by Daniel Owen Madden, a London journalist from Mallow, Co. Cork, who claimed that *The Nation* 'infused a spirit and life into the Agitation, which the tirades of O'Connellism would never have produced … Before its appearance, the Repeal Politics of Ireland were written with miserable insipidity and tameness.'[19] *The Nation* was founded by Charles Gavan Duffy, Thomas Davis and John Blake Dillon, and while Duffy was not a Trinity College graduate like Davis and Dillon, he was far more experienced as a professional journalist.[20] These young men who already belonged to the Repeal Association saw that supporting Repeal with their own newspaper was the most expedient way of promoting Irish nationalism, believing that newspapers would 'be for many a day, the stimulating power in Ireland.'[21]

The Dublin Repeal papers and the work of the Repeal Association

During its first volume, *The Nation* provided resolute support to the organization that was campaigning to repeal the Act of Union. There were no less than six other Dublin newspapers that already represented the Loyal National Repeal Association, published either daily, tri-weekly or weekly, which meant that Ireland already had an extensive coverage of Repeal news even before the advent of *The Nation* in the middle of October 1842. The proprietors of the Dublin newspapers that supported Repeal included Dr John Gray (part-owner) of *The Freeman* group of papers, *The Daily Freeman's Journal*, *The Evening Freeman's Journal* (tri-weekly) and *The Weekly Freeman's Journal*,

[18] 'Senanus', *Nation*, 12 Nov. 1842. This correspondent, using a pseudonym, may have been one of the Irish patriots living in Paris at this time.

[19] Madden, *Ireland … Part the First*, p. 303. Although Madden was a friend of Thomas Davis, he was not uncritical of his politics.

[20] While Davis and Dillon had worked together on *The Morning Register* in 1841, Davis also wrote for *The Citizen*, which became the *Dublin Monthly Magazine* in 1842; Duffy, too, had been a journalist on *The Morning Register*, before, as we shall see later, working on the *Belfast Vindicator*. Many secondary sources provide the background to the establishment of *The Nation*. See, for example: Richard Davis, *The Young Ireland Movement* (Dublin: Gill & Macmillan, 1987), pp. 13–27.

[21] 1st LA, *Nation*, 15 Oct. 1842.

Michael Staunton of *The Dublin Morning Register* (which ceased publication in January 1843) and *The Dublin Weekly Register*, and also Richard Barrett of *The Pilot* (tri-weekly), O'Connell's strongest supporter in the press.

Provincial newspapers also supported Daniel O'Connell and his Repeal Association; for example, *The Cork Examiner*, a tri-weekly newspaper established in 1841, was conspicuous for its role in assisting the Dublin nationalist press in their 1850s campaign for tenant right. Prior to the foundation of *The Nation*, Charles Gavan Duffy was an editor of the bi-weekly Catholic *Belfast Vindicator*, begun in 1839, which also supported the Repeal cause. These newspapers were especially useful for their coverage of the impressive Repeal meetings that took place throughout the country, where their journalists' reports of these events could also be reprinted in the Dublin Repeal newspapers, thus reaching a wider public. There were, of course, newspapers opposed to the repeal of the Union, such as the tri-weekly *Dublin Evening Mail*, launched in 1823 and strongly anti-Catholic; another was *The Warder*, a weekly newspaper established the year before and run by young middle-class Protestants.

Despite the number of Dublin Repeal newspapers and their wide distribution throughout Ireland, including some coverage in Britain, little progress had been achieved by the Repeal cause since the founding of the Repeal Association in 1840, until the arrival of *The Nation* two years later. It was not just the impact that *The Nation* seemed to have on the Repeal cause that was significant, but also its impact on the already established Dublin Repeal press. Despite the appearance on the market of yet another Repeal paper, it is noticeable that rather than decreasing, during 1843 the stamps issued to each, except Staunton's, had significantly increased from the year before (see Table II). This suggests that *The Nation* may have had an inspirational effect on the other Dublin Repeal papers, sharpening their ability to compete for readership, even if the proprietors were motivated by commercial reasons. However, it so happened that from the autumn of 1842 the Repeal Association strengthened its grassroots structure and increased its activities, thus giving the Dublin Repeal press far more to report, particularly throughout 1843, which no doubt also helped to boost sales.[22]

The organizational model for the Repeal Association was based on the successful campaign for Catholic Emancipation, when in 1823 Daniel O'Connell founded the Catholic Association and transformed its initially narrow following into a popular mass movement throughout Ireland. While the Dublin nationalist press was highly influential in the Emancipation

[22] William J. O'Neill Daunt, *Ireland and her Agitators* (Dublin: John Browne, 1845), pp. 236–40.

Table II Average number of stamps per issue of Dublin nationalist newspapers from 1842 to 1847

	1842	1843	1844	1845	1846	1847
Freeman's Journal	736	1,152	1,494	1,375	1,431	1,365
Evening Freeman	253	308	538	481	519	423
Pilot	649	835	1,093	836	699	523
Weekly Register	2,115	1,692	1,942	1,394	1,550	1,481
Weekly Freeman	3,558	5,106	5,462	3,981	4,038	4,558
Nation	4,583	7,856	8,606	6,327	5,760	5,096

Source: Based on 'Return of Number of Stamps issued at One Penny to Newspapers in United Kingdom, 1837–50', HCP, 1852 (42) XXVIII.497.

campaign, it was to have an even greater role in the early 1840s Repeal movement, especially with the presence of the innovative *Nation*. Though *The Nation*'s remit was to draw the middle and upper classes into the Repeal Association, the paper was also intended to appeal to the lower classes. *The Nation*'s writers believed that there was a 'growing love of reading among the operative and agricultural classes,' and took a direct interest in raising their standards of knowledge and literacy, supplying a number of reading societies with a variety of free newspapers each week and encouraging the development of Repeal reading rooms.[23] Clearly, in its appeal to all sections of Irish society, *The Nation* was in the vanguard of the Dublin Repeal press in assisting the Loyal National Repeal Association's quest of attaining wide public support.

As recruitment from the higher classes with their wealth and status would be highly advantageous to Repeal, the Association strove to present an image of respectability, along with aims that seemed viable and just. The Dublin Repeal press played a vital part in providing this information by publicizing both the proceedings of the weekly Repeal Association meetings

[23] 'Popular Reading Societies', *Nation*, 18 March 1843. See also: 'Popular Reading Societies', *Nation*, 1 April 1843. O'Neill Daunt, a leading Repealer, noted that T.M. Ray, Secretary of the Repeal Association, initially established Repeal reading rooms in the autumn of 1842: O'Neill Daunt, *Ireland and her Agitators*, p. 283. For *The Nation*'s involvement with Repeal reading rooms see, for example: 'Repeal Reading Rooms', 30 Nov. 1844. A good secondary source on this topic is: Roisín Higgins, 'The *Nation* Reading Rooms', in James H. Murphy (ed.), *The Oxford History of the Irish Book, vol. IV, The Irish Book in English, 1800–1891* (Oxford: Oxford University Press, 2011), pp. 262–73.

at the Dublin Corn Exchange and the public Repeal demonstrations and meetings that took place throughout the country and in Great Britain. Reports in the Repeal press of the Association's various meetings revealed that its leaders were able to express its policies articulately and intelligently, while providing the appearance of an efficient, well-structured and highly motivated organization that conducted its affairs in a business-like, professional manner. Furthermore, it was important that O'Connell and the movement he represented maintained a high public profile. The Repeal press made all this possible, particularly *The Nation*, due to the enormous popularity it achieved during its first year of existence.

Daniel O'Connell's concern for respectability was reflected in his delight when support was given to the Repeal Association by people from the upper ranks of Irish society. This can be demonstrated, for example, by his response to the admittance of an important new recruit, a baronet, at a Repeal dinner in Waterford: 'The accession of such a man was ominous of victory, and eloquently demonstrated the true character of the movement; for the support of such a man as Sir Richard Musgrave was not to be expected if it were not based upon justice and truth.'[24] Sir Richard, who had chaired the Repeal meeting earlier that day, was a prize catch for the Association as he was not only an aristocratic landlord, but also a Protestant. The acquisition of recruits of wealth and status in society enhanced the image of the Association and was a testament to its respectability. It was important, therefore, that information about recruits such as these was widely publicized in the Dublin Repeal press, demonstrating the growing diversity of the Association in terms of class and creed, and providing an inducement for others in the upper echelons of society to join the Irish nationalist cause.

At the core of the idea of respectability, the most powerful image that O'Connell wished to convey to Irish society and the British government was that of the emphatically peaceful nature of the Repeal Association, and the Dublin Repeal press was an important medium in conveying this image. O'Connell's call for non-violence in the meetings that he and his associates conducted was reiterated incessantly, almost like a mantra, and reported in the Dublin Repeal press. At his meetings, O'Connell expressed his abhorrence of physical force groups, whether open or conspiratorial. He dissociated Repealers from the Chartists, whose movement he believed was tainted by violence, and called on Repeal supporters to actively discourage Ribbonism, Catholic conspiratorial groups involved in crime and disaffection. O'Connell advocated the moral force of public opinion to achieve Repeal. He hoped that the power of the will of the nation, of

[24] 'Grand Repeal Meeting in Waterford', 9 July 1843, *Nation*, 15 July 1843.

the thousands upon thousands of enrolled Repealers, and the even more numerous attendees at the public Repeal gatherings, would persuade the government to grant Repeal. Mirroring O'Connell, as Charles Gavan Duffy, *The Nation*'s editor, remarked in his history of Young Ireland: 'the will of the people was the weapon by which they expected to accomplish their purpose.'[25] Furthermore, O'Connell thought that the Association could only be suppressed by the government if his followers violated the law; in other words, the 'shield of law' would protect the Repeal movement, provided that it remained peaceful.[26] The Repeal press fully supported Father Theobald Mathew's Temperance crusade which, without a doubt, contributed to the peaceful nature of the Repeal movement. Importantly, those not present at the Association's meetings to hear the Repeal rhetoric would know by the reports in the newspapers that non-violence was a creed adopted by O'Connell, which he believed was paramount to the advancement and eventual success of the Repeal movement. *The Nation* was especially useful in conveying this message as it attracted a much wider circulation than the other Dublin Repeal papers. But this peaceful policy was not advocated just by the reports of Repeal meetings in the press; it was strongly reinforced by the Dublin Repeal newspaper journalists in their leading articles. In May 1843 *The Dublin Weekly Register* declared, 'Let Ireland now triumph in this peaceful and constitutional struggle.'[27] It was evident, then, that the Repeal press played a vital role in endorsing and propagating Repeal policy.

While the Repeal Association and its press advocated non-violence and distanced itself from conspiratorial and seemingly violent organizations, a highly significant group of recruits drawn into Repeal was the Catholic clergy. The assistance of local priests had previously been shown to be beneficial to the work of the Catholic Association. Not only were Catholic priests at the grassroots level politically involved in the Repeal cause, support also came from the Catholic hierarchy. At a Corn Exchange meeting on 20 March 1843, O'Connell claimed that the majority of the bishops of Ireland were members of the Repeal Association.[28] Catholic clerical support was indeed pivotal; for instance, while providing anecdotal evidence of the sufferings of the people, which the Association could use as testimony to justify the political argument for Repeal, priests could also deliver compelling rhetoric conducive to the cause. An example of the latter can

[25] Duffy, *Young Ireland*, p. 339.

[26] Repeal banquet in Cork, 21 May 1843, *Nation*, 27 May 1843.

[27] 1st LA, *The Dublin Weekly Register*, 27 May 1843.

[28] *Nation*, 25 March 1843.

be cited at a Repeal banquet in Castlebar on 30 July 1843 when the Most Reverend Doctor MacHale, the Archbishop of Tuam, expressed praise for the leader of the Repeal movement and a justification for its existence; he 'resolved to be an uncompromising Repealer,' a solid testimony of support from an eminent clergyman.[29] There is no doubt that press reports of Repeal meetings showing how the Catholic hierarchy and the local priests were involved in the nationalist movement encouraged people to support the Repeal Association, one of the reasons for the increasing number of Repeal recruits and the thousands who arrived at Repeal demonstrations and meetings throughout the country during 1843.

Another indication of the respectability of the Repeal cause was the fact that, though male-dominated, the Repeal Association welcomed women into its ranks. Standing newspaper advertisements for the Dublin Corn Exchange weekly meetings, for example, indicated that women were permitted to observe free of charge in the gallery.[30] Press reports of Corn Exchange meetings noted the admittance of women into the Association.[31] At Repeal gatherings around the country, women and children formed a constituent part of the supportive crowds that greeted leading Repealers during their arrival at various venues, and could also be seen at the large meetings themselves. The Repeal press was certainly intended for both men and women. The fact that women were meant to be included in the readership of these newspapers was indicated by the regular articles on fashion and society news. For example, in March 1843 *The Nation* featured 'The newest London and Paris fashions for February, 1843'; and *The Weekly Freeman's Journal* provided society news in its regular 'Fashionable Intelligence.'[32] Of the Dublin Repeal papers *The Nation* could perhaps be seen as the most female-orientated, probably due to its extensive cultural and literary columns. However, the advancement of the Repeal Association did not rely solely on its inclusive nature; its survival and strength also relied on the structure and workings of the organization, and this is where the Dublin Repeal press had the opportunity to excel as its representative.

Reporting the weekly Repeal Association meeting at the Corn Exchange in the Dublin Repeal press was crucial to the Repeal cause.[33] This

[29] *Nation*, 5 Aug. 1843.

[30] Persons not enrolled into the Association had to pay a shilling for admission into the Corn Exchange.

[31] For example, Corn Exchange mtg., 7 Nov. 1842, *Nation*, 12 Nov. 1842.

[32] *Nation*, 11 March 1843; *The Weekly Freeman's Journal*, 22 July 1843.

[33] The Dublin Repeal press sometimes took note of regular provincial Repeal meetings. For example, *The Pilot* reported on 3 Feb. 1843 that a recent 'weekly meeting of the

meeting, conducted by the leading Repealers, was a focal point for the Repeal Association. Commenting on Repeal events was an ideal platform, providing publicity that would encourage new recruits, and information for those already belonging to the Association. A principal task of this meeting concerned enrolment where new supporters could be proposed, often accompanied by reasons why they wished to join the Repeal cause. Subscribers' contributions could be announced by the meeting's speakers, revealing a variety of support for the Association that reflected its inclusiveness. It was announced at a Dublin Repeal Association meeting on 18 July 1843, for example, that Sir Charles Wolseley, an English baronet, had sent in the subscriptions of forty-six English agriculturists who were duly admitted to the Association.[34] At a Corn Exchange meeting that September Duffy handed in 'the subscription of twenty English ladies from Everingham, in Yorkshire.'[35] Subscriptions would also come from Repeal reading rooms; for instance, at a Dublin Repeal Association meeting on 22 August 1843 a letter was read out which enclosed subscriptions from the Repeal Reading Rooms in Trim, Co. Meath.[36] Disclosing information about subscribers may have been a morale booster for those who were already supporters of Repeal, besides being an incentive for prospective recruits. Duffy, along with Dr Gray of *The Freeman* group, was particularly prolific in proposing new subscribers for admission into the Association. Importantly, an indication of the value of the press to the Repeal cause was the role of the newspaper office as a focal point of contact for those wishing to communicate with the Association.

Besides reporting Corn Exchange meetings, the Dublin Repeal press also performed an administrative function by printing comprehensive lists each week of those who had paid their subscriptions. These payments were known as the Repeal rent, reminiscent of the 1820s campaign conducted by the Catholic Association. There were three levels of subscriptions: the vast majority of supporters, known as Associates, paid a penny a month; for those who could afford more, Members paid £1 a year and Volunteers £10 a year.[37] Previously incorporated into the weekly Repeal meetings, from 6 February 1843 the acknowledgements of subscribers were too numerous to

Waterford Repeal Association was numerously attended, at which Counsellor Walsh presided.'

34 *Nation*, 22 July 1843.

35 Corn Exchange mtg., 11 Sept. 1843, *Nation*, 16 Sept. 1843.

36 *Nation*, 26 Aug. 1843.

37 Now disbanded, the Volunteers, a paramilitary group, had been formed during the American War of Independence to protect Ireland from possible French invasion, but was used by the patriots to help force concessions from the British government.

be read out and were henceforth printed separately in a new format as lists in the Dublin Repeal press. O'Connell attached particular importance to them; when *The Nation* and *The Dublin Weekly Register* initially omitted these receipts, they were severely reprimanded by him at a Corn Exchange meeting on 27 February 1843.[38]

From mid-October 1842, when *The Nation* joined the Dublin Repeal press, the weekly acknowledgements of subscribers grew in the columns of the Repeal papers in parallel with an ever-increasing total amount of Repeal rent collected. Most of these subscriptions were submitted by an individual on behalf of other people: this could include a collection from those residing in a particular area, such as 'Dunlavin, county Wicklow,' or 'Beragh, county Tyrone'; sometimes a parish priest would forward subscriptions from his parishioners, such as 'Rev. Edm. Prendergast' of Ballingarry; the rent often came from a group of workers or employees, for example, the 'Boot and Shoemakers,' the 'Dairymen of Dublin,' or the 'Chemical Works, St. Helen's, Lancashire.'[39] Although the total amounts fluctuated each week, partly as they were submitted on an *ad hoc* basis, overall they increased dramatically in *The Nation*'s first year. When *The Nation*'s first number was issued the Repeal rent collected for that week amounted to £57 9s 11½d; by the following June it had peaked at £3,104 7s 6½d.[40] These figures were a strong measure of the advance of the Repeal Association, and a morale booster for its supporters. Sometimes at the Dublin weekly meeting, when an amount was particularly significant, it was announced amidst vociferous cheering. Apart from testifying to Repeal's wide geographical dispersion throughout Ireland and Great Britain, these subscription lists printed in the Dublin Repeal press were indicative of the Repeal Association's success in terms of recruitment and finance since the initial publication of *The Nation*.

Many subscriptions to the Association arrived from Great Britain, where there was much support for the Repeal cause and *The Nation* newspaper, mostly, expectedly, from Irish immigrants. Near the end of January 1843, for example, a correspondent from Liverpool wrote to the editor of *The Nation*: 'the columns of your paper make the chords of our hearts vibrate with a feeling of unforgetfulness of the cradle of our race.

[38] *Nation*, 4 March 1843.

[39] 'Repeal Association', 'Return of Repeal rent for the week ending the 12th June, 1843', *Nation*, 17 June 1843.

[40] 'Loyal National Repeal Association', *Nation*, 15 Oct. 1842; *Pilot*, 23 June 1843. The Repeal rent was even higher the following year, when O'Connell and other leading Repealers were imprisoned: Repeal rent for week ending 17 June 1844 was recorded as £3,389 14s 8d, *Nation*, 22 June 1844; from then it began to decrease, e.g. for week ending 15 July 1844 it was £1,688 14s 3d, *Freeman's Journal*, 19 July 1844.

Here, in this large town, there are many of us who meet to feast upon its contents.'[41] In November 1842, about 2,000 persons reportedly attended a Repeal meeting in Liverpool, and more than three times that figure was recorded at another Repeal meeting there the following September; even though the presence of Daniel O'Connell, Junior, may have drawn more people, this increase in numbers was impressive.[42] Evidence from readers' letters and numbers of attendees at Repeal gatherings certainly suggests a correlation between *The Nation* and the advancement of the Repeal Association in Great Britain.

An important group within the Repeal movement was the Repeal Wardens whose supporting role at grassroots level was an integral part of the structure of the Repeal Association. While their duties were essentially ministerial, including arranging the collection of the Repeal rent in their local areas, they also ensured meetings were conducted peacefully, and actively discouraged secret societies. Repeal Wardens also assisted the Association in the dissemination of its publicity by arranging the regular despatch of Dublin Repeal newspapers around their localities and distributing them to those who would ensure their widest circulation.[43] Remembering that newspapers were highly expensive, many of those who would otherwise have had little chance of accessing them could now be reached. The Repeal Wardens' task of distributing these papers, which also often involved reading them aloud at local Repeal meetings, was a strong indication that the Association's leadership attached great importance to the printed word of the Dublin Repeal press. Not surprisingly, *The Nation* was the paper most requested throughout Ireland, evidenced by the Repeal Wardens' communications with the Association that were noted in the Corn Exchange meetings.

The Nation and the other Dublin Repeal newspapers certainly helped

---

[41] Letter from C. Magher, 28 Jan. 1843, *Nation*, 4 Feb. 1843.

[42] 'Great Repeal demonstration in Liverpool', 17 Nov. 1842, *Nation*, 19 Nov. 1842; 'Magnificent Repeal demonstration in Liverpool', 12 Sept. 1843, *Nation*, 16 Sept. 1843.

[43] Duties of Repeal Wardens relating to the Dublin Repeal press: 'The ninth duty of the Repeal Wardens is, *to take care that there shall be transmitted from* the association to each locality a WEEKLY NEWSPAPER for every two hundred associates, or a three-day paper for every four hundred, enrolled in that locality, as the case may be. The sum of ten pounds collected and forwarded to the association, entitles the Repealers of the district, whence it comes, to a weekly paper (THE NATION, the *Weekly Freeman*, or the *Weekly Register*) for the entire year *gratis*; and the sum of twenty pounds entitles them to the *Pilot* or *Evening Freeman* newspaper for the same period, if they prefer either to *two* weekly papers. The tenth duty of the Repeal Wardens is, to have the newspapers to which each parish or district may be entitled, *put into the hands of such persons as will give the greatest circulation to their contents*, so that each paper may be read by, and its contents communicated to, as many people as possible', *Nation*, 1 July 1843.

to enhance the image of the Repeal Wardens. Not only were their activities publicized in the Repeal press but they were also highly praised by Daniel O'Connell. At a Corn Exchange meeting in October 1842, O'Connell reportedly announced that: 'Their names would one day be as glorious as those of the Volunteers of '82; and he hoped to see the day when there would be a column erected in College-green large enough to have engrossed on it the names of every Repeal Warden.'[44] Even though O'Connell's style of public expression tended to be theatrical, not uncommon for a politician, a comment like this indicated the intrinsic value he attached to the Wardens' work. An occasional female could be numbered in their ranks; for example, it was announced at an adjourned Corn Exchange meeting on 22 March 1843 that Miss Maryanne Murphy had become a Repeal Warden.[45] Furthermore, a Miss Kate Carey was appointed to the higher position of Inspector of Repeal Wardens for the Swords district, Co. Dublin, at a Corn Exchange meeting on 18 July 1843.[46] Members of the clergy were also included amongst the numbers of Repeal Wardens; for instance, at a Corn Exchange meeting on 25 January 1843, O'Connell appointed the Rev. Mr A. Nolan, Parish Priest of Dunkerrin, King's Co., as an Inspector of Repeal Wardens in his district.[47] The Association preferred clergymen rather than lay people to be designated as Inspectors of Repeal Wardens, probably because of their knowledge of the local people and the authority that accompanied their ecclesiastical role in the community. Publicizing the work conducted by Repeal Wardens in the Dublin Repeal press suggested not only respectability among the Association's grassroots personnel, but demonstrated a seemingly efficiently run organisation.

Another function of the Dublin Repeal press was the provision of general publicity services for the Association's meetings, where notices and advertisements placed by the Association brought financial gain to these newspapers. The Corn Exchange weekly meeting, for instance, had a standing advertisement in the Dublin Repeal press. Requisitions for meetings throughout the country were advertised in the Dublin Repeal newspapers. A June 1843 issue of *The Pilot*, for example, printed the names of 116 people who had requested that a Repeal meeting be held for 'the Gentry, Clergy, and People of the County of LOUTH' in Dundalk on 29 June 1843, testimony to the socially inclusive nature of the Repeal cause.[48]

---

44 Corn Exchange mtg., 24 Oct. 1842, *Nation*, 29 Oct. 1842.

45 *Nation*, 25 March 1843.

46 *Nation*, 22 July 1843.

47 *Nation*, 28 Jan. 1843.

48 *Pilot*, 26 June 1843.

Resolutions of meetings in Repeal newspapers were another form of publicity, for these were the official declarations of the attendees at the Association's meetings throughout the country. For example, on *The Nation*'s front page on 19 August 1843, and repeated the following week, Repealers in the Barony of Ennishowen in Ulster gave notice of their Repeal resolutions following their Baronial meeting on 7 August 1843. One of these resolutions was intended to dispel the view in the north that the Catholic Repealers desired a Catholic ascendancy, thus promoting the Association's principle of unity of creed.

Apart from the leading articles in the Dublin Repeal press, many others appeared – sometimes a whole series of articles – that contributed to the work of the Association, either recording its activities or through educative means. For instance, a series entitled 'Repeal – the Movement' recorded the progress of the cause in *The Nation*.[49] *The Dublin Weekly Register* and *The Nation* also published the 'Repeal Catechism,' comprising a number of chapters spread over several issues.[50] Written from a nationalist perspective and expressed in colloquial language, each chapter was structured on a question and answer basis between a farmer and a Repeal agitator; it presented an historical insight into the Irish Parliament, and how the Union was created. Instructive and informative, the 'Repeal Catechism' explained and reiterated in a different format the arguments that were continually expressed in Repeal meetings throughout the country and in the Corn Exchange. While using reasoned argument, this series also included fiery rhetoric similar to that uttered by the Repeal Association's speakers. Initially unacknowledged, it was O'Connell himself who had written these chapters, directly using Repeal newspapers as a medium to convey his critique of British rule.[51] The Repeal press also sought other means of persuasion. On 17 December 1842, *The Nation* began a series, 'Political Text Book,' and in the first part it reprinted a quotation from John Locke about a people's right to dislodge an abusive legislature, suggesting that this piece of political philosophy could be applied to the Union. This tactic of persuasion was more likely to appeal to the higher classes as they would have been more familiar with political theorizing than the lower classes. With a variety of articles, therefore, the Repeal press could communicate political messages that were adapted to Irish society's different social groups.

A particularly popular column in *The Nation* was 'Answers to Correspondents' which essentially printed brief replies to letters from readers

[49] See, for example: *Nation*, 8 July 1843.

[50] Examples: *Nation*, 5 Nov. 1842 and *Weekly Register*, 7 Jan. 1843.

[51] Duffy, *Thomas Davis*, p. 94.

who may have submitted positive comments, criticism or queries; sometimes readers' poetry was printed. Occasionally, Duffy admitted, readers' letters were invented by the paper's writers in order to convey information relevant to the Repeal cause or to make or reinforce a particular point, perhaps to refute or agree with an invented opinion.[52] With its small snippets of print, this column was yet another form of nationalist teaching, attracting an overwhelming number of letters to *The Nation*.

The Dublin Repeal press also provided a platform for the dissemination of future Repeal policy. For example, once Repeal was achieved, the Association envisaged a remodelled Irish House of Commons, household suffrage, a ballot and a redistribution of parliamentary seats.[53] These and the Association's other aims, such as a new landlord and tenant arrangement, showed that the Association had a practical and democratic vision for a future society under Irish rule. In the meantime, O'Connell began plans for the establishment of a Council of Three Hundred, an idea he developed during 1843, which could be likened to a parliament-in-waiting. Another policy, suggested by Dr Gray, was immediately acted upon: the appointment of arbitrators in every parish who, in place of the petty sessions courts, could settle disputes between people.[54] These arbitrators were initially intended to replace those magistrates who had been dismissed by the government for supporting the Repeal Association. O'Connell thought highly of the arbitration scheme; at a Repeal banquet on 30 July 1843 at Castlebar, Co. Mayo, he reportedly saw the 'appointment of arbitrators as one of the most important and momentous steps that had been taken since the commencement of the Repeal movement.'[55] Publicity and support in the Dublin Repeal press was conducive to the practical application of this policy; arbitrators were named, their progress was monitored, and these courts were shown to be workable and effective.[56] Dr Gray had a pivotal role in the research and implementation of the Arbitration Courts, a key example of the close links between the Association and the personnel of the Dublin Repeal press.

The Repeal Courts of Arbitration were not destined to last however. In the context of the arrests and indictments of the leading Repealers at

[52] Charles Gavan Duffy, *My Life in Two Hemispheres, vol. I*, (London: T. Fisher Unwin, 1898) p. 73.

[53] Address from O'Connell 'To the people of Ireland', Corn Exchange mtg., 5 June 1843, *Nation*, 10 June 1843.

[54] Corn Exchange mtg., 18 July 1843, *Nation*, 22 July 1843.

[55] *Nation*, 5 Aug. 1843.

[56] See examples: 'Arbitration Court, Blackrock – yesterday', *Nation*, 30 Sept. 1843; 'The Arbitration Courts', *Weekly Freeman*, 7 Oct. 1843.

the end of the year, although deemed 'very successful' at a weekly Repeal meeting on 19 February 1844, a resolution was passed dissolving the link between the Repeal Association and the Courts. Following the conviction of O'Connell and other leading members that month for conspiracy, Repealers had no wish to place the Association 'at a disadvantage' and incur a further attack from the government.[57] Importantly, the formation of the Courts of Arbitration and their administration was indicative of the essence of Irish nationalism in action, the process whereby the Irish people were attaining the power to govern themselves by superseding British law, albeit on a small scale. These courts were a forerunner of the future when the Land League of the late 1870s to early 1880s established its own land courts to settle agrarian disputes in defiance of the law, and when, in the early twentieth-century, republican nationalists founded the Sinn Féin Courts of Arbitration.

There is little doubt that the Dublin Repeal press was crucial for the progression of the Repeal cause. Most of the columns of the Dublin Repeal press were dedicated, directly or indirectly, to the affairs and policies of the Association. During 1843 the Repeal cause was so eventful that many issues of the Dublin Repeal newspapers included free supplements to accommodate all the reporting of the Association's activities.[58] Many of those persons connected with the Dublin nationalist press were active Repealers, some of them (such as Duffy and Gray) sitting on the Association's General Committee. Furthermore, a variety of testimonies by leading Repealers can be cited to show the worth of the Dublin Repeal press to the Repeal cause. At an Association meeting in March, addressing the chairman, O'Connell himself declared: 'We are sir, singularly fortunate in our Repeal press, and I sincerely believe that no country was ever better served than Ireland now is by the newspapers which advocate our cause.'[59]

At another meeting that August, referring to the huge public outdoor Repeal gatherings that took place throughout the country, O'Connell stated that

> An elevated space ought to be reserved for the exclusive use of the

---

[57] *Freeman's Journal*, 20 Feb. 1844. Near the end of 1844, O'Connell asked Dr Gray to assist him in reviving the Arbitration Courts, but without any connection with the Repeal Association (by then Repeal newspaper editors had resigned from the Association), but this does not seem to have made much progress: 'Arbitration Courts – Mr. O'Connell', Letter from O'Connell to Gray & his reply, 10 Nov. 1844, *Nation*, 16 Nov. 1844.

[58] For example: *Weekly Freeman*, 3 June 1843; *Pilot*, 5 July 1843; *Weekly Register*, 5 Aug. 1843.

[59] Corn Exchange mtg., 22 March 1843, *Nation*, 25 March 1843.

> gentlemen of the press; and it should be railed in so as to prevent pressure upon the gentlemen of the press (hear, hear) – for it was impossible for them to report with anything like care or accuracy when they were pressed and pushed about on all sides.[60]

This remark suggests recognition of the importance and concern for the quality of the reporters' work, and perhaps a certain respect for them that may have been missing from earlier years.[61] Denis Holland, the future proprietor of the 1858 *Irishman* newspaper, noticed that during his speeches at the large outdoor meetings in the 1840s, 'O'Connell kept his hands occupied by gently twisting and untwisting the long hair of journalists seated in front of him.'[62]

Another indication of the value of the Repeal press to the Association is given by the toasts that were proposed at Repeal dinners and banquets that followed these large meetings. Toasts were usually reserved for matters and people of significance, the most frequent being directed at the Repeal cause and the Queen. However, they were often proposed to the Repeal press in general, and sometimes to particular Repeal newspapers and their proprietors or editors. At the end of a Repeal banquet in Mullingar, Co. Westmeath, on 14 May 1843, it was reported that the chairman, the Bishop of Meath, proposed a toast to: '"The health of Dr. Gray, and the *Freeman's Journal*;" and he would also add to the toast, "THE NATION, the *Pilot*, the *Weekly Freeman*, the *Weekly Register*, and the *Drogeda* [*sic*] *Argus*."'[63] At a Repeal banquet following a large meeting in Tullamore, King's Co., on 16 July 1843, it was reported that, 'The Chairman said the next toast was one that claimed the gratitude of the Irish people – the palladium of their rights – the Repeal Press of Ireland.'[64] Members of the nationalist press were often given the opportunity to directly address Repeal supporters. That August at a Repeal dinner in Tara, Co. Meath, reportedly seating over 1,000 people, Dr Gray declared 'on behalf of the national press of Ireland, that the members of it were politicians in the strongest sense of the word ... and as an Irishman he was ready to strike out boldly for the political

[60] Corn Exchange mtg., 14 Aug. 1843, *Nation*, 19 Aug. 1843.

[61] For a summary of O'Connell's treatment of reporters in the previous two decades see: Inglis, 'O'Connell and the Irish Press 1800–42', *IHS*, pp. 18–20.

[62] Denis Holland, 'Daniel O'Connell', *Emerald* (New York), vol. 4 (82), 28 Aug. 1869, pp. 58–9, in Paul Bew and Patrick Maume, 'The Great Advocate', (a review of Patrick M. Geoghegan, *King Dan: the Rise of Daniel O'Connell, 1775–1829*) *Dublin Review of Books* (8), Winter 2008–09, http://www.drb.ie, accessed 27.06.2009.

[63] *Nation*, 20 May 1843.

[64] *Nation*, 22 July 1843.

liberty of his country (hear, hear, and cheers).'[65] This statement typifies the commitment, loyalty and dedication of the nationalist journalists to the Repeal cause at this time, and was reflected in the rhetoric of their compelling leading articles.

Realizing its intrinsic value, O'Connell wielded much power and influence over the Dublin Repeal press at this time, although, as we shall see in the next chapter, of the Dublin Repeal newspapers *The Nation*, much to O'Connell's disquiet, was the most independent of both himself and the Association. The Dublin Repeal press was not only an essential aid in strengthening O'Connell's position as leader of the Repeal movement, it was also where he conducted much of his political leadership. O'Connell possessed the desirable qualities that a political leader needed in order to achieve success. He was a charismatic, strong and focussed leader of the Repeal movement throughout most of 1843. His rhetoric, whether it was delivered orally or in print, was skilled and impassioned. Being his main power-base, the Dublin Repeal press enhanced the cult of personality that surrounded him and his role as leader of the nationalist cause. Much of this was achieved through the extensive coverage those newspapers gave to O'Connell and his work in the Repeal Association. Requests for financial support for O'Connell also appeared regularly in *The Nation* and the other Dublin Repeal papers, such as the series entitled 'The O'Connell Tribute.'[66] Following his tenure as Lord Mayor of Dublin, 1841–42, which had raised his status in society, O'Connell was able to concentrate fully on Repeal matters. A particular event that accorded an enormous amount of publicity in the Dublin Repeal press was the Mansion House debate on the Repeal of the Union, from 28 February to 2 March 1843, where O'Connell successfully opposed Isaac Butt, an anti-Repealer and Protestant barrister. Of the Repeal newspapers, *The Nation* was particularly useful to O'Connell, due to its enormous popularity.

Although other Repeal leaders attended demonstrations and meetings, it was O'Connell's presence that caused the most excitement. Reporting his meetings at the Corn Exchange and especially his personal appearances throughout the country, with the many thousands of people in attendance, was paramount to the progress of Repeal. O'Connell was not only greatly praised and revered, but his presence sometimes caused such euphoria that reporters were unable to find words to describe the spectacles they witnessed. At a huge Skibbereen Repeal gathering in June 1843, for instance, a reporting

[65] 'Great "Monster" Repeal meeting on the hill of Tara', 15 Aug. 1843, *Nation*, 19 Aug. 1843.

[66] See, for instance: *Weekly Freeman*, 24 June 1843.

journalist did 'not have language to describe the extraordinary character of the scene' that the people of Skibbereen presented O'Connell on his arrival in the town. At the meeting itself, when he appeared before the people, the reporter observed 'indescribable affection, delight, and jubilee.'[67] Of course, many attendees at large meetings like these, unable to hear the Liberator's rhetoric, would later have access to his words in the Repeal newspapers. Not only did the Dublin Repeal press publicize O'Connell's speeches and addresses to the people, and describe his personal appearances at the ever-grander public gatherings week after week, they also wrote leading articles in support of his policies. During much of 1843 the Dublin Repeal press, O'Connell and the Repeal Association had the appearance of being locked together in a harmonious effusion of Irish nationalism.[68]

The most successful activities of the Repeal Association were the large public demonstrations and meetings that took place throughout the country. These the Dublin nationalist press could fully exploit with colourful reports and strident editorial comments. Repealers often assembled at historic places to evoke a sense of perceived past injustice by the British or of Irish gallantry. It has to be said, though, that reported calculations of the numbers present at these events were rough estimates but, even allowing for exaggeration, the figures were impressive for the time. Most of the social groups in Irish society, especially the lower classes, were represented at these venues, where speeches were delivered by the Repeal leadership and prominent supporters. Repeal banquets or dinners followed these large gatherings, with further speeches, and were usually attended by the higher classes of society, such as MPs, aldermen, priests, members of the bar, gentlemen and, though far less common, aristocratic landlords, most of whom would have been present at the preceding meeting. These large Repeal gatherings were reported in the Repeal press, both locally and nationally. *The Times* referred to them as 'monster meetings' and during 1843 this phrase came to be used by Repealers themselves and, since then, by historians.[69]

Reporting these monster meetings in the Dublin Repeal press had several advantages. For the thousands of persons attending them, hearing the speeches without the assistance of modern day technology would have

[67] 'Repeal demonstration in Skibbereen', *The Cork Examiner*, 22 June 1843, reprinted in *Nation*, 1 July 1843.

[68] There was, however, friction between *The Nation* and *The Pilot*, the latter being critical of the Young Irelanders. See, for instance: 1st LA, *Nation*, 28 Jan. 1843. This antagonism will be discussed in the next chapter.

[69] *The Times*, 1 July 1843, reported by O'Connell at the 'Great Trades Demonstration in Dublin', 3 July 1843, *Nation*, 8 July 1843.

proved difficult, and it was therefore useful that they were printed in the Repeal press. Furthermore, it demonstrated to those not present that there were respectable and key members of society in attendance. The Repeal press could also record the remarkably peaceful behaviour displayed at these outdoor gatherings. Significantly, the monster meetings exhibited a sense of unity and solidarity within the Repeal movement, and also between the different social classes in Irish society. Although political in intent, these meetings were also enjoyed as shared social experiences, important for the cohesiveness of the movement and thus for the development of Irish nationalism. Repeal journalists reported on the highly emotive speeches delivered at these events, while also describing the impressive visual images and activities experienced by those present. Emblems of Irish nationalism, such as houses decorated with green foliage, the erection of triumphal arches of green boughs and bands playing nationalist music were common; special floats were sometimes created that represented the support of specific trades. The publicity for the monster meetings provided by the Dublin Repeal press coincided with increased support for Repeal, and the more they were publicized from the autumn of 1842 and during 1843, the grander they became. The relationship between the Repeal Association and the Repeal press, when the sales of these newspapers soared during 1843 (see Table I), is a key reflection of the reciprocal nature between the nationalist press and the organizations it supported.[70]

The Dublin Repeal press' reports of these monster meetings, like the printed lists of those contributing their Repeal rent, are highly valuable to the historian, providing evidence, not only of an indication of the approximate numbers of people in attendance, but also their occupations and social status in Irish society. In Waterford, for example, the procession that preceded a meeting in July 1843 consisted of various trades, such as 'Carpenters, Farriers, [and] Shoemakers,' while those on the platform included Daniel O'Connell, the Mayor of Waterford, the editor of *The Waterford Chronicle*, at least one barrister, town councillors and numerous priests.[71] This was typical of the social mix at these meetings and, while providing an insight into those groups who supported Repeal, was further testament to the inclusiveness of the Repeal cause that was encouraged by the Dublin Repeal press. Notably, the characteristics and the development of the Repeal cause in Ireland and Great Britain in the early 1840s could

[70] It can be seen from Table II that this trend continued during 1844, probably due to the trial and imprisonment of Daniel O'Connell and other leading Repealers, including newspaper personnel.

[71] 'Grand Repeal meeting in Waterford', 9 July 1843, *Nation*, 15 July 1843.

be identified through the varied publicity services provided for the Repeal Association by the Dublin Repeal newspapers.

During *The Nation*'s first year of existence, these monster meetings became progressively more impressive in their expression of support for the Irish nationalist cause, not only in terms of the enormous numbers of people who arrived at the designated meeting places, but also in the ever-increasingly elaborate displays of support for the Repeal Association, and especially for O'Connell. While attendance figures at the large public meetings fluctuated, the overall trend was upwards.[72] Two Repeal demonstrations in November 1842, one in Waterford and another at Birr, King's County (now Co. Offaly), were each reportedly attended by an estimated 60,000 persons.[73] Six months later, in Cork on 21 May 1843, an estimated 500,000 people gathered for a demonstration, where numerous trades were represented in a procession that reportedly took three hours and five minutes to pass O'Connell's stationary carriage; and at the banquet in the evening 900 people were noted as seated.[74] The number of those who attended on horseback was also indicative of the increasing support for the monster meetings. On his way to a large Repeal gathering at Wexford in July 1843, *The Nation*'s reporter noted that when O'Connell arrived 'At Ferns he was met by upwards of six hundred horsemen from Enniscorthy, composed of the most respectable and wealthy men in the town.'[75] At a Corn Exchange meeting on 12 September 1843, O'Connell remarked that at his huge meeting in Loughrea, Co. Galway, two days previous, 'There could not be less than ten thousand horsemen.'[76] The following week in the same county, at a monster meeting in Clifden, the Repeal press reported the presence of 12,000 horses and ponies, of which the 'peasant cavalry' numbered 600.[77]

It was, in fact, the prospective number of horse riders and how

---

[72] Attendance figures at meetings varied and could depend, for example, on the strength of local support or the number of inhabitants living in a district. At a large Repeal demonstration in Trim, Co. Meath, in March 1843, the reporter estimated an attendance of only 20,000 people, noting 'the very scattered population of Meath', but the influential presence of the many wealthy inhabitants was thought to compensate for the comparatively low turnout: 'Great Repeal demonstration at Trim', 19 March 1843, *Nation*, 25 March 1843.

[73] 'O'Connell in Waterford. Great Repeal demonstration', 10 Nov. 1842, *Freeman's Journal*, 12 Nov. 1842; 'Great Repeal demonstration at Birr', 13 Nov. 1842, *Freeman's Journal*, 15 Nov. 1842.

[74] Report from *Cork Examiner* in *Nation*, 27 May 1843.

[75] 'Another "monster" meeting. The Wexford demonstration in favor [*sic*] of repeal', 20 July 1843, *Nation*, 22 July 1843.

[76] *Nation*, 16 Sept. 1843.

[77] 'Magnificent Repeal demonstration in Clifden', 16 Sept. 1843, *Nation*, 23 Sept. 1843.

they were to be mustered that was a key factor in the banning of the Clontarf meeting. Francis Morgan, a solicitor, took it upon himself to issue instructions to those intending to arrive on horseback; handbills were posted around Dublin and advertisements were placed in newspapers that riders should form into troops, led by officers.[78] The government proclamation that banned the meeting at Clontarf specifically referred to the riders: 'Advertisements and Placards have been printed and extensively circulated, calling on those Persons who propose to attend the said Meeting on Horseback to meet and form in Procession, and to march to the said Meeting in Military Order and Array.'[79] In the state trials that followed the arrests of the leading Repealers, an advertisement in *The Nation* entitled 'Repeal Cavalry,' placed a week before the Clontarf meeting, was cited as incriminating evidence by the Solicitor-General.[80] From the government's perspective, it could have seemed as though O'Connell (who, in fact, had not authorized this publicity) was amassing his own personal army – albeit without weapons – which provided the authorities with what they deemed a good enough reason to prohibit this meeting.[81]

The monster meeting held on the Hill of Tara drew the largest number of attendees. Remembered as the seat of the ancient high kings of Ireland, reporters estimated that 750,000 persons gathered there on 15 August 1843.[82] Even taking into consideration the likely exaggeration and guesswork of the statistics of these monster meetings, they do suggest a correlation between the publicity that appeared in the Dublin nationalist press and their overall increasing attendances, depending on location, with the advance of time.

On the same day as the Tara meeting, another took place at Clontibret in Co. Monaghan. Its location was important, noted by *The Nation*'s reporter as 'a glorious demonstration in the heart of Protestant Ulster'; it was there that Hugh O'Neill defeated the English in the 1595 Battle of Clontibret.

---

[78] Francis Morgan claimed responsibility for placards in Dublin, adjourned R.A. mtg, 11 Oct. 1843, *Freeman's Journal*, 12 Oct. 1843; 'Meeting of the Corporation', 20 Oct. 1843, *Freeman's Journal*, 21 Oct. 1843.

[79] 'The Coercion – The Proclamation', *Nation*, 7 Oct. 1843, 2nd ed.

[80] 'Repeal cavalry. Clontarf meeting', *Nation*, 30 Sept. 1843; 'The State trials', 9 Feb. 1844, *Freeman's Journal*, 10 Feb. 1844.

[81] The phrase 'Repeal Cavalry' was not new. At a Repeal meeting on 11 January 1841, O'Connell remarked on the 'farmers there, mounted on their horses. They were his Repeal cavalry (cheers and a laugh)': 'Great Munster Provincial meeting', *The Cork Southern Reporter*, reprinted in *Freeman's Journal*, 14 Jan. 1841.

[82] *Nation*, 19 Aug. 1843. At a Corn Exchange meeting on 22 August 1843, O'Connell estimated that at least a million men, women and children were there, and possibly even one and a half million, *Nation*, 26 Aug. 1843. *The Illustrated London News* presented an engraving of the meeting on Tara Hill in its 26 Aug. 1843 issue.

Leading Repealer W.J. O'Neill Daunt was present and delivered a rousing discourse on Repeal to the reportedly 300,000 attendees. Mr M.G. Conway, editor of *The Newry Examiner*, was also there and 'addressed the meeting in a brilliant and effective speech'; this was one of many occasions when members of the provincial Repeal press worked alongside the Repeal leadership.[83] Co-operation between the provincial Repeal press and the Dublin Repeal press conveyed an impression of a truly national campaign, an image that the Repeal leaders were anxious to relay to the British government.

Although the meeting at Tara was the one most remembered by Irish nationalists and historians, another important gathering was given even more publicity by the Dublin nationalist press, the demonstration at the Rath of Mullaghmast, Co. Kildare. Although there were fewer people present than at Tara, of all the monster meetings this was perhaps the most representative of the Irish nation and Irish nationality. In Parliament that September, when the Queen's Speech confirmed that Repeal would not be granted, in a marked challenge to British ministers, a Requisition was issued by the people of Leinster to hold a meeting at Mullaghmast on 1 October 1843. This Requisition consisted of an unprecedented number of names, over 2,308, which was not to be exceeded in the later Repeal years.[84] *The Nation* viewed the Requisition for this meeting as 'an unique document – one to which few other countries could produce a parallel – a document indicative of the resolution, patriotism, and unanimity of the Irish masses.'[85] The logistics of collecting and printing all these names (and their locations) in the mid-nineteenth century was a mark of the level of determination of Repealers and their newspapers. It was announced in the Dublin Repeal press a week after the meeting that this Requisition had been 'signed by TWO HUNDRED AND EIGHT CLERGYMEN, ONE HUNDRED Members of the Corporate Bodies, and above TWO THOUSAND of the Gentry, Freeholders, Burgesses, and other inhabitants of the province.'[86] (There is no evidence to suggest that these names were printed without permission or that false names were submitted to the press.) The publication of this enormous list of names prior to the Mullaghmast meeting was an outpouring of Irish nationalism in an act of unity and defiance against the British government, expressed through the medium of the Dublin Repeal press.

Like many of the other monster meetings, the site of Mullaghmast

---

83 'Repeal in Ulster', *Nation*, 19 Aug. 1843.
84 *Nation*, 23 Sept. 1843, with additional names on 30 Sept. 1843.
85 'The Great Leinster meeting', *Nation*, 23 Sept. 1843.
86 'Leinster declaration for Repeal', *Nation*, 7 Oct. 1843.

was chosen for its historical relevance to the Irish nationalist cause. As a reminder to its readers of the perceived truth of this historical event, a fortnight before the monster meeting, *The Nation* told them: 'The Rath of Mullaghmast has been selected for this great meeting, as the scene of a massacre atrocious even for the Saxon. The Earl of SUSSEX, shortly after the "Reformation," having invited FOUR HUNDRED CHIEFTAINS of Leinster to a conference on this hill, murdered them in cold blood.'[87] The day prior to this meeting, *The Nation* predicted that 'it will be the monster of the Monster Meetings. In numbers it will equal Tara – in intensity of feeling and importance of character it will surpass it ... Mullaghmast of the Martyrs will become Mullaghmast of the Victors – not a place of tears, but of triumph.'[88] The Mullaghmast meeting on 1 October 1843 was a highly successful celebration of the Repeal cause and Irish nationalism; it was estimated that half a million people were present, representing all sections of society. The pre-meeting publicity in the Dublin Repeal press had attracted the 'presence of a special government reporter' and 'several English gentlemen of all shades of politics.' Representatives of Irish cultural nationalism also attended, including John Hogan, the renowned Irish sculptor, John Cornelius O'Callaghan, the historical author, Henry MacManus, the Irish historical painter and W.H. Holbrooke, the Repeal Association's engraver and lithographer. In a piece of theatre, an offering was made to O'Connell by this group when Hogan placed a specially created 'Irish National Cap,' in a style reminiscent of the 'old Milesian crown,' on O'Connell's head.[89] This whole demonstration at Mullaghmast, at once a celebration of Irish nationalism and intended to discredit the Anglo-Saxon race and the British government, brought an emotional response from the Dublin nationalist press. *The Dublin Weekly Register* remarked:

> This great event, which has for some weeks absorbed the interest of public expectation, both amongst ourselves and in the country of the Saxon, has at length come and passed away, and its glories have left an impression never to be effaced – graved indelibly on

[87] 3rd LA, *Nation*, 16 Sept. 1843. For a brief reference to this incident, see: Hiram Morgan, 'Mullaghmast, massacre of', in S.J. Connolly (ed.), *The Oxford Companion to Irish History*, 2nd ed. (Oxford: Oxford University Press, 2002), p. 390, where it is stated that more than forty Irish chieftains were massacred by the English in the sixteenth century, not the figure of 400 claimed by the Repeal press. Whatever the historical truth of this incident, it served its purpose as an example of what Irish nationalists perceived as English cruelty, thus reinforcing justification for political separation.

[88] 3rd LA, *Nation*, 30 Sept. 1843.

[89] '"Monster" Repeal meeting at Mullaghmast', *Nation*, 7 Oct. 1843.

> the souls of all who were fortunate enough, to witness or to bear a part in so magnificent a manifestation of the national will.[90]

Despite the presence of fewer people than at Tara, never before had there been such an open display of unity for the nationalist cause in Irish society than surrounding this meeting at Mullaghmast, made memorable at the time by the reports and comments of the journalists of the Dublin Repeal press.

At the root of the Repeal cause was a critique of the poor quality of life of the lower classes. It was no surprise, then, that the Repeal movement would appeal to this group as it was they who, according to Repeal rhetoric, would be the greatest beneficiaries once Repeal of the Union was granted. As W.J. O'Neill Daunt noted, 'Repeal is emphatically the poor man's question.'[91] One of the many advantages of Repeal for the lower classes was its democratic aspiration. The Association, for instance, advocated universal male suffrage and voting by ballot, another legacy of the United Irishmen. In the meantime, the poorer classes could express themselves politically by supporting the Repeal cause. They could attend the Association's meetings, and had access to nationalist information in the Repeal press, where their subscriptions were publicly acknowledged. Importantly, the lower classes' poor quality of life and sufferings were recognized and publicized in the Repeal press. In July 1843, for example, at a Corn Exchange meeting, the Rev. Mr O'Gara, parish priest of Dromcliffe and Kilpatrick in Co. Sligo, submitted £6 and 8s from 128 Repealers, and it was noted that, 'In handing in that sum he begged leave to remark that that was the fourth remittance from a poor locality on the western shores of Ireland.' He further mentioned the 'universal state of poverty' there, where 'extermination [land clearance] was carried on by [*sic*] wholesale.'[92] This information provided two pieces of knowledge: it showed that the poor (albeit influenced and urged on by their priests) were willing to support a political movement in order to improve their lives, and it lent further evidence, from the Association's perspective,

---

90 'Repeal. The answer of Ireland to the Saxon', *Weekly Register*, 7 Oct. 1843. While the truth of the Mullaghmast massacre is unclear, Irish nationalists have their own version of events. For example, in this report *The Weekly Register* continues: 'The flippant audacity Saxon scribblers [*sic*] have sought to falsify the records of the past, and to cast discredit on truth itself in their zeal for the maintenance of their own domination and our degradation, is unworthy of more than a passing notice of contempt on the same day and hour that we chronicle the event, from whose glory and utility they vainly endeavoured to detract.'

91 Letter read out at Corn Exchange mtg., 10 Oct. 1843, *Nation*, 15 Oct. 1843.

92 Corn Exchange mtg., 11 July 1843, *Nation*, 15 July 1843.

for the justification of the Repeal cause. Having their plight recognized in the Repeal press possibly empowered the poorer classes to a certain extent, but importantly it was an incentive for others like them to join the Repeal Association; perhaps it was also an indication to the wealthier classes of the moral fibre of the poor, who were willing to make financial sacrifices for the Repeal cause.

Much of Repeal's critique of the Union centred on economic issues where they received extensive coverage in the Repeal press. Repealers often conducted their own research on behalf of the Association. For example, travelling through Leinster in the autumn of 1842, gathering information on manufactures, O'Neill Daunt reported a universal complaint about the decay of the linen trade and the total unpopularity of the poor laws.[93] And when T.M. Ray, Secretary of the Repeal Association, and then also Repeal Missionary for Munster, visited the district around Charleville in Co. Cork in November 1842, he reported the existence of great poverty, and children unable to attend school as they lacked adequate clothing. Ray found that impoverishment on the land was due to high rents and a lack of manufactures, relating it to 'that fatal act which robbed Ireland of her industrial occupations, and her people of their spirit and nationality.'[94] In the Dublin Repeal newspapers during the first week of January 1843 O'Connell set out in full what he envisaged to be the aims of the Association; they included the attainment of fixity of tenure to benefit tenants, the protection and encouragement of native manufactures, and an end to absenteeism, where many aristocratic landlords resided away from their estates, mostly in England. Above all, O'Connell argued, a repeal of the Union was the overarching goal whereby these individual aims could be attained; that is, through an independent Irish parliament. Repealers believed that the country's economic decline could only be reversed by a repeal of the Act of Union. In substantiating their arguments, Repealers frequently provided statistical data to compare the economic differences between the quality of life under the Irish Parliament of 1782–1800 and the present. Much of this information was conveyed by the press reports of the weekly meeting of the Repeal Board of Trade conducted by Daniel O'Connell's son, John.[95] For

[93] Corn Exchange mtg., 10 Oct. 1842, *Nation*, 15 Oct. 1842. Besides placing too great a burden on small tenant farmers, the poor laws failed to adequately help those in need of its services.

[94] Corn Exchange mtg., 28 Nov. 1842, *Nation*, 3 Dec. 1842.

[95] Voluntary groups of Boards of Trade to promote Irish manufacture in the early part of the nineteenth century were developed into the Repeal Board of Trade by Daniel O'Connell. See: Paul A. Pickering, '"Irish First": Daniel O'Connell, the Native

example, at a meeting reported in a February 1843 issue of *The Nation* it was stated that at the time of the Act of Union nearly 1,000 operative hosiers were employed, whereas they now numbered fewer than 100.[96] Economic arguments in favour of Repeal were repeated continually by the Repeal leadership at the Association's Corn Exchange meetings; they also formed part of the rhetoric at the monster meetings throughout the country. With compelling articles in the Dublin Repeal press, concern over economic issues received considerable coverage, and contributed to what leading Repealers believed was a powerful case against the Union and a justification for the Repeal cause. Revisionist scholarship has since challenged the claims of Irish nationalists that economic hardship was mainly due to the Act of Union however.[97]

Of all the critiques propagated by the Dublin Repeal press and the Association's leadership, the relationship between landlords and tenants received the most systematic attack. While modern scholarship challenges the extent of nationalist anti-landlord indictment during the nineteenth century, this cannot detract from the sufferings endured by many people at that time.[98] Notably, the Devon Commission, which began investigating the legal arrangement between landlord and tenant in 1843, reported two years later of its oppressive nature.[99] Newspaper reports of Repeal speeches at meetings and banquets, and leading articles, produced some of the most vitriolic and impassioned rhetoric against the landlord and tenant system. *The Nation* was the most consistently outspoken of the Dublin Repeal newspapers; an article published in early December 1842 applied political theory to this issue, referring to the division of people into two classes, 'the

---

Manufacture Campaign, and Economic Nationalism, 1840–44', *Albion: A Quarterly Journal Concerned with British Studies*, vol. 32 (4), Winter 2000, pp. 599 and 604–5.

96 'Repeal Board of Trade', 5 Jan 1843, *Nation*, 11 Feb. 1843.

97 Modern scholars cite factors such as: the decline of Ireland's cottage industry after 1800 due to factory production in Great Britain and north-east Ulster; the price of grain fell steeply after the Napoleonic wars, during which much food had been supplied by Ireland; a rising population led to land shortages and rural unemployment. See: L.M. Cullen, *An Economic History of Ireland Since 1600,* 2nd ed. (London: Batsford, 1987) and L.M. Cullen (ed.), *Formation of the Irish economy* (Cork: Mercier Press, 1969). Examples of the Repealers' perspective on pre-famine economic issues can be seen in: 1st LA, *Nation*, 15 July 1843 and 1st LA, *Freeman's Journal*, 9 Aug. 1843.

98 An overview of revisionist writing on the land question in Ireland can be found in: Michael J. Winstanley, *Ireland and the Land Question 1800–1922* (London: Methuen, 1984).

99 Peel instigated this Royal Commission in response to the Repeal agitation; its recommendations, one of which was compensation for outgoing tenants for their improvements to the property, were rejected by the House of Lords.

master and the slave' with 'one of them living in luxury and idleness, and the other enduring burdens and privations' that had originated in the conquest of Ireland by the English. Though this rhetoric seemed to be couched in a socialist discourse, *The Nation*'s writers were emphatic about not advocating socialism; they believed in a society where every man would be 'most certain of enjoying the fruits of his own labour.' The article continued, referring to the place of aristocratic landlords in Ireland's history:

> a few hundred years ago, some hungry adventurers possessed themselves of the lands of the country, and reduced the inhabitants to a state of serfdom. Since that time the descendants of those robbers … have kept the whole political power of the country in their own hands, and have had recourse to every expedient which they thought best calculated to weaken the native inhabitants whom they plundered, and to confirm their own iniquitous domination.[100]

This article, which contributed to the Repeal debate on aristocratic landlordism, presents *The Nation*'s argument in a cogent manner, combining emotive imagery and political theory. While the Great Famine was to add a new intensity to the rhetoric against the landlord class and its association with English conquest and rule, it certainly was present before then, forming a key part of nationalist writing in the early 1840s Dublin Repeal press.

There were difficulties, however, with the Association's approach to the landlord question. To a certain extent, it challenged its own policy of attempting to unify all classes in Irish society; by criticizing the landlords, Repealers were risking their alienation. But they argued that the law between landlord and tenant could be changed following a Repeal of the Union, by such measures as the introduction of fixity of tenure, which would greatly reduce the endemic rural crime that was present in Irish society, thus benefiting both tenants and landlords. At a meeting of the Association on 16 May 1843, O'Connell reportedly explained:

> Who could contemplate without horror the revolting murders which were perpetrated, on the one hand, by the landlords, in turning their wretched tenants homeless and houseless on the world's bleak common, to die of starvation or the typhus fever in dykes or ditches – and, on the other, by the infuriated tenantry, who driven to desperation by oppression, madly and impiously took into their own

[100] 1st LA, *Nation*, 3 Dec. 1842.

> hands the administration of that vengeance which was the exclusive prerogative of the Most High (cries of hear, hear).[101]

O'Connell tried to emphasize that Repeal would have reciprocal advantages for landlords and tenants, that the rights of both would be protected.

In their attempt to strike a balance between railing at landlords and trying to entice them into joining the nationalist cause, Repealers were eager to show that there were decent landlords as well as bad ones. It was advantageous, then, for the Association to acquire the support of a landed proprietor who could appeal to others of his own class to join the movement. At one Corn Exchange meeting, O'Connell drew attention to Mr John A. O'Neill of Bunowen Castle, whose 'tenantry were comfortable and happy.' O'Neill, who had hitherto been 'distinguished for his high Orange feeling, and his strenuous opposition to the Catholic claims,' had now become a committed advocate for Repeal, and attempted to induce other landed proprietors to join the Association.[102] While this type of publicity was beneficial to the Repeal Association, landlords' support for the Repeal cause was generally minimal.[103]

Although the landlord system assumed a high profile in Repeal rhetoric, it did not completely dominate the Irish nationalist cause at this time, as it would in later decades. The Repeal debate was conducted on a much broader landscape, and included many other grievances, such as the poor law system. However, the exposure of the hardship suffered by rural workers was deemed compelling evidence of the quality of life experienced under the Union, and naturally this topic received a considerable amount of attention in the Dublin Repeal press.

Another method of inciting negative feelings against the Union was the claim that the governing class of the Anglo-Saxon race not only possessed a different racial identity from the Irish but was also morally unfit to rule Ireland. It was as though the English were seen as an alien race. One word in particular that was frequently used by Irish nationalists when referring to the English was 'stranger.' At a Dundalk monster meeting in Co. Louth,

---

[101] *Nation*, 20 May 1843.

[102] Adjourned Corn Exchange mtg., 12 Sept. 1843, *Nation*, 16 Sept. 1843.

[103] Apart from the Association's own observations, the Dublin Repeal press used independent evidence to substantiate the landlord and tenant problem. A personal view was expressed by the Rev. Mr Davern, when he used *The Nation* to write a series of letters, begun on 21 Jan. 1843, to Viscount Hawarden, a Tipperary landlord, and proceeded to relay how badly tenants suffered on his estate; Lord Harwarden vociferously denied any wrong-doing and an indictment was brought against Charles Gavan Duffy in 1844 following the death of Rev. Davern, but the charge was dropped.

for instance, at the end of June 1843, O'Connell remarked that the 'Saxon and the stranger domineered over them.'[104] Capitalizing on this idea, a perceived exposé of English immorality formed part of the Repealers' publicity programme; in particular, an indictment was directed against the execution of the British government's colonial and imperial policies. Referring to the 1798 rebellion, the Very Rev. Dr Howly claimed that England 'drenched the fields of Ireland with blood'; rhetoric that referred to 1798 could produce strong emotional feelings in many.[105] In January 1843 *The Nation* severely censured Britain's military presence in Afghanistan.[106] A critique of British imperialism was an important component of later Irish nationalist newspapers; the Fenians in the 1860s particularly attacked the morality of British policies abroad.

Although Irish nationalists mostly directed their censure at British rulers, the nature of English society was also targeted. For instance, the conduct of popular English and Irish political groups was compared; O'Connell claimed that whereas the English Chartists gathered in mobs that 'appeared to be comparatively brutal,' they, the Irish Repealers, assembled in 'peace, tranquillity, and, he would say, civilised decorum marked all those meetings.'[107] More specifically, flattering his countrymen, he believed that, 'The delicacy of the treatment extended by the males to the females at all those meetings was such as could not be surpassed in the most polished circles of society.'[108] The Repealers also attacked the capitalist culture of England. At an Association meeting in Dublin near the end of March 1843, according to O'Connell, comparisons between rich and poor in England made 'humanity shudder.' In reinforcing and developing O'Connell's rhetoric, *The Nation*'s first leading article in the issue containing that report claimed that the people of England were not to be trusted as they had been both physically and spiritually ruined by the capitalist system, referring to them as 'the slaves and ministers of our bitter tyrant.'[109] During a Repeal meeting in May 1843 O'Connell was reported as stating that 'He would refer to the evidence of [parliamentary] committees as to the morality of

---

[104] 'O'Connell in Dundalk', 29 June 1843, *Nation*, 1 July 1843.

[105] 'Great Repeal demonstration in the South Riding of Tipperary', 23 May 1843, *Nation*, 27 May 1843.

[106] 1st LA, *Nation*, 14 Jan. 1843. For a secondary source on the topic of British imperialism and Irish nationalism see, for example: Niamh Lynch, 'Defining Irish Nationalist Anti-imperialism: Thomas Davis and John Mitchel', *Éire-Ireland*, vol. 42 (1/2), Spring/Summer 2007, pp. 82–107.

[107] Corn Exchange mtg., 29 May 1843, *Nation*, 3 June 1843.

[108] Corn Exchange mtg., 23 Aug. 1843, *Nation*, 26 Aug. 1843.

[109] Corn Exchange mtg., 27 March 1843, *Nation*, 1 April 1843.

the Irish people, and contrast with it the foul immorality and irreligion that pervaded England (loud cries of hear, hear, and cheers).'[110] Comments such as these produced by Repealers and their press, which delineated the differences between the two races in terms of moral and civilized behaviour, underpinned their argument that as the Irish were shown to be superior to the English, they should not remain politically united with their neighbour. Ironically, while Repealers were trying to detach themselves politically and culturally from Britain, as Michael de Nie's research shows, the British press viewed the Celtic Irish as racially inferior to the Anglo-Saxon and saw the Act of Union as propitious for remodelling Ireland in its own, perceived superior image.[111] Both the British press and the Irish nationalist press capitalized on the issue of race, the British in their effort to Anglicize the Irish, and the Irish nationalists in their resistance to this Anglicization.

Apart from trying to justify Repeal, the Association's leaders needed to convince the people of Ireland that it was attainable. During its first year *The Nation*, and the other Dublin Repeal papers, through the words of leading Repealers and journalists, claimed that Britain was weak and divided, and that its domestic, foreign and imperial policies were fragile. This state of affairs, they believed, gave Ireland the opportunity to pursue the Repeal campaign with vigour. The Repeal Association also needed to convey the impression that it was a formidable organization that would stand up to opposition from the government. For this reason Repeal rhetoric was often rendered in varying degrees of militancy. At a meeting in Skibbereen in June 1843, Edmund Burke Roche MP cautioned the government: 'I say if they dare attack the people, the people are prepared (vehement applause).'[112] At a Repeal demonstration in Cashel in May 1843, the Very Rev. Dr Howly declared that 'all the cannon of Great Britain could not put down the Repeal agitation (tremendous cheers).'[113] The Very Rev. Mr Hughes, a parish priest

---

[110] Corn Exchange mtg., 29 May 1843, *Nation*, 3 June 1843. See also O'Connell's comments a couple of weeks prior to this meeting, when 'he had only to look back to the reports of committees of both houses of parliament, and he found, upon the testimony of unwilling witnesses, and proclaimed by Lord Morpeth, and was proved by daily experience and irrefragable evidence, that the best husbands, brothers, kindliest relations – the most dutiful of children, and the purest and most faithful of wives, were, in competition with other nations, to be found in Ireland (cheers)': 'Glorious Repeal meeting and banquet at Charleville. Co. Cork', 18 May 1843, *Nation*, 20 May 1843. George Howard, known as Lord Morpeth, was Chief Secretary for Ireland, 1835–41.

[111] Michael de Nie, *The Eternal Paddy: Irish Identity and the British Press, 1798–1882* (Madison: The University of Wisconsin Press, 2004).

[112] 'Repeal demonstration in Skibbereen', 22 June 1843, *Nation*, 1 July 1843.

[113] 'Great Repeal demonstration in the South Riding of Tipperary', 23 May 1843, *Nation*, 27 May 1843.

from Claremorris, Co. Mayo, was reported as stating, referring to Peel, the Tory Prime Minister, and Wellington, Commander-in-Chief of the Army: 'let them see what they have to contend with, should they commence the work of slaughter against the Irish people ... let the motto of every Irish Repealer be – "Death, or victory."'[114] Despite O'Connell's appeals for non-violence, even he sometimes veered towards militant rhetoric. Repeal's fiery words had two purposes. One was to persuade the government that if it attempted to suppress the Association by force, Repeal supporters would be unyielding in the event of an attack. This stern rhetoric was also psychologically useful in rallying the support of followers and inspiring them with confidence. Importantly, because of the extensive press coverage, rhetoric of this nature was disseminated to a far wider audience than attendees at regular Repeal Association meetings and the monster meetings. Of the Dublin Repeal newspapers, *The Nation* was the most combative, with much of its verse expressed in a warlike tone, and while this seemed in keeping with the high passions of 1843, it was to be used against the Young Irelanders in the 1846 split between them and O'Connell.

It is noticeable that some of the fieriest Repeal rhetoric emanated from the Catholic priesthood, of which the last two quotations above are examples. Having the support of the Catholic Church was a distinct advantage to the Repeal cause as the people listened to, and trusted, their priests. However, the overwhelming support for the cause reported in the press endorsed the perception that Repeal was a Catholic cause, with Catholic interests. This was intensified by O'Connell's image as the Liberator, inspiring Catholics to join the cause, but potentially discouraging Protestant involvement in the Association. The success of Catholic Emancipation, therefore, worked for and against O'Connell in attempting to acquire allegiance to the Repeal cause. For the Catholic majority this achievement demonstrated his strength and encouraged involvement in Repeal, but for the Protestant minority it could produce apathy or fear. Paradoxically, while the Repeal press gave strength to the argument for Repeal, it could discourage unity of creed, a prime objective of the Repealers, and indeed of Thomas Davis and *The Nation*.

The Catholic image of the Association, though, was mitigated to a certain extent by news in the Dublin Repeal press on the progress of Protestant support for the cause. Often at the Corn Exchange meetings, subscriptions from Protestants were read out, and subsequently published in the Repeal newspapers. Thirty-one Orangemen in Dungannon, Co. Tyrone, for example, sent a letter to O'Connell enclosing subscriptions on behalf

[114] 'Another "Monster" Repeal meeting in Mayo', 30 July 1843, *Nation*, 5 Aug. 1843.

of 100 associates in support of Repeal.[115] Furthermore, the Repeal press in the north was valuable to the Association, and received much praise from O'Connell. Mr K.T. Buggy, the editor of *The Belfast Vindicator*, provided a positive assessment of support in the north by Protestants. In a letter addressed to the Association's Secretary, dated 25 February 1843, and read out at a Corn Exchange meeting, he optimistically claimed: 'The long slumbering North has at length shaken off its apathy, and in the good and glorious struggle for Legislative independence, the brave patriots of Ulster, including many of the honest and determined Presbyterians, will be found rivalling the South, and I fear excelling the West.'[116] (The Presbyterians had played a significant part in the United Irishmen's movement.) But just writing about Protestant recruits in the Repeal press could not help to draw more of them into the cause; access to the Association's specific policies relating to Protestants would be essential if they were to even consider trusting Repealers.

Reproducing policies of the Association clearly and firmly in print, rather than just through speeches at Repeal gatherings, which were mainly attended by Catholics, was important if Protestants were to be recruited to the cause. The arguments that O'Connell used at his meetings to assuage Protestant fears were then printed in the Repeal press. He attempted to distance himself from Catholic Emancipation by stating that Repeal 'had become a more national and a more highminded movement.'[117] One of the main Protestant fears about Repeal was that of Catholic ascendancy. O'Connell argued that, following the Repeal of the Union, Protestants' rights would be protected by a majority in the House of Lords and also by a Protestant monarch; there would be 'equality for all – ascendancy for none.'[118] According to the rhetoric of the Repeal journalists, Protestants had nothing to fear from Repeal of the Union. *The Freeman's Journal*, whose editor John Gray was a Protestant, argued, for instance, that a post-Repeal society would not be disadvantageous to Protestants but, indeed, would be beneficial to them.[119] This stance continued beyond 1843, when *The Freeman's Journal* insisted that

> A Catholic ascendancy is not possible. With the power of England, Scotland, and Ulster, combined to defend the religious liberties of the Protestants of Ireland, the idea of such a thing is so preposterous

---

[115] Corn Exchange mtg., 11 July 1843, *Nation*, 15 July 1843.
[116] Corn Exchange mtg., 27 Feb. 1843, *Nation*, 4 March 1843.
[117] Corn Exchange mtg., 29 May 1843. *Nation*, 3 June 1843.
[118] Committee Report, Corn Exchange mtg., 7 Nov. 1842, *Nation*, 12 Nov. 1842.
[119] 1st LA, *Freeman's Journal*, 28 July 1843.

> ... Repealers ... are most anxious to conciliate and satisfy Protestants of all sects – to merge all distinctions in love of Ireland.[120]

However, the Protestant community needed far more convincing, and of the Dublin nationalist newspapers, *The Nation* was at the forefront of concerted attempts to allay Protestants' apprehensions. A dialogue, for instance, took place in *The Nation* between the Dublin Protestant Operative Association (a working-class group founded in 1841 to oppose O'Connell's politics) and *The Nation*, whose writers were attempting to convince the operatives that their poverty was due to the Union.[121] More importantly, a series of letters in *The Nation* from a Protestant tried to persuade those of his own faith to join the Repeal cause. The author of this series was Thomas Davis, although he remained anonymous to readers. Believing there should be mutual forgiveness for the past, he saw Protestants as a constituent part of the Irish nation, the collection of people now residing in Ireland.[122] The past as a shared experience in the same land, rather than being divisive, should now bind them together; as Duffy commented in his history of Young Ireland, *The Nation*'s writers believed that 'if men loved and served the country they were Irish.'[123] Theorizing about Irish nationhood and supporting the Repeal Association's argument in relation to a post-Repeal society were two approaches adopted by Thomas Davis and *The Nation* in attempts to win over Protestants.

The Nation also fiercely attacked Protestant bigotry, an obstacle to any meaningful form of unity. As Duffy said of his newspaper, 'The rights and feelings of Protestant Irishmen were discussed with scrupulous respect and fairness, but their monopolies and prejudices denounced.'[124] In a leading article in August 1843, when addressing *The Warder*, the newspaper run by young Protestants, *The Nation* defended its non-sectarian policy:

> They should remember that the Catholics of Ireland are their countrymen – are men, not beasts – have hearts and feelings like their own, and like themselves, too, have a COUNTRY worth fighting for ... Do they believe that the object we have is to emancipate Ireland only to make Protestants slaves? Let them read

---

[120] 2nd LA, *Freeman's Journal*, 29 July 1844.

[121] 3rd LA, *Nation*, 24 June 1843; 'Address of the Protestant Operatives', *Nation*, 1 July 1843 and 2nd LA, *Nation*, 8 July 1843.

[122] 'Letters by a Protestant on Repeal' began on 17 Dec. 1842 in *The Nation*.

[123] Duffy, *Young Ireland*, pp. 155–6.

[124] Duffy, *Young Ireland*, p. 66.

> our writings, our political disquisitions, and our songs, and say is there *one line* to be found in them indicative of hatred to our own fellow-countrymen? ... We really do ask our countrymen, who have the enormous power of the press at their disposal, to reflect whether they are quite justified in teaching the growing Protestant youth of Ireland to fear, to shun, and to hate the Catholic youth, only because of their creed?[125]

The Nation's writers were attempting to dissipate the perceived destructive differences between Catholic and Protestant, to draw both creeds together in a cause they could share. As Duffy naturally appreciated, the power of the press was highly instrumental in framing and diffusing sectarianism, which he hoped would be countered by *The Nation*'s non-sectarian rhetoric.

The Dublin Repeal newspapers took a keen interest in parliamentary affairs, where a part of their role was to comment on Irish issues that were raised at Westminster. Unusually, Irish affairs had a high profile during 1843 in the Houses of Parliament, due to the Repeal agitation throughout Ireland and the debates over an Arms' Bill, which was intended to restrict the use of arms in Ireland. In a leading article that July, *The Nation* supported the Irish parliamentary speakers in a debate on the motion of forming a committee into Irish grievances. The Repealer E.B. Roche, MP for Cork, received special praise from *The Nation* for his contribution to this debate, especially his 'fearless and uncompromising tone.' In particular, William Smith O'Brien, a liberal-unionist, who had forwarded this motion, was acclaimed by *The Nation*: 'He has done more to break down the power of English tyranny in Ireland than any other man now attending the House.'[126] Repealers had to be careful, though, not to be hostile to the Irish liberal-unionists, a group composed of Liberal and Whig MPs, who were fighting for similar issues as the Repealers.[127] In August 1843, when Davis was visiting Cork, he wrote to Duffy to inform him of a recent *Nation* article on the Whigs that had offended many people. He claimed that it 'looked like a cruel attack when the Irish Whigs at least were doing nobly in the house. Take some opportunity

---

[125] 4th LA, *Nation*, 5 Aug. 1843.

[126] 3rd LA, *Nation*, 15 July 1843. Despite the arguments presented by Irish members, this motion was rejected.

[127] Robert Sloan shows how, in the voluntary absence of most Repealers from Parliament at this time, forty liberal-unionists led by Thomas Wyse and William Smith O'Brien launched a co-ordinated attack on the government in relation to the grievances of Catholic Ireland: Robert Sloan, 'O'Connell's liberal rivals in 1843', *IHS*, vol. 30 (117) May 1996, pp. 47–65. See also: Robert Sloan, *William Smith O'Brien and the Young Ireland Rebellion of 1848: The road to Ballingary* (Dublin: Four Courts, 2000), p. 82.

to distinguish that you did not mean them (O'Brien & the like) in attacking the Whigs.'[128] Davis recognized it was important that *The Nation* should not alienate those Irish MPs who, though not Repealers, nevertheless supported some of their grievances. This was wise advice, for William Smith O'Brien was eventually to join the Young Irelanders.

Another aspect of the Repeal Association's campaign was the exploitation of Ireland's relationship with France and America. These countries empathized with the Repeal movement from an ideological perspective, and the Repealers, especially those associated with *The Nation*, capitalized on this. Repeal newspaper rhetoric emphasized that both of these nations had suffered under oppressive governments and had broken free of them through violent revolution, implying that Ireland could follow the same path if Repeal was not granted or if the Repeal organization was attacked by the British authorities; not so long before, Irish nationalists, in particular Theobald Wolfe Tone, had collaborated militarily with France during the Anglo-French wars. Single articles and series of articles relating to France and America were particularly common features in *The Nation*, and it was through the Repeal press that the Castle officials, as well as the people, could see how much support was forthcoming from America and France for the Repeal movement. Apart from attempting to unnerve the government, it was a way of elevating the Repeal cause by showing there was support from nations outside Ireland.

The Dublin Repeal press reported a thriving Repeal movement among the Irish in America, where *The Nation* newspaper had a particular impact. For instance, the series 'Songs of The Nation' was copied from *The Nation* by the Repeal press in America, which, it was claimed, 'animate[d] the decaying spirit of liberty in the human system.'[129] The Repeal Association received steady moral and financial support from America, and when news came of a threat of civil war from the British government against the Repeal movement in Ireland, the reaction was decisive.[130] On 14 June 1843, a meeting took place in New York, reportedly attended by 20,000 persons, where the following resolution was proposed: 'That it is the opinion of this meeting that, if England invades Ireland, she will do it with the assured loss of the Canadas by American arms.'[131] Support for Repeal also

---

[128] Letter from Davis to Duffy, 29 Aug. 1843, Duffy Papers, NLI, MS 5756/53.

[129] 'Letters from America', 'No. V', 15 April 1843, *Nation*, 27 May 1843.

[130] Peel speaking in 'House of Commons – Tuesday, May 9' and 1st LA, *Freeman's Journal*, 12 May 1843.

[131] 1st LA, *Nation*, 1 July 1843. Two decades later, a group of American Fenians unsuccessfully adopted a similar policy.

came from the most important person in America, President John Tyler, which he declared in a communication, printed in *The Philadelphia Ledger*, to the Committee of the Irish Repeal Association in America.[132] As for the ordinary citizen, in *The Nation* series 'Letters from America,' an Irish immigrant declared: 'Every town of consequence in the United States is moving for your freedom.'[133] Practical support, in the meantime, came from donations to the Repeal Association; at the beginning of July 1843 *The Dublin Weekly Register* reported in its leading columns that 'the magnificent remittance of FIVE THOUSAND DOLLARS reached the Association' from America.[134] However, while Repealers appreciated American support and exploited it to their advantage, they were more circumspect in their dealings with France.

The attitude of Repealers to French support was more complex. Of the Dublin Repeal papers *The Nation* had the most contact with France. France was an inspiration to *The Nation*'s writers because of its political and cultural achievements. French writers, poets, politicians and historians were given considerable attention in *The Nation*'s columns. *The Nation* admired *Le National*, the French radical newspaper; when *The Nation* was founded, *Le National* saw it as 'an ally,' and sometimes reprinted its articles.[135] The French poet and politician, Alphonse de Lamartine, visited Ireland in 1842 and, inspired on reading the prospectus of *The Nation*, decided to start a weekly 'religious and poetical' paper on 1 November, named *La Patrie* (*The Homeland*).[136] Expressing an affinity with the French served as an indirect warning to the government of the physical force power of the masses, although this was tempered by O'Connell's insistence on non-violence. The Repeal leadership was more guarded in its references to France, and the relationship between *The Nation*'s writers and the Repeal Association over this issue, while causing some tension within the organization, did not disturb its unity at this time.

132 'Latest news from America', *Nation*, 22 July 1843.
133 Letter from 'An Exile', 'On the Hudson, near New York', 25 Aug. 1843, *Nation*, 9 Sept. 1843.
134 'Topics of the week', *Weekly Register*, 1 July 1843.
135 Duffy, *Young Ireland*, pp. 184, 283.
136 'Answers to correspondents', *Nation*, 5 Nov. 1842.

Irish nationality and *The Nation*'s literature

Whether communicating orally or in print, language used by the Repeal Association suggested that its existence emanated from one conception, an overwhelming sense of loss of Irish nationality. It was not just the political loss of an Irish parliament from 1782 to 1800 and economic regression since then, which Irish nationalists blamed on the Act of Union. They also mourned a deepening dispossession of their national identity. Repeated references were made by Repealers to restoring Ireland's nationhood; at a meeting in May 1843 in Tipperary, O'Connell was reported as saying that 'Ireland should be, what she ought to be, a nation again.'[137] This sentiment was echoed regularly in the Dublin Repeal press. A leading article in *The Weekly Freeman's Journal* referred to 'the great struggle for nationality.'[138] This sense of loss of Irish nationality and the campaign for its recovery was often conveyed to the people through poetic prose. O'Connell spoke of liberation from the slavery of the stranger, in a cause of 'purest patriotism,' which men should think of as a sacred and public duty to follow; and a few days later, he was reported as saying that the soul of the nation was in this national movement.[139]

While the Repeal Association was more concerned with what it saw as the political and economic losses of the Irish people since 1800, *The Nation* strongly lamented what it perceived as the growing cultural dispossession of Irish nationality. In a leading article on 29 July 1843, *The Nation* claimed that before the present nationalist agitation, 'Men were beginning to forget they had a country – they looked to England for opinions, tastes, and customs, as well as for laws.'[140] Speaking at a Repeal banquet in Castlebar, Co. Mayo, John Blake Dillon, a co-founder of *The Nation*, delivered an eloquent and fiery speech. He told his audience that '[The Saxons] have stripped you of your wealth, your commerce, your arts, your liberties, your genius – all of those things that combine to fashion and to educate the mind of a people.'[141] An important element of a national identity was a native language. Thomas Davis believed that 'The language, which grows up with a people, is conformed to their organs, descriptive of their climate,

137 'Most important demonstration of the North Riding of Tipperary', 25 May 1843, *Nation*, 27 May 1843.

138 1st LA, *Weekly Freeman*, 22 July 1843.

139 Magnificent Repeal demonstration in Galway', 25 June 1843, *Nation*, 1 July 1843; 'O'Connell in Dundalk. The Banquet', 29 June 1843, *Nation*, 1 July 1843.

140 3rd LA, *Nation*, 29 July 1843.

141 'The Banquet', 30 July 1843, *Nation*, 5 Aug. 1843.

constitution, and manners, mingled inseparably with their history and their soil, fitted beyond any other language to express their prevalent thoughts in the most natural and efficient way.'[142] Its erosion was a particular mark of Irish society in the mid-nineteenth century, especially in the context of the Great Famine, and it was not until the Gaelic Revival that a truly concerted effort came about to restore its usage in society.

Mourning what it believed was the loss of an Irish cultural identity, *The Nation*'s mission was to seek ways of promoting its regeneration. For example, a leading article in September 1843 stated:

> The materials of nationalisation – the food to nourish a healthy and permanent knowledge and love of country in the minds of all classes – each after its own fashion – are scanty and defective. They must be increased. We want national books, and lectures, and music – national paintings, and busts, and costume – national songs, and tracts, and maps – historical plays for the stage – historical novels for the closet – historical ballads for the drawing room – we want all these, and many other things illustrating the history, the resources, and the genius of our country, and honoring her illustrious children, living or dead. These are the seeds of permanent nationality, and we must sow them deep in the People's hearts.[143]

The young writers of *The Nation* believed that awakening in the Irish people an interest in their history and culture would not only help to halt what they perceived as the erosion of the Irish nation, it would also justify the political argument that, being culturally different from Great Britain, Ireland should have her own Irish rulers, a policy to be pursued by later Irish nationalists. *The Nation*'s cultural nationalism certainly had an impact on later important Irish nationalists such as Arthur Griffith, the main founder of the Sinn Féin movement, and leaders of the 1916 Rising, Patrick Pearse and James Connolly.[144] In his newspaper, *The Harp*, Connolly echoed Davis's sentiments: 'Nationality is reflected in our music, in our language, in our literature, in our customs, in our manners, in our games and pastimes.'[145] Davis's writings in particular continued to resonate into

---

[142] 'Our National Language', *Nation*, 1 April 1843.

[143] 1st LA, *Nation*, 9 Sept. 1843.

[144] *Sinn Féin* has been translated as 'ourselves alone,' 'we ourselves,' but is more commonly accepted as 'ourselves.'

[145] 'Eoin', *The Irish Nation*, 19 June 1909, in 'How to Realise the Ideals of Thomas Davis', *The Harp*, July 1909.

the twentieth century, testifying to the enduring nature of his thinking on Irish nationalism.

The Nation's task of inculcating an awareness and an appreciation of Irish culture into the people of Ireland was mainly communicated through its literary columns. Thomas Davis was the main cultural researcher for *The Nation*, but there were others, such as his friend, John Edward Pigot, who 'descended into the neglected fields of Irish literature, and formed societies, like the Archaeological, to rescue from oblivion our ancient manuscripts.'[146] Drawing attention to Irish cultural figures was a priority for *The Nation* and it dedicated a series to them called the 'National Gallery.' The second part of this series, published on 10 December 1842, featured a review of the life of Gerald Griffin and a line drawing of him. Griffin, who was born in Limerick in 1803 and died in 1840, wrote plays, novels and poetry, but is particularly known for his prose and his depictions of Irish life.[147] Also that December, an article appeared on Patrick MacDowell, the Irish sculptor from Belfast who was honoured by the Royal Academy.[148] MacDowell practised his art in London, and *The Nation* argued that if Ireland had the prestige of being an independent nation, such people of distinction would remain at home.

Other ways of helping to further Irish culture were promoted by *The Nation*. The article 'Hints for Irish historical paintings' from the series 'Popular Projects' complained of the absence of Irish national art. Helping to remedy this deficiency, a list of historical subjects, such as 'The Landing of the Milesians,' was compiled for prospective painters and sculptors to produce work with 'truth and vigour'; another idea was to recreate works depicting Ireland's social life, either from observation or from other sources, for example, the stories of Gerald Griffin.[149] Through the influence of Thomas Davis, the Repeal Association itself became actively involved in fostering the creation of Irish culture. Davis compiled a report, read out at a Corn Exchange meeting on 21 September 1843, which outlined the need for an Irish national culture and ways of achieving it:

> if the Repeal Association could induce the people of Ireland universally to use Irish music, to employ a style of architecture suitable to the climate, history, and character of Ireland; and if it could lead Irish artists to paint, model, and sculpture subjects

---

[146] 'S' (P.J. Smyth), an obituary of John Edward Pigot, *Nation*, 8 July 1871; see also: 'The late JOHN EDWARD PIGOT', Young Ireland (1), NLI, MS 3225.

[147] *Nation*, 10 Dec. 1842.

[148] *Nation*, 24 Dec. 1842.

[149] *Nation*, 29 July 1843.

> connected with the history, manners, and scenery of Ireland, it would serve the cause of Ireland and Repeal materially.

Davis suggested promoting the creation of works on Irish subjects by Irish artists, and prizes awarded for the best exhibits, to be sponsored by the Repeal Association.[150] Encouraging active participation in cultural nationalism was potentially a positive way for *The Nation* to strengthen the Repeal movement.

The other Dublin Repeal papers also supported cultural nationalism, albeit to a much lesser extent. *The Daily Freeman's Journal*, for instance, printed a regular literary review column.[151] *The Dublin Weekly Register* included some verse in its series 'The Poet's Corner,' and also had an occasional literary article, such as a review of a new publication, *Old Songs of Old Ireland*. In its introductory paragraph, *The Dublin Weekly Register*'s review echoed the sentiments of *The Nation*: 'Her [Ireland's] national airs and ballads have ever been made by her bards the medium of transmitting to posterity the many sad and bright eras of her annals.' *Old Songs of Old Ireland* was compiled by Rev. Joseph Fitzgerald, and the music composed by the popular Wellington Guernsey. One of their poetic tributes was dedicated to Gerald Griffin, the writer admired by *The Nation*. Another song was written in honour of the famous early eleventh-century battle at Clontarf, the air of which was described in the review as 'teeming with harmony and bold musical expression.' On the same page as the review, 'The Poet's Corner' featured 'The Clontarf Congress. October 8th, 1843,' written by Rev. Fitzgerald in anticipation of the grand Repeal monster meeting planned for the next day.[152] However, while the other Dublin Repeal newspapers had some literary items, it was *The Nation* that was the most passionate about literature and what it could do to advance the Irish nationalist cause.

Although the journalistic pages of *The Nation* were dominated by Repeal affairs, its literary contributions were far more than an adjunct to the Repeal Association's campaign: they provided historical perspective, political comment on the present struggle for Repeal and, by their very presence, they also promoted a sense of the value of literature composed by Irish people. What was important was that *The Nation*'s writers were not just passively passing on knowledge about Irish literature; they were actively engaged in its creation, especially through their verse. While used for the political purpose of stirring feelings of antipathy against the Union,

[150] *Nation*, 23 Sept. 1843.

[151] For example: short reviews of two books and a review of the current issue of the *Dublin University Magazine* appear in 'Literature', *Freeman's Journal*, 3 June 1843.

[152] *Weekly Register*, 7 Oct. 1843.

The Nation's literature also promoted images of the differences between the English and the Irish, justifying the creation of an Irish nation that was separate in character from England.

The Nation used the mediums of prose and poetry to remind the people of their history. For example, 'The Martyrdom of William Orr,' number three in the series 'Illustrations of Irish History,' was a prose account of Orr's death as a United Irishman.[153] *The Nation* believed that the most effective way of informing people about their past was through 'publishing historical ballads, the most powerful of all possible auxiliaries in the work of spreading a knowledge of history among a People.'[154] This policy was confirmed by Duffy in his later history of Young Ireland: 'Historical ballads of singular vigour and dramatic power made the great men and great achievements of their race familiar to the people.'[155] Much of the subject matter of *The Nation*'s verse was composed of historic battles and heroic characters, celebrating the martial ardour of Irishmen, and their martyrdom. The first poem of the series 'Historical Ballads,' 'Lament for the Death of Owen Roe O'Neill,' concerned a renowned general of the seventeenth-century Catholic Confederacy.[156] Verse such as this was intended to inspire people to enlist in the Repeal cause; it was meant to instil pride by relating the heroic exploits of their Irish ancestors, and provide an opportunity to identify with those who had gallantly fought for Ireland in the past.

Verse was also present in *The Nation* as a direct comment on current political affairs. In January 1843, the first poem in the series 'Lays for Landlords,' entitled 'The Extermination,' relates the tale of a widow and her infant who had been evicted from their home; after it was burnt down they were left to perish on 'the desolate moor.'[157] Such verse was intended to highlight the reality, and perceived inhumanity, of the landlord and tenant relationship, understood and criticized by both Repealers and the Irish liberal-unionist MPs, such as William Smith O'Brien. At the beginning of July 1843 a protest poem was printed in *The Nation* called 'The Irish Arms' Bill.'[158] At the time hotly debated in Parliament by Irish MPs, this bill, intended 'to prevent improper persons from having arms in *Ireland*,'

---

153 *Nation*, 16 Sept. 1843.

154 'Irish Sedition', *Nation*, 9 Sept. 1843.

155 Duffy, *Young Ireland*, p. 165.

156 *Nation*, 19 Nov. 1842. In a series on 'The Ulster Milesians,' as a contrast, an historical prose account was written on Owen Roe O'Neill, *Nation*, 7 Jan. 1843.

157 *Nation*, 14 Jan. 1843.

158 *Nation*, 1 July 1843.

was seen by the Repealers and their press as another example of slavery under the government of the Union.[159] As these examples demonstrate, it was evident that poetry in *The Nation* was not just a means for drawing attention to Irish political grievances, but was intended as a bitter critique of the government and its laws in relation to Ireland, and a justification for the Repeal of the Union.

The Nation's verse was also a reflection of the success of the monster meetings. 'The Voice of Labour,' for instance, was written in response to the large procession of numerous trades that preceded a Repeal meeting in Dublin on 3 July 1843.[160] Later in the month, referring to Repeal monster meetings in general, 'The Repealers' March' appeared in *The Nation*'s 'Poet's Corner.' Composed to the familiar air of 'O'Sullivan's March,' the first verse runs:

> March to the gathering! – pour from the valley;
> Rush from the craggy cliff's thunder-charged cloud;
> Men of the hills from your dark mountains sally,
> Where the eagle's cry swells o'er the waterfall loud –
> March from the heaths where the red deer are bounding yet,
> Where the Gaelic of glory's old tones are resounding yet –
> March from the woods where your fathers did rally
> Which ne-er to the axe of the Sassanach bow'd![161]

Both of these poems were examples of spirited and defiant effusions of Irish nationalism; they celebrated the success of the large Repeal campaign meetings, and were a rallying cry for others to join the movement. Emulating the United Irishmen's press, which had used verse and stories to promote their cause, this effective tactic was also practised by later Irish nationalists.

Recruitment into the Repeal cause was naturally far more of a challenge in the north, mainly due to its overwhelming Protestant population. By trying to enlist supporters from this region, *The Nation*'s poetry frequently reminded northerners of their contribution to the Irish nationalist cause during the 1790s, especially with references to the United Irishmen. But *The Nation* also went further back into the past to show the strength and resolution of the people of Ulster against their enemies. The fourth poem in the series 'Songs of the Nation' was 'The Song of Ulster,' which celebrated

---

159 'Abstract of the Arms' Bill', *Nation*, 9 Sept. 1843. This Bill restricted the possession of arms through licensing; it became an Act on 22 Aug. 1843.

160 *Nation*, 8 July 1843.

161 *Nation*, 29 July 1843.

the unity and strength of the men of the north against the English. The following is verse four:

> Oh! proud was the day, when the Chief of the Gael,
> Like a thunderstorm scattered the sons of the pale;
> And the strength of the Saxon, like stubble went down
> Before the strong septs of the cross and the crown.
> The Men of the North.[162]

The psychological dimension of this verse was important, praising the men of the north who possessed superior militant ardour in their fight against the enemy. Indirectly, this poem implied that Repeal success would be likely if the northern counties joined the present battle between Irish Repealers and their British rulers. Poems in *The Nation* also supported Repeal ideology in relation to unity of creed. In 'Poet's Corner' an item entitled 'Song for July 12th, 1843' by J. De Jean encouraged Protestant and Catholic unity, the fourth verse stating:

> The same good soil sustaining both,
> Makes both united flourish
> But cannot give the Orange growth,
> And cease the Green to nourish.[163]

This verse, as with the previous one, suggests that Protestants and Catholics needed to join together if they were to be successful and win Repeal. There is an allusion here to the nationalism espoused by Davis, who believed that their living in the same land and sharing the same past should promote these religious sects' unity, not divide it.

As evidenced by the excerpts above, verse was a crucial medium for drawing people into the Irish nationalist cause. Like the prose reports from Repeal meetings and the newspaper articles, verse showed Irish nationalism as being on an elevated plane, using words such as 'sacred' and 'holy.' This style in prose and poetry was characteristic of the language used by Irish nationalist writers from the United Irishmen up to 1916 and beyond. With the trappings of poetical devices and a license to exaggerate, to draw on folklore and to kindle the emotions, verse could exert an even greater impact than prose when set to an old tune. 'Repeal' in the series 'Poet's

[162] *Nation*, 11 March 1843. The phrase 'strong septs of the cross and the crown' refers to the well-known arms of the confederated chiefs of Ulster.
[163] *Nation*, 8 July 1843.

Corner' is an example of this, intended to be sung to the well-known air of 'Garryowen'; here is the chorus:[164]

> Yes, Freedom! *thine* is our morning hymn,
> Our mid-day wish, and our ev'ning song;
> FOR REPEAL, we will peril life, name, and limb –
> Be the fight soon or late – be it short or long.

Verse such as this could be highly effective, not least due to its simplicity, its link with a familiar air and also, Ireland being a Christian country, its religious allusions.

Martial verse like 'Repeal' suggested the possibility of physical force, which may have given the Repeal cause strength. According to Repeal rhetoric, the Association's supporters would be prepared to die for Ireland in defensive action should the need arise. O'Connell was also aware that from the government's perspective this unprecedented campaign of monster meetings appeared so menacing that this vast resource of supporters could, theoretically, be engaged offensively in military combat. The Duke of Wellington was concerned with the sheer power that the Repeal leadership exerted over this mass movement.[165] Frederick Shaw, an independent Irish member, spoke in the House of Commons on 30 May 1843 during the adjourned debate on the Arms' (Ireland) Bill. He believed that 'Ireland was at the present moment in an alarming state' and connected it to *The Nation*, pointing out the dangers of its writings: 'In a weekly paper, a leading one of that party, and one conducted with great ability – the *Nation* – there was a programme of their intentions, and an institution of the means by which they were effected.' Shaw quoted recent extracts of the paper as evidence, including prose with the phrase 'ourselves alone' and a version of the traditional rebel song 'Shan Van Vocht' ('Poor Old Woman'), two important emblems of Irish nationalism, the latter being an eighteenth-century personification of Ireland.[166] 'Ourselves alone' originated from verse composed by Young Irelander John O'Hagan in December 1842 when *The Nation* advocated separation from the Union and faith in the Irish nation as the only realistic way of regenerating Ireland, believing it was necessary 'To

[164] *Nation*, 20 May 1843.

[165] Leslie A. Williams, *Daniel O'Connell, the British Press and the Irish Famine: Killing Remarks*, William H.A. Williams (ed.) (Hampshire & Vermont, America: Ashgate Publishing Ltd., 2003), pp. 42–3.

[166] *Nation*, 3 June 1843. The extracts Shaw refers to appeared in 1st LA, *Nation*, 20 May 1843.

do at once what is to do/ And trust OURSELVES ALONE.'[167] This phrase became an important symbol of Irish separatism and, eventually, republican nationalism. In May 1843, however, while *The Nation* wished to rouse the spirit of the people to support the Irish nationalist cause, its writers were not advocating violence; as the editor explained, 'We are literary agitators, not military enthusiasts.'[168] The defiant tone in some of *The Nation*'s columns, though, appeared to be popular, as suggested by the paper's increasing sales throughout 1842–43.

The Nation's writers were under no illusion about the quality of their verse during this first year. Referring to the publication of *The Spirit of the Nation*, a collection of verse reprinted from *The Nation*, it was admitted in the 'Answers to Correspondents' column: 'We are far from estimating the bulk of these songs highly; but any national are better than the best alien verses. A beginning has been made, and the carrying out must be left to abler hands.'[169] The Young Irelanders were more concerned about conveying the nationalist message than the quality of its literary expression. *The Nation*'s verse did improve over the years, when female poets made a noticeable contribution.[170] However, verse was intended for all the people, not just the minority of those with a privileged education.

Although literary purists might find much of it lacking in high literary quality, there was considerable contemporary praise for *The Nation*'s verse in 1843. Reviewing *The Spirit of the Nation* inspired *The Waterford Chronicle* to estimate its worth in a similar romantic tone to the poems themselves:

> We have pored with delight over this beautiful wreath of genuine Irish song, which may aptly be termed a Rosary of National Feeling – its every verse, and line, and word, breathing scorn for the foe – love of native land – defiance to the oppressor – freedom for the slave – death to tyranny, and invoking the light of liberty, pure, bright, and unshackled as the breeze or beam of Heaven, for all who deem the glorious gift worth struggling for.[171]

The quality and effectiveness of *The Nation* are also attested to by those

167 'Songs of the Nation. No. III. – OURSELVES ALONE', *Nation*, 3 Dec. 1842.

168 'Answers to Correspondents', *Nation*, 5 Nov. 1843.

169 *Nation*, 20 May 1843.

170 See, for example: Brigitte Anton, 'Women of *The Nation*', *History Ireland*, vol. 1 (3), Autumn 1993, pp. 34–7. A more comprehensive account can be found in: 'An essay on the Women of Young Ireland', [Typescript, March 1948], NLI, MS 10,906.

171 *Nation*, 17 June 1843.

who were opposed to Repeal politics. The editor of *The Quarterly Review*, a Conservative political and literary periodical, noticed that

> There has recently been established in Dublin a weekly newspaper, the most violent as well as the *most able* of all the organs of agitation, and which assumes the emphatic title of "THE NATION" ... This paper has published ... a great many short poetical pieces, some of them of considerable beauty of language and imagery.[172]

In a review of *The Spirit of the Nation*, the *London Morning Post*, which supported the government, stated: 'Formerly the ballads for the Irish common people were distinguished for nothing but humorous slang of the coarsest kind, but here are verses fit to STIR THE HEART OF MEN.'[173] Opinions from those who disagreed with Repeal politics are valuable as they had no vested interest in praising their opponents, except as a warning of their effectiveness in the advancement of the Repeal movement.

Powerful and well-written language can be highly useful for the progress of a nationalist press campaign. This was certainly the case with Repeal in 1843, when *The Nation*'s verse in particular seemed to strike an emotional chord. For example, when referring to *The Spirit of the Nation*, *The Planet*, a London literary journal, stated:

> There is a soul – there is an energy in this collection of poems, such as are only brought forth in times when the hearts of men are moved, as if by a mighty convulsion ... These are specimens of the Irishman – not as he is in paltry Irish stories, and worse farces, but in his grief and his daring – these are the thoughts of the Irishmen of 1843.[174]

This was the intention of *The Nation*, to express the thoughts and feelings of the Irish people. As one article stated, 'We attribute our reputation to the sentiments we reflect, the opinions which we echo, the public opinion which we record, and which, we trust, we sometimes guide – honestly at all events.'[175] However, on balance, *The Nation* probably did more to create and stimulate public opinion than to reflect it, and much of this was due to the effectiveness of its poetical rhetoric.

---

172 'The Quarterly Review and the Nation', *Nation*, 16 Sept. 1843.
173 *Nation*, 15 July 1843.
174 3rd LA, *Nation*, 29 July 1843.
175 'The Quarterly Review and the Nation', *Nation*, 16 Sept. 1843.

Without a doubt *The Nation* was a newspaper of quality that had a distinct impact on those who had access to its contents. Friends and foes of the Repeal movement alike testified to this. Not unnaturally, much appreciation and praise of *The Nation* came from supporters of Repeal. For instance, at a Corn Exchange meeting in March 1843 a message was read out from Mr P. Barrett, a Repeal Warden from Collooney, Co. Sligo, who stated, 'The tone and talent ... of that excellent newspaper, THE NATION, has rendered incalculable benefit to Repeal.'[176] At another Association meeting attention was drawn to a letter dated 12 May 1843 from Denis Davis, Riverstown, Co. Cork, addressed to Duffy, and accompanied by subscriptions of £4 and 1s on behalf of eighty-one Repealers. The letter praised 'the hard-working and ill-requited peasantry' for their support, adding that

> Daniel Cashman, labourer ... deserves particular notice, who, after nine weeks' unabated idleness, has cordially given the first shilling earned by him during that period. This ardent and never-dying zeal is mainly due to the unrivalled spirit so brilliantly diffused through the columns of your invaluable journal, to which they are constant subscribers, and which has given to that immortal cause a powerful impetus.[177]

This, of course, the encouragement of local priests notwithstanding, is further evidence that *The Nation*'s writers influenced the lower classes.

Comments from those diametrically opposed to the concept of Repeal are particularly valuable for estimating the quality and effectiveness of *The Nation*. Isaac Butt, a co-founder of *The Dublin University Magazine* and an editor for four years from 1834, reportedly stated at a Protestant Anti-Repeal Meeting in the Rotunda on 14 June 1843 that *The Nation* 'was written with *real ability and talent*, and labours to excite the passions of the people (loud cries of hear, hear, hear).'[178] About two months later, *The Nation* printed an extract from *The Warder* that observed that *The Nation*'s huge circulation figure was 'multiplied indefinitely by the eager transference of each copy from hand to hand.' *The Warder* claimed that it was not alone in thinking that *The Nation* was 'the *most ominous and formidable phenomenon* of these strange and menacing times.' Furthermore, *The Warder* remarked of *The Nation* that 'It represents the opinions and feelings of SOME MILLIONS OF MEN, reflected with vivid precision in its successive pages – and ... is

---

[176] Corn Exchange mtg., 20 March 1843, *Nation*, 25 March 1843.

[177] Corn Exchange mtg., 15 May 1843, *Nation*, 20 May 1843.

[178] 'The Spirit of The Nation', *Nation*, 1 July 1843. Butt later became a Conservative MP and would also act as defence lawyer for some of the Young Irelanders and the Fenians.

a genuine and gigantic representative of its vast party.'[179] Statements such as these demonstrate the effectiveness of *The Nation*'s writing in furthering the Repeal cause, even suggesting that it was the main instrument of power within the Repeal movement.

The influence of *The Nation* can also be judged by the eagerness of its readers to submit unsolicited contributions. The submission of articles and verse to this newspaper was a demonstration of active participation in literary nationalism. As early as December 1842, *The Nation*'s office was already 'oppressed with a too abundant harvest'; by the following March 1843, the editor claimed that enough articles had been submitted to fill three or four *Nations* a week.[180] Much of the unsolicited verse was, according to the editor, unsuitable for inclusion, but even if these contributions, prose and poetry, were not of a standard suitable for publication, one can see that readers were inspired by *The Nation* to put pen to paper on the Irish nationalist cause.

The zenith of the Repeal movement, 1843

The Repeal movement achieved great strides in Irish society both quantitatively and in terms of its inclusivity during *The Nation*'s first year, and there is a considerable amount of evidence to substantiate this claim. The growth in the collection of Repeal rent during this period, for example, is an indication of numerical and financial support for the Association. The most telling evidence of the progress of Repeal in Irish society during 1843 was the growing attendance at the monster meetings, accompanied by their increasingly ostentatious nationalist displays. Much testimony in relation to Repeal's progress came from parliamentarians at Westminster; for example, dramatic warnings were expressed during the 1843 summer debate on the 'State of Ireland' in the House of Commons. On 4 July, William Smith O'Brien, who was not a Repealer at this time, stated that:

> the agitation or organisation for Repeal was not confined to the lower classes, but nearly one-half of the middle classes of the Roman Catholics, and nearly the whole of the Catholic clergy, were mixed up with it, and took an active part in promoting it. And although up to the present time not many of the Catholic nobility had joined in the agitation, if they did not they would soon stand alone. In addition to this, if matters were allowed to remain as they

[179] 4th LA, *Nation*, 5 Aug. 1843.

[180] 'Answers to Correspondents', *Nation*, 17 Dec. 1842 and 18 March 1843.

> were, the agitators for Repeal might reasonably expect a junction of a large number of Protestants.[181]

A week later, Lord John Russell, leader of the Whig opposition party, commented in Parliament that 'Disguise from ourselves we cannot, that Ireland is in a most critical situation (hear, hear). That assemblages, not merely of great multitudes, but comprising people of every class, except the highest, are daily assembling in various parts of that country, at the call of one individual.'[182] These observations not only demonstrated that the number of people involved in the cause was significant, but also that Repeal's aim for a unity of classes within Irish society to support the nationalist movement was gaining momentum, which, for the government, signalled a threat to the viability of the Union and a concern for the safety of the Empire. The government's citing of evidence such as this suggests that the Repeal movement was making considerable progress, and there is no doubt that the Repeal press, and *The Nation* in particular, had a significant role in producing this effect. A leading article in the radical London *Morning Chronicle* was of the opinion that during 1843 Repeal was 'one of the most formidable organizations that ever yet menaced the integrity of this empire.'[183]

Repealers themselves naturally voiced their positive comments on the progress of the Repeal cause. For instance, at a Corn Exchange meeting on 14 August 1843, O'Connell himself claimed that 'The most astonishing unanimity prevailed amongst them, such as was never exhibited before by any country on the face of the globe.'[184] In a letter dated 15 May 1843, which was read out at a Cork repeal banquet, the Archbishop of Tuam made known his positive assessment of the progress of Repeal:

> The most wretched peasantry on earth swelling the funds of the Repeal Association with their weekly contributions – the chief corporations of Ireland ... giving the measure the approval of their municipal authority – a priesthood ... giving it the sanction of their blessing – Protestants ... now mingling with the people in a requisition for a native parliament. Such an array of rank, of wealth, of intelligence and of number ... [185]

[181] *Nation*, 8 July 1843.
[182] *Nation*, 15 July 1843.
[183] 1st LA, *The Morning Chronicle*, 9 Oct. 1843.
[184] *Nation*, 19 Aug. 1843.
[185] 'The Liberator in Cork. The Banquet', 21 May 1843, reprinted from *The Cork Examiner* in *Nation*, 27 May 1843.

All the Dublin Repeal papers spoke regularly in positive terms about the progress of Repeal. In August 1843, *The Nation* provided its own assessment of the Repeal movement since the previous year. It stated that

> The enrolled Repealers were scarcely a couple of hundred thousand – they are now running towards two millions. It had then half-a-dozen Protestant members – it has now thousands, from the wealthiest of the gentry to the most stern of the democracy. The entire Catholic Hierarchy and Priesthood have given it open support or tacit assent ... Most of the Counties of Leinster and Munster, and some in Ulster and Connaught, have come in masses together to declare that they are ready to make any sacrifice – money, repose, or life – to achieve their independence.

But recruitment to the Repeal cause was not the most important point; leading members in various committees of the Association were making plans in preparation for government. As *The Nation* continued in this article: 'Ireland is changing into a nation. She is obtaining all the machinery of one – public opinion, order, taxation, justice, legislation.'[186] Some of this, of course, was already being put into action, such as the Arbitration Courts. O'Connell claimed that 1843 was Repeal year, and as the year progressed the Repealers' rhetoric intensified in the Dublin Repeal press and at Repeal meetings, and it seemed to them as if Repeal was increasingly within their grasp.

The most telling evidence of the strength of the Repeal movement was the response from Robert Peel's Tory government: it sought to break the power of the Association and of the Dublin Repeal press. The last monster meeting of the year, to be held at Clontarf on 8 October 1843, was prohibited and indictments were brought against O'Connell and other leading Repealers for conspiracy, including editors and proprietors of the Dublin Repeal press. While this action was a turning point in the advancement of Repeal, when the future unity of the leaders was severely challenged, it was also the catalyst for the admission of a significant new recruit into the Repeal movement.

Probably the most prized acquisition to the Repeal cause was William Smith O'Brien, and *The Nation* had a key role in his decision to join the Repeal Association. Born into the Protestant gentry, and a descendant of the medieval king Brian Bóruma, he was to emerge as one of the most singularly outstanding figures in Irish nationalism in the mid-nineteenth century. Smith O'Brien was admitted into the Repeal Association at the meeting on 23 October 1843, where a letter was read out from him explaining his

---

[186] 1st LA, *Nation*, 12 Aug. 1843.

position. He had initially been strongly against Repeal of the Union when it was first mooted, believing that Catholic Emancipation heralded a new era in which

> the statesmen of Great Britain would spare no effort to repair the evils produced by centuries of misgovernment – that the Catholic and Protestant would be admitted to share, on equal terms, in all the advantages resulting from our constitutional form of government – that all traces of an ascendancy of race or creed would be effaced.[187]

These reforms failed to happen. But what finally convinced O'Brien was the government's ban on the monster meetings and its indictment of O'Connell and other leading Repealers, which deprived the people of the freedom to express their political discontent. Believing it was a way to help the Irish cause, O'Brien joined the Association as it seemed respectable and worthy in its operations. Importantly, the ideology of *The Nation* had a bearing on O'Brien's decision, seen, for example, in a private letter from O'Brien to Davis in which he writes: 'I am delighted with the article in yesterday's Nation respecting the prospect of an Union between Orange and Green. It makes me for a moment believe that the dream of my life is about to be realised.'[188] Although written in August 1845, this letter is reminiscent of the one he sent to the Repeal Association in October 1843. Furthermore, by the time of O'Brien's recruitment to Repeal he had already become impressed by *The Nation*; in his history of Young Ireland, Duffy observed that a private note written by Davis remarked of O'Brien that 'He is the most extravagant admirer of the *Nation* I have met.'[189] Throughout its first year and beyond, *The Nation* emphasized its vision of an Ireland composed of Catholics and Protestants living in harmony and prosperity as one nation, a vision shared by O'Brien.

Conclusion

According to the Loyal National Repeal Association, Repeal of the Union was the panacea for all Irish grievances under British rule. Although Repeal

[187] Letter from Smith O'Brien, 20 Oct. 1843, *Nation*, 28 Oct. 1843.

[188] Letter from William Smith O'Brien to Thomas Davis, 3 Aug. 1845, Thomas Davis Papers, NLI, MS 2644.

[189] Duffy, *Young Ireland*, p. 387.

was not achieved at this time, its ideological policies of unity of class and creed did have some success during 1843, although this was to be short-lived. The Association reached out to all sections of Irish society irrespective of class, creed, race, occupation, gender and age, particularly reflected in the phenomenon of the monster meetings. Compelling testimony as to the advancement of the Repeal cause not only came from the vast numbers of people who supported the Association, whether attending meetings or contributing to the Repeal rent, but included evidence from the Catholic priesthood and also those parliamentarians who were opposed to Repeal. The Dublin Repeal press was a formidable campaign machine, a window into the Repeal Association's organization, revealing its policies and activities. These newspapers were responsible for much of the success and empowerment of Irish nationalism from the autumn of 1842 to the autumn of 1843. Of the Dublin Repeal papers, *The Nation* was the most widely distributed and had the most influence over the fortunes of the Association. The success of *The Nation* during its first year is attested to by its high circulation and readership figures, which coincide with a dramatic increase in public support for the Repeal Association. It was only after the launch of *The Nation* that the middle classes and a few of the upper classes were drawn into the Repeal movement. *The Nation*'s non-sectarianism encouraged Protestants to join the Association, and the most important recruit was William Smith O'Brien. Readers' response to *The Nation* indicates that the nationalism it espoused had struck a chord with the Irish people. *The Nation* gave a voice to the Young Irelanders' concept of Irish nationalism, adopting a holistic approach in which the creation of a cultural nationalism was just as important as political nationalism. Whilst working for the Repeal Association, the very success of *The Nation* as a newspaper gave exposure and prominence to those who were involved in its writing and production, to the Young Irelanders and, in particular, Thomas Davis, whose impact on contemporaries and future Irish nationalists was truly inspirational.

CHAPTER 2

The role of the Dublin nationalist press in events leading to the downfall of the Irish nationalist movement in 1848

'They stand up and declare themselves men of war, and advocates of bloodshed, and revolutionary violence ... I therefore arraign Young Ireland as being treacherous to Repeal,' Daniel O'Connell, Repeal Association meeting, 3 August 1846.[1]

WHILE 1843 COULD BE SEEN as the highest point in the development of Irish nationalism in the mid-nineteenth century, three years later the Repeal cause encountered a momentous setback when the Young Irelanders seceded from the Loyal National Repeal Association. Much of the success of Irish nationalism during 1843 had been largely due to a certain harmonious spirit that had prevailed within the Repeal movement, particularly between the Repeal Association and *The Nation*, the most powerful nationalist newspaper at this time. From 1844, however, dissension between *The Nation*'s writers and the Repeal leadership caused irreparable damage to the nationalist ideology embraced by the Repeal Association.

The concept of unity among Irish nationalists in modern Irish history, particularly in the 1840s Repeal movement, was considered in theory to be a prerequisite for the attainment of independence from Great Britain. Advances in the unity of class and creed, and especially a strong degree of unity and solidarity within the Association itself, empowered the Repeal cause in 1843. From the end of that year, loss of faith crept into the Repeal organization and disunity within the Irish nationalist community manifested itself in a series of conflicts. *The Nation* newspaper was at the epicentre of this discord, leading to a turbulent rupture in the Repeal Association. This split was followed by the formation of the Irish Confederation, an organization identified with *The Nation*, but in early 1848 it, too,

[1] *Nation*, 8 Aug. 1846.

suffered dissent. That year *The United Irishman*, the first in a series of rebel newspapers, was founded in opposition to *The Nation*. As a consequence of these splits in the Repeal movement, Irish nationalism failed to recover the strength and unity that had been achieved in Irish society in 1843 and would have to wait for the Parnell era before this was restored.

Prior to the founding of *The Nation*, Daniel O'Connell exercised complete power over the Repeal Association. This power, however, was challenged by *The Nation* when four significant issues arose that brought those connected with this newspaper into conflict with O'Connell and undermined his authority in the Repeal movement. These issues were Federalism, religion and religious education, the Whig alliance and the use of physical force. O'Connell's overriding wish to help the Irish Catholic population, whether it was related to Federalism or to a Whig alliance, drew him into situations where he became involved in political manoeuvring. To *The Nation*, more intransigent in its approach to Repeal than O'Connell, this action seemed to compromise the aim of the Repeal movement. As a representative of the Irish Catholics, O'Connell expressed concern for their moral welfare, as demonstrated in 1845 by his critical reaction to the so-called 'godless' colleges that Robert Peel, the Tory Prime Minister, intended to establish. The new colleges, however, were essentially welcomed by *The Nation*, whose writers believed in the idea of an inclusive and pluralist society. For O'Connell, unity of creed was related more to the expediency of achieving Repeal than a basis of nationhood, whereas *The Nation* believed that being Irish defined a person's nationality more than adherence to a particular creed.

Probably the most persistently contentious basis for disagreement among Irish nationalists in the 1840s, and a key issue in both the 1846 and 1848 secessions, was the tension between physical force and moral force. While in 1846 the notion of physical force centred on a theoretical argument, in the second secession it was a major practical concern when the more extreme members in the Irish Confederation sought to dominate Irish nationalism's policy-making decisions. Motivated by what they perceived as a highly negative response to the Great Famine from the government and the landlords, the Irish Confederates issued several advanced nationalist newspapers in 1848 that preached physical force. The balance of power in the Irish nationalist movement had by then shifted from the dominance of the Repeal Association's leadership during the early days of *The Nation* to the extremist nationalist press six years later, culminating in an attempted rebellion and the collapse of Irish nationalism as a movement.

Conflicts between *The Nation* and the Repeal leadership from 1844

Many historians believe that there was, at root, a conflict between *The Nation*'s romantic nationalism and the more moderate and pragmatic variant espoused by Daniel O'Connell. In providing in-depth analyses of the Young Irelanders, however, Richard Davis concluded that there was not a great difference between the thinking of Young and Old Ireland within the Repeal movement.[2] Roy Foster, differentiating the Young Irelanders from European romantic nationalists, believed that in 'many ways the spirit of the *Nation* was as modernist and utilitarian as O'Connell.'[3] Given, then, that the two groups may have had much in common, why did their conflicts prove so contentious and sometimes intractable?

The Young Irelanders were defined and separated within the Repeal Association by their link with *The Nation*, making them a unique force with a strong voice in the Repeal movement. Despite upholding Repeal principles and ideology, the Young Irelanders evolved, perhaps unwittingly, into an elitist group ready to challenge O'Connell. Their separateness in the Association was notably promoted by the O'Connellite organ, *The Pilot*. O'Connell allowed this newspaper to contrive an image of the Young Irelanders as a disparate group within the Repeal Association. The challenge to O'Connell's policies played a significant part in the events leading up to the 1846 secession. It was not just the nature of the conflicts inherent in the challenges to O'Connell, but also the mere fact of these confrontations themselves. O'Connell's authority was undermined, disturbing the balance of power in the Repeal movement.

In the past, O'Connell firmly controlled the Dublin papers that had supported him. He was able to do this as they were financially reliant on the publicity sought by his political organizations. As far as he was concerned, O'Connell was putting into practice the conception of newspapers as a fourth estate, to criticize the government (more difficult in Ireland than in Britain owing to the uneasy relationship between the two countries) and in doing this, was expecting his followers in the press to support him unconditionally. According to Brian Inglis, tensions had arisen in the 1820s and 1830s between the principle of freedom of the press and O'Connell's determination that he alone should lead Irish nationalist opinion; what made this worse was O'Connell's propensity to change his policies. Michael Staunton in particular was highly critical of the way he was expected to

[2] Davis, *Young Ireland*; see in particular p. 259.

[3] R.F. Foster, *Modern Ireland 1600–1972* (London: Penguin Books, 1989), p. 311.

accept and publish policies that O'Connell had previously denounced.[4] In the early 1840s, though, relations between the Dublin Repeal press and O'Connell were far more cordial, in large part due to the success of the Repeal movement at that time.

However, a group of young journalists emerged who had the effrontery to challenge Daniel O'Connell, the great Liberator and leader of Irish Catholics in Ireland and Great Britain. At an Association meeting several months after the first secession, O'Connell stated, to the amusement of his faithful audience, that the Young Irelanders were 'merely writers for a newspaper ... this is a dissension between the Repeal Association on the one side, and a compositor's room of a newspaper on the other. (Laughter and cheers.)'[5] Ironically, that was the reality, and a reason why the Dublin nationalist press played a highly significant role in the fate of Irish nationalism at this time. Despite any common ground, from the end of 1843 a series of confrontations defined the nature of the relationship between the Young Irelanders and the O'Connellites in the Repeal movement and this was destined to have a marked impact on the development of Irish nationalism.

Relations between *The Nation* and the Repeal Association from October 1842 to October 1843 were generally harmonious, mainly because of the reciprocal nature of the alliance between these two groups. In practical terms, *The Nation* received money from Repeal advertisements and notices, and the Repeal Wardens aided the paper's circulation throughout Ireland and Great Britain. More importantly, ideologically, they shared the same ultimate aim, the repeal of the Act of Union. And while *The Nation* speedily became an outstanding success as a Dublin nationalist newspaper, what was written in its columns greatly assisted the progress of the Repeal Association. However, as a consequence of this success *The Nation*'s writers developed a sense of empowerment that was to lead to friction within the Repeal movement.

Initially, *The Nation* accepted that O'Connell possessed unsurpassed power over the Irish nationalist cause, respecting and obeying his leadership. Looking back over the past, Charles Gavan Duffy, *The Nation*'s proprietor and editor, recorded that O'Connell 'had jealously reserved to himself the initiative in opinion and action, and maintained it by a constant censorship of the press. The young men knew this well, and cheerfully accepted him

[4] O'Connell's relationship with the Irish nationalist press in the early part of the nineteenth century is explored in Inglis, 'O'Connell and the Irish press 1800–42', *IHS*, pp. 1–27; see also Inglis, *The Freedom of the Press*, pp. 220–4.

[5] Repeal Association (RA) meeting, 14 Dec. 1846, *Nation*, 19 Dec. 1846.

as the leader from whom the word of command, and the plan of the campaign, would emanate.'[6] This view was reflected in the pages of *The Nation* where, especially at the beginning, deference, if not subservience, was shown to O'Connell's leadership. O'Connell, for his part, welcomed *The Nation* as another liberal paper fighting for the Repeal cause. During its first year, however, underlying tensions began to appear between *The Nation* and the hierarchy of the Repeal leadership. From Duffy's perspective there were signs at the beginning that O'Connell was encroaching on his editorial control and independence. A few minor resentments arose, such as complaints about the amount of space allocated to Repeal news. In the second week, for example, *The Nation* announced: 'The space occupied by the proceedings of the Repeal Association, compels us to hold over the first Portrait in our NATIONAL GALLERY till our next number.'[7] Even so, irritations of this nature were almost negligible compared to the potentially more serious conflicts of interest that emerged later between *The Nation* and O'Connell.

One of the cornerstones of *The Nation*'s policy was a belief in a free press. Its writers thought that they had the right to express their own views 'upon all questions not fundamental to the existence of a Repeal party.'[8] They kept within this remit during the first year when, apart from a difference of opinion over the Poor Law, it was unnecessary to challenge O'Connell's authority on Repeal policy. Nevertheless, during this time *The Nation* did express views that were at variance with those of the Repeal Association, but any discord between the two sides was minor and did not seem to damage its unity. One episode of contention in 1843 concerned O'Connell's disapproval of praise bestowed on Tory writers by *The Nation*.[9] When *The Nation* refused to agree with O'Connell's judgement on 'literary questions,' it demonstrated its determination to be independent.[10]

A more serious disagreement centred upon the Repeal Association's policy on the Poor Law. In 1838 an Act of Parliament established workhouses throughout Ireland that were financed out of local rates. Much of O'Connell's criticism of the current Poor Law was based in his belief that it was too hard on the small tenant farmers, while not providing

6 Duffy, *Young Ireland*, p. 165.

7 'Answers to Correspondents', *Nation*, 22 Oct. 1842.

8 Duffy, *Young Ireland*, p. 166.

9 Article, 'Irish writers' and RA mtg., 20 Feb. 1843, *Nation*, 25 Feb. 1843; RA mtg., 27 Feb. 1843, *Nation*, 4 Mar. 1843. The writers in question included William Maginn and Charles Lever.

10 Duffy, *Young Ireland*, pp. 169–70.

enough help to those most vulnerable. Unlike O'Connell, though also berating the Poor Law, *The Nation* opposed its abolition, openly stating in a leading article in December 1842 that 'we shall stand firm, even should we stand alone, in defence of what we have got. We shall never consent to see the People deprived of the slight protection which the present Poor Law affords them, until some more effectual protection is substituted in its place.'[11] But, following a report compiled by a committee of the Repeal Association that had embraced the differing opinions on the Poor Law, O'Connell announced that 'he was thoroughly convinced that a legislative poor law, instead of diminishing pauperism or lessening public distress had the very opposite effect,' but seeking its amendment rather than its repeal was more practical.[12] From *The Nation*'s perspective, this may have seemed like a small victory, perhaps giving its writers more confidence, but it did not mean that O'Connell was bowing to their views; rather, he was choosing the option that was more achievable. Worryingly, *The Nation* had articulated its opposition in a highly defiant manner, foreshadowing the future. Even though Duffy acknowledged that 'O'Connell was little accustomed to criticism within his own party,' and conceded that 'no journal had hitherto maintained itself in the confidence of the people without the support of O'Connell,' he was willing to voice the independent opinion of *The Nation* and risk O'Connell's censure.[13] *The Nation*'s refusal to be cowed by O'Connell proved to be a sign of its growing prestige within the Repeal community. However, while the Irish nationalist cause was achieving great strides throughout much of 1843, these relatively minor squabbles did not hinder its progress.

It was *following* the *débâcle* at Clontarf that the serious conflicts between the hierarchy of the Repeal leadership and *The Nation*, which endangered the unity of the movement, began to emerge. Some Young Irelanders, like Duffy, claimed retrospectively that this discord had already begun with their disappointment at O'Connell's decision to abandon the Clontarf monster meeting in response to the government's proclamation of 7 October 1843

---

[11] 1st LA, *Nation*, 31 Dec. 1842.

[12] RA mtg., 19 Jan. 1843, *Nation*, 21 Jan. 1843; RA mtg., 30 Jan. 1843, *Nation*, 4 Feb. 1843. See also: Letter of complaint over the Poor Law from John O'Connell, 'To the Editor of the Nation', 4 Jan. 1843, and *The Nation*'s reply; John O'Connell refers to a letter from his father in which he implies that he would look to '*amend* the poor law' in parliament (suggesting that he was considering this option at the time as well as abolition), RA mtg., 5 Jan. 1843, *Nation*, 7 Jan. 1843; Letter from 'Mr O'Connell on the Poor Laws' to *Cork Examiner*, 14 Jan. 1843, *Nation*, 21 Jan. 1843; 1st LA, *Nation*, 4 Feb. 1843.

[13] Duffy, *Young Ireland*, pp. 172 and 166.

that had outlawed the event.[14] O'Connell was certainly determined to avoid bloodshed and, at that time, *The Nation* firmly endorsed his judgement; a leading article implored: 'People of Ireland! obey more implicitly than ever him whose solicitude, wisdom, and intrepidity, averted this calamity.'[15] What is clear is that after Clontarf and the arrests of Daniel O'Connell, his son John, newspaper proprietors Dr John Gray, Richard Barrett and Duffy, and other Repealers, an atmosphere of uncertainty and tension crept into the Repeal Association. Ironically, that October the Association's move into Conciliation Hall, its new premises, coincided with the beginnings of a distinct downward spiral in the relationship between O'Connell and *The Nation*. O'Connell claimed that the name 'Conciliation' was meant to reflect his policies: 'I wish to conciliate every class of my fellow-subjects – I wish to conciliate every man of every persuasion, Catholic, Protestant, Presbyterian, and Dissenter … I have no wish to conciliate the Whigs, for they are a dangerous party.'[16] Although meant as an affirmation of O'Connell's plans, these well-intentioned policies were to cause much dissension within the Repeal movement.

The first serious public confrontation between O'Connell and *The Nation* occurred over the issue of Federalism. Following the Repealers' trials, in February 1844 they were convicted for conspiring to repeal the Union by illegal means and sentenced to prison on 30 May. It was after a reversal of the verdicts by the House of Lords on 4 September 1844, when the Repealers were released from prison, that the conflict over Federalism arose. Around this time there had been growing support for Federalism among both Tories and Whigs in England and Ireland.[17] Supporters of this policy included Protestants of rank and influence, such as William Sharman Crawford, a large northern landowner and a radical MP. The principle of Federalism in Ireland meant having an Irish Parliament with sovereignty over its own soil, and representation in an imperial congress dealing with non-domestic affairs. England and Scotland would have the same arrangement, if so desired. Repeal of the Union, on the other hand, sometimes referred to as 'simple Repeal,' meant possessing a completely independent Irish Parliament, while sharing a common crown with Great Britain. It was, in essence, to be a reorganized restoration of the 1782 constitution whereby Ireland had its own parliament but without any interference from Westminster.

---

14 Duffy, *Young Ireland*, pp. 377–8.

15 2nd LA, *Nation*, 14 Oct. 1843.

16 RA adjourned mtg., 24 Oct. 1843, *Nation*, 28 Oct. 1843.

17 See, for example: *Nation*, 28 Sept. 1844.

Finding Repeal as elusive as ever, O'Connell was now drawn once again to the idea of a move towards Federalism, which he had briefly entertained the previous year. At an Association meeting on 9 September 1844, he enthused over a pamphlet on Federalism by the Protestant John Grey Porter, former High Sheriff of Co. Fermanagh, seemingly offering him the leadership of the Association in a bid to entice the co-operation of the Federalists.[18] One week later, O'Connell announced that, despite preferring 'unconditional Repeal,' a Federal parliament would be acceptable. In turn, *The Nation* was willing to 'give this plan a fair trial.'[19] But, in a further development, in a letter read out at an Association meeting on 14 October 1844, O'Connell revealed that he now preferred Federalism to 'simple Repeal.'[20]

Believing that O'Connell was completely abandoning Repeal, without consulting his colleagues who were away from Dublin, Duffy drafted a respectful, but resolute letter for publication in *The Nation*, stressing the need to preserve the Repeal principle. Duffy's main objection to Federalism centred on the continuation of the connection between Ireland and Great Britain with representation at Westminster. Compared with full legislative independence, Federalism would mean less power for the Irish parliament. Furthermore, Duffy asked, how could an Irish minority in a new imperial parliament have much say when they were already virtually powerless at Westminster? Under a Federal structure the aristocracy would be likely to gravitate towards London rather than remain in Ireland, especially as some Federalists did not envisage an Irish House of Lords; as a consequence, apart from increasing landlord absenteeism, Ireland's prestige as a nation would be diminished. More importantly, under a Federal system the Irish people would be dominated culturally, morally and intellectually by England, which was abhorrent to *The Nation*, whose aim had always been to resist the growing influence of Englishness upon Ireland.[21] The Federal issue thus came to reflect the fundamental differences of emphasis over the attainment of Irish nationality; as an advocate of cultural as well as political nationalism, *The Nation* wanted far more than what it perceived as O'Connell's narrow political settlement, which failed to embrace the Irish nationalist aspirations of the Young Irelanders.

Other contributors to *The Nation* expressed disapproval of O'Connell's new policy. Michael Joseph Barry, for example, wrote to William Smith O'Brien: 'If any change to Federalism be made in the constitution of

[18] *Nation*, 14 Sept. 1844.

[19] RA mtg., 16 Sept. 1844 and 1st LA, *Nation*, 21 Sept. 1844.

[20] Daniel O'Connell's letter, 2 Oct. 1844, *Nation*, 19 Oct. 1844.

[21] 1st LA column, *Nation*, 19 Oct. 1844.

the Association I will resign as a member.'[22] In another letter to Smith O'Brien, Thomas Davis explained: 'My opinion is, you know, what I have always avowed in the Nation namely that Federalism is not & cannot be a final settlement.'[23] But despite saying this, it does appear that Davis was not against the idea of Federalism as an interim step towards full independence; Duffy recalls that Davis had 'looked upon it as a possible and honorable compromise' after Clontarf.[24] Furthermore, during October 1844 Davis had travelled to the north to attend a meeting with the Belfast Federalists, who were discussing their plans for the future. In light of his more flexible approach towards Federalism, Davis may have been less willing than Duffy to publicly reject what appeared to be O'Connell's total conversion to Federalism; however, Davis remained loyal to Duffy's public reproach, which had far-reaching consequences for future relations between O'Connell and *The Nation*.

The contrast between Duffy's reaction in 1844 and when the Federal principle had become a contentious issue in the Repeal Association the previous year demonstrates how the relationship between *The Nation* and O'Connell had changed during this time. In October 1843, O'Connell had announced at an Association meeting that, without relinquishing the Repeal cause, he would be prepared to accept a Federal arrangement.[25] While *The Nation* disagreed with Federalism, it recognized the possible positive effects, stating that to avoid division in the Association it would not oppose this policy. Supporting O'Connell, *The Nation* wrote: 'The only man whom the country trusts or believes in has pronounced for it; and if we could draw any popular opinion from his views to ours, it is only too obvious that to that extent we would weaken the national strength … we dare not peril the cause.'[26] However, in private Duffy met with O'Connell to remonstrate against his adhesion to Federalism.[27] But no sooner had he begun moving

---

[22] Letter from M.J. Barry to Smith O'Brien, 27 Oct. 1844, William Smith O'Brien Papers, NLI, MS 434/1258.

[23] Davis to Smith O'Brien, 18 Oct. 1844, Smith O'Brien Papers, NLI, MS 434/1295. See also: Duffy, *Thomas Davis*, p. 261; W.J. O'Neill Daunt, *Personal Recollections of the late Daniel O'Connell, M.P., vol. II* (London: Chapman & Hall, 1848), pp. 220–1; Letter from Thomas Davis to D.O. Madden, [n.d.], Charles Gavan Duffy Papers, NLI, MS 5758/6.

[24] Charles Gavan Duffy, *Short Life of Thomas Davis 1840–1846* (London: T. Fisher Unwin, 1895), pp. 258–9 in Denis Gwynn, *Young Ireland and 1848* (Cork: Cork University Press, 1949), pp. 28–9.

[25] RA mtg., 16 Oct. 1843, *Nation*, 21 Oct. 1843.

[26] 1st LA, *Nation*, 21 Oct. 1843.

[27] Noted later in 2nd LA, *Nation*, 22 Aug. 1846.

towards Federalism, O'Connell felt compelled, with opposition from other Repealers, to make a public retreat at an Association meeting on 30 October 1843.[28] One year on, when O'Connell raised the issue of Federalism for the second time, Duffy was prepared to 'peril the cause' by publicly challenging him in *The Nation*.

It is difficult to explain why Duffy took such a bold course of action. Had it worked, allying with the Ulster Protestant Federalists may have gone a long way to fulfilling *The Nation*'s unity of creed, and would have especially appealed to Davis. Perhaps Duffy had genuinely lost faith in O'Connell's judgement and leadership. Certainly, he pressed this point in his later highly subjective histories, accusing O'Connell of weakness and vacillation following Repeal's retreat at Clontarf. Duffy also feared that in adopting Federalism O'Connell would be drawn closer to the Whigs and could again compromise the nationalist cause by abandoning Repeal, as he had done in 1835 with the Lichfield House Compact, when he had agreed that Repeal MPs should support the Whigs against the Tories in return for limited reforms for Ireland. The relationship between O'Connell and *The Nation*, which had soured following the prosecution of the Repealers in the 1844 trials, heightened tensions; on more than one occasion, O'Connell complained bitterly about being implicated in *The Nation*'s indictments.[29] As for Duffy, being the proprietor and editor of the most renowned Irish nationalist newspaper in Ireland and Great Britain for the last two years probably gave him what he believed was the authority to voice his opinions in this way, and having been among those convicted alongside O'Connell gave him stature within the Repeal movement.

Following the publication of Duffy's letter to O'Connell on 19 October 1844, *The Nation* remained defiant; a few weeks later, a leading article declared: 'This [i.e. Repeal] is what Ireland wants. On this we insist. For this we and Ireland were ready to take issue, even with O'CONNELL.'[30] Much of the nationalist press throughout Ireland had, in fact, given Federalism a muted response and had not appeared too critical of Duffy's letter. Now, fired by a new confidence, it almost seemed as though *The Nation* had, on this issue, superseded O'Connell as the authoritative voice of the Repeal movement.

O'Connell decided to retreat from Federalism for the second time, thereby implying that *The Nation*'s opposition to his policy had forced a change of strategy. Referring to this incident a couple of years later, *The*

[28] *Nation*, 4 Nov. 1843.
[29] For example, RA mtg., 9 Sept. 1844, *Nation*, 14 Sept. 1844.
[30] 1st LA, *Nation*, 16 Nov. 1844.

Nation claimed that 'the great bulk of the Press, English, American, and Irish – from the *Quarterly Review* downwards – treated the issue as the defeat of Mr. O'CONNELL by THE NATION.'[31] Apart from *The Nation*'s associates, there was opposition to Federalism from other Repealers, most notably William Smith O'Brien. Showing how much he valued Smith O'Brien, O'Connell had sought his opinion on Federalism, stressing that he would not proceed with this new policy without his support.[32] However, wishing to remain neutral in this controversy, Smith O'Brien composed a conciliatory letter, which was read out at the Association's weekly meeting on 4 November 1844, stating that although there should be co-operation between Federalists and Repealers, he personally preferred Repeal.[33] When he returned to the Association on 25 November 1844, O'Connell tried to save face and assert his authority. Assuming a defensive position, he denied ever fully committing himself to Federalism (which was correct as he was awaiting approval from Smith O'Brien), 'Yet a cry was raised – a shout was sent forth by men who doubtless thought themselves more fitted to be leaders than I am (oh! oh!), and several young gentlemen began to exclaim against me.'[34] Henceforth, O'Connell accused the Young Irelanders of challenging his leadership in the Repeal Association. While his commanding influence over the Catholic population could never be usurped, overall the Federal debate marked a definitive change in the balance of power between *The Nation* and O'Connell, most notably appearing to increase the power of *The Nation*, while reducing the power of O'Connell. As the British radical *Tait's Magazine* remarked at the time, 'The Agitator [as O'Connell was then known in England] has ceased to be master of the agitation.'[35]

Though less volatile, a few other issues arose from 1844 that were symptomatic of the worsening relationship between *The Nation*'s Young Irelanders and the O'Connellites. One was related to the Repeal Association's income. While the Dublin Repeal press showed that the Association appeared to be well run, there was one particular aspect that troubled not only the Young Irelanders but also potential supporters. That September a letter of complaint from John O'Connell to Smith O'Brien concerned a Committee meeting from which he and his father had been absent and

[31] 2nd LA, *Nation*, 22 Aug. 1846.

[32] Letters from O'Connell to Smith O'Brien, 1 & 21 Oct. 1844, William Smith O'Brien Papers, NLI, MS 434/1245 & 1254.

[33] Smith O'Brien's letter, 31 Oct. 1844, *Nation*, 9 Nov. 1844.

[34] *Nation*, 30 Nov. 1844. See again: O'Connell's letter, 2 Oct. 1844, *Nation*, 19 Oct. 1844.

[35] Duffy, *My Life in Two Hemispheres, I*, p. 105.

at which aspersions were cast against Daniel O'Connell over the handling of the Repeal Association's finances. John O'Connell claimed that these charges were 'unjust, ungenerous & utterly unfounded.'[36] This seemed like another attack on Daniel O'Connell, who was the Association's treasurer, suggesting that he was incapable of properly managing its funds. The Young Irelanders wanted the Repeal accounts to be publicized, believing that accountability would have rendered them more efficient, especially as an open rather than a secretive approach may have attracted more Protestant support; this was an issue which, according to Duffy, 'tortured men like O'Brien, Davis and his comrades.'[37] In 1846 the subject was raised again in a Repeal Association meeting when Young Irelander John Martin revealed that many of his fellow-Ulster Protestant countrymen who may have been inclined to join the Association questioned why Repeal's finances were not made public.[38] The *Dublin Evening Mail*, a newspaper opposed to Repeal, called for the publication of the Association's accounts, as did *The Nation*; the former hoped to destroy the credibility of the Association and to cause dissension, while *The Nation* saw the transparency of finances as beneficial to the cause.[39] But the Association's leadership refused the request.

The unity of the Repeal organization in 1844 was to be further seriously compromised by the conflicts over religion, and particularly religious education. During the Federal debate, a religious conflict was simultaneously taking place in the Irish press when *The Nation* was attacked by other newspapers for allegedly writing irreligious articles.[40] This charge against *The Nation* was led by 'An Irish Priest,' Rev. Patrick A. Murray, a Maynooth professor, in *The Dublin Weekly Register* on 19 October 1844.[41] He was provoked by several items that had appeared in *The Nation* the previous week, wherein, for example, Davis had praised a recently published work by

---

[36] John O'Connell to Smith O'Brien, 11 Sept. 1844, Smith O'Brien Papers, NLI, MS 434/1240.

[37] Duffy, *Young Ireland*, p. 639.

[38] RA mtg., 23 Feb. 1846, *Nation*, 28 Feb. 1846.

[39] 3rd LA, *Nation*, 14 March 1846.

[40] For an in-depth account of this affair see: Duffy, *Thomas Davis*, pp. 269–80, and Duffy, *Young Ireland*, pp. 610–21; for a revisionist interpretation see: Maurice R. O'Connell, 'Young Ireland and the Catholic Clergy in 1844: Contemporary Deceit and Historical Falsehood', *The Catholic Historical Review*, vol. 74 (2), April 1988, pp. 199–225.

[41] In a letter to his wife, John Blake Dillon told her that Murray admitted later that he had been mistaken about *The Nation*'s infidelity and had apologised to Duffy: Extracts of letters from Dillon to his wife, Aug. 1847 and biographical material compiled by William Dillon, son of J.B. Dillon, John Blake Dillon Papers, Trinity College Dublin (TCD), MS 6457 d.

D.O. Madden (*Ireland and its Rulers*) that had been critical of O'Connell and the Catholic religion. Failing to see how his remarks might have caused offence to his mainly Catholic readership, Davis was privately furious with 'the bigot attacks on The Nation' for, he believed, ultimately, 'the question at issue is religious liberty.'[42] While providing ammunition for *The Pilot*, a paper always ready for an excuse to tarnish *The Nation*'s image, this row did not bode well for the forthcoming troubles within the Repeal Association. As for O'Connell, he was convinced that *The Nation* was in the wrong, and did not intervene when entreated by Davis, via Smith O'Brien, to use his influence to stop the attacks.[43] Duffy believed that newspapers accusing *The Nation* of irreligious writing were being encouraged by John O'Connell; he also thought that they could have been sanctioned by Daniel O'Connell, who emphatically denied such charges.[44]

Nevertheless, John O'Connell did have a particular stake in undermining *The Nation* since secularism, though reflecting the Young Irelanders' theory of nationality, confronted the Association's most ardent supporters in the hierarchy of the Catholic Church; indeed, the bishops who followed Dr John MacHale, Archbishop of Tuam, believed that the Association should be fighting their corner more specifically on Catholic issues. It was to John O'Connell's advantage to demonstrate that he fully supported Catholic matters in order to secure the alliance of these bishops when the time came to choose a successor to his father's leadership. The other contender for this position was William Smith O'Brien, the Protestant, who, like *The Nation*, viewed the Association as a secular organization; he was a natural successor to O'Connell, second in status to him in the Repeal movement. For the MacHalite bishops, it was preferable for them to have John O'Connell as the head of the Association rather than Smith O'Brien, for they would also see the power of *The Nation* weakened. Duffy believed that, John O'Connell seemed increasingly to be transforming the Repeal Association into a sectarian organization from the summer of 1845. Davis reinforced Duffy's view of John O'Connell's growing influence on the Association's policies. That July he wrote to Young Irelander John Mitchel: 'O'C., under Johnny's culture, promises to throw up more bigotry.'[45] From John O'Connell's

[42] Letter from Thomas Davis to Smith O'Brien, 3 Nov. 1844, Smith O'Brien Papers, MS 434/1282.

[43] Letter from Daniel O'Connell to Smith O'Brien, 9 Nov. 44, Smith O'Brien Papers, MS 434/1273; Letter from Thomas Davis to Smith O'Brien, 27 Oct. 1844, Smith O'Brien Papers, MS 434/1296.

[44] 'Autograph letter of Daniel O'Connell to Thomas Davis', 30 Oct. 1844, NLI, MS 129.

[45] Letter from Thomas Davis to John Mitchel, postmark 7 July 1845, John Mitchel,

perspective, *The Nation* needed to be discredited for its treatment of his father over Federalism, its challenge to the O'Connell leadership and its support of Smith O'Brien.

In the meantime, a bitter controversy arose between the Young Irelanders of *The Nation* and Daniel and John O'Connell over a proposed government bill to establish non-denominational colleges at Belfast, Cork and Galway. Using the phraseology of Tory MP Sir Robert Inglis, Daniel O'Connell labelled these colleges as 'Godless' owing to their lack of provision for religious instruction. *The Nation* and William Smith O'Brien, albeit critical of certain elements of the bill, approved its principle of mixed education, believing it could be an opportunity to reconcile and unify Catholics and Protestants. After much argument in the nationalist press and in Conciliation Hall, this conflict reached an emotional climax at a defining Association meeting on 26 May 1845, where O'Connell challenged Davis's views: 'The principle on which the present bill is founded has been lauded by Mr. Davis, and was advocated in a newspaper professing to be the organ of the Roman Catholic people of this country, but which I emphatically pronounce is no such thing.' When O'Connell then referred to 'the Young Ireland party, anxious to rule the destinies of this country,' Davis denied any factions in the Association, and stressed that they were all working for Irish nationality.[46] Although there followed a reconciliation between O'Connell and Davis, Duffy noted that 'poisonous seeds of distrust and division' had been sown.[47] Writing to Smith O'Brien on 15 June 1845, Davis reported that in a Committee meeting on the previous day 'O'Connell seemed anxious that the supporters of mixed Education should secede from the Association; but none of us did so.'[48] Two and a half months later, in another letter to Smith O'Brien, Davis wrote: 'How very long it will take to get over the ill effects of the Education Row & the worse effects of the bigotry shown during & since it took place.'[49] It was evident that the quarrel over religious education was indicative of a deepening rift between *The Nation* and the O'Connellites.

The Last Conquest of Ireland (Perhaps), (Glasgow: Cameron, Ferguson & Co., [1876]), p. 88; first published in book form by (Dublin: *The Irishman*'s office, 1861); latest printing: Patrick Maume (ed.) (Dublin: University College Dublin Press, 2005). John Mitchel (1815–75) was one of the most iconic Irish nationalists of the mid-nineteenth century, whose journalism, as we shall see, was to have a dramatic effect on events leading to the attempted 1848 rebellion.

[46] *Nation*, 31 May 1845.

[47] Duffy, *Young Ireland*, pp. 705–8.

[48] Duffy, *Young Ireland*, p. 717.

[49] Thomas Davis to William Smith O'Brien, 28 Aug.[1845], William Smith O'Brien Papers, NLI, MS 432/ 881.

While this debate reflected a difference of opinion over the principle of mixed education, it demonstrated too O'Connell's belief that *The Nation* was again usurping his authority and leadership. Even though he had previously been favourable to mixed education, O'Connell now based his present stance on trying to protect the moral well-being of his Catholic supporters.[50] Encouraged by John, he took the opportunity to make a stand against the Young Irelanders, and denounced *The Nation* for failing to represent or support its overwhelmingly Catholic readership, thereby trying to discredit the paper in the eyes of the Repeal movement. From *The Nation*'s perspective, the O'Connellites were attacking the Young Irelanders' right to hold their own opinions and to publicize them freely; as a leading article complained: 'Men who attempt to coerce individuals or the press out of their honest opinions, do us incurable injury … It is for liberty we are fighting, not for slavery.'[51] Indeed, this principle of the right to differ was a tactic used by *The Nation* to defend itself in the final split in the Association.

With the O'Connellites and *The Nation* becoming increasingly polarized towards the end of 1845, the Young Irelanders believed that it was important to secure the alliance of William Smith O'Brien in order to bring more authority and kudos to their group. Entrusted with the temporary leadership of the Repeal Association while O'Connell was imprisoned in 1844, Smith O'Brien was by far the most prestigious person next to him in the Association. Furthermore, viewing Repeal as a secular movement, Smith O'Brien was attuned to *The Nation*'s concept of Irish nationality, which was now in danger of being compromised by John O'Connell's increasing power within the Association. While the Young Irelanders conducted much private correspondence with Smith O'Brien behind the scenes, such as seeking his advice and keeping him *au fait* with current Repeal matters when absent from Dublin, it was ultimately their support for him in *The Nation* that drew Smith O'Brien to their side.

One defining event finalized Smith O'Brien's adhesion to the Young Irelanders, although it further damaged the relationship between O'Connell and *The Nation*. When Smith O'Brien refused to sit on a Parliamentary railway committee because it was unconnected with Ireland, he was brought into contempt of the House of Commons, where he was duly imprisoned. While O'Connell disapproved of Smith O'Brien's behaviour and was reluctant to allow the Association to display sympathy for him, in their leading articles in May 1846 *The Nation* justified and applauded his

[50] For further information on O'Connell and mixed education see, for example: Davis, *Young Ireland*, pp. 68–74 and 174–5.

[51] 2nd LA, *Nation*, 18 Oct. 1845.

action.[52] By reprinting articles from other newspapers, *The Nation* further demonstrated that there was much support for Smith O'Brien throughout the country.[53] Duffy also wrote to Smith O'Brien expressing 'the sympathy of the men connected with the *Nation* in your present stand for Ireland.'[54] In addition, on 14 May 1846, the Young Irelanders arranged a deputation to London from the Eighty-Two Club (an exclusive offshoot of the Association that encouraged the membership of Protestants) with an address of praise to Smith O'Brien in prison, duly reported in *The Nation*.[55] Evidence of further support for Smith O'Brien that month came from '147 petitions from places in nearly every county in Ireland' urging his release.[56] With a growing tide of Repeal supporters in favour of Smith O'Brien, O'Connell changed course, treating him on his release from incarceration 'as a soldier returning from a victorious campaign.'[57] There is little doubt that *The Nation* was both leading and reflecting public opinion over this issue, thereby again seeming to challenge O'Connell's authority and judgement. O'Connell was further undermined by *The Nation*'s praise of Smith O'Brien when a leading article on 16 May 1846, written by the poet John Fisher Murray, stated, 'Let us contemplate the nobility of the work this man has set himself down to do; let us fill ourselves full of the greatness of a man leading the forlorn hope of his country's nationhood.' Not only was the tone of this rhetoric similar to that usually conferred upon O'Connell by *The Nation*, but there also seemed to be an indirect comparison between the two men; referring to Smith O'Brien, this article noted that 'He does not blow hot and cold upon Repeal.'[58] Apart from siding with Smith O'Brien against O'Connell's wishes, *The Nation* also unwisely criticized the Liberator, creating even more uneasiness within the Repeal hierarchy.

Smith O'Brien, naturally, was impressed by how the Young Irelanders and *The Nation* responded to his imprisonment, compared to O'Connell's reaction. He had written to Duffy from his confinement in the House of Commons expressing much disappointment with the Association.[59] It was

---

52 1st LA, *Nation*, 2 and 9 May 1846.

53 'Smith O'Brien and his constituents'; 'The Irish Press on the imprisonment', *Nation*, 9 May 1846; 'Public Opinion', 16 May 1846. See also: 2nd LA, *Nation*, 30 May 1846.

54 Duffy to Smith O'Brien, [n.d.], William Smith O'Brien Papers, NLI, MS 441/2243.

55 3rd LA, *Nation*, 16 May 1846.

56 'House of Commons – Monday', 18 May 1846, *Dublin Weekly Register*, 23 May 1846.

57 Charles Gavan Duffy, *Four Years of Irish History, 1845–1849. A Sequel to "Young Ireland"* (London & New York: Cassell, Petter, Galpin & Co., 1883) p. 143.

58 1st LA, *Nation*, 16 May 1846.

59 Smith O'Brien to Duffy, May 1846, '59 Letters from W.S. O'Brien to C.G. Duffy', 1845–1855, NLI, MS 2642.

during the Peace Resolutions' debate in Conciliation Hall towards the end of July 1846 that Smith O'Brien decisively sided with the Young Irelanders against the O'Connellites. These resolutions, drawn up by the Repeal leadership, stated that the Association's policy was to repudiate physical force in all circumstances. While the Young Irelanders agreed to this policy as far as the Repeal Association was concerned, they refused to agree with the principle of abhorring physical force in any situation, which brought them into a serious conflict with the O'Connellites. During a discussion of this issue at an Association meeting on 27 July 1846, Smith O'Brien spoke of his recent imprisonment and acknowledged that

> The gentlemen connected with THE NATION were kind enough to approve of my conduct – I must say they spoke the sentiments of a great majority of the Repealers of Ireland ... if there be an attempt to cut off THE NATION newspaper from the Association, or exclude these gentlemen from the committees, I shall feel it impossible, until these gentlemen be restored, to co-operate with the Association.[60]

This statement testifies to the direct link between *The Nation*'s support of Smith O'Brien and his decision to align himself with the Young Irelanders. Their response to Smith O'Brien's imprisonment, though clinching the alliance between himself and the Young Irelanders, drove a further wedge between the O'Connellites and *The Nation*, appearing to the Old Irelanders (a name now conferred upon O'Connell's closest supporters in the Association) to be yet another serious challenge to O'Connell's leadership. This disquiet was made worse by the O'Connellites' newspaper, *The Pilot*, which for the past few years had been persistently fuelling antagonism between them and the Young Irelanders.

From the beginning of *The Nation*'s existence, Richard Barrett's *Pilot* had been its unrelenting adversary. As another Repeal paper, *The Nation* posed a threat to *The Pilot* both commercially and politically, especially in terms of its status within the Repeal movement. *The Pilot* therefore attacked *The Nation*, referring to its writers as the 'Clique,' identifying them and isolating them as a dangerous group within the Association. Any criticism of O'Connell and his followers by *The Nation* elicited a disparaging response in *The Pilot*. For instance, in a leading article published in May 1846, *The Pilot* asked: 'What, then, *is* Young Ireland? The *Nation* is Young Ireland – its creed, "what will make the *Nation* sell?" – its means, down with O'Connell

60 *Nation*, 1 Aug. 1846.

and the Priests, and up with … College Bills, and latitudinarianism.'[61] In this manner, Barrett sought to undermine *The Nation*'s standing within the Repeal movement; thus he attacked the paper's non-sectarianism, accusing it of being not only irreligious, but also at odds with Ireland's mostly Catholic population. Barrett also edited the short-lived *Old Ireland* (10 October 1845–7 February 1846), a Catholic weekly paper that had been founded as another weapon with which to attack *The Nation*'s views on mixed education. Furthermore, knowing how much the people loved O'Connell, *The Pilot* even accused *The Nation* of expressing hatred towards him.[62] Barrett repeatedly charged *The Nation* with trying to usurp O'Connell's position as head of the Repeal movement, for example, when *The Pilot* asked 'whether the Repeal cause and the Irish people are to be governed, conducted, and led by the *Nation* clique in future.'[63] *The Pilot* had its critics though; among them Frederick Lucas, proprietor of *The Tablet*, a London Catholic newspaper that supported O'Connell, who highly disapproved of Barrett's journalism. In a letter to O'Connell in August 1846 Lucas wrote: 'I loathe the man and his doings with my whole soul and my private notion is that he is rather injuring the cause than serving it.'[64] *The Pilot*, it seemed, wished to destroy *The Nation*, even if this imperilled the unity of the Repeal movement.

The 1846 secession between Young and Old Ireland and its aftermath

One of the earlier (though not the earliest) published histories of events leading to the 1846 secession was written by Duffy who, while chronicling the preceding friction between the Young Irelanders and the O'Connellites over the issues of Federalism and religious education, maintained that the split in the Repeal Association was ultimately due to O'Connell's alliance with the Whig party.[65] Although this view still has its supporters,

[61] 1st LA, *Pilot*, 4 May 1846.

[62] 1st LA, *Pilot*, 25 May 1846.

[63] 1st LA, *Pilot*, 20 May 1846.

[64] Frederick Lucas to Daniel O'Connell, 29 Aug. 1846, Maurice R. O'Connell (ed.), *The Correspondence of Daniel O'Connell 1846–7, vol. VIII* (Dublin: The Blackwater Press, 1980), pp. 92–3. A letter from Charles Gavan Duffy, 5 Nov. 1845, to the editor of *The Tablet*, summarizes *The Pilot*'s attacks on *The Nation* and himself: *Nation*, 8 Nov. 1845.

[65] Duffy, *Young Ireland* and *Four Years of Irish History*. See also: Duffy, *My Life in Two Hemispheres, I*. Among the earliest published histories of the Young Ireland era was: Michael Doheny, *The Felon's Track or History of the Attempted Outbreak in Ireland*

F.S.L. Lyons suggested that the split may have been caused by the basic difference between the Young Irelanders and O'Connell over the issue of physical force. Lyons was much influenced by Maurice O'Connell, who believed that the Peace Resolutions were introduced mainly to safeguard the principle of moral force; he in turn had been influenced by Frederick Lucas, who pointed out in *The Tablet* on 8 August 1846 that O'Connell was greatly concerned to crush any notion of physical force.[66]

It could be argued that the split in the Repeal Association in 1846 was ultimately caused by the increasingly bitter power struggle between *The Nation* newspaper and the O'Connellites over the direction of Irish nationalism. Federalism and religious education in particular were issues that caused growing unease between the O'Connellites and *The Nation*. On the question of Federalism, *The Nation* appeared to triumph over the leader of the Repeal Association. From this point, John O'Connell seemed determined to crush *The Nation* to avenge his father and to safeguard his succession to the Repeal leadership, which had been threatened by the popularity of Smith O'Brien. Whilst O'Connell may have thought that *The Nation*'s stand on religion and religious education was inappropriate for the Repeal Association, which was essentially supported by Ireland's Catholic population, he and John used the debate over religious education to reduce the power of the Young Irelanders. Davis, on the other hand, was determined to champion his belief in non-sectarianism in *The Nation* even though it was inviting criticism and causing friction. Key issues in this secession, apart from the underlying principle of aspiring to self-determination, were *The Nation*'s resistance to the Whig alliance and its attitude towards physical force, and both were intimately intertwined. The crucial Peace Resolutions' debate at the end of July 1846 was dominated by what had been printed in *The Nation*. By this time, however, the O'Connellites and *The Nation* were already divided into two antagonist camps, poised for a final showdown over who should control the political direction of the Repeal Association.

O'Connell was now departing from the Association's policy of being independent of other parties. He realized that the Young Irelanders would

---

Embracing the Leading Events in the Irish Struggle from the year 1843 to the close of 1848, Arthur Griffith (pref.) (Dublin: M.H. Gill & Son Ltd., 1914); 1st ed. (New York: W.H. Holbrooke, 1849).

[66] Maurice O'Connell drew this article to the attention of Lyons and also allowed him to read an essay he wrote on this issue that was published in *The Irish Times*, 30 Dec. 1971: F.S.L. Lyons, *Ireland since the Famine*, 2nd ed. (London: Fontana Press, 1985), pp. 106–7. See also: 'O'Connell, Young Ireland and violence' in Maurice R. O'Connell, *Daniel O'Connell. The Man and his Politics*, Conor Cruise O'Brien (foreword) (Dublin: Irish Academic Press, 1990), pp. 61–88.

resist his alliance with the Whigs, given what had been printed previously in *The Nation*, most notably its long-standing objection to combining with any other party. *The Nation*'s opposition to the possibility of an alliance between Repealers and Whigs had been reiterated periodically; at the beginning of March 1844, a leading article headed 'No Compromise' warned the Whigs to leave the Repealers alone.[67] The Young Irelanders reminded their newspaper's readers of the perceived dangers of allying with the Whigs. Bearing in mind the 1835 Lichfield House agreement between Whigs and Repealers, *The Nation* believed that if the Whigs came into power and were supported by O'Connell, the national cause would be compromised or even lost. During an Association meeting in June 1846, when O'Connell's followers were denying a rumour of a Repeal-Whig alliance, leading Young Irelander John Mitchel correctly predicted that 'if any overture could be made by him [O'Connell] for a compact with any English faction whatever … then this Association commits suicide, [and] abandons the principle … that Ireland is entitled to govern herself.'[68] At the beginning of July 1846, after Lord John Russell had come into power, and a Repeal-Whig coalition became a possibility, *The Nation* reaffirmed its opposition. O'Connell was equally resolute in seeking to co-operate with the Whigs to achieve concessions for Ireland in the short term, and possibly Repeal in the long term. These two intractable positions left little room for manoeuvre or compromise by either *The Nation* or the O'Connellites.

But what strengthened O'Connell's determination to seek a Whig alliance was the partial failure of the potato crop in the winter of 1845–46 that caused famine in the countryside. One of the concessions that O'Connell had hoped to gain from the Whigs was 'An act for the establishing throughout Ireland of the TENANT-RIGHT,' intended to provide some form of security to tenants; this had been one of the aims of the Repeal Association before the Great Famine, but it was now needed more urgently than ever to reduce the rising number of evictions and the growing unrest in rural areas.[69] O'Connell empathized greatly with his suffering people and in the circumstances of the Famine prioritized relief over Repeal, believing that the Whigs would do more to help the rural poor than the Tories. John Mitchel, one of O'Connell's chief adversaries, admitted that 'To the last he laboured on the "Relief Committees" of Dublin, and thought every hour lost unless employed in rescuing some of the doomed.'[70]

[67] 1st LA, *Nation*, 2 March 1844.

[68] RA mtg., 15 June 1846, *Nation*, 20 June 1846.

[69] RA mtg., 6 July 1846, *Nation*, 11 July 1846.

[70] Mitchel, *Last Conquest*, p. 136.

As a consequence of Thomas Davis's death in 1845, John Mitchel, an Ulster Protestant solicitor on the periphery of the Young Ireland group at that time, was invited by Duffy to join his editorial staff as a full-time writer. Davis had died on 16 September of that year, a week after informing Duffy that he was suffering from scarlet fever.[71] His death deeply shocked friends and foes alike; John Blake Dillon wrote: 'This calamity makes the world look rather bleak. God knows I am tempted to wish myself well out of it.'[72] *The Pilot*, bitter opponent of *The Nation*, joined the chorus of mourners:

> The warmth of his love for Ireland was brightly reflected in the burning eloquence of his pen. To those who enjoyed the friendship of Mr. Davis the bereavement is irreparable – to those who revered his high-souled honor and the virtues of his character a model of emulation has been lost, ... – and to the country, which we do believe he so fondly and so truly loved, the absence of that genius, which breathed and lived only for her sake, is a calamity deplorable.[73]

Davis's loss was to have serious repercussions for the future of *The Nation*.

With his fiery prose, Mitchel brought a far more strident tone to *The Nation* than had previously been adopted by Davis, and he soon incurred O'Connell's wrath. Near the end of 1845, much offence in particular was caused by a leading article reacting to what Mitchel deemed provocative language against the Repeal Association in the English Peelite newspapers *The Morning Herald* and *The Standard*, the latter of which had suggested how railways could be militarily advantageous to the government in suppressing treason. Mitchel responded in *The Nation* by suggesting that if the government decided to suppress the Repeal Association by force, the railways, on the contrary, could be utilized to defend the people against enemy aggression, with instructions passed on locally by Repeal Wardens.[74] Within days O'Connell visited *The Nation*'s office to remonstrate against this article, and forced the paper to state in its next issue that *The Nation*

[71] Two letters from Davis to Duffy, [9 & 11 Sept. 1845], RIA, MS 12 P 19 Box III (2). See also: Duffy, *Young Ireland*, pp. 751–4.

[72] Letter from Dillon to Duffy, [n.d. but '45' added later], Duffy Papers, NLI, MS 5756/129.

[73] Extract from *Pilot*, 17 Sept. 1845, reprinted in *Nation*, 20 Sept. 1845. Whether or not this moving tribute to Davis by *The Pilot* was intended to be genuine, there was much truth in its sentiments; the paper was not slow, however, to continue its previous criticism of him.

[74] 1st LA, *Nation*, 22 Nov. 1845.

had 'neither connexion with, nor control over, Repeal Wardens.'[75] Even so, on 10 January *The Nation* published a personal letter from Duffy 'To the Repealers of Ireland' in defence of Mitchel's railway article and *The Nation*'s journalism. Earlier that week, an indictment for seditious libel had been issued against Duffy, as proprietor of *The Nation*, for the railway article which, it was alleged, intended to cause disaffection among the people against the government.[76] The court hearing took place on 17 June 1846, but the jury's failure to agree on the verdict led to the case being thrown out the next day, suggesting there was insufficient evidence to show that *The Nation* had broken the law.[77] As far as O'Connell was concerned, however, *The Nation*'s speaking on behalf of the Repeal Association and dictating policy, particularly on the delicate issue of physical force, was yet another example of its usurpation of his authority. Furthermore, he saw *The Nation* as a liability at a time when he was seeking an alliance with the Whigs.

O'Connell was aware that the Whigs would prove unenthusiastic about his continued association with *The Nation* because of its outspoken opposition to their party and its more radical nationalist stance within the Repeal movement. This was confirmed by Lord John Russell, leader of the Whig Party, who claimed in a speech in Parliament on 15 June 1846 that those persons who represented *The Nation* desired not Repeal of the Union but complete separation, achieved by violence.[78] By way of response, *The Nation* denied the accusation, remaining defiant: 'We mean to go on writing in THE NATION exactly as we have done … If we are guilty of high treason, perhaps he [Russell] would like to prosecute us.'[79] It was, of course, to the Whigs' advantage to see the Repeal movement weakened by dissension. At a Conciliation Hall meeting on 31 August 1846, O'Connell claimed that Russell's speech had prompted him to initiate the Peace Resolutions to distance the Repeal Association from *The Nation*.[80] It seems that O'Connell's main motive in introducing these resolutions was to sever relations with *The Nation* in order to demonstrate to Russell his commitment to the Whig alliance, ostensibly claiming that the legal safety of the Association needed protection as *The Nation* was now, he argued, inclining too far towards militant rhetoric.

---

[75] Duffy, *Four Years of Irish History*, pp. 116–8; 'Threats of coercion', *Nation*, 29 Nov. 1845.

[76] 'The State prosecution', *Nation*, 10 Jan. 1846.

[77] '"The Nation" prosecution', *Nation*, 20 June 1846.

[78] House of Commons, *Weekly Register*, 20 June 1846.

[79] 3rd LA, *Nation*, 20 June 1846.

[80] *Nation*, 5 Sept. 1846.

From its early days *The Nation*'s combative image, expressed largely through its poetry, distinguished it from the rest of the Dublin nationalist press. However, from the start *The Nation*'s policy was not to sanction the use of physical force, and after Davis's death Duffy continued to abide by that policy, 'To complete the work of education and conciliation which Davis had begun.'[81] Later, when Mitchel's rhetoric appeared to veer towards militancy near the end of 1847, Duffy's disapproval of this direction forced Mitchel's resignation from *The Nation*. It has to be remembered that O'Connell's own Repeal rhetoric in 1843 was sometimes suggestive of physical force, and while he condemned *The Nation*'s writings that were cited against him in the 1844 trials, the prosecution had also considered O'Connell's own speeches just as seditious.[82] Since then, however, O'Connell had become more circumspect about the issue of physical force, which he fully exploited in 1846 to distance the Association from the Young Irelanders and their newspaper.

One way to dissociate the Repeal Association from *The Nation*, and hence weaken the paper's authority, was to oust its associates from Conciliation Hall. It was testimony to the influence *The Nation* held over public opinion at that time that O'Connell deemed it necessary to take such action; as Mitchel remarked retrospectively: 'The *Nation* still remained the most widely circulated and influential journal of the Irish Nationalists.'[83] Knowing, therefore, that the Young Irelanders would jeopardize his alliance with the Whigs, O'Connell drew up the Peace Resolutions to isolate, and then drive them, from the Repeal Association. Writing to Young Irelander Michael Joseph Barry, Mitchel stated, 'You must know the "Peace Resolutions" were framed *avowedly* to get rid *of us*. O'C. said so openly in the Committee, & especially said he "could not work with *me* at all" or with anyone holding my opinions.'[84] Nor was this view confined to *The Nation*'s writers. Towards the end of July 1846 a two-day debate on the Association's Peace Resolutions took place in Conciliation Hall, and on the first day Smith O'Brien observed: 'Now, I am afraid that the tendency of the resolutions … is to drive those persons who are identified in opinion with THE NATION newspaper to leave the Association.'[85]

Leading up to this debate, in a crucial Association meeting on 13 July

---

81 Duffy, *Four Years of Irish History*, p. 22.

82 O'Connell complained, for instance, at RA mtg., 9 Sept. 1844, *Nation*, 14 Sept. 1844.

83 Mitchel, *Last Conquest*, p. 110.

84 'Letter from Mitchel to Barry on the Secession', [n.d.], Duffy Papers (2), RIA, MS 12 P 16, Box II (15).

85 RA, mtg., 27 July 1846, *Nation*, 1 Aug. 1846.

1846, John O'Connell had brought up the question of the Peace Resolutions, stating that those who 'don't subscribe unconditionally and unequivocally to those principles of peaceable agitation and utter repudiation of physical force under any circumstances' would have to leave the Association. While Mitchel's response was 'to disavow solemnly all intention of exciting our countrymen to insurrection,' he could not assent to the abstract and universal principle of denouncing the use of physical force in all circumstances, which was, in any case, irrelevant as *The Nation* and the Young Irelanders unequivocally supported moral force as it related to the Repeal Association. This argument did not satisfy the Liberator, who stated: 'I drew up this resolution to draw a marked line between Young Ireland and Old Ireland. (Cheers.) I do not accept the services of any man who does not agree with me both in theory and in practice.'[86] Daniel O'Connell was determined to firmly assert his authority, once and for all, over the Young Irelanders and *The Nation*. Five days later, a leading article in *The Nation* admitted its belief in the possibility of violence occurring during the monster meeting era when 'all Ireland arose to the trumpet-call of nationality, and sprung to an attitude of defiance and resistance.'[87] This confession dramatized the conflict, providing more ammunition for the O'Connellites, who attacked *The Nation* at the following Association meeting on 20 July.[88] Duffy responded to this reaction in a letter to the Association the next day, in which he admitted *The Nation*'s mistake in misinterpreting speeches from Repeal leaders in 1843.[89]

Duffy's letter was used as a key piece of evidence against him on 28 July 1846, the second day of the debate; to the Old Irelanders it was proof that *The Nation* supported the use of physical force. Towards the end of the debate that day, when Young Irelander Thomas Francis Meagher was in the midst of his eloquent often-quoted 'sword' speech about the abstract principle of the justification of physical force, he was interrupted by John O'Connell, who ordered him to leave the Association for what he, John O'Connell, deemed dangerous language.[90] Smith O'Brien defended

---

86 *Nation*, 18 July 1846.

87 1st LA, *Nation*, 18 July 1846.

88 *Nation*, 25 July 1846.

89 For Duffy's letter see 3rd LA column, *Nation*, 25 July 1846.

90 Thomas Francis Meagher (1823–67) was born in Waterford. Educated by the Jesuits in Co. Kildare and in Lancashire, after briefly studying law in Dublin, he chose a political career and joined the Irish Confederation in 1847. William Makepeace Thackeray gave him the name of 'Young Meagher of the Sword', a sarcastic reference to his stirring speech in Conciliation Hall. Following his involvement in the attempted 1848 rebellion, Meagher was exiled to Tasmania the following year. In America he became a brigadier-general in the Union Army of the American Civil War.

Meagher, and John O'Connell presented an ultimatum to the effect that his father (who was not at this meeting) made the Association's rules and if anyone disagreed with him, he, Daniel O'Connell, would leave the Association. Responding to this threat, Smith O'Brien 'abruptly left the Hall,' accompanied by the Young Irelanders.[91]

In many respects, the O'Connellites had a weak case against the Young Irelanders over this issue of physical force. For example, if the Young Irelanders agreed to abide by O'Connell's no violence rules, there seemed little justification in contriving their expulsion. It would appear, therefore, that the debate, though ostensibly raging over the Young Irelanders' defence of the theoretical principle of physical force, was related more to their resistance of the Whig alliance. Locked into a mindset of opposition that had been seriously brewing since 1844, both sides were determined not to give way. O'Connell's authority had already been challenged over Federalism, religious education and Smith O'Brien's imprisonment, and from their editorials O'Connell knew that *The Nation* would resist the Whig alliance. What the argument over physical force shows is that O'Connell believed that *The Nation* was powerful enough to thwart his plans of pursuing a Whig alliance, and because of the Young Irelanders' opposition he drew them into a debate about physical force, which he knew was likely to end in their expulsion from the Repeal Association. Furthermore, it was John O'Connell, during the Peace Resolutions debate, who presented the Young Irelanders with the final ultimatum of staying or going. What was at stake for him was not only who was to have the dominant say over Repeal policy, but also his own succession to the Repeal leadership. It was to John O'Connell's personal and political advantage that the power of the Young Irelanders and Smith O'Brien be curtailed, that they were denied a voice in the Association and, importantly, that *The Nation* could not speak on behalf of an organization it no longer represented.

Like a high court drama, the O'Connellites used the issue of physical force to attack the Young Irelanders, accusing them of treason and stating the case for the prosecution in the Association's weekly meetings. In the week following the secession, at an Association meeting on 3 August 1846, O'Connell announced:

> They stand up and declare themselves men of war, and advocates of bloodshed, and revolutionary violence … I therefore arraign Young Ireland as being treacherous to Repeal … I am going to move that the committee of the Association should consider whether there

[91] *Nation*, 1 Aug. 1846.

> be any such connexion between the Repeal Association and THE NATION newspaper as would require for our safety the severance of that connexion.[92]

While the Young Irelanders' views could no longer be heard in Conciliation Hall, *The Nation* met every attack uttered there, repeatedly stating its unequivocal adherence to a moral force policy in relation to the Repeal Association. This acrimonious conflict continued for many months after the secession, the O'Connellites frequently maligning *The Nation* with the charge of preaching physical force doctrines. *The Nation*'s admission of the possibility that violence could have occurred during the monster meeting era of 1843 was a gift to the O'Connellites, wielded relentlessly against the Young Irelanders and their newspaper.

Over the years, owing to its success, *The Nation* had increasingly given the Young Irelanders more authority within the Association. Without the power of *The Nation* behind them, the Young Irelanders would have been more reticent about challenging O'Connell over the issues that had divided them. The O'Connellite organ, *The Pilot*, was nowhere near as popular as *The Nation* and consequently less effective than it could have been in discrediting the Young Irelanders in the Association. Importantly, *The Nation*'s role in supporting the Young Irelanders in the Association is indicative of the power the press could wield in raising the influence of the political groups it represented. However, it was, ironically, the prestige *The Nation* conferred on the Young Irelanders that played a part in splitting the Repeal movement in July 1846.

The power struggle developing over the previous few years, and played out by the O'Connellites and *The Nation*'s associates, had now reached a peak. During the Repeal Association debate on 27 July, the O'Connellite John Reilly spoke disparagingly of the Young Irelanders, whose 'attempt is made all but openly to sap the confidence of the people in the Liberator of Ireland. They display a feverish anxiety to call him their leader, and to dub him their chief, yet they were covertly working to upset his power and oppose his doctrines.'[93] On 28 September 1846, at an Association meeting, Captain Broderick, O'Connell's cousin, claimed that the Young Irelanders 'wished to rule the Association, and at last they brought matters to that pass that it should be decided whether Old or Young Ireland should guide its councils.'[94] The disdain of O'Connell's supporters for *The Nation*'s associates

[92] *Nation*, 8 Aug. 1846.
[93] *Nation*, 1 Aug. 1846.
[94] *Nation*, 3 Oct. 1846.

is highly evident in O'Connell's correspondence. Some weeks before the 1846 secession, one of O'Connell's closest allies, Thomas Steele, wrote to him: 'It has given your own Old-Ireland people joy beyond measure that ... you intend putting these scamps in their proper position.'[95] O'Connell's authority had been challenged over the years by *The Nation*'s circle of writers, in print and in Conciliation Hall, and much to the delight of his closest supporters, he had made a final stand against them with the Peace Resolutions. Of course, it had not been *The Nation*'s intention to usurp the Liberator, as he was loved and respected by the mostly Catholic population, but the Young Irelanders were determined to have a powerful voice within the Repeal movement.

The initial response of the other Dublin Repeal papers to the physical force debate typified their respective political positions in relation to Old and Young Ireland. While *The Freeman* group felt 'deep pain' over the split in the Association, *The Dublin Weekly Register* and *The Pilot* were pleased with the outcome of the Peace Resolutions debate.[96] Although *The Freeman* papers tended to take the O'Connellite side, and were reproachful of Young Ireland, they adopted a conciliatory tone, hoping that Smith O'Brien's departure was temporary and that unity would be reinstated for the sake of the Repeal movement. *The Dublin Weekly Register*, by contrast, an ardent O'Connell supporter, called for the secession to be final.[97] It claimed that 'Young Ireland had grown dogmatical, and *insisted* not only that itself was right, but that it was right that everybody else should adopt its prophecies, and follow its guidance.'[98] *The Nation*'s bitter opponent, *The Pilot*, even saw 'good' in the split, positive proof of what it had long advocated, that a clique existed in the Association, 'that the *Nation* was its organ, and anti-O'Connellism its object.'[99] Referring to *The Nation* in a leading article on the secession, *The Pilot* was adamant that, 'The writers on it were members of the Association, and, to his [O'Connell's] very teeth, opposed him in that assembly, and tried to divide it into two parties, of one of which they and their paper should be the heads.'[100] In other words, *The Pilot* claimed that the secession was caused by *The Nation*'s writers vying for power against the O'Connellites in the Association.

---

[95] Letter from Thomas Steele to Daniel O'Connell, 16 June 1846, O'Connell (ed.), *The Correspondence of Daniel O'Connell*, p. 48.

[96] 1st LA, *Weekly Freeman*, 1 Aug. 1846.

[97] 1st LA, *Weekly Register*, 1 Aug. 1846.

[98] 2nd LA, *Weekly Register*, 8 Aug. 1846.

[99] 1st LA, *Pilot*, 31 July 1846.

[100] 1st LA, *Pilot*, 24 Aug. 1846.

A fundamental issue emerged from this conflict: the principle of the right to differ. A leading article in *The Nation* at the beginning of August 1846 declared: 'Free and independent opinion, the right, the sacred "right to differ," is banned in the Hall called of "conciliation."'[101] And in the following month *The Nation* queried, 'Is the law of the Association this – that whoever differs from Mr. O'CONNELL, or Mr. JOHN O'CONNELL, on any subject, even when they differ from their former selves, ceases *ipso facto* to be a member, or to possess the common right of remonstrance or dissent?'[102] As we saw earlier in this chapter, Inglis noted that the Dublin papers that had supported O'Connell in the 1820s and 1830s had then complained about his behaviour concerning these very issues. Staunton, the most critical of O'Connell in the past, now unequivocally aligned himself with Barrett (O'Connell's ever-faithful follower) against *The Nation*. It seems that the success of the Repeal Association during 1842–43 had fostered a much stronger tie than in the previous two decades between O'Connell and his old Dublin press supporters. Of course, Staunton and Barrett, now comparative veterans in the newspaper world, still considered *The Nation*'s writers as upstarts, and may have been envious of the paper's vast circulation sales.

In addition to *The Nation*'s protests against the O'Connellite edicts denying the expression of free speech, many Repealers throughout the Association also voiced their concern. In Great Britain, for example, a meeting of Repealers in Salford passed resolutions protesting against the Association while 'supporting THE NATION newspaper, as the genuine organ of free and fair discussion.'[103] A few days later, the Repealers of Liverpool, many of whom disagreed with *The Nation*'s doctrines, argued 'that an Association struggling for freedom should not itself invade the legitimate liberty of the press.'[104] So even those who did not necessarily concur with *The Nation*'s opinions could identify with the principles of the right to differ from the Repeal leadership and the freedom of the press, issues which the Young Irelanders exploited. On the latter point in particular *The Nation* could effectively defend itself and win support against the O'Connellites.

After the split there followed much initial support for Old Ireland, mostly promoted by those priests who had come to believe that *The Nation* was an irreligious newspaper. *The Pilot* seemed to take delight in presenting

---

[101] 2nd LA, *Nation*, 1 Aug. 1846.
[102] 2nd LA, *Nation*, 12 Sept. 1846.
[103] 'The Repealers of Salford', mtg., 27 Sept. 1846, *Nation*, 3 Oct. 1846.
[104] 'The Repealers of Liverpool', mtg., 30 Sept. 1846, *Nation*, 10 Oct. 1846.

an English establishment perspective of the secession by reprinting an extract from *The Times* that stated: 'The *Nation* party is proved not to be the "national" party; the people follow their pastors; their pastors are guided by their prelates; the hierarchy are devoted to O'Connell.'[105] Furthermore, a directive from O'Connell that *The Nation* should not in future be ordered by the Repeal Wardens meant that its circulation, particularly in terms of group reading, was reduced, especially in rural areas where the priests, many of whom were Repeal Wardens anyway, exercised a great deal of control over their local communities. Nevertheless, according to official figures, *The Nation* retained its position after the 1846 secession as the leading Repeal paper. It appears that while there was a decrease in circulation for all the Repeal papers from 1844 to 1845, they made a recovery in 1846, with the exception of *The Pilot* and *The Nation*, whose circulations that year continued to decline (see Table II). The figures suggest that *The Nation*'s circulation may have been damaged by the first secession to the advantage of the other Repeal papers, apart from *The Pilot*. However, over the whole of 1846 and 1847 *The Nation* sold more copies than any other Dublin Repeal paper, which suggests that it was not greatly affected financially by the split, but as there are no quarterly or half-yearly stamp returns for these years the immediate effect on the sales of the paper remains uncertain.

Following the secession increasing bitterness directed against *The Nation* in the weekly Association meetings was led by O'Connell. With the Dublin Repeal papers widely distributed throughout Ireland and Great Britain, the dissension between *The Nation* and the O'Connellites was given much publicity, which polarized opinion throughout the Repeal movement. For example, that September an article in *The Nation* stated: 'We are informed that the Repealers of Belfast are about equally divided between the Seceders and their opponents.'[106] Along with numerous Repealers objecting to Conciliation Hall's behaviour was a more formal response in the form of Remonstrances, when resolutions by those attending meetings in various localities were passed in support of the Young Irelanders. The most impressive was in Dublin, reportedly signed by seventy-four Repeal Wardens (out of 120), at least 300 members and upwards of 1,000 associates of the Repeal Association.[107] Repealers throughout the movement defied directives from Conciliation Hall. There is evidence that Repeal reading rooms were ignoring the order to replace *The Nation* with other Dublin Repeal

105 *The Times*, 13 Aug. 1846, reprinted in 2nd LA, *Pilot*, 14 Aug. 1846.

106 5th LA, *Nation*, 12 Sept. 1846.

107 3rd LA, *Nation*, 31 Oct. 1846. The names and addresses of many hundreds of Dublin Remonstrants were printed in *The Nation*, 10, 17, 24 and 31 Oct. 1846.

newspapers. Repealers in Loughrea, Co. Galway, resolved on 2 September 1846 that 'THE NATION having been excluded from the Repeal reading-room, and the working classes and associates of the Repeal Association deprived thereby of the excellent political teaching and instructive articles of that paper,' they would subscribe to it independently.[108] Despite O'Connell's influence over public opinion, *The Nation* was not crushed by its exclusion from the Association.

The secession of 1846 was a devastating blow to the Repeal movement. *The Nation*'s survival undermined the strength of the Repeal Association and with the amount of time consumed maligning the Young Irelanders, it seemed as if the Association's energies were directed more at *The Nation* than at repealing the Act of Union. Early in September *The Nation* asked, 'is it against the Legislative Union, or against THE NATION, they are agitating now in Conciliation Hall?'[109] Edward Brady, Vice-President of the People's Hall, Cork, wrote to the Association on 13 October 1846:

> This suicidal and anti-national policy, adopted by the committee of the Repeal Association on the return of the Whigs to power – and since so recklessly persevered in – has produced the most disastrous results. It has chilled the enthusiasm of the people, enkindled suspicion in the hearts of the earnest and uncompromising, and is producing daily throughout the country wide-spread bitterness and fatal division.[110]

Another letter that October from a Repeal Warden in Dundee stated that, due to O'Connell's behaviour towards *The Nation*, he and his colleagues would 'cease working for the Repeal cause.'[111] Reflecting the poor state of the Repeal Association, at the meeting on 30 November 1846, O'Connell solemnly declared: 'We are divided – our forces are scattered.'[112] Reconciliation between the two opposing groups was attempted towards the end of the year but unsuccessful, each side blaming the other for its failure. The Association managed to soldier on despite its diminishing authority. As for the Young Irelanders, cast out of the Association, they no longer supported Repeal as members of a political nationalist organization. Furthermore,

---

108 'The Repealers of Loughrea', *Nation*, 12 Sept. 1846.

109 3rd LA, *Nation*, 5 Sept. 1846.

110 'Letter from E. Brady, esq., V.P., People's Hall, Cork', *Nation*, 17 Oct. 1846.

111 Letter from William Sweeney, 13 Oct. 1846, 'Repeal *versus* The Repeal Association', *Nation*, 31 Oct. 1846.

112 *Nation*, 5 Dec. 1846.

their contributions to *The Nation* decreased; as Duffy complained to Smith O'Brien, '[Michael Joseph] Barry, [Richard] O'Gorman & Meagher have not written one line in the *Nation* since the Secession.'[113] The Young Irelanders were, for the present, in limbo.

The impact of the Great Famine on the 1848 secession

In the meantime, Smith O'Brien had conceived a project to form a literary group to present the views of the seceders, and promote Repeal of the Union and Irish nationality. Weekly contributions of about four items were to be placed in a dedicated section of *The Nation* entitled 'The Irish Party.' *The Nation* described it as 'a Literary Repeal Association, as it were – a plan which would attain at once the freedom of individual opinion and the force of combination'; a letter from Smith O'Brien explained that contributions were to be drawn from any subject, history, science or the arts, 'which may be made instrumental in inspiring a spirit of nationality.'[114] Beginning on 28 November 1846, its writers included the leading seceders, such as Smith O'Brien, Meagher and Mitchel. 'The Irish Party' in *The Nation* became a specific forum, a rallying point maintaining the identity of the Young Irelanders as a viable opposition group to Old Ireland.

This project drew the seceders together and, supported by the Dublin Remonstrants, who had sided with the Young Irelanders, 'The Irish Party' evolved into a new political organization, 'The Irish Confederation.' Established in opposition to the Repeal Association, it further undermined Old Ireland's authority. With *The Nation*'s writers among the leaders of the Irish Confederation, this paper was naturally its mouthpiece, propagating its policies and aims, which were, in fact, essentially the same as those adopted by the Repeal Association. However, at the first meeting of the Irish Confederation on 13 January 1847, resolutions were proposed for its 'absolute independence of all English parties' and 'an abstinence from all subjects likely to lead to religious differences,' issues that had led to dissent in Conciliation Hall.[115] These policies were endorsed in *The Nation* that

[113] Letter from Duffy to Smith O'Brien, [n.d.], William Smith O'Brian Papers, NLI, MS 440/2215.

[114] Short editorial intro. followed by letter, 29 Oct. 1846, 'Smith O'Brien – Repeal Projects', *Nation*, 31 Oct. 1846. See also: Letters from Duffy to Smith O'Brien, first two, [n.d.], 10 Nov., [n.y. but '1846' added], Duffy Papers, NLI, MS 5758/13–20, 45–50 and 94–7.

[115] *Nation*, 16 Jan. 1847.

week in the hope that 'the Irish Confederation, if it be fit for its work, may mould the scattered and jarring elements of Irish society into a NATION.'[116] Still surviving after a year, the Irish Confederation reported having 11,000 enrolled members.[117] With the other Dublin Repeal papers supporting Old Ireland, it seems unlikely that the Irish Confederation would have emerged, let alone succeeded, as a new, independent group within the Repeal movement without the direct involvement of *The Nation*. Clearly, what this demonstrated was the important role of a newspaper as a lifeline for political survival.

Like the Association, the Irish Confederates viewed persuasive argument in the press that supported their organization as an essential tool. Much of their rhetoric was concerned with defending their part in the secession and discrediting Old Ireland. In attacking the Association, one of their most serious charges was their claim that the Whig alliance in 1846 had led to the suffering of thousands of Irish people from the political economy policies of the Whig government. Thus, when John O'Connell refused to agree that Repealers should take a pledge against place-hunting in the forthcoming elections in the summer of 1847, an opportunity arose for the Confederates to go on the offensive. A leading article in *The Nation* referred back to O'Connell's 1835 compact with the Whigs when 'Place-begging became the order of the day' and Repeal was abandoned, paralleling it with the conflict of 1846, 'which gave Ireland to famine and the Whigs, and gave places to so many O'CONNELLS and O'CONNELLEENS.'[118] However, whatever credit the Irish Confederation hoped to gain by this line of attack, much of its high moral ground was lost with the death of Daniel O'Connell.

After months of illness, O'Connell died on 15 May 1847. That June *The Nation* incurred further alienation from Old Ireland supporters when it printed a letter addressed to the editor from the radical nationalist Father John Kenyon from Tipperary, a member of the Irish Confederation, who criticized the paper's highly respectful response to O'Connell's death, adding: 'I think that Mr. O'Connell has been doing before his death, and was likely to continue doing as long as he might live, very grievous injury to Ireland; so that I account his death rather a gain than a loss to the country.'[119] Kenyon also warned the Council of the Irish Confederation

---

116 1st LA, *Nation*, 16 Jan. 1847.

117 Anniversary mtg., 12 Jan. 1848, *Nation*, 15 Jan. 1848.

118 1st LA, *Nation*, 3 July 1847. Place-hunting involved adopting a particular political line in order to get the reward of a position (or promotion) in government office.

119 'The Rev. Mr. Kenyon on O'Connell's Position and Career', *Nation*, 5 June 1847. See also: 1st LA, *Nation*, 29 May 1847.

that 'your cooperation in this public honour to his remains will be used (and justly) to cut your own throats, & what is worse (for *you* deserve it) to cut the throat of your own country.'[120] From Kenyon's perspective, by publicly admiring O'Connell's lifetime political achievements, though less effusively than the other Dublin nationalist papers such as *The Pilot*, *The Nation* was unwittingly damaging the Young Irelanders' image, thereby bringing more retribution to bear on them by their enemies. In other words, praising O'Connell's accomplishments gave the impression that their action leading up to the secession may have been wrong. Here was an opportune moment for Old Ireland, led by *The Pilot*, to criticize the Young Irelanders, most notably by accusing them of betraying O'Connell, even harming his health and hastening his death. Unsurprisingly, O'Connell's death wrung particular hostility from lower-class Old Ireland supporters, especially unruly mobs who attempted to disrupt the Irish Confederation's meetings or attacked members on their return home.[121] To those who had remained loyal to Old Ireland it seemed that the Young Irelanders held much responsibility for O'Connell's death. There was a ring of truth in Kenyon's prediction for this was to haunt them in the many months ahead.

Following O'Connell's death *The Nation* was in a weakened position, and the only way forward was to concentrate on expanding the Irish Confederation in order to regain its former authoritative voice in Irish nationalism. Summer 1847 was a low point for the Repeal movement generally, as acknowledged that August by John Blake Dillon, who wrote to his wife: 'Every day brings fresh conviction to my mind that some new agitation must soon commence, or *repeal* must be abandoned as a word that has lost all meaning. And I shd [*sic*] not be surprised if this latter were to be the result.'[122] However, following the formation of the Irish Confederation, a few local groups had begun to meet on a regular basis. Reading rooms were organized, and in Dublin these groups evolved into Confederate Clubs. Meagher recognized their potential value and shared his optimism with Smith O'Brien: 'These Confederate Clubs will be admirable instruments – they will distribute … our principles and spirit, and call the people into action.'[123] Reportedly, by the middle of July, the Swift Confederate Club

120 Letter from Kenyon, 30 May 1847, Minutes of the Council of the Irish Confederation, 4 June 1847, RIA, MS 23 H 44.

121 Reported, for instance, in the Irish Confederation mtg., 29 July 1847, *Nation*, 31 July 1847.

122 Dillon Papers, TCD, MS 6457 d.

123 Letter from T.F. Meagher to Smith O'Brien, [n.d.], Smith O'Brien Papers, NLI, MS 440/2203.

claimed over 100 members.[124] These Clubs, fully encouraged by *The Nation*, began to inject new hope and life into the Repeal movement; indeed, on 20 July 1847, their value to the Confederation was reflected at a Council meeting, where it was believed that such Clubs should be organized throughout Ireland and Great Britain.[125]

Promoted by *The Nation*, the Clubs gave the Irish Confederation structure and coherence, and a proactive role in the Repeal movement. The Young Ireland newspaper encouraged the development of the Clubs in its editorials and, by publishing reports of their meetings, inspired others to form. The effectiveness of *The Nation*'s support for the Clubs can be seen in London's Chelsea Repealers, whose report of their meeting on 27 September 1847 stated:

> The inert mass of Repealers in this metropolis is now beginning to exhibit unequivocal symptoms of vitality ... The report of the committee on organisation, as published in THE NATION a few weeks back, with rules and regulations for the formation and guidance of Confederate Clubs, has at once dispelled speculation and hesitation, by giving a proper direction to the minds and feelings of all patriotic Irishmen, and sincere Repealers.[126]

Soon afterwards, writing from Limerick, Dr William Griffin (brother of the writer Gerald Griffin) informed Smith O'Brien that: 'I have been regularly attending and watching the progress of the Sarsfield Club every evening of meeting [*sic*] ... It is winning adherents in all the small towns about which will eventually give it the command of the County as well as the City. We already number nearly 200.'[127] It is evident that publicity in *The Nation* did much to advance the expansion of the Confederate Clubs, thus strengthening its opposition to Conciliation Hall. During the first half of 1848, leading up to the attempted rebellion, the appearance of the Dublin rebel newspapers was to coincide with a dramatic increase in the formation of Clubs, perhaps numbering over 235. Notably, whereas many priests had sided with O'Connell in the 1846 secession, they were now to constitute a high proportion of the membership of these Clubs.[128]

---

124 First public mtg. of Swift Confederation Club, 14 July 1847, *Nation*, 24 July 1847.

125 'The Irish Confederation', *Nation*, 24 July 1847.

126 'Chelsea Repealers and the Irish Confederation', *Nation*, 2 Oct. 1847.

127 Letter from William Griffin to Smith O'Brien, 13 Oct., [n.y.], Smith O'Brien Papers, NLI, MS 440/2184.

128 Address book of members of Irish Confederation in Irish towns, RIA, MS 23 H 40.

Running parallel with this political activity was the reality of famine; while it had a bearing on the first secession, the Great Famine became a driving force behind the second.[129] The failure of the potato crop was to continue after 1845–46 for several more years, the worst being a total crop failure in the winter of 1846–47. Very little was done by the government to alleviate the suffering of victims from starvation and disease, a failure made all the more striking by the fact that not only was Ireland a constituent part of the United Kingdom but Britain, Ireland's next-door neighbour, was the wealthiest nation in the world. The reason for the government's inaction lies partly in its adherence to the orthodox policy of non-interference with market forces. Furthermore, from the government's perspective, prior to the Famine, Ireland was viewed as over-populated and the prevailing agricultural system seen as neither productive nor efficient. Two contrasting ideas of how to beneficially transform Irish agriculture had been projected by political economists. One was linked to the orthodox view of property and the belief that the diminution of both the number of smallholdings and what was thought a surplus population would enable Irish agriculture to prosper; the Famine brought about the conditions for both of these to occur. An alternative idea for improving the state of agriculture in Ireland was favoured not just by Irish nationalists but by others such as the political economist J.S. Mill; its proposals were based on the well-being of the local people and called for parliamentary legislation to provide tenants with rights that would provide incentives for improved farming practice.

With the onset of the Great Famine, *The Nation* deemed that rights for tenants were needed more than ever. In its belief that nothing could be gained from the Whigs to save the rural population, the Young Irelanders remained unyielding. At the beginning of January 1847, just before it evolved into the Irish Confederation, *The Nation*'s Irish Party argued: 'As an ultimate remedy for Irish famine, *we* can propose nothing but self-government.'[130] The approach of the government to the 1840s Great Famine provided the Dublin nationalist newspapers with what they deemed to be undeniable evidence of how badly the British ruled Ireland. Whig government relief included a public works scheme, continued in the short-term from the Tory administration. Workhouses remained the main source of relief, and while soup kitchens were opened for a limited period during 1847 and a Poor Law Amendment Act was passed that allowed provision of some temporary

129 One of the foremost works on the Great Famine is: Christine Kinealy, *This Great Calamity, 1845–52*, 2nd ed. (Dublin: Gill & Macmillan, 2006).

130 John B. Dillon, Chairman, 'Address of the Committee of "The Irish Party" to the People of Ireland', *Nation*, 2 Jan. 1847.

outdoor relief, all of this proved to be highly inadequate in addressing the severity of the crisis.[131] The Poor Law Amendment Act, for example, had a clause stating that tenants possessing more than a quarter acre of land would be refused relief. Starvation forced many to leave their homes. *The Nation* was in the vanguard of the attack by the Dublin nationalist press on the Russell government for what it deemed its failure to prevent numerous people dying every day of disease and starvation, seizing on this state of affairs as a compelling argument for Irish independence.

As Repealers aspired to self-determination through constitutional means and believed that this could only be achieved by a unity of classes, *The Nation* took the opportunity to encourage the engagement of the upper echelons of society in addressing the devastation of the Great Famine. For example, at the first meeting of the Irish Confederation in January 1847, Smith O'Brien, himself from the landed gentry, focused on the necessity 'to unite all Irishmen' in the present crisis of the Famine, and praised the efforts of many landed proprietors with whom he had been meeting, to discuss the problems of feeding and employing rural people.[132] That year the Irish Council was formed to meet the crisis of the Famine. Its members were drawn from every class and profession; it was to be above political affiliations, and included O'Connellites and Young Irelanders. *The Nation* initially supported this organization, but later in the year criticized it for failing to go far enough on the question of tenant right.[133] Unable to reach a consensus on the landlord-tenant relationship, the Irish Council proved ineffective. In another attempt to combat the effects of the Famine, a group of Irish MPs convened a meeting on 2 November 1847. They issued thirty-five resolutions which *The Nation* saw as 'impotent' and berated them for omitting tenant right.[134] This lack of progress in ameliorating the devastation in the countryside further radicalized some members of the Irish Confederation. Instead of uniting

---

[131] That so little was done by the British government to ease the suffering of the Famine's victims can be placed into perspective by showing that the total amount of money spent on famine relief in 1845–50 was about 8 million pounds, whereas 69 million pounds were to be used on the military expenditure of the 1854–56 Crimean War: Joel Mokyr, *Why Ireland starved: A quantitative and analytical history of the Irish economy, 1800–1850*, 2nd ed. (London: Allen & Unwin, 1985), p. 292, noted in Peter Gray, *Famine, Land and Politics. British Government and Irish Society 1843–1850* (Dublin: Irish Academic Press, 1999), p. 333.

[132] 'The Aggregate Meeting. Formation of the Irish Confederation', 13 Jan. 1847, *Nation*, 16 Jan. 1847.

[133] 'Meeting of peers and commoners convened by the Irish Council', 6, 9 and 11 Nov. 1847, where John Mitchel in particular argued the case for tenant right; 2nd LA, *Nation*, 13 Nov. 1847.

[134] Article, 'The Council of National Distress', *Nation*, 20 Nov. 1847.

Irishmen as the Young Irelanders had hoped, the Famine fragmented the Repeal movement even more, which now manifested itself in dissension between Duffy and Mitchel, the leading associates of *The Nation.*

As Mitchel's divergence from Duffy was to have significant consequences for the development of Irish nationalism, both in the short and the long term, it is important to understand the thinking behind his actions. It is necessary to show how Mitchel was affected by the distress caused to the Irish people by the government's handling of the Great Famine, and how he used the press to articulate his views and persuade others to accept them. Accompanied by Meagher, Mitchel had travelled down to Galway to join other Irish Confederates in opposing a government candidate in an election in February 1847. On his journey Mitchel directly witnessed the devastation of the Famine, seeing

> in front of the cottages, little children leaning against a fence when the sun shone out, – for they could not stand, – their limbs fleshless, their bodies half-naked, their faces bloated yet wrinkled, and of a pale, greenish hue, – children who would never, it was too plain, grow up to be men and women.[135]

Mitchel was to recall several images of the Famine in his writings, such as 'how maniac mothers stowed away their dead children to be devoured at midnight.'[136] Duffy did not quarrel with Mitchel's view of the Famine as the defining proof that Britain was unfit to govern Ireland. What Duffy objected to was Mitchel distancing himself from *The Nation*'s policy of seeking Repeal by peaceful means and veering towards the suggestion of the use of physical force. From believing, around the time of the Peace Resolutions' debate, that 'peace is our true *policy* – our only policy,' this digression of Mitchel was to develop into extremism in his advocacy of a complete severance from Britain by physical force, and the formation of a republic whereby there would be no connection with what he deemed a brutal and heartless government.[137] What Mitchel wrote in the Dublin nationalist press had a direct bearing on the attempted rebellion of 1848.

---

135 Mitchel, *Last Conquest*, pp. 147–8. The government candidate won (it seems through bribery) by a very small margin, but in the general election later in the year he was deposed. See also: Duffy, *Four Years of Irish History*, pp. 363–5.

136 John Mitchel, *Jail Journal*, Arthur Griffith (pref.), 2nd ed. (Dublin: M.H. Gill & Son Ltd., [1913]), p. xxxix; reprinted from *The Citizen* newspaper, New York, 14 Jan.–19 Aug. 1854.

137 Letter from Mitchel to *The Tablet*, [n.d.], reprinted in Duffy, *My Life in Two Hemispheres, I*, p. 165.

Although John Mitchel's thinking was influenced by what he believed to be both the government's lack of an effective response to the Great Famine and the negative attitude of the landlords, he was swayed even more by the writing of James Fintan Lalor. Lalor, a man destined to have an important impact on Irish nationalist ideology, suggested proposals for relieving the distress suffered by the poor in rural Ireland. In January 1847 he had begun to send private letters to *The Nation* through which his theories circulated among the Young Irelanders.[138] Lalor believed that the Famine was destroying the social framework of rural Ireland, aided by the government and the aristocracy in order to turn the countryside into a stock farm. If the landlords neglected to help their tenants, Lalor anticipated a spontaneous peasant uprising, and the establishment of a peasant proprietary whereby cultivators of the land would also own the soil. Invited by *The Nation*'s staff to publicize his views, in his first communication to landowners in April 1847, Lalor called for a 'new structure of society' with the creation of 'a secure and independent agricultural peasantry.'[139] Back in the autumn of 1842 *The Nation* had suggested a similar policy: 'the People of Ireland ought to … call with one voice for a complete remodelling of the laws affecting landed property.'[140] Responding to Lalor's proposal, Mitchel wrote to Smith O'Brien:

> I wish you wd [*sic*] read carefully the paper signed J.F. Lalor in today's Nation. I do believe the landed proprietors, if they would even now, or any considerable number of them, take to heart that proposal, cd [*sic*] make fair & honourable terms for themselves, & become the most popular & powerful aristocracy on earth … P.S. … I do think it is still in the power of the aristocracy to save this nation & themselves at the same time. And I wish & pray earnestly that they may find it in their hearts to do so.[141]

It is evident that in seeking the co-operation of the landlords Mitchel was suggesting a conservative, non-aggressive approach to the Famine.

By September, however, Mitchel was beginning to despair of the

---

[138] First letter from Lalor, 11 Jan. 1847, Duffy Papers (2), RIA, MS 12 P 15, Box I (5). Also printed in *James Fintan Lalor. Patriot and Political Essayist 1807–1849*, L. Fogarty (ed.), Arthur Griffith (pref.) (Dublin: Talbot Press; London: T. Fisher Unwin, 1918), pp. 1–6; 2nd ed. (Dublin: Talbot Press, 1947).

[139] 'A New Nation', *Nation*, 24 April 1847.

[140] 1st LA, *Nation*, 3 Dec. 1842.

[141] Letter from Mitchel to Smith O'Brien, 24 April 1847, William Smith O'Brien Papers, NLI, MS 438/1882.

landlords; writing to Smith O'Brien, he warned that 'the time has nearly come when affairs must take a decisive turn either in the one way or the other. I sincerely hope it will be in the moderate direction.'[142] These letters are indicative of the progression of Mitchel's thoughts towards a more radical tone, which increasingly found an expression in *The Nation*, much to Duffy's disapproval. William Dillon, Mitchel's most competent biographer, has remarked on 'how long he clung to the hope that the landed gentry' would 'take their stand on the national side as the natural leaders of the people.'[143] And John Dillon, son of John Blake Dillon and a major figure in the Irish Parliamentary Party, noted in 1888: 'By nature John Mitchel was much more conservative than radical. He was averse to change, and by no means fanatically opposed even to Irish landlordism.'[144]

Like the other *Nation* writers, Mitchel had hoped that, apart from helping to ease the suffering of the countryside people, here was an opportunity for the landlords to support the nationalist movement, a step towards the ideal of unity of class, and indeed of creed. Instead, Mitchel lost all faith in the landlords following their seeming failure to help the Great Famine's victims, now combined with their support of a government coercion bill introduced into Parliament at the end of November 1847 that was intended to counter crime arising from rural distress. As a consequence, he sought extreme means to ameliorate the effects of the Famine. Duffy, on the other hand, who was determined at this time to remain strictly within the law to avoid alienating the landlords, which he believed would harm Repeal, refused to allow Mitchel to continue expressing his increasingly advanced opinions in *The Nation*. At the end of the year Mitchel severed his connection with Duffy's paper.

Mitchel was trying to steer the policy of *The Nation* and, indeed, the policy of the Irish Confederation towards accepting the possibility of physical

---

142 Letter from Mitchel to Smith O'Brien, 8 Sept. 1847, William Smith O'Brien Papers, NLI, MS 439/1983.

143 William Dillon, *Life of John Mitchel, vol. I*, John Dillon (intro.) (London: Kegan Paul, Trench & Co., 1888), p. 143.

144 Dillon, *Mitchel*, pp. xiv–xv. It should be noted that some landlords faced hardship during the Great Famine and there were those who tried to help their tenants. In light of the above observations by the two Dillons, it is notable that Mitchel defended the South and its way of life in the American Civil War, where two of his sons died and another was wounded after enlisting in the Confederate army; Mitchel was also critical of the capitalist society that was emerging in America and he had an aversion to nineteenth-century liberalism. For a discussion of Mitchel's ideology, especially in relation to his support for the institution of slavery, see: James Quinn, 'John Mitchel and the rejection of the nineteenth century', *Éire-Ireland*, vol. 38 (3/4), Fall/Winter, 2003, pp. 90–108.

force, while Duffy remained committed to moral force. Mitchel, whose plan of action was, at this time, far too radical for Duffy, 'had watched the progress of the Famine-policy of the Government, and could see nothing in it but a machinery, deliberately devised, and skilfully worked, for the entire subjugation of the island, – the slaughter of a portion of its people, and the pauperization of the rest.'[145] Influenced by one of Lalor's theories – the feasibility of 'moral insurrection,' but only with the backing of 'military force' – Mitchel argued that a policy of 'passive resistance' should be put into place, for example, 'a combination amongst the people to obstruct and render impossible the transport and shipment of Irish provisions,' but with the option, where necessary, 'to try the steel.'[146] Although the potato crop had failed, other food markets in Ireland were thriving, and produce such as grain and meat continued to be carried off to ports for distribution in Britain. Mitchel's plan included withdrawing rents (already advocated by Lalor) and rates, resisting ejectments and arming the people. After he left *The Nation*, Duffy accused Mitchel of 'abandoning the policy at which we had both been labouring, the policy of reconciling classes, and fusing the discordant elements of the Irish nation into one common power.'[147] For Mitchel, this policy seemed irrelevant with the shadow of death spreading throughout the land, but he failed to convince most of the other members of the Council of the Irish Confederation to accept his views, especially Duffy and Smith O'Brien.

Now concerned about the image of the Confederation, Smith O'Brien drew up ten resolutions in opposition to Mitchel's radical plan, reminiscent of O'Connell's Peace Resolutions. There followed a debate from 2 to 4 February 1848, and as Meagher remarked on the last day, it was in a 'nut-shell' a decision of whether or not the Confederation should relinquish 'constitutional agitation.'[148] Resolutions were passed in favour of the moderates by 317 to 188, indicating that there were many in the Confederation sympathetic to Mitchel's views. Following this vote, Mitchel, together with two of his most ardent supporters, John Martin and Thomas Devin Reilly, resigned from the Council, signalling the second secession. While the issue of physical force was a theoretical argument in the first secession, it was at the heart of the second secession, a real issue of whether

[145] Mitchel, *Last Conquest*, p. 157.

[146] Private letter from Lalor to Irish Confederation, 25 Jan. 1847, later printed in 6th LA col., *The Irish Felon*, 1 July 1848; Mitchel, *Last Conquest*, p. 157.

[147] 'The Nation – Mr. Mitchel and Mr. Duffy'; see also Mitchel's view on why he left *The Nation*, letter to Duffy, 7 Jan. 1848, *Nation*, 8 Jan. 1848.

[148] 'Meeting of the Irish Confederation', *Nation*, 5 Feb. 1848.

or not physical force should be adopted as a policy by *The Nation* and the Irish Confederation that would mark a significant change in the direction of Irish nationalism at this time.

Barred not only from *The Nation*, but now also from the Council of the Irish Confederation, Mitchel lacked a medium to disseminate his changed political beliefs. Remedying this predicament, he established his own Irish nationalist newspaper in Dublin, *The United Irishman*, the title recalling the name of the organization that had been involved in the 1798 rebellion, thus underlining Mitchel's extremism. Having editorial control over his own paper meant that he did not have Duffy's restraining influence. In the present circumstances of the Great Famine, Mitchel appealed to the lower classes, and called for defensive action against what he came to believe was the virtual annihilation of the Irish people by the English government. Dismissive of both sections of the Repeal movement, and seeking to strike a distinctive pose, his prospectus declared that *The United Irishman* 'believe[s] the world is weary of Old Ireland, and also of YOUNG IRELAND.'[149]

Established in opposition to *The Nation* and sold at a penny cheaper, *The United Irishman* was of a similar format, intended to prove a formidable opponent and threat to Duffy's paper. Assisted mainly by Devin Reilly, the first issue of Mitchel's newspaper was published on 12 February 1848. Numerous agents were appointed to sell *The United Irishman* throughout Ireland, which included Belfast; and in Great Britain London, the north and Glasgow were also represented.[150] As with the first issue of *The Nation*, demand vastly exceeded supply. Mitchel wrote to John Martin the day after it first appeared: 'If we could have fully supplied the demand, we might have got off fifteen thousand copies. As it was, we could only get from the press five thousand.'[151] On 24 February, Lord Stanley, a peer in the House of Lords, informed his colleagues: 'This paper was published at 5d., but, as I am informed, when the first number appeared, so much was it sought after, that, on its first appearance, it was eagerly bought in the streets of Dublin at 1s. 6d. and 2s. a number.'[152] During 1848 *The United Irishman*'s total stamped figure indicates that its average weekly circulation of 8,125 was higher than *The Nation*'s figure of 5,433.[153] For both papers, the number of

149 Advertisement, *Nation*, 22 Jan. 1848.

150 The list of agents in Ireland and Great Britain numbered sixty-four, *The United Irishman*, 26 Feb. 1848. In contrast, *The Nation* began with more agents, its first issue on 15 October 1842 naming eighty agents in Ireland, with others in Liverpool and Manchester.

151 Letter from Mitchel to John Martin, 13 Feb. 1848, Dillon, *Mitchel*, p. 204.

152 'The English Parliament. House of Lords', *United Irishman*, 4 March 1848.

153 Based on 'Return of Number of Stamps issued at One Penny to Newspapers in

those who had access to their contents through sharing copies and group reading would have been considerably larger than the official figures.

Certainly, Mitchel's defiance hurled weekly against the government in *The United Irishman* caught the imagination of many people. Young Irelander Michael Doheny stated that 'In every corner of the island the influence of the *United Irishman* was instant and simultaneous' and that 'every word struck with the force and terror of lightning.'[154] In a letter addressed to John Russell in *The United Irishman*, Mitchel drew his attention to the correlation between the sale of his newspaper and the state of the country:

> It has reached only its tenth number … yet never [a] newspaper in Ireland reached such a circulation before in so short a time, and that circulation, remember, is amongst the very poorest of the people both in town and country … Why do poor men club their pence to buy it, and get it read to eager crowds every Saturday evening and Sunday morning? Why? – Because it utters for them the deep and inextinguishable hatred they all bear in their inmost souls against the 'Crown and Government' of Britain.[155]

Duffy observed of Mitchel that 'The boldness with which he threatened and assailed the Government in *The United Irishman* delighted the people.'[156] With rhetoric of this nature, during its short lifespan of less than three and a half months, *The United Irishman*'s intention was to foment disaffection among the people, and frighten the government into repressive measures against the paper and its proprietor, whereby the Whig ministry would be forced to pack a jury to achieve conviction; this outrage, Mitchel believed, would 'ripen the Revolution.'[157] Although *The United Irishman*'s plan was to prove successful for Mitchel, it was to set in motion actions that would herald the downfall of the Irish nationalist movement that summer.

United Kingdom, 1837–50', HCP, 1852 (42) XXVIII.497.

[154] Doheny, *The Felon's Track*, p. 127.

[155] 1st LA column, *United Irishman*, 15 April 1848.

[156] Duffy, *Four Years of Irish History*, p. 548.

[157] Mitchel, *Jail Journal*, p. xliv.

The rebel press and the collapse of the Irish nationalist cause

Meanwhile, although the followers of the Repeal cause had now split into three warring groups – those who rallied around either John O'Connell at Conciliation Hall, Duffy's *Nation* or Mitchel's *United Irishman* – a defining event occurred which could have provided an opportunity for their unification. In February 1848 King Louis-Philippe of France was deposed, which stunned Europe. A popular revolution in which regime change was accomplished with hardly any bloodshed or destruction of property was applauded by both European moderates and radicals. As the French Revolution of 1789 had influenced the ideology and actions of earlier Irish radicals, especially Wolfe Tone, so the 1848 French Revolution inspired the 1840s Irish nationalists. The fall of Louis-Philippe and the proclamation of the Second Republic (22 to 24 February 1848), with its little bloodshed and peaceful aftermath, filled the Confederates and Repealers alike with awe. It seemed to be an ideal revolution. Many of the leaders of the revolution were linked with radical newspapers and the poet Alfonse de Lamartine became head of France's provisional government.[158] *Le National*, the newspaper most closely linked to the rising, commented on 25 February 1848 that 'Never was a victory more rapid, more unexpected. And after the victory, nothing was more impressive than the good order.'[159] *The Nation* remarked in the following week that it was 'liberty without anarchy.'[160] The success of the Paris insurgents was contagious and other European cities caught the revolutionary fever, staging their own rebellions. In an atmosphere of elation, the Dublin nationalist press convinced itself that Ireland's opportunity had arrived.[161]

Mistakenly believing the government might think that revolutionary France could attack Britain, combined with what they perceived to be a threat to social stability posed by the British Chartists, whose press also exploited an imagined threat from France, Irish nationalists hoped that the government's resistance to Repeal might weaken.[162] France, however, had no intention of attacking Britain and Chartism did not seriously threaten

[158] As we saw in Chapter 1, back in 1842 Alfonse de Lamartine had been inspired by *The Nation*'s prospectus.

[159] Roger Price (ed.), *1848 in France* (London: Thames and Hudson Ltd., 1975), p. 63.

[160] 1st LA, *Nation*, 4 March 1848.

[161] For example: 2nd LA, *Nation*, 4 March 1848.

[162] The spring and summer of 1848 saw some solidarity between Chartists and Repealers, especially in Britain. For example, a 'Repeal meeting in Manchester' in March 1848, with a reported number of about 8,000 present, was attended by Feargus O'Connor,

the government's formidable powers of law and order.[163] Nevertheless, in the meantime, Irish nationalists joined the revolutionary excitement captured across Europe, their newspapers creating a conscious belief that the tide of events had turned in favour of Ireland's future independence.

Above all, all three disparate groups of Irish nationalists and their newspapers recognized that the time for unity had arrived. This perhaps was best symbolized by a meeting of many thousands of Dubliners who were addressed by opposing Confederate leaders, including Smith O'Brien and Mitchel; even more encouraging, on a procession after this meeting, as it proceeded close by Conciliation Hall, Old Ireland Repealers emerged from their own meeting and cheered the marchers with much enthusiasm.[164]

Later that year, however, when Conciliation Hall Repealers and Irish Confederates attempted a reconciliation by forming the Irish League, an organization intended to replace the Association and the Confederation, its effectiveness was compromised by the desertion of John O'Connell. While agreeing to the dissolution of the Association, he refused to join the League, which is not surprising considering the past bitterness between him and the Young Irelanders.[165] More importantly, another serious disturbance took place in France at the end of June, which resulted in much bloodshed, frightening off many prospective supporters from joining the new Irish League.

Following the overthrow of Louis-Philippe in February 1848, even though Mitchel, Martin and Reilly were reinstated on the Council of the Irish Confederation, the two factions essentially remained separate, the differences between them defined and strengthened by their respective newspapers. One area of contention that prevented an alliance between these groups in the Irish Confederation was a fundamental disagreement over the concept of unity of class. This policy, strongly supported by *The Nation*, was continually undermined by Mitchel's paper. Smith O'Brien complained that Mitchel's 'writings in the *United Irishman* had alienated

---

the Chartist leader, accompanied by Meagher and Doheny, *Manchester Guardian*, [n.d.], in *Nation*, 25 March 1848.

[163] When Smith O'Brien and Meagher led a delegation to France to present a congratulatory address on the revolution, hoping for possible support for their cause, Alphonse de Lamartine was reluctant to commit himself, not wishing to endanger relations with Britain; this outcome did not change the minds of the Irish Confederates, who were more determined than ever after February 1848 to repeal the Act of Union.

[164] 'France and Ireland. Great Meeting of Trades and Citizens of Dublin', 20 March 1848, *Nation*, 25 March 1848.

[165] Charles Gavan Duffy speaking at Irish Confederation mtg., Music Hall, 'A.B.', 21 June 1848, Police reports on political activities in Ireland, 1848, TCD, MS 2037.

from the cause of Repeal and from [the] Confederation an incalculable number of persons belonging to the higher and wealthier classes of society.'[166]

Mitchel also antagonized those of the lower classes who supported Old Ireland. Responding to criticism of O'Connell in *The United Irishman*, in Limerick on 29 April 1848 an angry mob carrying an effigy of Mitchel, and a flag bearing 'death to Mitchel,' hurled stones at a building in which Mitchel, Meagher and Smith O'Brien were attending a meeting by invitation.[167] Smith O'Brien was furious with Mitchel and disgusted with the mob, especially as he was assailed on leaving the building and badly injured in the face. The following morning Mitchel wrote to Smith O'Brien: 'I am deeply grieved & ashamed at your having been so brutally treated.'[168] Nevertheless, as a consequence of their political differences, and following this incident, Mitchel once more left the Council, again demonstrating the gulf between him and his newspaper and the comparatively more moderate Confederates.[169]

Inspired by the February French Revolution, *The Nation* had, however, developed a more defiant tone, and this was reflected in the behaviour of Council members at Confederate meetings. For example, the following month a leading article in *The Nation* stated: 'We believe a NATIONAL MILITIA and a NATIONAL COUNCIL have become essential to our very existence.'[170] When the leaders of the Confederation began initial preparations for a Council of Three Hundred and a National Guard, Lord Clarendon, the Viceroy, issued a proclamation on 29 April 1848 declaring them illegal.[171] In response, at a Confederation meeting in the Music Hall, on the evening of 3 May 1848, '*Mr. Duffy* read the *Proclamation by the Lord*

166 Written retrospectively in a personal memorandum, Smith O'Brien Papers, NLI, MS 449 in Denis Gwynn, *Young Ireland and 1848* (Cork: Cork University Press, 1949), p. 165.

167 Extracts of reports of the meeting that appeared in local newspapers were reprinted by Mitchel's paper: 'Meeting in Limerick', *United Irishman*, 6 May 1848. As their political policies were now so diverse, had he known that Mitchel also had an invitation, Smith O'Brien would not have attended this meeting. However, despite their opposing political views, Smith O'Brien believed that Mitchel was 'pureminded and truthful': Draft Address of William Smith O'Brien, 1848', William Smith O'Brien Papers, NLI, MS 464/45–7 in Sloan, *Smith O'Brien*, p. 231.

168 Letter from Mitchel to Smith O'Brien, Smith O'Brien Papers, NLI, MS 440/ 2202.

169 Mitchel's letter of resignation to the Council of the Irish Confederation with accompanying comments: 3rd LA, *United Irishman*, 6 May 1848.

170 2nd LA, *Nation*, 11 March 1848.

171 Minutes of the Irish Confederation, 27 & 29 March, 19 April 1848, RIA, MS 23 H 44.

Lieutenant, tore it and *flung it to the winds*.'[172] Meagher then proceeded to read a counter-proclamation from the Council of the Irish Confederation (signed by Smith O'Brien) refusing to accept the legality of Clarendon's document.[173]

But, despite *The Nation*'s increasing radicalism, ideological differences between its supporters in the Confederation and those involved with *The United Irishman* remained as far apart as ever. *The United Irishman* called for an agrarian insurrection and, under the influence of the ideology of Thomas Paine, in the tradition of Wolfe Tone and inspired by the French Revolution, this was to be followed by the establishment of a republic. By comparison, *The Nation* moderately sought a Council of Three Hundred, a militia and Repeal. Although the French Revolution failed to unify the two factions in the Irish Confederation, it prompted both *The Nation* and *The United Irishman* to become bolder in their militant rhetoric. It was, in fact, to be the government's repressive measures in response to this militancy that finally fused these two factions into making plans together for an insurrection that summer.

Like *The Nation* and Young Ireland in their early years, the success of *The United Irishman* imbued Mitchel with power, making him unwilling to compromise his beliefs. He claimed that *The United Irishman* was 'by far the most widely circulated paper in Ireland. It was read in all military and police-barracks, – was clubbed for in all parishes, – and duly read on Sundays to eager crowds in all chapel yards.'[174] William Dillon, Mitchel's biographer, noted that *The United Irishman* 'exercised a far greater influence over the minds of the Irish masses than any other journal then published in the country.'[175] Certainly, with *The United Irishman*'s success Mitchel was even more determined to challenge both the government and the moderates in the Confederation. Despite remaining at odds with the Council leaders, especially Smith O'Brien, Duffy and Dillon, *The United Irishman* had a special hold over the Confederate Clubs. For example, the proliferation of Clubs throughout Ireland and Great Britain that had emerged after the outbreak of the February French Revolution included names such as 'The United Irishman' and 'John Mitchel.'[176] But the influence of Mitchel's newspaper was especially reflected by the government's determination to suppress *The United Irishman* and silence its proprietor.

[172] 'C.D.', 4 May 1848, Police reports, TCD, MS 2037.
[173] *United Irishman*, 6 May 1848.
[174] Mitchel, *Last Conquest*, p. 170.
[175] Dillon, *Mitchel*, p. 235.
[176] 'The Clubs', *Irish Felon*, 1 July 1848.

Initially intended to deal with Mitchel, a new law, the Treason-Felony Act, was hurriedly promulgated on 22 April 1848 to tackle what the British government deemed the anarchical writings and speeches of the Irish Confederates. Responding to what it perceived as a military threat from the Confederates – especially with Mitchel's references to the United Irishmen, a republic and physical force – the government was determined to thwart their power. Instead of charges for sedition, this new act was intended to treat writings and speeches that were thought to incite rebellion against the government as a criminal offence, thus bearing a much harsher punishment. Earlier, on 21 March 1848, Mitchel, Meagher and Smith O'Brien had been arrested; Mitchel was indicted for seditious articles in *The United Irishman*, and the other two Confederates for seditious speeches in the Music Hall on 15 March 1848.[177] These charges of sedition did not intimidate Mitchel or halt his vitriolic rhetoric; he saw them as a further step towards a climactic confrontation between the government and the people. Addressing a letter 'To the Right Hon. The Earl of Clarendon, Her Majesty's Executioner-General and General Butcher of Ireland,' Mitchel announced:

> the Irish nation and the British government are now finally at issue. Whichsoever field of battle you prefer, the Queen's Bench or the streets and fields – whichsoever weapon, packed juries or whetted sabres – I trust, I believe, you will now be stoutly met. One party or the other must absolutely yield: you must put us down, or we will put you down.[178]

Meagher and Smith O'Brien were brought to trial that May; their juries were not packed, and they were found not guilty. But Mitchel's *United Irishman* was deemed so dangerous by the government that his charges of sedition were dropped and he was re-arrested on the evening of 13 May 1848 under the new Treason-Felony Act. Writings in *The United Irishman*, which the Whig government considered treasonable, formed the basis of the new indictment against him when he appeared in court a week later.[179]

---

177 'State Prosecutions', *United Irishman*, 25 March 1848.

178 Letter, 24 March 1848, 1st LA column, *United Irishman*, 25 March 1848.

179 The Clerk of the Crown read Mitchel's indictment, being mainly a speech delivered by him at Limerick and printed in *The United Irishman* on 6 May 1848, an article, 'The *Times* on Rebellion' and a letter to the Protestant farmers, both in *The United Irishman* on 13 May 1848: 'The State Prosecutions. Trial of Mr. Mitchel', *United Irishman*, 27 May 1848.

One of the indicted items was a 'Letter to the Protestant farmers, labourers, and artizans, of the North of Ireland,' urging their support in joining forces with the nationalists in the south in their quest for 'an IRISH REPUBLIC' to be won '*In arms*, my countrymen, in arms. Thus, and not otherwise, have ever nations of men sprung to liberty and power.' He further urged their co-operation in preventing food from leaving the country, for that 'simple act of self-preservation will at one and the same blow prostrate British dominion and landlordism together.'[180] The image of food leaving the country while the Great Famine's victims were starving to death was a major indictment against the Whig government, one of the themes to which Mitchel was to return in his later writings on this period of Irish history.[181] While he was determined to overturn the government, Mitchel was also clearly advocating a class war in *The United Irishman*, seeing Irish nationalist aspirations intimately entwined with the disempowerment and eventual removal of the upper classes.

The suppression of *The United Irishman* and Mitchel's conviction and deportation marked another turning point for the Irish Confederation. *The United Irishman* made its final appearance on 27 May 1848, the day Mitchel was sentenced to fourteen years abroad in penal servitude after being convicted by a packed jury. He had, in fact, hoped that his conviction would ignite a daring rescue by the Dublin Clubs, thereby triggering a spontaneous uprising throughout Ireland. Despite the Clubs' willingness to act and Meagher's initial agreement to the rescue, following consultations between Duffy and other leading Confederates, it was decided that it could not be accomplished successfully; this was due to a lack of military preparation by the Clubs and the government drafting 10,000 extra troops into Dublin in response to *The United Irishman*'s rhetoric of an impending insurrection. However, a police report on a meeting of Confederates in the Music Hall in early June 1848 noted Meagher's warning that 'their destinies were changed, they now must be prepared to lose their lives in the cause of Freedom … He vowed to follow Mitchel, and if possible to complete the work he had in hand.'[182] Reflecting the belligerent mood of the Clubs, the following month at a Council meeting Smith O'Brien asked if 'all the leaders were apprehended, could the Clubs be restrained from attempting a rescue: all the delegates, but one, answered "no."'[183] Responding to the injustice of a packed jury and the harsh sentence, the Confederation's leaders

[180] *United Irishman*, 13 May 1848.
[181] Mitchel, *Last Conquest*, p. 112.
[182] 'C.D.', 6 June 1848, Police reports, TCD, MS 2037.
[183] 'C.D.', 12 July 1848, Police reports, TCD, MS 2037.

and the Clubs adopted a far more militant tone following Mitchel's trial, which had been the intention of *The United Irishman*.

After the suppression of Mitchel's paper and his deportation, three other short-lived Dublin weeklies sprang into print: *The Irishman*, *The Irish Tribune* and *The Irish Felon* appeared in June and July that year.[184] These papers continued Mitchel's seditious and militant rhetoric, thereby reflecting the willingness of his followers to emulate *The United Irishman* in confronting the government. *The Irish Tribune* and *The Irish Felon*, each costing fivepence, and similar to *The United Irishman* with their highly-charged rhetoric against the Irish aristocracy and the British government, proved even more aggressive and rebellious than Mitchel's mouthpiece. So sought after were these papers that it was claimed 'when a day old, their value often run [*sic*] up to half a crown and three shillings a copy.'[185] *The Irishman* was the least militant of these papers and with a lower cost of one penny and fewer pages, its content was narrower in scope. Claiming a circulation of 15,000, this paper listed thirty-two agents from the north and south of Ireland and Great Britain at the beginning of July, an increase from the nineteen agents that were listed in its first issue a few weeks earlier, suggesting a rise in circulation.[186] Notably, *The Irishman* continued Mitchel's appeal for Protestants to join the cause.[187] Other short-lived penny weeklies were founded in the spring of 1848 that also followed the tone of *The United Irishman*. Confederates John Savage and J. De Courcy Young published *The Patriot* until it was stopped by the authorities, whereupon they became involved with *The Irish Tribune*; another paper, *The Young Irishman*, issued for several weeks from 25 March 1848, was linked to *The Irishman*, which it preceded.[188] *The Irish National Guard*, regularly advertised in *The United Irishman*, was a rebel weekly that had begun in April 1848, costing 1d, or, if posted, 2d, and could be bought in the south and north of Ireland and also in England; lasting three months, this paper represented both nationalist and Chartist interests.[189]

184 These 1848 papers had only a short life: *The Irishman*, 10 June–1 July, *The Irish Tribune*, 10 June–8 July, and *The Irish Felon*, 24 June–22 July.

185 John Savage, *'98 and '48: The Modern Revolutionary History and Literature of Ireland*, 3rd ed. (New York: Redfield, 1856), p. 322.

186 *Irishman*, 1 July 1848.

187 'To the Protestants of Ireland', *Irishman*, 10 June 1848.

188 Savage, *'98 and '48*, pp. 323–4. According to Savage, *The Young Irishman* was issued by George Wright Draper. *The Irishman* bears Draper's signature on the front pages of two of its surviving issues in the British Library, 24 June and 1 July 1848, and his initials accompany some of the poems in *The Irishman*.

189 Michael Huggins suggests that *The Irish National Guard*, published from 22 April to

Planned even before the suppression of Mitchel's paper, *The Irish Tribune* was established and edited by medical students Kevin Izod O'Doherty and Richard D'Alton Williams, who aptly stated in their first issue that they wished to 'heal the broken-hearted spirit of the nation.'[190] Along with O'Doherty and Williams, the new paper was funded by members of the Irish Confederation, mainly Dr Thomas Antisell, and also John Savage, J. De Courcy Young and Walter T. Meyler; they, with Confederates Stephen Joseph Meany and Michael Doheny, wrote articles for the new paper.[191] Urging preparation for war, *The Irish Tribune* demanded that the Confederation should 'make the possession of arms and *ammunition* an absolute and indispensable qualification of membership.'[192] An item entitled 'Our War Department,' which had also featured in *The United Irishman*, gave practical hints for prospective combatants. Nor was there any shortage of tirades directed against the government and the landlords. For instance, following the line of rhetoric from *The United Irishman*, which stated that the Great Famine was killing the people aided by the government with the aim to murder what it deemed Ireland's surplus population, at the beginning of July *The Irish Tribune* declared: 'The famine ... [was] deliberately made by our English tyrants and their landlord slave-drivers' and called on its readers to 'exterminate the English despots, and crush with them the anti-Irish aristocracy for ever!'[193] Although highly-charged rhetoric of this nature was written in the context of the anguish and anger felt during the Famine, the idea of British government culpability was to gather momentum in later decades.

Meanwhile, the Tory *Belfast News-letter* considered *The Irish Tribune*

> an exceedingly neatly got-up paper ... The matter is rather more cleverly and scholarly written than that of the *United Irishman*, and will prove a formidable rival to the *Nation*. It is bitterly opposed to John O'Connell's assumption of leadership ... it clearly appears

---

22 July 1848, was essentially a Chartist paper: 'Democracy or nationalism? The problems of the Chartist press in Ireland', in Joan Allen, Owen R. Ashton (eds.), *Papers for the People. A study of the Chartist press* (London: The Merlin Press Ltd, 2005), pp. 129–45.

[190] 1st LA, *Irish Tribune*, 10 June 1848. This paper listed sixty-four named agents throughout Ireland and in Great Britain, many of whom had been agents for *The United Irishman*.

[191] In his history of 1848, John Savage commented that two other men, both 'distinguished,' also funded and wrote for *The Irish Tribune*, but did not wish to expose them: Savage, *'98 and '48*, pp. 321–2.

[192] 1st LA, *Irish Tribune*, 17 June 1848.

[193] 1st LA, *United Irishman*, 4 March 1848; 3rd LA, *Irish Tribune*, 1 July 1848.

> that the TRIBUNE is independent of both the Confederates and Conciliation-hall humbugs.[194]

Certainly, the writers of *The Irish Tribune*, representing the extreme Confederates, along with those of the other rebel papers, distanced themselves from the now beleaguered Irish League, believing that militancy was the only way forward for Irish freedom. This approach, though, merely reinforced the divisions within the Irish nationalist movement.

Seeking to make a more practical and effective stand against the government than the other rebel papers, *The Irish Felon* started preparations for its own military group. This paper was founded by John Martin and Thomas Devin Reilly, who were joined by James Fintan Lalor, now free to publicly extrapolate on the radical theories that he had passed on to Mitchel and the Irish Confederation. In particular, he emphasized his idea of moral insurrection: 'We must only try to keep our harvest, to offer a peaceful, passive resistance, to barricade the island, to break up the roads, to break down the bridges, – and, should need be, and favourable occasions offer, surely we may venture to try the steel.'[195] Urging the people to arm, Lalor declared the intentions of *The Irish Felon*:

> We have determined to set about creating, as speedily as possible, a military organization, of which the FELON Office shall be the centre and citadel … our object is to gather together a number of men competent to lead in cases of necessity, and a staff of contributors competent to take the conducting of this journal, if its present Conductors should be removed by death or exile.[196]

A week after Lalor's invitation to his readers to join the paper's militant Felon Club, Joseph Brenan, a dedicated Mitchelite and regular contributor to *The Irish Felon*, announced in the paper that 'a huge pile of letters' had been received from those wishing to be enrolled.[197] These letters mirrored the militant spirit of the rebel press. For instance, an Irish Chartist who

---

[194] 'Opinions of the Press', *Irish Tribune*, 24 June 1848.

[195] 5th LA, *Irish Felon*, 8 July 1848. Notice that Mitchel used Lalor's phraseology of 'passive resistance' and 'to try the steel' when writing his history in *Last Conquest*, p. 157.

[196] 3rd LA, *Irish Felon*, 1 July 1848.

[197] 3rd LA, *Irish Felon*, 8 July 1848. Joseph Brenan (1828–57) belonged to the Cork Historical Society. Besides writing for *The Irish Felon*, he also wrote prose and poetry for the 1848 rebel newspapers *The United Irishman* and *The Irish Tribune*. As we shall see, following imprisonment, in 1849 Brenan became an editor of the semi-advanced *Irishman*.

was president of the Mary Mitchel Club in Stalybridge, Manchester, offered his services both as a prospective *Felon* contributor and a fighter, stating that he had 'written several pamphlets' and was 'quite fit to lead a section of pikemen.'[198] Another, a doctor's son and Dublin student, declared that he was 'ready to fight for a free Republic.'[199] The response of readers in letters such as these is testimony to the effectiveness of the rhetoric in the rebel press of 1848. There was certainly no equivocation about *The Irish Felon*'s total dismissal of constitutional agitation and its intention to incite an uprising. A letter written by John Martin in *The Irish Felon*'s last issue prior to its suppression by the government urged members of the Clubs to:

> Stand to your arms! … though thousands of us be butchered by the enemy's cannon and bayonets, and our streets and native fields be purpled with our blood – never shall the struggle for Irish freedom cease but with the destruction of that monstrous system of base and murderous tyranny, or with the utter extermination of the Irish people![200]

While *The Irish Tribune* had a lower circulation of 4,800, official statistics suggest that with average weekly stamp returns at around 10,000, *The Irish Felon* was even more popular than Mitchel's paper, probably due to its aim to 'take up the mission of THE UNITED IRISHMAN' and its call to arms through the Felon Club.[201] All these rebel papers of 1848, in their attempt to mobilize the Irish people in their crusade of defiance, reflected a great outpouring of anger against the British government for its indictment of Mitchel and its approach to the Great Famine.

Despite the new Treason-Felony Act and the successful prosecution of Mitchel by a packed jury, well aware of the fate that awaited them, these journalists continued to assail the government. The split between Duffy and Mitchel, and the departure of Mitchel to found his own militant newspaper – actions crucial to the direction of Irish nationalism – inspired

---

[198] B. Treanor to Joseph Brenan, 4 July 1848, James Fintan Lalor Papers, NLI, MS 340/154. Mary was the name of John Mitchel's mother.

[199] James Marroll, 12 Charlotte Quay, to *The Irish Felon*, [n.d.], Lalor Papers, NLI, MS 340/41.

[200] 1st LA, *Irish Felon*, 22 July 1848. A warrant had been issued for John Martin, who contributed to his paper in hiding, which he continued after he surrendered to the police on 8 July 1848.

[201] Based on 'Return of Number of Stamps issued at One Penny to Newspapers in United Kingdom, 1837–50', HCP, 1852 (42) XXVIII.497. 'Mr. Lalor's letter', 21 June 1848, *Irish Felon*, 24 June 1848.

a militancy in other papers that followed the course of *The United Irishman*. Even *The Nation*, in direct competition with its commercial rival, had become increasingly more defiant in its tone. Mitchel believed that 'The *United Irishman* had also forced the *Nation* to adopt the insurrectionary policy, and to publish plain instructions on pike-exercise, and the like, – or else go unread.'[202] Attempts were made by Clarendon from the spring of 1848 to discredit the leading Confederates and portray them as a danger to society, thus to draw support away from them. In his attack Clarendon not only arranged for the issue of pamphlets and posters, but employed the services of the disreputable James Birch and his newspaper, *The World*, to morally blacken the characters of these Confederates. But Clarendon failed. Unsurprisingly, the popularity of the militant rhetoric in the rebel newspapers and the escalating defiance of *The Nation* prompted the government into taking repressive measures. That July the voice of militant Irish nationalism was officially silenced when newspaper proprietors and writers were arrested and their papers suppressed. Duffy himself was arrested on Saturday 8 July 1848, and on 29 July *The Nation*'s last issue under production was seized by police.[203]

The suspension of habeas corpus on 22 July 1848 was the final trigger for the insurrection, although the original intention of the Confederate leaders was to wait until after the harvest. The Confederates lacking military training, weaponry and resolute leadership, the people demoralized and still suffering from the effects of the Great Famine and being urged by their priests to resist the call to fight, the attempted rebellion that month, led by Smith O'Brien, was easily defeated.[204] Though the newspaper rebellion had also been crushed, residual resistance to the government persisted in the months that followed; John O'Mahony, for example, the future American Fenian, was engaged in guerrilla tactics on the hills bordering Kilkenny and Waterford. Some Confederates managed to flee from the authorities; Dillon, Reilly and Savage escaped to America. Of those arrested, Martin and O'Doherty were convicted of treason-felony and sentenced to deportation; charges against Duffy and Williams failed, while Confederates such as Lalor, Brenan and Meany were temporarily imprisoned. Smith O'Brien,

---

202 Mitchel, *Last Conquest*, p. 172.

203 Like John Martin, Duffy continued writing for his paper from Newgate Prison.

204 Smith O'Brien was shown to be a reluctant leader; Duffy wrote to him on 17 June 1848, 'I am perfectly well aware that you don't desire to lead or influence others': Charles Gavan Duffy Papers, RIA, MS 12 P 19. In his in-depth study on Smith O'Brien, Robert Sloan aptly demonstrates how Smith O'Brien was drawn into the leadership of the Young Irelanders, and eventually into the responsibility of being at the head of the Irish Confederates' attempted rebellion: Sloan, *Smith O'Brien*.

Meagher and others were convicted of high treason and sentenced to death, but this was commuted to penal servitude abroad. Irish nationalism as a political movement was effectively destroyed that summer.

Conclusion

The Dublin nationalist press was at the forefront of the events that led to the downfall of the 1840s Irish nationalist movement. The policies of unity of class and creed, including the political independence of the Repeal Association, were severely tested from the end of 1844. *The Nation*'s resistance to the proposed adoption of the Federal principle by Daniel O'Connell and an alliance between O'Connell and the Whigs weakened the political integrity of the Association. Federalism was perceived by *The Nation* as an unacceptable compromise over the aspirations of Irish nationalists for self-determination, while the British government was totally opposed to the notion of any break-up of the United Kingdom. However, even if Duffy believed that O'Connell was abandoning Repeal, had *The Nation* supported him, and provided the Federalists could work with him, it is not impossible to believe that Federalism (as envisaged then) could have temporarily satisfied Irish nationalist aspirations. Tension between *The Nation's* non-sectarianism and its representation of a movement that was mostly Catholic was a source of conflict and fully exploited by the O'Connellites. What impacted on these issues – and what many historians have recognized as a clash of the Young Irelanders' idealism with O'Connell's pragmatism – was their respective approaches to the meaning of Irish nationalism. Given what was written in *The Nation*, while O'Connell was prepared to accept a political solution to Ireland's future, the Young Irelanders looked to a purer, more holistic nationalism, embracing Irish politics and Irish culture, devoid of English influence. While *The Nation* saw that being part of the Irish nation meant embracing the ideal of the unity of creed, for O'Connell its tactical value in achieving Repeal was superseded by his loyalty to the dominant Catholic population. The Young Irelanders could not resist challenging O'Connell's authority in *The Nation* and in the Association when it conflicted with their own vision of Irish nationalism. What intensified these divergent perspectives of Irish nationalism was *The Nation*'s championship of its right to challenge O'Connell's autocratic leadership of the Repeal Association. Ultimately, the 1846 secession was caused by the shifting balance of power between the O'Connellites and *The Nation*, a conflict over who was to decide the future policy of the Repeal Association. However, while the Young Irelanders survived through their newspaper and founded the Irish Confederation, the Repeal Association was severely damaged, never recovering its former prestige and influence within the Repeal movement. The impact of personal rivalries certainly played a part in both secessions. The Young Irelanders of *The Nation* dared to challenge Daniel O'Connell, the great Liberator, and were a threat to John O'Connell's aspiration to leadership of the Repeal Association. The disagreement between Charles Gavan Duffy and John Mitchel, following the latter's departure from *The Nation*, intensified when Mitchel established his *United Irishman* in opposition to *The Nation*.

An event that partly influenced the secession of July 1846 but impacted considerably on the secession of February 1848 was the Great Famine, when the Dublin nationalist press criticized what it perceived as the negative response of the government. The Famine had a profound impact on the development of Irish nationalism in the mid-1840s, particularly prompting Mitchel to adopt a strident editorial policy to help those who were suffering from its effects. While the image of Ireland as a victim had been portrayed by Irish nationalists before the Famine, it now became solidly entrenched in Irish nationalist ideology. Promoted by the nationalist press, justice for Ireland was to become a mantra more than ever after the Famine. The Irish nationalist press, in particular the more advanced Dublin nationalist papers of 1848, articulated a collective emotional response to the government's handling of the Famine, fomenting a sense of belonging, a common experience necessary for national identity, felt and shared by the people, more powerful and enduring than Repeal grievances and henceforth duly exploited by Irish nationalist newspapers. Saving the people came to be equated with saving the Irish nation and preserving Irish nationality, an important theme in the 1860s Fenian press.

The Irish Confederation, despite making progress through its Club system, was compromised by Mitchel's conflict with Duffy over the future policy of *The Nation*. A power struggle between the Duffyites and the Mitchelites was waged in their respective newspapers, *The Nation* and *The United Irishman*. It was now a clash of policy over whether Irish nationalists would abandon moral force and replace it with physical force. Repeal's ideal of the unity of class, an attempt to embrace the collective strength of all classes against the Union, was abandoned when militancy increasingly became the order of the day. *The United Irishman* played a significant role in changing the course of Irish history, forcing the pace and direction of action. Influenced by James Fintan Lalor, Mitchel's social and political radicalism was a direct response to the devastating effects of the Great Famine. Reacting to the government's management of the Famine, and despairing of the landlord class, Mitchel was driven to extremism, believing that the power of his newspaper could save the Irish nation. It was almost as if, in his eyes, the immense popularity of *The United Irishman* made his policies invincible. With the success of his paper Mitchel created a dedicated following in the Confederate Clubs and his school of thought dictated actions that ultimately led to the failed 1848 rebellion.

The French Revolution had a decisive effect on the thinking of Irish nationalists. Their reaction to the fall of Louis-Philippe that February is a compelling example of the idealistic nature of Irish nationalism, an idealism that conflicted with reality. To expect a population dying of hunger and disease to take part in an armed rebellion was unrealistic. Irish nationalist thinking, particularly in *The Nation*, *The United Irishman* and the other rebel papers, was too linked to the heart rather than the head, and this imbalance led to consequences that were damaging to the Irish nationalist movement. These newspapers set in motion a consistently more determined attitude towards physical force tactics, and this approach survived to manifest itself in the 1916 rebellion. Revolutionary republican nationalism was revived by Mitchel through *The United Irishman* in response to the Great Famine, and became an established part of Irish nationalist orthodoxy. Divisions in the Dublin nationalist press over the direction of Irish nationalism grew from 1844 and in the summer of 1848, fuelled by the government's Famine policy, in despair, the rebel press appeared to spiral out of control. All this was highly damaging to the development of Irish nationalism. The destructive side of the Dublin nationalist press became firmly entrenched in the mid-nineteenth century and was to be played out, time and again, in Irish nationalist politics.

CHAPTER 3

Survival and revival

The Dublin nationalist press from 1849 to 1859

'The *Nation* revived is but the ghost of its former self – bloodless and weak. Prison-chains seem to have crippled Mr. DUFFY's right hand,' *The Irishman*, Sept. 1849.[1]

FOLLOWING THE ATTEMPTED REBELLION against British rule in the summer of 1848, the Irish nationalist movement was in a disconsolate state. Its most active advocates in the Dublin nationalist press and in the field were scattered; some were in prison awaiting trial and others became fugitives, a few of whom fled abroad. The country was still in the grip of famine, lasting in some places until 1852. Yet, despite all this turmoil, the Dublin nationalist press kept the Irish nationalist spirit alive. Some Irish nationalists refused to be quiescent after the turbulence of the Young Ireland era. Not only did Irish constitutional nationalism attempt an innovative revival, Irish revolutionary nationalism also reasserted itself in the form of secret conspiracy. The Dublin nationalist press, while implicated in the downfall of Irish nationalism as a movement, had a significant role in ensuring its survival and recovery. Though promoting constitutional nationalism, it also encouraged a revival of the extreme nationalist ideology characteristic of the earlier months of 1848 that was eventually to play such a prominent part in Irish history.

The years immediately following Young Ireland's attempted rebellion were unsettling and challenging for the Dublin nationalist press. Two moderate Dublin Repeal papers, *The Pilot* and *The Dublin Weekly Register*, ceased publication, the former in February 1849, and the latter in September 1850. Dr John Gray's *Freeman's Journal*, with its weekly and evening counterparts, continued to keep the idea of Repeal of the Union alive,

[1] 1st LA, *The Irishman*, 1 Sept. 1849.

especially when the Repeal Association was revived in October 1849, although, lacking sufficient support, this organization was gone within two years.[2] Constitutional nationalism, however, was given a boost in the autumn of 1849 by Charles Gavan Duffy's reissue of *The Nation*, which, after its 1848 militancy, now followed a strict moral force approach. Duffy also formed the Irish Alliance, a nationalist group that was middle-class led and espoused the new political tone of the reissued *Nation*. When Frederick Lucas's ardent Catholic newspaper, *The Tablet*, transferred at the beginning of 1850 from London to Dublin, it became a useful ally to the Dublin nationalist press.

A major consequence of the Great Famine was a reduction in Ireland's population, mostly affecting the poorest rural classes. From 8.2 million in 1841, the population of Ireland had declined to 6.6 million by 1851; by the turn of the century, it was around 4.5 million. Much of this decline was due to emigration, which, as we shall see in the next chapter of this book, particularly alarmed the 1860s IRB journalists. While beleaguered tenants were already subject to high rents and evictions even before the Famine, from the mid-1840s an overwhelming number of people were driven from their homes. Furthermore, the Famine accelerated the change from tillage farming to the more profitable grazing farming, which in turn led to more evictions. This state of affairs was compounded by the Encumbered Estates Acts of 1848–49, which allowed bankrupt Irish landlords to sell their estates on the open market, and further increased the number of evictions. A key topic in this chapter is the role of the nationalist journalists in addressing the plight of the tenant farmers.

From the political perspective, the burgeoning of the tenant right movement in the early 1850s created much hope for the promotion of constitutional nationalism, when Gray, Duffy and Lucas committed themselves and their respective newspapers to the collaboration of Ireland's northern and southern counties and the founding of an independent Irish party in Parliament. The progress of these projects, however, was compromised, partly by the issue of religion. *The Nation*'s ideal of unity of creed, which seemed to have held out much promise, was crushed. Irish constitutional nationalism reached a low ebb, symbolized by Duffy's departure from Ireland towards the end of 1855.

An important theme of the period 1849 to 1859 was the emergence of

---

[2] RA mtg., 2 Sept. 1850, where it was announced that subscriptions were now so low that rent for the hall could not be met in future. Repeal rent for that week only amounted to £8 0s 9d: *Nation*, 7 Sept. 1850. However, the Association did manage to hold a few more meetings the following year.

physical force nationalism as a long-term voice in the Dublin nationalist press. One of the early protagonists in this venture was the important Young Irelander, James Fintan Lalor. In 1849 he was involved in a conspiracy of resistance against the government while also attempting to establish an advanced Irish nationalist newspaper. Whereas the Dublin nationalist press of the 1840s Repeal years was mostly characterized by moral force and was led by the middle class, in January 1849 *The Irishman* was launched, ostensibly of a constitutional nature but evolving into an advanced nationalist newspaper. Later that year, it was to become the mouthpiece of the Irish Democratic Association (IDA), a working-class nationalist organization with social and political aspirations that was founded to compete with Duffy's Irish Alliance. When *The Irishman* was overshadowed by Duffy's reissue of *The Nation* that September, bitter rivalry between these two papers for nationalist support ended with financial losses for *The Irishman*. Following the demise of *The Irishman* in May 1850, the voice of advanced nationalism in the Dublin press lay dormant for the next few years until the appearance of *The Tribune* in the mid-1850s.

A split in the new Irish parliamentary party in this decade left a vacuum into which physical force nationalism reasserted itself in response to Britain's involvement in the Crimean War (1854–56). For some Irish nationalists this event signalled the opportunity for a potential uprising and the advantage of having an army ready to strike when Britain found itself in a vulnerable military position. In the absence of a strong constitutional nationalist movement, another advanced nationalist paper, also called *The Irishman*, was established in Belfast in 1858; it had offices in both Belfast and Dublin, but operated solely from the Irish capital the following year. Outlasting the short-term tenures of the 1849 *Irishman* and *The Tribune* and the 1848 rebel papers, the 1858 *Irishman* heralded the beginning of a long era of advanced Irish nationalist opinion in print.

From 1849 the extreme Dublin nationalist press, following the rebel papers of the previous summer, modelled themselves on *The Nation* and espoused cultural as well as political nationalism. Conscious of falling foul of the law, though, they were not as openly militant as *The Nation* and the rebel papers had been in the spring and summer of 1848. However, whether it was attempting to resuscitate moral force nationalism or militant nationalism, this period from 1849 to 1859 marks the determination and the resilience of the Dublin nationalist press to survive in the wake of the failure of the attempted 1848 rebellion and the devastation of the Great Famine.

Recovery of the Irish nationalist cause and *The Irishman*, 1849–50

The early post-1848 years were a time of reflection on the nature and future prospects of Irish nationalism. In 1849, for instance, John Blake Dillon commented gloomily on Irish nationality when he wrote to his wife from exile in America, asking her to convey to Duffy his belief that 'The old forms of society, the old laws, and the old language have perished irrecoverably.'[3] There was much truth in this statement. Dillon knew this when he founded *The Nation* with Thomas Davis and Duffy in 1842. Back then, *The Nation*'s intention had been to salvage the remnants of Irish nationality. Now, after the *débâcle* of the summer of 1848, believing it to be a completely hopeless cause, Dillon wanted Duffy to abandon 'Celtic Nationality' (i.e. the struggle for complete Irish independence), concentrate on the Rights of Man, and reissue *The Nation* from London, pursuing a 'Federal Republic' for Ireland and Great Britain.[4] But what, in fact, was left of Irish nationality to be saved, as Ireland had already become much Anglicized? What remained or was distinct enough of Irish society in the mid-nineteenth century to constitute Irish nationality and thus justify independence from Great Britain? Given that both countries were Christian, espousing similar moral values and because Ireland had absorbed much of English law and civic institutions, was Irish society that unlike the English? Certainly two big differences between England and Ireland were the latter's predominantly rural way of life, and its Roman Catholicism and dominance by priests. While intellectuals like the Young Irelanders were concerned about the Anglicization of Ireland in political and cultural terms, what was more relevant to the mostly rural population was that the way the law was structured caused them economic and social hardship. Rather than being concerned about preserving what remained of a distinct or unique culture, was Irish nationalism more to do with a reaction against the perception of being badly and unjustly governed? Perhaps so, but there were those in the Dublin nationalist press who were unequivocal in their belief that as England and Ireland were distinct nations, Ireland should have complete control over her own destiny. After the political failures of 1848, though, the constitutional nationalist journalists accepted that independence was not achievable in the short term.

Despite the suppression of all the advanced Irish nationalist newspapers in Dublin during the summer of 1848, many journalists associated with

[3] Duffy, *Two Hemispheres, II*, pp. 3–4.
[4] Duffy, *Two Hemispheres, II*, pp. 2–3.

these papers who had experienced prison life did not cease to support their cause through the press, and continued to do so from 1849. While some of them, like Duffy, would revert to constitutional nationalism, others would pursue the path of advanced nationalism. One such was James Fintan Lalor, who was possessed of an almost obsessive belief that a newspaper was essential to disseminate his views, and hoped thus to gain support for his critique of aristocratic landlordism in Ireland. After his release from prison in November 1848, Lalor was still determined to fight for the Irish nationalist cause, both as a journalist and as a revolutionary conspirator. He sought Duffy's assistance in launching a new advanced nationalist newspaper to accompany his participation in an emerging conspiratorial movement.[5] Following Duffy's refusal to be involved, with help from the future Fenian, Thomas Clarke Luby, Lalor persisted in trying to establish his new nationalist newspaper, which he named *The Public Press*.[6] He was also assisted by Stephen Joseph Meany, a former contributor to *The Irish Tribune* who had been imprisoned for his suspected participation in the rebel activities in 1848.[7] In the middle of September 1849, though, both the newspaper project and the conspiracy suffered failure, not least due to the leadership rivalry between Lalor and Joseph Brenan, the latter also a former writer for *The Irish Felon*. Following these setbacks Lalor again wrote to Duffy, and in a mood of pessimism about the future of the nationalist cause, commented: 'The coffin-lid has closed on the last hope of the living generation.'[8] Nonetheless, Lalor asked Duffy if he could now write for *The Nation* despite their opposing political views. According to Luby, Duffy's reply was 'favourable,' but it appears that the political gulf between them was too wide.[9] When Duffy reissued *The Nation* that September he conducted his paper, along with the new Irish Alliance that it represented, on moderate constitutional lines. Believing, in opposition to Duffy, that the militant approach was the only way forward for Irish nationalism,

---

[5] Letter from Lalor to Duffy, Duffy, *Two Hemispheres, I*, pp. 315–6.

[6] 'Mr. James F. Lalor. "The Public Press"', *The Limerick and Clare Examiner*, 4 Aug. 1849; 'The new national weekly journal. Public Meeting', *Limerick and Clare Examiner*, 11 Aug. 1849. See also: *The Irish Nation* (New York), 31 Dec. 1881, in Thomas P. O'Neill, 'Fintan Lalor and the 1849 movement', *An Cosantoir: The Irish defence journal*, vol. 10 (4), April 1950, p. 174.

[7] In 1843–44 Meany had an influential editorial position on *The Freeman's Journal* where he was known as 'O'Connell's Reporter': John Savage, *Fenian Heroes and Martyrs. Edited, with an historical introduction on "The Struggle for Irish Nationality"* (Boston: Patrick Donahoe, 1868), pp. 232 and 239.

[8] Letter from Lalor to Duffy, 28 Sept. 1849, Duffy Papers, NLI, MS 5757/215–6.

[9] Luby's letter to the Editor, *Irishman*, 23 Feb. 1850.

Lalor consulted Luby about establishing what would have been a rival organization to the Irish Alliance. In conversation with Edward Keatinge, a former Confederate, Lalor had reportedly told him: 'I will CRUSH THE ALLIANCE in a month; it is sinking fast into *O'Connellism*.'[10] This comment indicated how far Duffy had now moved the political direction of *The Nation*. Determined to oppose this course, Lalor asked another future Fenian, John O'Leary, to assist him in 'setting up a paper on more advanced lines than those of the new *Nation*'; but Lalor died in December 1849 before it got under way.[11] Although suffering from ill health, Lalor's resolve to fight for his cause during 1848–49 was unbounded. Importantly, despite a comparatively limited involvement with Irish nationalist journalism, what Lalor unwittingly bequeathed to posterity in the Dublin press has given him an iconic place in Irish nationalist history.

Lalor belonged to the movement that evolved out of the 1848 attempted insurrection, which ushered in the formation of secret revolutionary societies. They amalgamated in the following year when plans were formed for a simultaneous rising in several places on 16 September 1849. The leading participants involved in this venture were mostly journalists and, besides Lalor, included Irish Confederates Joseph Brenan, Philip Gray, Thomas Clarke Luby and John O'Leary. One of the most indefatigable leaders of this group was Gray, secretary of the Swift Confederate Club. After the suspension of habeas corpus in July 1848, and accompanied by fellow Confederate John Savage, Gray joined the future leader of the Fenian Brotherhood John O'Mahony in the Comeragh Mountains. In the south of Ireland Gray organized an association based on European secret societies and, owing to his success in recruiting the peasantry, the rebel leaders decided to stage a rebellion in 1849. Their main encounter was at Cappoquin, Co. Waterford, when it was reported that conspirators unsuccessfully attempted to attack a police barracks.[12] Compared with the mass of written work by contemporaries and historians alike on the events surrounding the 1848 attempted rebellion, much less is known of the 1849 conspiracy. But it was out of this secret nationalist movement that Fenianism grew. Notably, in the mid-1850s Luby and Gray were to be involved with the publication of *The Tribune*, ostensibly the first Fenian newspaper in Ireland, and in the

---

10 Luby's letter to the Editor, *Irishman*, 23 Feb. 1850.

11 John O'Leary, *Recollections of Fenians and Fenianism, vol. I*, (London: Downey & Co., 1896), p. 42; reprinted with intro. by Marcus Bourke (Shannon: Irish University Press, 1969).

12 *Limerick and Clare Examiner*, 22 Sept. 1849. The Cappoquin incident received only sparse and conflicting eyewitness coverage in the provincial and Dublin press.

early 1860s Luby and O'Leary were to become leading writers for the IRB's paper, *The Irish People.*

Joseph Brenan, one of the 1849 conspirators, was fully involved in nationalist journalism while immersed in revolutionary activities. During an imprisonment for suspected participation in the 1848 rising, Brenan had contributed prose and poetry to *The Irishman*, a new weekly newspaper first issued on 6 January 1849, costing 6d, which was to last less than a year and a half. Following his release from Newgate that March (when the suspension of habeas corpus was lifted), until a hasty departure to America after the failure at Cappoquin, Brenan became the paper's editor, and with some ex-Confederate associates he strove 'to kindle anew the smouldering fires of nationality in the hearts of his compatriots.'[13] There appears to be no evidence to suggest, however, that Bernard Fullam, *The Irishman*'s proprietor, was actively involved in the '49 conspiracy. Brenan, though, foreshadowed future Fenian strategy by using the press as a vehicle to influence public opinion while covertly planning an insurrection against the British government.

Although vehemently denied by Bernard Fullam, Charles Gavan Duffy, imprisoned when *The Irishman* began, was convinced that Fullam wanted the public to believe that his new paper was a reissue of the suppressed *Nation*. Originally entitled *The National* and published from *The Nation*'s office, where the latter paper's subscribers and country agents were solicited for its sale, Duffy thought that Fullam wished to take over *The Nation*'s old circulation.[14] In fact, several reviews from other newspapers compared the quality of *The Irishman* favourably with *The Nation*.[15] Issuing a warrant for Fullam's arrest before its publication, the government also believed that his paper was to be a reprise of the 1848 *Nation*, until convinced by Fullam that it would not advocate physical force policies. However, though *The Irishman* was not initially an advanced nationalist paper, it became more daring in its tone after a few months, especially when Joseph Brenan assumed editorial control. From the autumn of 1849, when *The Irishman* came to represent the IDA, its language became even more extreme. Increasingly veering towards a revolutionary tone, *The Irishman* was, by then, beginning to resemble the suppressed *Nation*.

In January 1849, despite Fullam's protestations that his paper was not *The Nation* under another name, *The Irishman* commenced its short life by

---

13 'Joseph Brenan by [Young Irelander] Michael Cavanagh', Young Ireland Papers (I), NLI, MS 3225.

14 Duffy, *Two Hemispheres, I*, pp. 310–11.

15 '"The Irishman." Opinions of the Press', *Irishman*, 13 Jan. 1849.

trying to re-ignite the spirit of *The Nation*'s early days that had inspired so many people. Until that September, unlike the Dublin nationalist papers earlier in the decade, *The Irishman* did not initially support or advocate the formation of a nationalist organization. Despite its wish to fill the void left by the defeat of 'the true-hearted nationalists of '48' and the silence of their press, *The Irishman* did nothing more than encourage the people to establish reading rooms and form associations to discuss Irish nationalism.[16] Thomas Davis and John Mitchel were to provide the main focus of these groups; for instance, *The Irishman* asked its readers to consider 'What is Nationality? ... that fired the muse of DAVIS – that nerved the soul of MITCHEL.'[17] *The Irishman* especially extolled the nationalist virtues of Mitchel, saying: 'He will live enshrined and cherished with the memories of our purest martyrs.'[18] The paper's focus on Mitchel reflects the ambivalent nature of *The Irishman.* While it adopted Mitchel's radical social policies and was highly critical of constitutional methods for furthering Irish nationalism, *The Irishman* did not openly preach revolutionary politics and occasionally even warned against physical force. The role of *The Irishman* up to that September was essentially educational, encouraging people not to forget the Young Irelanders, and keeping Irish nationalism alive by reproducing selective sentiments and ideas from both *The Nation* and *The United Irishman.*

With the imprisonment or flight of many Confederates and the devastating impact of the Great Famine, hope of a political revolution was completely untenable at the beginning of 1849. Though recognizing that any advance in the nationalist movement would be a slow process, *The Irishman* refused to lose hope in the idea of the Irish nation for 'While a remnant of that Nation exists, it has deep within it the elements of resuscitation.' Reminiscent of Davis's dictum in *The Nation*, 'Educate, that you may be free,' *The Irishman* believed that the principle of education, linked to its encouragement of discussion forums, was the key to unlocking 'a heritage of chains.'[19]

In keeping with the need for education, and echoing *The Nation*'s promotion of culture, *The Irishman* urged the recovery and the creation of an Irish national literature. Looking back to the past, *The Irishman* spoke of the importance of the songs of the bards of old, who represented defiance against alien rule. The threat they had posed to the government, claimed

16 1st LA, *Irishman*, 7 April 1849.
17 3rd LA, *Irishman*, 31 March 1849.
18 1st LA, *Irishman*, 31 March 1849.
19 Article with this title, *Nation*, 5 Oct. 1844; 2nd LA, *Irishman*, 13 Jan. 1849.

The Irishman, resulted in the extirpation of the 'tinkling harp-strings of Celtic patriots.'[20] The music and songs of the bards was a poignant theme of Irish nationalist newspapers, not least for their powers in stirring emotions. Denis Holland, for example, proprietor and editor of the 1858 *Irishman*, in an emotive celebratory article, saw the bards intimately linked to the life of the Irish nation: 'Our glorious music, the purest and most distinctive token of our nationality, is still preserved amongst us – indestructible whilst the Irish race itself exists upon the earth – living like an immortal fire kept ever burning on the altar of a nation's hopes.' The 1858 *Irishman* adopted a more optimistic approach than its earlier namesake, for even though the 'sweet songsters and patriot martyrs' were dead, the very existence of their music will survive as long as the Irish people live.[21]

Lamenting the loss of the bards, the 1849 *Irishman* saw their disappearance to be synonymous with a dying language and a dying nationality. Just when nineteenth-century models of nationalism focused on language, the use of Gaelic was dramatically decreasing in Ireland. Thomas Davis had certainly seen language as an essential component of nationality, bringing a uniqueness to the people of a country, and *The Irishman* reiterated this idea: 'The identity, the independence, the very existence of a nation, is intimately connected with its language.'[22] Although most Irish nationalists in the mid-nineteenth century accepted that the Irish language was now irretrievable for everyday use, the idea of its loss and recovery had its place in Irish nationalist rhetoric. *The Irishman* stated, for example that 'Though they [tyrants] crush a nation, though they slaughter, exile, or enslave its people and parcel out its fair fields to the instruments of their guilt – it is not enough – they are never satisfied – they never feel secure, till they have exterminated its language.'[23] Irish nationalists believed that it was something else the conquerors had taken away in the continuous stripping of the Irish nation. Thus the revival of the Irish language was encouraged by *The Irishman*:

> we are proud to say this Gaelic speech of ours is not extinct. It was, like every other Irish thing, long a proscribed rebel … Give us one who learns, or *attempts* to learn, the Irish language (and of such

---

20 4th LA, *Irishman*, 3 Feb. 1849.

21 'Ireland's Mighty Dead. The Bards', *Irishman*, 4 Sept. 1858. S.C. Lanier argues that the harp, used as a nationalist political symbol from the 1790s, is devalued as a musical instrument in its own right as part of Ireland's heritage: S.C. Lanier, '"It is New-Strung and Shan't be Heard": Nationalism and Memory in the Irish Harp Tradition', *British Journal of Ethnomusicology*, vol. 8, 1999, pp. 1–26.

22 'A Nation's Language', *Irishman*, 27 Oct. 1849.

23 'A Nation's Language', *Irishman*, 27 Oct. 1849.

> there are thousands), and you give us a patriot … We say *attempts* to learn; for if he acquires a few phrases or words, and is proud of them, it is enough; the raw material of nationality is in him, and it will be manufactured some day.[24]

While *The Irishman* accepted the use of the English language, Gaelic was not forgotten; promoting the recovery of the Irish language continued the age-old defiance against British rule and was also a way of preserving what was left of Irish nationality.

The importance of keeping the Irish language alive was reflected later in the decade when the Society for the Promotion and Cultivation of the Irish Language was founded in 1858. The Society had two main objectives. Studying Irish would provide 'an intimate acquaintance with the grand History and exalted Literature of this long oppressed land,' particularly desired by Irish nationalist journalists; there would also be an opportunity for Ireland's youth to 'acquire the mastery of their native tongue.'[25] When the Society sought William Smith O'Brien's 'patronage and approval,' his positive response in a letter of 3 August 1858 was printed in *The Irishman*; he stressed the importance of the Society's work, remarking that 'To those who desire to preserve the vestiges of our nationality this study is the more indispensable because the time is fast approaching when Irish will no longer be spoken as a vernacular language.'[26] Furthermore, Smith O'Brien's advocacy in the 1858 *Nation* of a revival of Gaelic was received with a positive response from Irish nationalists.[27] That year a 'Gaelic Department' appeared in *The Nation* featuring literary items and even lessons in the Gaelic language. Towards the end of the nineteenth century, in a literary renaissance, the revival and encouragement of the use of Ireland's native language was promoted by the Gaelic League, founded in July 1893, which became a significant expression of Irish nationalism. While not suggesting that there was a literary revival in the 1850s, in the absence of any formidable nationalist political activity in this decade and in the 1890s, whether constitutional or revolutionary, it was an alternative expression of rebellion against the English and an assertion of national identity. And, of course, nationalist newspapers provided valuable publicity and encouragement in promoting the Irish language.

---

[24] 'A Nation's Language', *Irishman*, 27 Oct. 1849.

[25] 'Address of the Provisional Committee of the Society for the Promotion and Cultivation of the Irish Language', 23 July 1858, *Irishman*, 31 July 1858.

[26] 'The Irish Language', *Irishman*, 21 Aug. 1858.

[27] For example, Letter from George Archdeacon to Smith O'Brien, 31 Aug. 1858, William Smith O'Brien Papers, NLI, MS 446/3061.

In line with the study of Gaelic, and following Davis's belief that apart from language, history and literature also defined nationality, the 1849 *Irishman* stressed that to promote a sense of Irish nationalism, people needed knowledge of:

> The various races who inhabited, and inhabit our island – their origin and chronicles – their dwellings and dress – their habits and dispositions, and particular influences on our national character at present, all are as yet either wholly overlooked, or only partially investigated. Our history is still waiting to be rescued from alien calumny, and from native prejudice – our annals, and scenery, and genius, stand forth teeming with romance and poetry, as tender, magnificent, and varied as our climate.[28]

Searching the past to rediscover the history and culture of Ireland was intended not only to legitimize the existence of an Irish inheritance and justify the campaign fought by Irish nationalist journalists, but also to demonstrate that the difference between the races of England and Ireland entitled the Irish to rule themselves. Arising from this standpoint a cultural distinction was drawn by *The Irishman* between England and Ireland, a ploy often used by the Irish nationalist press during the heyday of the Repeal campaign.

Going hand in hand with differences between the two countries in relation to their respective cultures was the formation of a person's character, which can be associated with environment and lifestyle. Irish nationalists wished to emphasize their belief that the people of England and Ireland each possessed distinct characteristics. Echoing Daniel O'Connell's Repeal campaign rhetoric, which was reaffirmed by *The Nation*, *The Irishman* saw a significant distinction between the characteristics of the English and the Irish, the industrialization of the former and the ruralization of the latter. Extolling Young Ireland's idealization of the Irish peasant, which was to be rekindled in the Gaelic Revival around the turn of the century, *The Irishman* believed that:

> A true love of freedom – an energy as powerful as their rushing streams – a spirit as stern as their tall mountains – these characteristics, from the days of HOMER to the present day, have distinguished those engaged in the care and tillage of land. And in the present day, when we see the difference between an Irish

---

[28] 4th LA, *Irishman*, 3 Feb. 1849.

> peasant, generous, good-humoured, frank, and fearless, and the brutalised, debased, and stupid denizens of English large cities, we cannot much regret that the bulk of our population is removed from the influences which tended to this result.[29]

The Irishman was drawing a distinction between what it deemed to be the low quality of life in British cities compared to the seemingly purer way of life of the rural Irish. According to *The Irishman*, it was not only the Irish people's environment that informed their behaviour and made them different from the English, but also characteristics inherited from the Celt; for example, *The Irishman* was 'indebted' to the Celt 'for our tenacity of Nationality, and spirit of resistance against oppression – a spirit indomitable because inextinguishable,' unlike the Saxons, who were passive when overthrown by the Normans.[30] From *The Irishman*'s perspective, praising the Irish character while denigrating the English, showing not only the difference between the two nationalities but the superiority of the Irish, further justified Ireland's independence.

The Nation's sense of a holistic nationalism in terms of the combination of politics and culture was also an important creed for *The Irishman*. It pointed out that while desiring a political separation from England, 'If we be foreign in our thoughts, foreign in our habits, foreign in our institutions, it matters little where the Legislature sits.'[31] In other words, cultural and political nationalism were inseparable. The first number of *The Irishman* in January 1849 stated that its principles could be summed up as '*Ireland for the Irish*,' one of those phrases used time and again by Irish nationalists (such as Daniel O'Connell in his speeches and Mitchel in *The Nation* and *The United Irishman*) epitomizing Irish nationalist aspirations.[32] *The Irishman* wanted, for example:

> the labour of Ireland to enrich Ireland and no other country – the wealth of Ireland to strengthen and nourish Ireland, and *not* England and her colonies – the Art of Ireland to adorn Ireland, and *not* English Houses of Parliament and English saloons – the rents which have sprung from the sweat of Ireland to be spent *in* Ireland, not at Derby, gambling, and in London, *the dansants* [tea dances] – the land of Ireland to feed, and clothe, and belong to

[29] 3rd LA, *Irishman*, 21 April 1849.
[30] 1st LA, *Irishman*, 10 March 1849.
[31] 3rd LA, *Irishman*, 20 Jan. 1849.
[32] A short introductory item placed before 1st LA, *Irishman*, 6 Jan. 1849.

> the people of Ireland, and not to feed, and clothe, and belong to Irish absentees and English Jews.[33]

This was the kind of argument that had influenced Duffy's firm stand against Federalism in 1844, justifying the need for Irish political sovereignty. Even if Ireland did possess its own culture, its own way of life, in qualifying for nationhood *The Irishman* was adamant that it must legislate for itself. An analogy was drawn with Scotland, which had its 'native genius, native art, native manufactures … and yet is not a nation … True Nationality … owes no allegiance to English-made laws.'[34] Having a separate cultural identity was not enough to qualify as a nation; nationhood had to include political autonomy.

In 1849, when Irish independence seemed as far away as ever, inspired by John Mitchel, *The Irishman* chose to appeal to society's lower classes in trying to achieve this goal. Taking its cue from Mitchel's paper, *The Irishman* championed the rights of the poorer classes, a policy that was developed throughout 1849 and into 1850.[35] Notwithstanding *The United Irishman* and the other rebel papers that followed its rhetoric in 1848, and the Chartist and nationalist aspirations of *The Irish National Guard* in that same year, *The Irishman* was the first Irish nationalist newspaper to focus on engaging the lower classes and place them at the heart of Irish nationalist aspirations. This plan was to be achieved through its connection with the IDA, into which the views of *The Irishman* were channelled.[36] The IDA was an urban-based organization in Ireland and Great Britain whose aims included

> The elevation of the character and condition of the working classes, so that our artisans may understand their true value; and the tiller of the soil, on whom all are dependent, his just and indefeasible

---

33 1st LA, *Irishman*, 7 April 1849.

34 2nd LA, *Irishman*, 16 June 1849.

35 See, for example: 1st LA, *Irishman*, 5 May 1849.

36 Vincent Geoghegan offers a very brief but interesting discussion on *The Irishman* and the IDA in 'The emergence and submergence of Irish socialism, 1821–51', in D. George Boyce, Robert Eccleshall and Vincent Geoghegahn (eds.), *Political Thought in Ireland since the Seventeenth Century* (London & New York: Routledge, 1993), pp. 113–7. Michael Huggins suggests that the Irish Universal Suffrage Association, founded by Irish Chartists in 1841, was a forerunner of the Irish Democratic Association, and he viewed the 1849–50 *Irishman* (as well as the 1848 *Irish National Guard*) as a Chartist newspaper: Huggins, 'Democracy or nationalism?' in Allen, Ashton (eds.), *Papers for the People*, pp. 129–43.

> claim to live happily on the land he has made productive by the sweat of his brow.

Echoing the policy 'Ireland for the Irish,' the IDA also intended to encourage 'Native Manufacture, and to lay down a plan for the revival of Irish trade' while also developing 'Irish talent, and the diffusion of a literature.'[37] *The Irishman*'s proprietor, Bernard Fullam, was prominent in founding the IDA in opposition to Duffy's new moderate, essentially middle class-led nationalist group, the Irish Alliance, which had been established following the reissue of *The Nation*. Tensions between these two groups were played out in *The Nation* and *The Irishman*, where they both had key roles in influencing and articulating their respective policies.

Even though Lalor and Mitchel were unable to bring about a social revolution and instead each attempted a political revolution, *The Irishman* and the IDA retrieved this mantle and, like them, initially sought a social revolution. If successful, this change in society would be followed by a political revolution transforming Ireland into a democratic and independent nation. In seeking to help the rural lower classes, central to *The Irishman* were theories and policies relating to the land that originated from Lalor and Mitchel, which its journalists readily adopted. In early September 1849 a leading article in *The Irishman* noted:

> MITCHEL first directed his attention to the land question. His pen made its importance understood. It taught us that the freedom of Ireland should be struggled for, not 'on the floor of the House,' but amid the golden corn. It proved to us that a social revolution should precede a political one – that we should destroy landlordism before we could overthrow imperialism. The former supported the latter, and, therefore, we should remove the one before we could rid the country of the other.[38]

Joseph Brenan was prominent in disseminating the views of his hero, Mitchel, especially when he assumed the editorship of *The Irishman*. For example, in a personal appeal 'To the People of Ireland,' following the Mitchelite argument from *The United Irishman* in relation to the Great Famine, Brenan attacked the premise of the political economists that Ireland had 'a surplus population.'[39] Lalor's thoughts in connection with

[37] 'Objects of the Irish Democratic Association', *Irishman*, 12 Jan. 1850.
[38] 1st LA, *Irishman*, 8 Sept. 1849.
[39] 1st LA, *Irishman*, 21 April 1849.

the land also had a high profile in *The Irishman*, where, for example, a leading article in April 1849 claimed: 'The soil of this island, called Ireland, all thereon, from the sod to the sky, belongs to the *people* of that island. It may be in the hands of the few, but it is the property of the many.'[40] Some of Mitchel's land arguments had been derived from Lalor before their appearance in *The Irish Felon*; Mitchel popularized them through *The United Irishman*, demanding the removal of Irish landlordism and the establishment of a peasant proprietary. *The Irishman* adopted similar arguments and objectives when discussing tenant right, a topic that was increasingly occupying the thoughts of Irish nationalists during 1849. However, while more specifically political issues, mainly the independence from Great Britain, were secondary concerns, by early 1850, although still campaigning for tenant right, it had become clear to *The Irishman* that 'It is idle to think of adjusting the land question, before we have asserted the independence of Ireland.'[41]

The Irishman's policies became more clearly focused and increasingly appealed to the lower classes with the founding of the IDA, whose many working-class members had belonged to the old Confederate Clubs. Arguments presented by *The Irishman* before the establishment of the IDA were now reiterated with more conviction and authority, such as a repudiation of 'the rotting influence of that which has been baptised "constitutional agitation"' and, more importantly, an appeal to the people to help themselves, an echo of the early *Nation*'s concept of self-reliance that was expressed in the phrase 'Ourselves Alone.'[42] But while *The Nation* saw this concept as inclusive, *The Irishman* believed there could be no reliance on past failed leaders and their organizations, urging only the lower classes to follow the path of 'Ourselves Alone,' for 'With this motto on our banners, what force shall impede our march to victory!'[43] In his *United Irishman*, John Mitchel had praised the value of the lower classes in a political movement:

> The tradesmen, and the labourers, and the farmers [i.e. small farmers], and the able-bodied paupers, are the men to lead: they led in Paris; they were, and will for ever be, the beginning, and middle, and end, the bone and muscle, nerve and spirit, aye, and heart and

---

[40] 1st LA, *Irishman*, 28 April 1849; although unacknowledged, this rhetoric is similar to: 'Mr. Lalor's letter. To the editor of "The Irish Felon"', *Irish Felon*, 24 June 1848.

[41] 2nd LA, *Irishman*, 12 Jan. 1850.

[42] 1st LA, *Irishman*, 5 Jan. 1850; for example, 'Ourselves alone', *Nation*, 3 Dec. 1842.

[43] 3rd LA, *Irishman*, 12 Jan. 1850.

> brain, of *any* great national movement, here and everywhere. Yes, our hope is in the People and the People alone.[44]

The idea in modern Irish nationalism of only depending on the power of the lower classes, originating with Mitchel, who was inspired by Wolfe Tone's reliance on '*the Men of No Property*,' was extended and popularized by *The Irishman* and the IDA.[45] Testimony to the composition of IDA members can be verified by reports of meetings; for example, the Secretary of a Dublin meeting in February 1850 claimed that 'the working men were the soul and sinew of that Association.'[46]

Evolving out of a concern for the lower classes, *The Irishman* turned increasingly to socialist rhetoric to lead the IDA, an approach which differentiated it even more from Duffy's reissued *Nation*. Terminology such as 'the *poor* man's rights' and 'grinding capitalist' characterized this strand of Irish nationalism, and while 'English tyranny' had to be rooted out, so had the 'tyrant of wealth.'[47] Striving for Irish independence, *The Irishman* was influenced by what it perceived as socialist rhetoric in *The United Irishman*. Despite a denial by Mitchel that 'we have never, in this journal, preached any of the systems which are called in France Socialism, Communism, Fourierism, St. Simonism,' he 'denounced the tyranny of Capital over Industry.'[48] Interpreting Mitchel's rhetoric in *The United Irishman* as supporting socialism, *The Irishman* claimed that 'JOHN MITCHEL clearly developed the doctrines of the Socialist catechism' seeing 'Socialism' as 'a protest against the existing system of society' where 'the good of the many is sacrificed to the miserable aggrandizement of the few.'[49] Socialism as preached by the 1849–50 *Irishman* was associated with improving and protecting the livelihoods of the lower classes from what were seen as oppressive laws of a foreign government. This thinking anticipated the work of Michael Davitt, architect of the 1879 Land League, and also James Connolly, one of the signatories of the 1916 Proclamation, who extensively used the press to propagate his socialist and nationalist doctrines. Connolly, a follower of Marx, believed that nationalism and

---

[44] 4th LA, *United Irishman*, 4 March 1848.

[45] Wolfe Tone's well-known rhetoric was printed every week before the leading articles of *The United Irishman*: 'Our independence must be had at all hazards. If the men of property will not support us, they must fall: we can support ourselves by the aid of that numerous and respectable class of the community, *the Men of No Property*.'

[46] IDA mtg., 18 Feb. 1850, *Irishman*, 23 Feb. 1850.

[47] 2nd LA, *Irishman*, 6 April 1850.

[48] 3rd LA, *United Irishman*, 29 April 1848.

[49] 1st LA, *Irishman*, 25 May 1850.

socialism were inseparable; in *The Harp* newspaper, which he edited, Connolly stated: 'Nationalism without Socialism – without a reorganization of society on the basis of a broader and more developed form of that common property which underlay the social structure of Ancient Erin – is only national recreancy.'[50] Another article in this newspaper contended 'that Socialism will lead to the highest, the purest, the holiest form of nationality.'[51] In *The Harp* Connolly paid tribute to the Dublin nationalist newspapers of the mid-nineteenth century, which included the 1849–50 *Irishman*.[52]

The ideological shift of *The Irishman* from a somewhat ambivalent constitutional position to an increasingly more extreme nationalist stance was sharpened from September 1849, which coincided with the reissue of *The Nation*. Constitutional nationalism was increasingly attacked by *The Irishman*, implying that militant nationalism was the only route to social and political justice for Ireland. Many years later, Fenian John O'Leary aptly remembered *The Irishman* as being 'not avowedly revolutionary, but neither could it be considered exactly legal and constitutional, and controversial it certainly was.'[53] The revived *Nation*, with its old formidable reputation to rely on, and a high-profile editor who had been in prison for Ireland (well publicized with O'Connell in 1844 and latterly) meant that *The Irishman* was faced with strong competition. Journalists on *The Irishman* now adopted a consistently more rebellious tone to compete with *The Nation*. An article in October 1849 stated that 'The true patriot is only he who gives his life for his country, on scaffold or battle-field.'[54] In line with this policy, at the first main meeting of the IDA on 5 March 1850, Andrew English, the organization's secretary, implored its members 'to abstain from Parlia-

[50] James Connolly, *Shan Van Vocht*, ['1896' crossed out later by hand and replaced with] Jan. 1897, reprinted in 'Socialism and Nationalism', *The Harp*, March 1909. *The Harp* was published monthly in New York from January 1908 to November 1909 and distributed throughout the United States, Canada, Ireland and Great Britain; from January to June 1910 it was published in Dublin. Connolly established the Irish Socialist Republican Party in 1896.

[51] [Details of original article added by hand:] 'Eoin', *The Irish Nation*, 19 June 1909, reprinted in 'How to Realise the Ideals of Thomas Davis', *Harp*, July 1909. A discussion of Connolly's views on nationalism and socialism are included in an essay by Richard English, 'Reflections on Republican Socialism in Ireland: Marxian Roots and Irish Historical Dynamics', *History of Political Thought*, vol. 17 (4), Winter 1996, pp. 555–70.

[52] James Connolly, 'Labour in Irish history', *Harp*, April and May 1910. Published in book form with the same title (Dublin: Maunsel & Co., 1910). Several editions have since followed.

[53] O'Leary, *Recollections*, *I*, p. 34.

[54] 2nd LA, *Irishman*, 20 Oct. 1849.

mentary agitation of every description' and to 'follow in the steps of John Mitchel and Thomas Francis Meagher.'[55] This daring rhetoric was mirrored in the recently established local branches of the IDA. For example, at a Cork Branch meeting on 15 April the chairman stated, 'Let no man join us who is not willing to sacrifice all that life holds dear, and who is not prepared, should the contingency arrive, to assert the rights of his country by the strength of his arm.'[56] With language of this nature, *The Irishman* and the IDA seemed to be moving towards adopting a revolutionary policy.

There was, however, a contradictory stance conveyed by *The Irishman* in relation to physical force. One leading article, for instance, while presenting strident Lalorite and Mitchelite arguments about the land rights of the lower classes, protected itself against prosecution by adding: 'I do not advise you to commit any illegality.'[57] This position was also reflected at an IDA meeting on 29 April 1850, when its 'Report on Organization' stated that 'prudence counsels us to keep within the law'; there was to be no rash physical force action.[58] The objective of *The Irishman* and the IDA was 'to convert the masses to Democratic principles, and to organize them into a dense, compact, and solid point, whether for resistance or attack,' believing, 'the way to prevent bloodshed is to make our movement so strong that it would be madness in oppression to hazard a battle.'[59]

In accomplishing this aim, the IDA was determined to include Ulster in its organization. As a leading article in *The Irishman* stated: 'we, Democrats, do not necessarily contemplate an armed insurrection; so far from it, we are persuaded that, when we shall have wound Orange Ulster and Catholic Ireland into a solid bond of fraternal friendship, cemented by mutual interests, not a blow shall be necessary.'[60] Taking its cue from Mitchel, *The Irishman* appealed for a union with the lower-class Protestants of Ulster. In keeping with this policy, echoing Thomas Davis, the IDA's rules were intended to preclude sectarian strife, for all creeds were to be respected.[61] Along with this thinking, there was to be no campaign for 'the destruction of the Church Establishment [i.e. the Protestant Church of Ireland]; with this our Association will not meddle – our object being union of creeds, and believing that the agitation of the same will only keep alive those bigoted

---

[55] *Irishman*, 9 March 1850.
[56] *Irishman*, 20 April 1850.
[57] 1st LA, *Irishman*, 12 May 1849.
[58] *Irishman*, 4 May 1850.
[59] 1st LA, *Irishman*, 27 April 1850.
[60] 1st LA, *Irishman*, 18 May 1850.
[61] 1st LA, *Irishman*, 23 March 1850.

hostilities.'[62] Again this mirrored Mitchel's policy of urging unity of creed for the advancement of Irish nationalism; and as we saw earlier, unity of creed had also been desired by other Young Irelanders and Daniel O'Connell for the progress of the Repeal movement. In an address to the working classes of Ulster, *The Irishman* told them: 'A social and political union involves no sacrifice of religious principle, and we ask you to make none … let us bind heart to heart in one long coil, folding itself round every corner of our island, and Ireland is safe.'[63] A conclusion can be drawn that, while not completely dismissing physical force tactics, any seemingly revolutionary rhetoric of *The Irishman* was related more to the image of the IDA, wishing it to be perceived as a formidable organization that supported the martyrs of '48, and sought independence from Britain by eliciting wide support from the lower classes, both Catholic and Protestant, as a step towards this reality.

One way of encouraging support from the lower classes was to become involved with the burgeoning tenant right groups that were now increasing towards the end of 1849. Both *The Irishman* and *The Nation* competed for a stake in the emerging tenant right movement. These newspapers both advocated that the land issue must be given precedence over anything else, although it was the IDA that initially prioritized this far more than the Irish Alliance. In the autumn of 1849 *The Irishman* had encouraged the establishment of tenant right clubs. Seen as a rallying point and a way of disseminating information, raising funds, and teaching self-reliance they would, suggested *The Irishman*, be 'ultimately subversive of English Rule. With this view, and to this end – the only end worth living or labouring for – we must always keep before us *The Nationality of Ireland!* All our thoughts, and feelings, and hopes, and actions must tend towards this grand consummation.'[64] But it soon became apparent that there could be no possibility of a union between the tenant right groups and the IDA. While the IDA and *The Irishman* saw the tenant right movement as part of a broader vision of Irish nationalism, a step towards independence, the tenant right campaigners were only concerned with a single issue. More importantly, *The Irishman* and the IDA were far too radical in their politics to be able to forge an alliance with a constitutional movement.

The other area of potential alliance with the IDA involved the British Chartists. Following Mitchel's link with them in 1848, *The Irishman* also sought their support.[65] Although this association was tenuous, involving

---

62 'The Democratic Movement', IDA mtg., 5 March 1850, *Irishman*, 9 March 1850.

63 1st LA, *Irishman*, 18 May 1850.

64 1st LA, *Irishman*, 8 Sept. 1849.

65 Early in 1848 John Mitchel promoted co-operation between the Irish Confederates

more rhetoric than action, a commonality existed between the Chartist movement in Britain and the IDA. There was, in fact, a limited co-operation between the two groups; for instance, at a meeting in April 1850 new members of the Liverpool Branch of the IDA included Chartists.[66] The old Confederate Clubs, many of whose members had now become absorbed into the IDA, did have Chartist supporters in their heyday; Young Irelander Richard O'Gorman, Jnr. had warned Smith O'Brien of 'a very violent spirit of Chartism' present in a few clubs which might divert members away 'from Irish business and make them Englishmen in their Policy.'[67] The IDA and Chartism both supported causes that sought to help the lower classes. *The Irishman*, for example, expressed a kindred feeling with the oppressed of England and Scotland, believing them to be common victims of the same tyrannical power, and urged unity with them.[68] Feargus O'Connor, the British Chartist leader, was highly supportive of *The Irishman* and the IDA. Contributing several addresses to *The Irishman*, he encouraged a union between British Chartists and the IDA, whose supporters had become known as the Irish Democrats. Feargus O'Connor, however, was not as radical as *The Irishman*'s writers; in an address to the people of Ireland, he advised against physical force and urged readers to work through constitutional means by organizing local election committees throughout the country.[69]

While the Irish Democrats believed it was advantageous to have British Chartist support and vice versa, there were important demarcations between them over aims and methods. The Irish Democrats refused to engage in constitutional activities, whereas the Charter, the petition to Parliament, itself formed the very essence of the campaign conducted by the British Chartists, although there were some who sought militant means of fulfilling their expectations. Furthermore, whereas Chartists desired more power within their own nation, the Irish Democrats not only wanted more political and social power, but an independent nation. Consequently, even though the Chartist press in Britain, such as *The Northern Star* and *Reynolds's Weekly Newspaper*, supported the IDA and *The Irishman* supported the British Chartists, it was unlikely that an enduring

---

and the Chartists in his newspaper; see for example, 'Movements in England – Chartism', *United Irishman*, 26 Feb. 1848.

[66] *Irishman*, 27 April 1850.

[67] Letter from Richard O'Gorman, Jnr., to Smith O'Brien, [n.d.], Smith O'Brien Papers, NLI, MS 441/2267.

[68] 2nd LA, *Irishman*, 6 April 1850.

[69] 'Original Correspondence. To the Irish People', *Irishman*, 1 Dec. 1849 (but this page misprinted as 31 Nov. 1849).

and meaningful ideological or tactical union could exist between these two agitating movements.[70] Even so, this did not prevent future attempts by English political activists and Irish nationalists seeking an alliance against the British government when circumstances appeared favourable.

In the mid-1860s advanced Irish nationalists were to see an advantage in collaborating with English radicals. Fenian leader James Stephens sent Frank Roney, a prominent IRB member, on a mission in 1865 to contact the British radical, Charles Bradlaugh.[71] A group emerging from the defunct Chartist movement that same year was the English Reform League, campaigning for manhood suffrage and the vote by ballot. Communication was made between IRB members and individual Leaguers with the intention of forming a possible alliance between the two groups.[72] A month after the IRB rising in March 1867 the radical newspaper *The Commonwealth* warned:

> Fenianism, so long as it is confined to Ireland, may excite little or no alarm; but what would become of the ruling powers if the English democracy were to shake hands with the democracy of Ireland. We do not advise it, but we could tell our Tory friends that such a union has been more than hinted at.[73]

While the Reform League sympathized with Irish grievances, physical force remained a major obstacle to a union between the extreme Irish nationalists and the English reformers. Although an Irish Reform League also existed in 1867 and had the same two aims as its English counterpart, this organization operated separately and was even more determined not to become involved in physical force tactics.

Thomas Clarke Luby, who later gained notoriety as a leading member of the Fenian movement in Ireland, was one of *The Irishman*'s writers.

---

[70] The Chartist movement in Britain had a large contingency of Irish members both as supporters and leaders, many of whom were sympathetic to Irish independence. More research needs to be undertaken to establish the extent of Chartism in Ireland and its contribution to the development Irish nationalism.

[71] Frank Roney, *Irish Rebel and California Labor Leader: An Autobiography*, Ira B. Cross (ed.) (Berkeley: University of California Press, 1931), pp. 118–9.

[72] See, for example: John Bedford Leno, *The Aftermath: with Autobiography of the Author* (London: Reeves & Turner, 1892), p. 71. Leno was one of the leaders of the English Reform League.

[73] 'Words of Warning', *The Commonwealth*, 27 April 1867. For more information on the relationship between Fenians and English radicals see: John Newsinger, 'Old Chartists, Fenians, and New Socialists', *Éire-Ireland*, vol. 17 (2), Summer 1982, pp. 19–45.

Luby particularly supported Mitchel's views; he advised the editor of *The Irishman* that Mitchel's 'ideas should be the guiding stars of all our policy.'[74] He also maintained that it was a duty to strive for freedom even if it were to fail, no doubt thinking of his part in the 1849 conspiracy. Luby belonged to the IDA, and fully endorsed its policies and tactics, making his views known in contributions to *The Irishman* early in 1850, which took the form of addresses and letters.[75] In the long-term divide between constitutional nationalism and physical force nationalism, which developed after the dramatic events of 1848, Luby had clearly chosen his path, reflected by his involvement in the '49 conspiracy, his writings in *The Irishman*, his support for the IDA, and his disdain for Duffy's constitutional Irish Alliance.

As both the IDA and the Irish Alliance strived to make headway, considering the IDA's beginnings, it was a feat that this organization achieved so much when taking into account the disadvantages and problems it encountered. Unlike the Irish Alliance, the IDA lacked prominent personnel and resources, and faced opposition from the higher classes and the clergy; for example, the IDA's Barnsley Branch in Yorkshire reported that, according to *The Kilkenny Moderator*, the IDA had been denounced by the Bishop of Kilkenny.[76] Luby remarked on the considerable progress of the IDA compared to that of the Alliance; the latter he saw

> commence its career under the most favourable auspices – cheered on by individuals highly influential and wealthy – individuals who freely support it by purse and patronage. ... I watched the career of those two bodies, and I saw the humble Democrats, gradually at first, and at last rapidly, grow ... without the aid of celebrity, influence, or wealth, steadily and surely gaining ground on the rival Association, and at last threatening to beat it hollow.[77]

---

[74] 'Original Correspondence. Truth versus Trickery – Manhood versus Milk and Water', *Irishman*, 2 Feb. 1850.

[75] According to fellow-Confederate John Savage, Luby was a leading writer for *The Irishman* in 1849 and, following Brenan's escape to America after the Cappoquin incident, he became an editor of that paper: Savage, *Fenian Heroes*, p. 318. However, in his memoirs, written for John O'Leary, Luby does not corroborate this information and only refers to his 1850 'letters' to *The Irishman*: Thomas Clarke Luby Papers, Feb./March 1881, NLI, MS 332. Savage was in New York during *The Irishman*'s existence and may not have been fully aware of Luby's work on it.

[76] Meeting of the 'Barnsley Branch of the Irish Democratic Association', 31 March 1850, *Irishman*, 6 April 1850.

[77] 'The Alliance – The Democratic Association – Ireland's Mission, to the Nationalists

In May 1850 *The Irishman* claimed that the IDA had about 250,000 enrolled members; based only on this evidence it appears that the IDA had a larger following than the forty thousand-odd members of the Irish Confederate Clubs in the summer of 1848.[78]

The progress of the Irish Democrats can be reflected in their meetings, two of which appeared particularly impressive. The first main meeting of the IDA on 5 March 1850 in Dublin's Music Hall, reportedly holding a capacity of 5,000 people, was filled with representatives from various branches; also present were Feargus O'Connor, many ladies, and some members of the 'higher classes.'[79] According to Luby, this first public meeting in Ireland, where the lower classes were not just spectators but also the main speakers, 'was a triumphant success.'[80] That May *The Irishman* further reported a highly impressive IDA demonstration in the provinces at Carrick-on-Suir, Co. Tipperary, reminiscent of the Repeal monster meetings. Despite attempts by the authorities to sabotage the meeting and intimidation by local landlords, the platform observers estimated that 'at least *ten thousand*' persons were present. *The Irishman*'s reporter saw this meeting as signalling 'the people's moral and intellectual progress, which startles and terrifies our enemies, and rekindles the faith and love of every friend of Irish nationality and popular liberty.'[81] And, of course, this had been the initial remit of *The Irishman* – to rekindle Irish nationality in the people after the summer of 1848.

The Irishman, a newspaper that reiterated Mitchelite ideas and, to a certain extent, fulfilled a leadership role, was of paramount importance to the promotion and expansion of the IDA. Its intention was to provide the Irish Democratic movement, composed of the lower classes, with a respectability and a voice. Like the relationship between *The Nation* and the Irish Confederation's clubs, *The Irishman* reported on the establishment of new branches of the IDA, which, in turn, inspired others to follow. The rules of the Association were printed in *The Irishman* providing the basis for the founding of branches.[82] At the formation of a branch in Sligo, for instance, Michael Dowlan 'read the rules and regulations, as printed in the *Irishman*

---

of Ireland', *Irishman*, 2 March 1850.

[78] 1st LA, *Irishman*, 18 May 1850; Gary Owens, 'Popular Mobilization and the Rising of 1848: The Clubs of the Irish Confederation' in Laurence M. Geary, *Rebellion and Remembrance in Modern Ireland* (Dublin: Four Courts Press, 2001), pp. 51 and 55–6.

[79] *Irishman*, 9 March 1850.

[80] Address 'To the Members of the Democratic Association', *Irishman*, 30 March 1850.

[81] 'Great Meeting of the Tipperary Democrats at Carrick-on-Suir', 12 May 1850, *Irishman*, 18 May 1850.

[82] 'Rules of the Irish Democratic Association', *Irishman*, 12 Jan. 1850.

of the 12th of January.'[83] *The Irishman* was also read aloud at the IDA's branch meetings; in Kilkenny, for example, 'Several articles of the *Irishman* were [then] read by different members, and elicited universal applause.'[84] Inspired by *The Irishman*, branches had also been formed in England. In Manchester a 'Democratic Club' was founded in response to the influence of *The Irishman*, a letter from whose members stated: 'The dormant spirit of the men of Manchester is at length aroused by the able teachings of the *Irishman*, under whose guidance alone we can ever hope for the restoration of that spirit of national independence which has been swindled from us by Whigism and O'Connellism.'[85] *The Irishman* also had supporters in Scotland, who informed the paper that 'the Glasgow Democrats retain as their text-book your invaluable journal, the *Irishman*.'[86] By May 1850, according to *The Irishman*, the IDA had also spread over much of Ireland and the north of England. *The Irishman* recognized its own influence in the progress of the IDA, believing it was due to the 'arms' of 'Principles, and a Press.' And in a celebratory note, *The Irishman* announced: 'The harp of Erin is no longer silent; its chords are struck to the wild notes of liberty, by the reverberating voices of an awakened Democracy.'[87]

While *The Irishman* may have been celebrating the success of its mission to place the lower classes at the forefront of Irish nationalism, the reissue of *The Nation*, priced at 6d, in September 1849, had in the meantime been causing financial problems for Fullam's paper. *The Nation*'s appearance presented a serious challenge to *The Irishman*, which gave rise to commercial rivalry, and manifested itself in two main areas of fierce contention. The first battle was related to *The Irishman*'s origin, when Duffy accused Fullam of issuing *The Irishman* under the guise that it was a revived *Nation* in order to boost its sales; this led to an acrimonious volley of invective between *The Irishman* and *The Nation*. Maurice R. Leyne, grand-nephew of Daniel O'Connell and a rebel of '48, working as an unpaid writer on *The Nation*, took it upon himself to argue on Duffy's behalf in relation to *The Irishman*'s origins.[88]

---

[83] Letter from John Gillin to *The Irishman*, 27 April 1850, 'Sligo Branch of the Irish Democratic Association', *Irishman*, 4 May 1850.

[84] Meeting of the 'Kilkenny Branch of the Irish Democratic Association', 28 April 1850, *Irishman*, 4 May 1850.

[85] Letter from 'Members of the Democratic Club' to *The Irishman*, 2 April 1850, 'Democracy in Manchester', *Irishman*, 6 April 1850.

[86] Letter from James Fairley to *The Irishman*, 29 April 1850, 'Glasgow Branch of the Irish Democratic Association', *Irishman*, 4 May 1850.

[87] 1st LA, *Irishman*, 13 April 1850.

[88] Andrew English, the Secretary of the IDA, having a vested interest in the paper

The other theatre of battle was *The Irishman*'s disapproval of *The Nation*'s return to constitutional nationalism. From the start of *The Nation*'s reissue it was unashamedly assailed by *The Irishman*. At the beginning of September 1849, for example, a leading article stated: 'The *Nation* revived is but the ghost of its former self – bloodless and weak. Prison-chains seem to have crippled Mr. DUFFY's right hand … He says, we cannot go back to the armed movement of "48."'[89] Fullam's paper also attacked John O'Connell, who re-opened Conciliation Hall that October with policies not dissimilar to the Irish Alliance. *The Irishman* railed against both of these constitutional groups; one leading article remonstrated: 'We condemn – and all true nationalists must condemn – these two agitating movements.'[90] In line with its attack on *The Nation*'s current policies, to strengthen its argument *The Irishman* cast aspersions on the nationalist loyalties of Duffy and Leyne, accusing both men of betraying the cause in 1848.

But in the battle of words between these two papers, *The Nation*'s evidence attesting to the origin of *The Irishman* and the loyalty of Leyne and Duffy seemed more convincing, and coincided with a downturn in *The Irishman*'s sales.[91] While the growth of the IDA had provided opportunities for more people to access *The Irishman*'s contents, this did not particularly assist the paper's sales, due to shared copies and group reading amongst the IDA's mainly lower-class supporters. Pursuing a more extremist stance from September 1849 and associating with the IDA may have driven away those readers who were able to afford the expensive price of a newspaper and could now turn to the more moderate *Nation*. At the end of the day, *The Irishman* seemed to have lost credibility, reflected by its diminished sales. On 25 May 1850 Fullam announced that the paper was to be suspended as it was no longer financially viable, admitting that the confrontation with Duffy and Leyne in *The Nation* had played a part in this.[92]

---

that was representing his organization, demanded proof of the accusations. Responding to this challenge, Leyne's evidence on 11 May 1850 seemed to prove much of Duffy's case. Fullam, in turn, refuted the charges in a statement that included a denial that his first editor's resignation was due to the identification of Duffy with *The Irishman*. See: 'Answers to Correspondents', *Nation*, 4 May 1850, 'Mr Leyne. To the members of the Irish Democratic Association. Letter second and final', *Nation*, 11 May 1850, 'Mr. Leyne's letter to the Democrats' *Irishman*, 4 & 11 May 1850 and 'Mr. M.R. Leyne's "Charges" and "Proofs"', *Irishman*, 18 May 1850.

89 1st LA, *Irishman*, 1 Sept. 1849. *The Irishman* would have had prior knowledge of the reissued *Nation*'s contents from its prospectus.

90 3rd LA, *Irishman*, 13 Oct. 1849.

91 Letter from Joseph O'Grady '*To the Editor of the Nation*', 27 May 1850, and Duffy's reply, 'The Carrick-On-Suir Democratic Meeting', *Nation*, 1 June 1850.

92 Untitled article from Bernard Fullam, *Irishman*, 25 May 1850.

However, the clash between these two newspapers was as much a difference of opposing ideologies as of personal bitterness and commercial rivalry. *The Irishman* struggled financially after the reissue of *The Nation*, in terms of both sales and advertisement revenue.[93] Fullam was eager for more subscriptions to maintain the solvency of his paper, but could not withstand the competition from *The Nation*, and despite urging members of the IDA to elicit more subscribers, eventually *The Irishman* became insolvent as a commercial enterprise.[94] In 1850 *The Nation*, adhering more than ever to constitutional nationalism, had a prominent role in the temporary eclipse of the advanced nationalist press in Dublin.

The black cloud that hung over the founding of *The Irishman* and its proprietor, Bernard Fullam, cannot detract from the paper's role in keeping alive the spirit of Irish nationalism in 1849 and beyond, and the sincerity of its writers in furthering their nationalist beliefs, many of whom were unpaid for their contributions. Furthermore, at that time the content of *The Irishman* as a newspaper was considered to be of a good standard. Joseph O'Grady, a member of the IDA, but with no direct connection to *The Irishman*, praised the paper for 'its great ability, its language sharp and clear like the ring of a rifle, and the intense earnestness with which it advocated what I conceive to be the only true policy for Ireland.'[95] Bearing in mind that they had a vested interest in the success of *The Irishman*, an issue of the British Chartists' *Reynolds's Weekly Newspaper* commented:

> In its miscellaneous news and intelligence, as also in its literary reviews, its critiques and its correspondence, it is at least equal to any journal that Ireland has heretofore produced, while in point of downright plain-spoken honesty of purpose, and devotedness to the political and social rights of the Irish people, it is without a competitor in the Irish press ... 'Tis a new phase, this, in the history of Ireland! – a real Democratic association! and a real Democratic journal![96]

---

[93] The stamp return for *The Irishman* in 1849 suggests an average weekly circulation of 808, but as there are no quarterly returns for this year it is difficult to properly assess how this paper fared either before or after the reissue of *The Nation*. See: 'Return of Number of Stamps issued at One Penny to Newspapers in United Kingdom, 1837–50', HCP, 1852 (42) XXVIII.497. When looking at these figures we must bear in mind that, at this time, official figures only represented a fraction of those who had access to newspapers.

[94] *The Irishman* was briefly reissued on 10 and 17 Aug. 1850.

[95] 'Mr. O'Grady. To the editor of the Nation', *Nation*, 22 June 1850.

[96] 'The Chartist Press', *Irishman*, 25 May 1850.

In its socialist rhetoric and its promotion of the IDA, *The Irishman* sounded the rights of the lower classes. Notably, *The Irishman* gave the rebels of 1848, such as Brenan, a voice to express their loyalty to the Irish nationalist cause where, dismissing constitutional nationalism, they indicated that the pursuit of physical force had not been forgotten in seeking Irish independence from Britain.

The Dublin nationalist press and the tenant right movement in the 1850s

While *The Irishman* represented the IDA and *The Nation* the Irish Alliance, Dr John Gray's *Freeman* group of newspapers remained the voice of Repeal. *The Freeman* was invaluable to the progress of Irish nationalism in the mid-nineteenth century, not least in the decade following the high drama of 1848. While its rhetoric was far more measured than the advanced Dublin nationalist papers in 1848, thus surviving the turbulence of that year, *The Freeman* continued to be as passionate as ever about the state of Ireland and the Repeal cause. Consequently, in October 1849, when John O'Connell revived the Repeal Association, Dr Gray welcomed its return. In a leading article, however, *The Freeman* gave the Association a cautious affirmation of its ability to succeed, intending to be a stern critic of its progress. *The Freeman* believed that the Repeal Association's potential would give Ireland a desperately needed organization to address 'The neglect of the government, the cruelty of the landlords, the monstrous grievance of the church establishment, the appalling effects of famine and pestilence, with the evils which all these brought in their train.'[97] However, while *The Freeman* wished the Association to succeed there was grave concern that the existence of the rival Irish Alliance would thwart its progress.

Worried about disunity within the Irish nationalist movement, *The Freeman* in fact condemned both John O'Connell's revived Repeal Association and Duffy's Irish Alliance over their rivalry. In a leading article that November *The Weekly Freeman* deplored with 'shame and sorrow' the division being created by these two rival organizations.[98] Disgusted with their undignified behaviour, the following week *The Freeman* likened their quarrel more to 'two urchins fighting for a seat at school, than men struggling for the deliverance of a nation,' implying that they did much to

[97] 1st LA, *Freeman's Journal*, 22 Oct. 1849.

[98] 1st LA, *Weekly Freeman*, 24 Nov. 1849.

lower the tone and dignity of the Irish nationalist cause.[99] *The Freeman*'s chastisement, however, could not overcome the historical animosity between the two groups or its leading protagonists, John O'Connell and Charles Gavan Duffy. However, firmly rooted in constitutional nationalism, *The Nation* was now far tamer than ever before, and there seemed to be much truth in *The Irishman*'s charge that Duffy's paper was 'the ghost of its former self.'[100] It was frustrating for *The Freeman* as both John O'Connell's supporters in the Repeal Association and the members of the Irish Alliance were probably closer in ideology and strategy in this period than they had ever been in the past, even though *The Nation* remained firm in refusing to renounce its stand on the theoretical principle of physical force which had been a central issue in the 1846 secession. However, what the latter months of 1849 demonstrated was that Irish nationalism was in rhetorical fighting form, even if much of it was directed at rival groups within the movement. But an issue that was emerging at this time and was to bring about a rapprochement between Duffy and Gray the following year was the growth of the tenant right movement, when their papers would work together for the same goal.

By the time of Duffy's release from prison in the spring of 1849, after unsuccessful attempts by the government to prosecute him, his priorities had changed. The land issue was to take precedence over Irish independence, and his refusal to become involved with Lalor's newspaper project, intended to support an emerging conspiratorial movement, was indicative of his wish to return to constitutional nationalism.[101] When Duffy turned to what he deemed to be the seemingly more achievable task of dealing with the land problem, this issue became especially more realisable when he began working with others such as the MP William Sharman Crawford, the Federalist and long-suffering proponent of tenant right, and also Frederick Lucas, who, on moving the Catholic paper, *The Tablet*, from London to Dublin in 1850, became more directly involved with the Irish nationalist cause. Neither Sharman Crawford nor Lucas would have worked with Duffy had there been any hint of physical force. Explaining his new direction in a letter to the exiled John Blake Dillon, while emphasizing that he had not abandoned the nationalist cause, Duffy had come to the conclusion 'that extermination and famine have conclusively eradicated all reliance on Irish landlords.'[102] Ironically, this is what Mitchel had been saying at the end of

[99] 3rd LA, *Weekly Freeman*, 1 Dec. 1849.
[100] 1st LA, *Irishman*, 1 Sept. 1849.
[101] Duffy, *Two Hemispheres, I*, pp. 315–7.
[102] Duffy, *Two Hemispheres, II*, p. 6

1847, and was one of the reasons for the founding of his *United Irishman* in opposition to *The Nation*. Shortly after his release from prison, Duffy held a private meeting with other Dublin nationalists whom, he recalled, were unanimous about his suggestion of reissuing *The Nation*. At this meeting Duffy explained his new policy: 'I told them that the protection of the farmers who were flying daily before the Exterminator seemed to me the most urgent business ... For nationality we could do little just now ... Ireland lay in ruins' and would have to be reconstructed very gradually.[103] Pessimistic about achieving an independent Ireland, Duffy now found it more expedient to concentrate on helping the small farmers.

However, even though the land question was a priority for *The Nation* when it was reissued in September 1849, the Irish Alliance, the organization it represented, was a political umbrella under which tenant right was just one of the many issues. This policy was reflected in the initial meeting of the Council of the Irish Alliance that December with the announcement of the formation of seven Committees that represented, amongst others, the Land, the Church Question and the Franchise.[104] Similar to the late Confederate Clubs that had sprung up to support the Irish Confederation, local groups called 'People's Institutes' were formed in Dublin to support the Irish Alliance 'for the purposes of Education and Organization,' which included tasks such as helping to return creditable candidates to municipal and parliamentary elections.[105] The general policy of the Irish Alliance tended towards inclusivity not only in terms of multi-tasking but also in relation to the composition of its supporters.

In contrast to the IDA, membership of the Irish Alliance was intended to include a cross-section of classes. Although essentially led by the middle class, when the council of this new organization was formed in December 1849 it was composed of 'landholders, professional men, tradesmen, and artisans.' The lower classes were included

> to show that the Alliance and the committee were determined that the working men of the city of Dublin should be fairly represented (hear, hear). They did that because they knew that in addition to the generous and noble efforts the artizans [*sic*] had always made for the benefit of the country they would bring practical knowledge

103 Duffy, *Two Hemispheres, II*, pp. 6–7.

104 'The Movement', mtg. 27 Dec. 1849, *Nation*, 5 Jan. 1850.

105 'The Movement. Portobellow People's Institute', mtg. 17 Feb. 1850, *Nation*, 23 Feb. 1850; 'The Movement. Linen-Hall People's Institute', mtg. 12 March 1850, *Nation*, 16 March 1850.

> and experience of the utmost importance into the future deliberations of the council (hear, hear).[106]

Apart from seeking more supporters in building a solid membership base, drawing in the lower classes may have been a ploy to keep them away from the more advanced rhetoric of *The Irishman* and the beginning of the new nationalist group that it represented, the IDA. A battle, in effect, was fought between *The Nation* and *The Irishman* to win the loyalty of the urban lower classes for their respective newspapers and emerging organizations.

By the spring of 1850, however, it was becoming clear to the IDA that *The Irishman*, its representative in the nationalist press, was becoming seriously insolvent. Anxious to safeguard his organization, Andrew English wrote a letter to Duffy. He detailed the progress of the IDA, arguing that as it was more successful than the Irish Alliance – which would not succeed 'without the Democracy' – he invited Duffy and the Irish Alliance to join the IDA.[107] When *The Irishman* collapsed in May 1850 and the IDA was bereft of a representative in the Dublin press, some members of its local clubs drifted to the Irish Alliance. With the IDA's membership now falling, again reflecting the importance of a newspaper's support for a political organization, the Irish Democrats had little choice but to abandon the IDA altogether or to amalgamate their organization with the Irish Alliance, which was represented in the press by the influential *Nation*. As for commonality of interest between the IDA and the Irish Alliance, both were ultimately striving for independence from Great Britain.

Following a conference between these hitherto opposing nationalist groups it was agreed that they should unify, and in August 1850 the Irish Democratic Alliance was formed.[108] What the IDA and the Irish Alliance have shown, especially the former, is that, despite the collapse of the Irish nationalist movement in 1848, the Dublin nationalist press still had the power to persuade numerous people to join nationalist organizations. The new Irish Democratic Alliance, however, was to be eclipsed following *The Nation*'s total involvement in an emerging tenant right movement, which offered a unique opportunity towards achieving the ideal of unity of creed.

With a groundswell of interest in tenant right, the tenant-landlord relationship evolved as the single most significant issue for the Irish nationalist press in the early 1850s. In response to the seemingly never-ending evictions

---

[106] 'The Irish Alliance', mtg. 19 Dec. 1849, *Weekly Freeman*, 22 Dec. 1849.

[107] 'Original correspondence', *Irishman*, 25 May 1850.

[108] 'Union of Nationalists' and 'The Creed of Independence', *Nation*, 17 Aug. 1850. See also: 'The Irish Democratic Alliance', *Nation*, 7 Sept. 1850.

in 1849, local tenants' groups began to flourish in the south. At the same time, farmers in the north, who had also suffered in the Great Famine, were becoming increasingly concerned about a new land bill introduced by the government which threatened their tenant right custom, which they now wanted legalized, allowing outgoing tenants to sell improvements they had made to the land. Strongly encouraged by the press, and their common problems, an opportunity was to present itself for north and south to act in concert in the spring of 1850.

Along with *The Nation*, *The Freeman* and *The Irishman*, *The Tablet* could now be included among the Dublin newspapers that reported extensively on the tenant meetings taking place in the country, which were accompanied by rousing editorials. Both *The Nation* and *The Irishman* had seen an opportunity in the growth of the tenant right movement to win the support of the tenant groups for the respective nationalist organizations they represented. Unsurprisingly, being more moderate in politics and more popular than its rival, *The Nation* had a far better chance of affiliating itself and the Irish Alliance with the growing tenant societies. However, although there were numerous local tenant groups, no central body existed like that of the Repeal Association in the early to mid-1840s, which had one strong voice representing the whole movement. Duffy therefore campaigned for a central authority, hoping that the Alliance would be that body and *The Nation* its representative in the press. That March it seemed that *The Nation* was making progress in the tenant movement when a leading article reported that at a recent meeting held at Baltinglass, Co. Wicklow, tenants 'adopted a resolution calling on the other Tenant Societies to rally round a common central Association – and set the example by at once affiliating itself to the Irish Alliance.'[109] However, a central organization, supported by a powerful press, could be even more meaningful and authoritative if it were to embrace tenant groups in both the north as well as the south.

It was, in fact, *The Londonderry Standard*, an important mouthpiece of Ulster's tenant right movement for the past three years that called for such a union. In June 1850 *The Londonderry Standard* announced:

> When we made our appeal to the Dublin press on the subject, some months ago, we had considerable misgivings as to the practicability of the measure, and as to the preparedness of the public mind to receive it; but THE NATION responded to the proposal promptly and warmly; the *Tablet* urged its importance and necessity with

[109] 2nd LA, *Nation*, 23 March 1850.

great energy, and, though last not least, the *Freeman's Journal* advocated it with all its characteristic ardour.[110]

But, having agreed with Duffy that there should be a central authority, *The Londonderry Standard* was adamant that the Irish Alliance should not be that organization. *The Nation* concurred with this wish, and hence removed the issue of tenant right from the Irish Alliance, noting that the central organization should be 'one whose sole and exclusive object should be to establish the rights of the tenant-farmers.' Importantly, it was to 'embrace men of all political parties and all churches.'[111] In the meantime, Duffy had been seeking the co-operation of Dr James McKnight of *The Banner of Ulster*, the leading tenant right newspaper of the north. The movement was further strengthened by the rallying of the provincial press in the south to the tenant right cause, especially *The Cork Examiner* and its proprietor John Francis Maguire. An observation by the future editor of *The Nation*, A.M. Sullivan, that 'in 1850 the *Derry Standard* and *Banner of Ulster* newspapers were as "seditiously" violent in language as the *Nation*, the *Cork Examiner*, or the *Freeman's Journal*,' suggested a mark of solidarity between the tenant right press of the north and south in a common cause.[112]

The manifestation of this novel unity between north and south, until to now only in rhetoric, was sealed when Duffy and Lucas summoned a national conference. An impressive assembly gathered in Dublin on 6 August 1850, followed by further meetings during that week. Present were Catholic and Protestant representatives from the main Irish newspapers of the north and south that supported the tenant right cause. Delegates from the tenant right societies throughout Ireland, including numerous Protestant and Catholic clergymen, and professional gentlemen, were also present. The success of the conference was reflected in the unification of two significant movements. The Ulster Tenant Right Association (one of the founders being Dr McKnight, who now took the Chair on the first day of the conference) was joined by the south's Callan Tenant Protection Society.[113] Established by Father Tom O'Shea and Father Matthew O'Keeffe, this latter society had been a focus and an inspiration for other southern farmers to form tenant groups.

Out of this conference the Irish Tenant Right League was formed, which had its first meeting that Friday.[114] Such co-operation between the

---

110 Reprinted in 'Union for Ireland', *Nation*, 29 June 1850, 2nd ed.
111 1st LA, *Nation*, 30 March 1850.
112 Sullivan, *New Ireland, vol. I*, p. 308.
113 'The Tenant Conference' and 'The Agrarian Congress', *Nation*, 10 Aug. 1850.
114 'Great Meeting of the Tenant League', 9 Aug. 1850, *Nation*, 10 Aug. 1850.

Protestant north and the Catholic south was rare. For *The Nation* this event was such a feat that its first leading article that week claimed it was lost for words, although it managed expressions of somewhat undisguised delight and optimism, for example: 'North and South, East and West, joined hands, and vowed to unclasp them no more. … In a country pitted in provincial division for eight generations, this event is of enormous significance.' The Tenant Conference had a special meaning for *The Nation*, which had long campaigned for a unity of creeds and races: 'If this were not an occasion that forbade all party triumph, we might be proud to remember that this memorable union is the consummation of hopes and principles long preached in THE NATION.'[115] This conference symbolized one of *The Nation*'s main aspirations, the ideal of nationality for Ireland in terms of creed and race seemingly realized. Attempting to solve the landlord and tenant problem appeared like the beginning of a new era of reconciliation and hope for the advancement of Irish nationalism.

Importantly, while the national and provincial press, both north and south, were largely responsible for the growth of the tenant right societies, many of their personnel were involved in the founding, organization and leadership of the Irish Tenant League, including Duffy, Gray, John MacNamara Cantwell (at this time co-owner of *The Freeman's Journal*), Lucas, James McKnight and John Francis Maguire. Support for the activists in this fledging, but highly promising, organization was to be promoted by remarkable press coverage, accompanied by impassioned articles. At the beginning of August *The Nation* anticipated the progress of the new Irish Tenant League with 'A Song for The League,' later followed by others in celebration of its success.[116]

But what was ultimately required to achieve the aims of the Irish Tenant League was a change in the law, the introduction of new legislation, as landlords would not voluntarily alter their terms of tenancy to their own disadvantage. Without representation in Parliament the tenants had little hope of changing the law. On the third day of the Tenant Conference, therefore, it was resolved that a bill should be prepared and submitted to Parliament.[117] Duffy and Lucas believed that the tenant right problem could be tackled successfully through moral force nationalism if a unified and independent Irish parliamentary party could be formed to represent the interests of the Tenant League.

---

[115] *Nation*, 10 Aug. 1850. For the positive response of several provincial newspapers to this event see: 1st LA, *Nation*, 17 Aug. 1850.

[116] *Nation*, 3 Aug. 1850.

[117] 'The Tenant Conference', *Nation*, 10 Aug. 1850.

An opportunity now presented itself for an idea that Duffy had sought to impress upon his fellow Confederates at the end of 1847. During his last imprisonment Duffy had already decided: 'I was resolutely determined to fall back upon the plan I had proposed to the Council of the Confederation – independent opposition and the gradual creation of confidence in a patriot party whom the country would trust and follow in any extremity.'[118] This idea had been included in an Irish Confederation report, read out by Duffy at a Council meeting, after Mitchel had left *The Nation*, suggesting a constitutional way forward for the Irish Confederation. Its proposal was opposed by a rival document presented by Thomas Devin Reilly on behalf of himself and Mitchel, causing tension and uncertainty amongst Council members, who decided that its adoption should be postponed.[119] Duffy's report had anticipated Joseph Biggar's innovative obstruction tactics in the 1870s, even suggesting that it was possible 'to stop the entire business of Parliament till the constitution of Ireland was restored.'[120] With changed circumstances, there was no equivocation, and this plan was now adopted by the newly formed Tenant League Council.[121] What lent optimism to its efficacy was the extension of the county franchise in 1850, which now included those farmers occupying land valued at £12 per annum, who, if not intimidated by landlords, could support the election of Tenant League MPs.

Coincidentally, Duffy was not alone in his thinking about the value of the tactical voting of Irish MPs in Parliament who shared the same policies. George Henry Moore, a member of a group of Irish MPs known as 'the Irish Brigade,' had encouraged a similar strategy when championing Catholic interests in Parliament. Using a tactic of voting together against government bills, the Irish Brigade MPs had acquired a degree of influence in the balance of power in Parliament. Believing that it was an expedient way of furthering the tenant right cause, Sharman Crawford encouraged Duffy and Lucas to affiliate the Tenant League MPs with the Irish Brigade MPs in August 1851. The price of unity, however, was an unwelcome compromise over the aspirations of the Tenant League MPs; a parliamentary

[118] Duffy, *Two Hemispheres, I*, p. 316.

[119] Minutes of the Council of the Irish Confederation, 31 Dec. 1847 and 11 Jan. 1848, RIA, MS 23 H 44; Letter from J.B. Dillon to O'Brien, 3 Jan. 1848 & Letter from M.J. Barry to O'Brien, 5 Jan. 1848, W.S. O'Brien Papers, NLI, MS 441/2347 & MS 441/2349.

[120] 'Report on the Ways and Means of Attaining an Independent Irish Parliament' referred to in Duffy, *Four Years of Irish History*, pp. 487–8 and *Two Hemispheres, I*, pp. 247–8. Joseph Bigger was a Fenian who became an MP in 1874.

[121] 'Great Meeting of the Tenant League', 9 Aug. 1850, *Nation*, 10 Aug. 1850.

bill prepared by Sharman Crawford only included two of the hoped for '3 fs,' fair rent and free sale (the latter being the right to sell the interest in a holding to an incoming tenant without interference from the landlord, similar to the Ulster custom), while fixity of tenure was dropped.

But, more importantly, any meaningful unity that the Brigaders and Leaguers may have had was to be challenged over their contrasting views in relation to Catholic issues. The Brigade was intent on tenaciously pursuing the interests of Catholics. This caused much tension in the League, whose membership included Protestants as well as Catholics. As the Brigade did not have a newspaper to promote its own policies, in January 1852 John Sadleir, a leading member of the group, decided to establish *The Weekly Telegraph*.[122] Sadleir's paper intensified religious bigotry, the antithesis of the League's belief in religious harmony and unity, and was assailed by tenant right leaders Duffy, Gray and Lucas in their respective newspapers, *The Nation*, *The Freeman* and *The Tablet*. A newspaper-waged war of words developed throughout the year, heightening tensions and promoting distrust between these two groups.

Nevertheless, the Tenant League MPs joined the Irish Brigade MPs in forming an independent parliamentary party. Included in this new party of MPs were newspaper proprietors and leading Leaguers: Duffy, Lucas and Maguire represented New Ross, Meath and Dungarvan respectively.[123] At a conference in September 1852 MPs in this Irish party accepted Sharman Crawford's compromised bill and agreed to abide by the innovative principle of independent opposition.[124] That week *The Nation* was effusive in its enthusiasm: 'At last we have witnessed a real IRISH PARTY, knit together by solemn pledges, buoyant with hope and ability, charged with a great mission, and girdled with the love and hopes of their country.'[125] Again, as after the conference of the north and south, *The Nation* saw this as a closer realization of its principles, such as ending place-begging, and the presence of a united Irish opposition to the British government. However, though this article (not written by Duffy, incidentally) intended to spread optimism and display confidence in this pact, it was overshadowed by the continuing newspaper war between the two factions of the new Irish parliamentary party.

---

122 Accompanying *The Weekly Telegraph* was a tri-weekly evening paper, *The Evening Telegraph*, but at 4d this did not undercut *The Evening Freeman*, and was gone by the end of 1852.

123 Gray stood for Monaghan in the election but failed to secure enough votes to win.

124 'Tenant Right Conference', 8 Sept. 1852, *Nation*, 11 Sept. 1852.

125 1st LA, *Nation*, 11 Sept. 1852.

Apart from the religious question, Duffy, Gray and Lucas were suspicious of the intentions of John Sadleir, and also of William Keogh, another leading Brigade MP. In their newspapers the Leaguers challenged commitment of these two MPs to the policy of independent opposition, although this was strongly denied by *The Weekly Telegraph*.[126] The new Irish parliamentary party, later to become known as the 'Independent Opposition,' was successful in helping to depose the Tories in December 1852 and, following the formation of a coalition government, it held the balance of power in Parliament.[127] However, the idea of independent opposition was betrayed by many of these MPs when they were offered, and accepted, government appointments, driving a division into the party; in particular, Keogh and Sadleir defected, the former became Ireland's Solicitor-General, the latter a junior Lord of the Treasury.[128] Furthermore, Paul Cullen, the Archbishop of Dublin, who had hitherto supported the tenant right MPs, now cooled in his support for them, for reasons which, J.H. Whyte says, remain unclear.[129] But what is well documented is Cullen's suspicion of Duffy and his link with the attempted 1848 rebellion.

The defection of those MPs from their pledge of independence now intensified the newspaper war between *The Weekly Telegraph* and the papers of Duffy, Gray and Lucas, which adversely affected the Tenant League and the Irish parliamentary party. The new Irish party was greatly weakened by the split, although it managed to survive until 1859, and even for a few years after that individual MPs who supported independent opposition continued to be elected, for example, John Blake Dillon in 1865.[130] The return of agricultural prosperity in the mid-fifties, though, diffused antagonism between landlords and tenants, taking away some of the urgency of the need for tenant right legislation. The Tenant League held its final meeting in 1858 and any hope that the tenant right movement or indeed an Irish parliamentary party could advance the Irish nationalist cause was gone for now, and would have to wait for another two decades.

The presence of *The Weekly Telegraph* had also adversely impacted *The Nation*, *The Weekly Freeman's Journal* and *The Tablet*. This was due to

---

126 For a flavour of the disquiet between the two groups see John Sadleir's letter to the Bishop of Cloyne, 6 Sept. 1852, 'The policy for Ireland', *Nation*, 11 Sept. 1852.

127 The term 'Independent Opposition' was first used in spring 1853: J.H. Whyte, *The Independent Irish Party. 1850–9* (London: Oxford University Press, 1958), p. 109. Whyte, who made extensive use of newspapers as a source for his book, provides a detailed account of the Independent Opposition MPs and the Irish Tenant League.

128 Whyte, *Irish Party*, pp. 89–109.

129 Whyte, *Irish Party*, pp. 115–6.

130 Whyte, *Irish Party*, pp. 153–4.

Sadleir's investment of many thousands of pounds into his paper, which he issued at 3d, half the price of the other three weeklies.[131] It is not surprising that *The Weekly Telegraph* was a commercial success. According to A.M. Sullivan, with its enormous monetary investment, Sadleir's new Catholic weekly 'swept the island' as it 'pandered to the fiercest bigotry' to appeal to the Catholic masses. Sadleir also attacked his newspaper rivals for their criticism of him, accusing Duffy and Lucas of being 'bad Catholics' and Gray, who was a Protestant, a 'heretic.' As a consequence of the battle between Sadleir and his opponents, both *The Nation* and *The Tablet* 'were almost fatally crippled.'[132] Of these two papers *The Tablet* suffered the most as it could not afford to lower its price in order to compete with *The Weekly Telegraph* and, as a result, its circulation dropped. As for *The Nation*, to safeguard its readership, money was invested into new projects (one being the issue of a free monthly pamphlet, which only lasted four months) so that its stamp returns for the years 1851 to 1854 showed little change after the foundation of *The Weekly Telegraph* (see Table III). While the circulation of *The Tablet* was reduced during this period, *The Weekly Freeman*'s sales increased, protected by a reduction in price from 6d to 4d from February 1852. Five years later, *The Weekly Freeman* ceased supporting the Tenant League and the independent Irish MPs, and changed its allegiance to the Liberal Party.[133] Lucas died in 1855, and three years later *The Tablet* returned to London.

There were serious consequences for the development of Irish nationalism in the early 1850s. It had suffered a severe setback, partly due to the adverse effect of Sadleir's *Weekly Telegraph* on the authority and finances of *The Nation*, and consequently on Duffy. But even as he entered Parliament in November 1852 as an MP for New Ross, Co. Wexford, Duffy was pessimistic about Ireland's future. This pessimism is revealed in a letter he wrote to William Smith O'Brien the day before taking up his seat in the House of Commons:

> the destruction of the people goes on without let or hindrance, and the very memory of our National hopes has died out of all but a few hearts. I recently had the List of local Confederates examined in some of the larger towns, and the number who have died, or gone to America or the Workhouse, is appalling. Many a time since

---

[131] Sadleir had an investment empire; in 1856, just before he was to be revealed as a fraudster, he committed suicide.

[132] Sullivan, *New Ireland, I*, p. 343.

[133] Whyte, *Irish Party*, pp. 124–41.

> you left Ireland in a prison-ship I have wished that I had gone too, rather than live among the sights that remained … it is a weary and disheartening task to go to the English Parliament with doubtful allies, and relentless enemies.[134]

When he joined the world of parliamentary politics, Duffy's pessimism was realized. *The Nation*'s original principles, particularly in assailing both religious bigotry and place-begging, were all under attack. The undisguised joy of *The Nation* following the Tenant Conference was now dissipated. It was not just the defection of Sadleir and Keogh that caused Duffy great disappointment, but what he also saw as the betrayal by Archbishop Cullen and most of the Catholic Church, who had taken the side of the defectors: 'The archbishop of Dublin who was foremost and loudest to pronounce for the principle of Independent Opposition lends all the weight of his authority to its opponents.'[135] It was a great hindrance to any progress in Irish constitutional nationalism not to have the support of the priests who wielded a powerful influence over the people.

Furthermore, *The Nation*, the foremost iconic voice of Irish nationalism, had been effectively compromised by *The Weekly Telegraph* when its religious bias, diametrically different from the Young Irelanders' ideal of the unity of creed, was disseminated on a large scale throughout Ireland. On a more personal level, the challenge from Sadleir's paper may also have affected Duffy's financial security.[136] He decided to sell *The Nation* and emigrate to Australia.[137] On 16 August 1855 Duffy rendered a sombre farewell address to both the New Ross electors and the readers of *The Nation*, despairing 'no more hope for the Irish Cause than for the corpse on the dissecting table.'[138] This is one of the most quoted images used by both Irish nationalists and historians. Duffy's departure from *The Nation*, and that November from Ireland, marked the end of an era in the development of Irish nationalism.

This episode in Irish history had a significant effect on the future direction of Irish nationalism. It weakened the cause of constitutional

---

134 Letter from Duffy to Smith O'Brien, 7 Nov. 1852, Duffy Papers, NLI, MS 5758/109.

135 'Mr. Duffy's Address', 1st LA col., *Nation*, 18 Aug. 1855.

136 Lucas suggested in a letter of 30 July 1855 to Archbishop MacHale of Tuam that Duffy left Ireland for financial reasons: Bernard O'Reilly, *John MacHale, Archbishop of Tuam. His life, times and correspondence, vol. II*, (New York; Cincinnati: F.R. Pustet & Co., 1890) p. 403, in Whyte, *Irish Party*, p. 120.

137 Duffy became the Prime Minister of Victoria in 1871 before returning to France to write his prolific histories of the Young Ireland era.

138 'Mr. Duffy's Address', *Nation*, 18 Aug. 1855.

nationalism and left a vacuum for the development of revolutionary nationalism. Had it not been for the defection of the Irish MPs, this strategy of independent opposition could have worked to the advantage of tenant right. Instead, its failure provided further justification and encouragement for the physical force nationalists. In 1847 there had already been an attempt to form an Irish parliamentary party to tackle the effects of the Great Famine, but MPs seemed incapable of voting together on Irish issues.[139] Both Smith O'Brien and John Mitchel believed that it was impossible to form an independent Irish parliamentary party in 1847; Mitchel wrote to Smith O'Brien that year:

> Speaking of a parliamentary party, I quite agree with you in your estimate of the difficulty, or rather impossibility of creating a genuine Repeal, that is, Young Ireland Party, in Parliament at all. We have neither the men, the money, nor the franchises. And, besides, by the time the elections arrive, I do believe all Irishmen will be so busy preserving their lives, and keeping themselves out of the workhouses, that there will be small interest about electing members to sit in so palpably useless and delusive an assembly.[140]

Another, far more committed, attempt to create and sustain a viable parliamentary party, and with more favourable conditions, had now also failed. However, with the power of a larger electorate twenty years later Parnell adopted the idea of independent opposition, and in his evidence to the Parnell Commission in 1889 he acknowledged that it originated with Duffy and Lucas in 1852:

> I had some knowledge … of Irish history, and had read about the Independent Opposition movement of Sir Charles Gavan Duffy and the late Mr. Frederick Lucas in 1852, and whenever I thought about politics I always thought that that would be an ideal movement for the benefit of Ireland.[141]

The time was not propitious for a successful Irish parliamentary party or land movement in the mid-nineteenth century, though, in hindsight, these

---

[139] See: *Nation*, 16 Jan. 1847 and 20 Feb. 1847.

[140] Mitchel's letter to Smith O'Brien, 19 March 1847, Dillon, *Mitchel, vol. I*, p. 155.

[141] Extract from the Official Report of the Parnell Commission, 1890, vol. VII, in Duffy, *Two Hemispheres, vol. I*, p. 251 (footnote).

ideas held promise for the future. The same cannot be said for the Irish Tenant League in terms of its unique character of bringing north and south together. Even though the idea of Protestants and Catholics uniting for social and economic reasons could have been important for Irish nationalist aspirations, it was not to be realized, despite all the support of the press in both north and south. However, while the Tenant League did not achieve its aims, the Dublin nationalist press, keeping the specific issue of tenant right before the public, was to play a prominent part in the 1879–82 Land War, when circumstances proved more promising for its success.

Table III Average number of stamps per issue of Dublin weekly newspapers involved in the early 1850s tenant right movement

	1851	1852	1853	1854
Weekly Freeman	3,462	4,788	5,654	6,231
Tablet	4,743	3,825	3,660	3,462
Nation	3,221	3,230	3,644	3,246
Weekly Telegraph	–	20,163	16,356	18,442

Source: Based on 'Return of Number of Stamps issued at One Penny to Newspapers in United Kingdom, 1851–53', HCP, 1854 (117) XXXIX.479 & 'Return of Number of Stamps … 1854', HCP, 1854–55 (83) XXX.497.

The 1855–56 *Tribune* and the reassertion of advanced nationalism

While the Independent Opposition MPs and the Tenant Leaguers were struggling in the mid-1850s, some Irish nationalists were imbued with renewed inspiration when the Crimean War broke out. Although there had been an absence of advanced nationalist newspapers in Dublin since the summer of 1850, when an opportunity arose later in the decade there were those willing to revive that journalistic challenge. Like the French Revolution of February 1848, which had a profound effect on the Irish nationalist movement, when Great Britain entered the Crimean War on 28 March 1854, Irish nationalists were once again optimistic about winning independence from England. The old dictum of 'England's difficulty is Ireland's opportunity' now seemed to offer them tangible hope. Whereas in 1848 there was only the speculative possibility of war with France, Britain was now actively engaged in military operations with France and Turkey allied against Russia in a major European conflict. Even so, there were two distinct disadvantages for any advance in Irish freedom at this time: unlike in 1848, when the network of Confederate Clubs was established and accompanied by highly emotive articles in the rebel papers, in 1854 there were only small knots of disaffected revolutionists and an absence of Dublin nationalist newspapers dedicated to propagating extremist views. Near the end of the following year, however, Irish nationalist hopes found a public expression in *The Tribune*, a new Dublin newspaper whose main theme was to persuade the Irish people to use Britain's involvement in the Crimean War to recover Ireland's national independence.[142]

A weekly of sixteen pages, *The Tribune* followed the prototype of *The Nation*, rooted in political and literary nationalism. It was at this time that newspapers could now take advantage of a change in the law in relation to the purchase of stamps. From 1855, papers that were not posted could cost a penny less. While it was an advantage for nationalists to have a cheaper press, newspapers were still expensive for most people, and access via shared copies, which included reading aloud, remained commonplace. This law meant that it was even more difficult to calculate a paper's circulation as stamp returns now only accounted for a part of a newspaper's sales figures. *The Tribune* was priced at 3d unstamped and 4d stamped, and although a penny cheaper than *The Nation*, it only survived for about three months, from 3 November 1855 to 9 February 1856. Without evidence to identify *The Tribune*'s unstamped circulation, there is no clear indication of its overall circulation, although official figures suggest that it sold far fewer stamped copies than its well-established rival.[143] Little is known about *The Tribune*, but its extreme political tone indicates an appeal to the working classes, while the cultural items could be appreciated more by the middle classes who tended to be better educated.

Unlike the Dublin nationalist papers of the last few years, political nationalism was to be a priority for *The Tribune*; it wished

> to give a voice again to the National yearning for Freedom: that yearning which is not dead, nor destined to die, while any fragment of the Irish race survives in Ireland … The Conductors of THE TRIBUNE, therefore, convinced by all history, deep reflection and sad experience, that Independence or Self-government is the

142 1st LA, *The Tribune*, 10 Nov. 1855.

143 Based on 'Return of Registered Newspapers and Publications in United Kingdom, and Number of Stamps issued, July 1855–December 1857', HCP, 1857–58 (489) XXXIV.259.

> very breath of a Nation's life – that Freedom is the highest earthly prize for the possession of which men have ever dared or died.[144]

A leading article in the first issue of *The Tribune* at the beginning of November 1855, pointing to the failure of 'Party politics,' believed that 'this question of Nationality' had to be addressed before any 'moral or material improvement' could be made. Following independence there would be two priorities for *The Tribune*: a 'revolution in the landed property of the country' and 'the abolition of the Anglican Establishment,' which could only be achieved by an Irish government.[145] A see-saw policy, particularly in the mid-nineteenth century, of whether a social revolution in the land should precede or follow a political revolution, depended on the circumstances of the time; Mitchel, for example, after failing to persuade the landlord class to accept reform, turned to the notion of armed rebellion against the government. This revolutionary direction was reignited by *The Tribune*'s policy of prioritizing 'Nationality' (i.e. Irish independence) to be followed by the other advanced nationalist papers in 1858 and 1863.

Among *The Tribune*'s founders were John Edward Pigot, Denny Lane, Father John Kenyon and Professor W.K. Sullivan, dedicated Irish nationalists who saw an opportunity to revive the cause. Luby was a sub-editor who wrote many of *The Tribune*'s leading articles; other contributors included Philip Gray, Charles Kickham and John Fisher Murray.[146] Many of those connected with *The Tribune* had been involved with the original *Nation*; Pigot and Lane, for instance, had belonged to Young Ireland's circle of friends and colleagues. The strong cultural influence of the early *Nation* was reflected in *The Tribune*, evident, for example, in a correspondent's translation into Irish of 'The Welcome,' a love poem by Thomas Davis; both versions were printed in *The Tribune*.[147] The advanced nature of *The Tribune* could be seen in the activities of some of its writers: Sullivan and Luby, for instance, had been involved in attempting to found a secret revolutionary organization near the end of 1848.[148] Luby and Kickham were to become leaders in the Fenian movement in Ireland and the foremost writers for the influential Fenian newspaper of the 1860s, *The Irish People*. As for

144 'The Tribune. A new weekly newspaper, *Tribune*, 3 Nov. 1855.

145 1st LA, *Tribune*, 3 Nov. 1855.

146 Luby's Papers, NLI, MS 332. As we saw in Chapter 2, John Fisher Murray was the poet who, at the expense of O'Connell, praised Smith O'Brien after his release from prison; and Father John Kenyon was the Irish Confederate who reprimanded the Confederation's Council for not being critical enough of O'Connell after his death.

147 *Tribune*, 10 Nov. 1855.

148 Luby's Papers, NLI, MS 332.

Philip Gray, had he lived, based on his dedicated commitment to the Irish nationalist cause, observed by his comrades, there is little doubt that he would have had a leading position in the Fenian organization in Ireland.

The Tribune, described by A.M. Sullivan as 'semi-revolutionary,' was the first Fenian newspaper in Ireland.[149] Although dismissing constitutional nationalism, like *The Irishman* before it, *The Tribune* needed to be more circumspect than the rebel papers of the summer of 1848 to avoid prosecution; it could not preach too much disaffection, such as directly calling people to arms, for this would risk being silenced by the government. Learning from the fate of the rebel journalists in 1848, *The Tribune*'s writers realized that while they could not deliver a passionate flow of martial rhetoric, their articles still needed to be powerful and inspirational enough to win recruits for any prospective nationalist organization that might emerge as a viable military force ready – when an opportunity arose – to seize independence by physical force.

One of the most direct ideological links between *The Tribune* and the 1860s Fenians was the notion of sacrifice for the nationalist cause, although this was not the messianic idea of martyrdom later espoused by Patrick Pearse and others in 1916. One leading article in *The Tribune* advocated that

> a nation's liberty must be gained with difficulty, by perils and struggles in the face of sword and fire, by sacrifice of life itself. Better a thousand times win liberty by the bloodiest sacrifices of war than (were it possible) by the demoralizing means of a peaceful and legal parliamentary agitation.[150]

The Tribune further argued that independence won by physical force rather than by peaceful means was an ennobling experience for both individual and nation, a poignant theme that was to reappear in *The Irish People.*

The Tribune developed a strategy that was also later adopted by *The Irish People*, to nurture public opinion into accepting that physical force was the only way of achieving independence from Great Britain. In line with this policy, *The Tribune* appealed to notions of manhood in persuading young men to become recruits for militant combat. However, *The Tribune* faced a more challenging task for, unlike *The Irish People*, which was founded to support an already well-established revolutionary conspiracy, it seems that in the mid-1850s only a small minority of Irish nationalists, involved in meetings and drilling, believed in revolution. Reminiscent of the '49

---

149 Sullivan, *New Ireland, vol. II*, 2nd ed. (1877), p. 85.

150 1st LA, *Tribune*, 12 Jan. 1856.

Irishman, *The Tribune* laid stress on the importance of public opinion and invited its readers to think positively about Irish nationalism. *The Tribune* wanted people not only to accept the possibility of a future revolution but also, where appropriate, to become active participants upon its arrival. But a seemingly insurmountable obstacle presented itself: how, after the failures of physical force activities in 1848 and 1849, could the Irish people, still recovering from the effects of the Great Famine, be persuaded that they could achieve a successful revolution?

The abiding aim of *The Tribune*'s writers was to shake off the spirit of apathy they believed was currently pervading the country and to inspire a renewed sense of Irish nationalism with the eventual hope of stirring people into revolution. They spoke initially of a sense of healing wounds, and laying no particular blame on Young or Old Ireland for past failures. In keeping with this statement, a lack of national unity among the people was identified as a major drawback to any hope of achieving independence. *The Tribune* believed that disunity was historical, due to septs or clans with their own individual loyalties, recognizing that

> there is no one thing, which has a greater tendency to perpetuate the bondage of Irishmen, than their existing incapability of comprehending the large idea of an Irish nation ... All notions of country in the popular mind of Ireland are vague and confused; or, if the people have any definite idea in connexion with patriotism, it is narrow, a strong feeling of partizanship in [*sic*] behalf of their province or their county, or still worse, their parish or their faction.[151]

Being loyal to a locality rather than embracing the larger idea of nationality was, according to *The Tribune*, a hindrance to the development of Irish nationalism. Instilling in the people a sense of national unity that transcended loyalty to a locality was a challenging ideal. A nationalist newspaper issued from Dublin, Ireland's capital city, was possibly an effective way of achieving this aim.

In galvanizing the whole of the country, however, there needed to be a central focus, and an identifiable concept that the people could relate to, binding them into one movement. But some of the rhetoric used by *The Tribune*'s journalists could be seen as too idealistic for the average Irish person to comprehend or accept. For example, when appealing for an understanding of the 'grand idea of independent nationality,' *The Tribune* suggested that

---

[151] 1st LA, *Tribune*, 19 Jan. 1856.

'Animated with such an idea, the people of a country will be continually striving to elevate their souls to diviner things, will be ever ready to pursue the path of duty, and to aspire to a life more heroic than the ordinary vulgar existence of men.'[152] While *The Tribune* attempted to place the concept of Irish nationalism on a higher plane, for those eking out a living off the land, survival, not abstract concepts of nationalism, was uppermost in their minds. However, newspapers that carried messages from a recognized leader of an organized group had the potential to unify society in the nationalist cause. Daniel O'Connell, for example, had provided that leadership both with his charisma and his image as the Liberator. To achieve the commitment of whole communities to a nationalist organization, the involvement of priests, who wielded much local power, was highly desirable. O'Connell and *The Nation* together were particularly inspirational in 1843 and, with the crucial support of the priests, they provided a national focus; a fragmented Irish society had been bound up in the momentum of the Repeal movement. The absence of these popular unifying forces rendered *The Tribune*'s role that much more difficult. It was not easy to rouse those in rural areas and make them comprehend a national idea; there was more potential in urban areas with their comparatively higher densities of population – greatly increased owing to the effects of the Great Famine – which provided the environment for the exchange of dialogue and ideas, particularly where there was easier access to newspapers. Despite various drawbacks, however, journalists kept faith with their nationalist ideals and communicated them to the people through the medium of *The Tribune*, their hopes reactivated by the Crimean War when Ireland was emptied of troops.

The Tribune charted the progress of the war and, in doing so, criticized Britain's war effort, especially its defeats, such as the Redan (18 June and 8 September 1855).[153] The Crimean War being the first to use the electric telegraph, news sometimes came comparatively quickly from the front, and had a more dramatic impact because of its immediacy. Britain's military prowess was a source of derision and hope for *The Tribune*, which delighted in the possibility that Ireland could achieve independence with Britain humiliated and weakened by the war. What hitherto could not be achieved by threats and agitation from Irish nationalists or working-class agitators in Britain could now potentially be realized by this military conflict. *The Tribune*, demonstrating that it was not short of poetic prose, commented in a leading article:

152 1st LA, *Tribune*, 19 Jan. 1856.

153 'War Intelligence', *Tribune*, 17 Nov. 1855. The Redan was a fortification that protected the Russian naval base of Sebastopol, which the allies had hoped to destroy.

> Tottering on the verge of the bottomless abyss! The pirate flag of England has been torn down and trampled on; her fleets baulked in the Pacific, skulking home from the Baltic, baffled or sunk in the Black Sea, the stormy waves of which now sing the dirge of her departed glory and her vanished fame.

Besides providing a possible opportunity for independence, *The Tribune* also saw the war in terms of retribution against what it perceived as England's historic behaviour at home and abroad:

> It has dealt a mortal blow to the vilest system of despotism that ever cursed this earth – a system which, not content with rapine, plunder, and spoliation, must needs rob and murder under the pretence of advancing the interests of Civilization and Religion – and it has given the victims of English misrule in every part of the world an opportunity of recovering the rights and dignity of Freemen.

Acknowledging potential internal danger from the impoverished lower classes in England, from Irish nationalists, the colonies and external threats abroad, *The Tribune* declared: 'the British Empire is doomed.' There was a palpable sense in *The Tribune* that the British Empire was on the verge of meltdown.[154]

Irish-American nationalists, refugees from 1848 and 1849, were also imbued with renewed inspiration for Ireland's independence by the advent of the Crimean War. Irish nationalists in America could communicate with those in Ireland through *The Tribune*. For example, at a convention on 4 December 1855 an emotive address, printed in *The New York Citizen*, was communicated by the American Irish Emigrant Aid Society 'To the Irish Race,' stating that their association was established to 'fulfil the destiny of the Irish nation.'[155] The address was reprinted in *The Tribune* to inspire its readers. Opinions and news of the activities of Irish nationalists in America were frequently charted in *The Tribune*, expressing their continuing criticism of British rule. Irish-American journalists sanctioned and praised *The Tribune*. *The New York Citizen* saw it as 'a new organ of great political power.'[156] Support also came from *The Irish American*

---

[154] 1st LA, *Tribune*, 24 Nov. 1855.

[155] 'Important from America – grand convention of Irish delegates in New York', 4 Dec. 1855, *Tribune*, 29 Dec. 1855.

[156] 'From the "New York Citizen"', *Tribune*, 19 Jan. 1856.

newspaper, which stated 'We can state on authority, that it has the cordial support and assistance here of such men as John Mitchell [*sic*], T.F. Meagher, J.B. Dillon, John O'Mahony, &c.,' and invited people to subscribe to it.[157] But *The Tribune* was short-lived; in February 1856 it ceased publication, possibly due to financial difficulties, and coinciding with the ending of the Crimean War, whereupon the Dublin advanced nationalist press fell silent for a couple of years.[158]

Many clubs had been formed in America since 1849 with the intention of keeping Irish nationalism alive. These clubs were mostly quiescent until the beginning of the Crimean War, when the Irish Emigrant Aid Society was founded in Boston, Massachusetts, and the Irish Military and Civil Association was formed in New York. The latter group was composed of two parts, a civil branch for married men with families, and an oath-bound military organization, the Emmett Monument Association, reportedly composed of some 3,000 men who intended to return to Ireland to assist those fighting for Irish independence.[159] Having disbanded at the end of the Crimean War and Ireland's missed opportunity, the Emmett Monument Association retained a committee that within a couple of years was to communicate with potential political activists in Ireland to reignite revolutionary nationalism on both sides of the Atlantic.

The strengthening of Irish nationalism from 1858: *The Nation* and *The Irishman*

Despite Duffy's pessimism about the future, the ebb and flow of Irish nationalism continued after his departure. As the middle years of the 1850s saw little activity in the progress of Irish nationalism, the return of William Smith O'Brien to Ireland heralded new hope. The Dublin nationalist press had already capitalized on Smith O'Brien's reportedly harsh treatment abroad, building up much sympathy for him; commenting on his subjection to 'beastly indignities,' *The Nation* saw Smith O'Brien as the 'noblest Irishman of his generation.'[160] Unconditionally pardoned

---

157 'The "*Tribune*" in America', *Tribune*, 2 Feb. 1856.

158 According to O'Leary, Thomas Mason Jones had been nominated proprietor and editor by the founders of *The Tribune* and his financial problems were responsible for the paper's demise: O'Leary, *Recollections, I*, p. 248.

159 'The Convention for Ireland', *The New York Times*, 5 Dec. 1855, reprinted in *Tribune*, 29 Dec. 1855.

160 3rd LA, *Nation*, 6 July 1850. See also, for example: 'Meagher's Message to Ireland, PART II', on Smith O'Brien's treatment, *Nation*, 3 Aug. 1850.

in 1856, Smith O'Brien returned to Ireland the same year.[161] Seeing him as a martyr and one of the most important and influential Irish patriots alive, Irish nationalists sought his approval for their projects.[162] Reluctant to become actively involved in another nationalist organization, however, much of Smith O'Brien's influence was exercised through the nationalist press, which became a medium for his authority and leadership.

Those associated with the nationalist press were particularly anxious to seek Smith O'Brien's advice and endorsement on nationalist issues, especially *The Nation*, his most ardent supporter since the 1840s. Following Duffy's departure in 1855, Alexander M. Sullivan became a part proprietor and an assistant editor of *The Nation*; within two years he became sole proprietor and editor.[163] A year later, both Sullivan and Dr Robert Cane, an ex-Confederate who now edited *The Celt*, a literary periodical, believed that a new national organization for legislative independence could be founded on a similar basis to that of the Irish Confederation. When Smith O'Brien wrote an extensive address on Irish nationalism, intended for publication in *The Nation*, he omitted to sanction this idea, which had already been suggested in *The Celt* and *The Nation*. Sullivan claimed that this omission would 'secure to the country *utter despair*' and 'extinguish the prospect of revival.'[164] Sullivan's reaction can be seen as a distinct example of what Irish nationalists deemed to be Smith O'Brien's power over public opinion. Consenting to Sullivan's request, Smith O'Brien amended a sentence in his address prior to its publication. The importance of this address, printed in ten parts in *The Nation*, was reflected by the fact that it was reprinted by many other newspapers. Sullivan believed that the address had 'sunk deep into the minds of all thinking Irishmen and will be

[161] Smith O'Brien was first pardoned in 1854 on condition that he would never return to Ireland.

[162] For example, Michael Dwyer, a former editor of the 1849–50 *Irishman* who was dismissed as an assistant editor from *The Tablet* in 1858 (the same year this paper returned to London), sought O'Brien's approval for a new Catholic and nationalist newspaper that was intended to challenge *The Catholic Telegraph and Irish Sun*, formerly *The Weekly Telegraph*: Letters from Michael Dwyer to Smith O'Brien, 4 and 7 Oct. 1858, Smith O'Brien Papers, NLI, MS 446/3068 & 3071. There is, in fact, no apparent evidence of this paper going further than the Prospectus.

[163] Sullivan, *New Ireland, II*, p. 371. While Duffy had been occupied with parliamentary duties, the editorship of *The Nation* was conducted by John Cashel Hoey, with Duffy only a contributor: 'Mr. Duffy', *Nation*, 28 July 1855. In 1855 Duffy sold *The Nation* to A.M. Sullivan and M. Clery: 'Mr. Duffy's Address', *Nation*, 18 Aug. 1855.

[164] Letters from A.M. Sullivan to Smith O'Brien, 17 and 23 March 1858, Smith O'Brien Papers, NLI, MS 446/3013 & 3015.

acted upon.'[165] Others unconnected with *The Nation* also saw its potential importance to Irish nationalism. For example, a letter to Smith O'Brien from George Archdeacon in Glasgow, on behalf of the Council of the Irish Protection Association, claimed that Smith O'Brien's 'magnificent Series of Letters' was responsible for the rekindling of 'the national spirit' throughout Ireland, noting in particular that 'plans for self-government, and your advocacy of the revival of the ancient Celtic Language have had the effect of inspiring the Irish Exile with high hope.'[166] Smith O'Brien's address was certainly a boost for Irish nationalism, and with subsequent contributions to *The Nation*, Sullivan believed that in the years after his return to Ireland 'he exercised a considerable influence on passing events.'[167]

Smith O'Brien's importance could also be seen in his potential usefulness to the advanced Dublin nationalist press. His help was sought by *The Irishman*, a new weekly nationalist paper initially founded in Belfast on 17 July 1858 by Denis Holland; it also had offices in Dublin and from April 1859 was issued solely from the capital, and continued to 1885. Priced 3d unstamped and 4d stamped, *The Irishman* was distributed in Ireland and Great Britain. The editor claimed that 'Between five and six thousand copies' of *The Irishman*'s first issue 'were in the hands of the people,' of which 4,000 were sold in the provinces; on the assumption that each copy was shared by at least twelve people, it has been estimated that the readership could have exceeded 60,000.[168] Like *The Tribune*, understandably, *The Irishman* had a lower stamped circulation figure than *The Nation*.[169] And following *The Tribune*, this paper's foremost priority was 'the inextinguishable Nationality of Ireland,' its secondary pursuits advocating 'the sacred rights of the wronged and oppressed tenantry,' and 'For the overthrow of that foul stronghold of persecution and fraud and social injustice, the Church Establishment, we shall never cease to labour with tongue and pen.'[170]

---

165 Letter from Sullivan to Smith O'Brien, 25 May 1858, Smith O'Brien Papers, NLI, MS 446/3041.

166 See again: Letter from George Archdeacon to Smith O'Brien, 31 Aug. 1858, Smith O'Brien Papers, NLI, MS 446/3061.

167 Sullivan, *New Ireland, II*, p. 108.

168 1st LA following 'Summary', *Irishman*, 24 July 1858.

169 Bearing in mind that stamp returns now accounted for only a part of the number of sales of a newspaper, in the second half of 1859 *The Irishman*'s stamped sales indicated an average of 962 per issue whereas *The Nation*'s figure was 1,462: based on 'Return of Registered Newspapers and Publications in United Kingdom, and Number of Stamps issued, June 1859–60', HCP, 1860 (593) XL.151.

170 'Prospectus', *Irishman*, 17 July 1858.

Anxious to secure the support of Smith O'Brien, John Edward Pigot, a contributor to *The Irishman*, wrote to him that December, saying:

> men who like Mr Holland earnestly and purely desire to exert themselves for that same cause which is yours as well as theirs … should have from time to time the benefit of your suggestions … I am quite sure the influence of your opinion would be always powerful in the conduct of the Irishman.[171]

Pigot even hoped that Smith O'Brien might 'share with the "Nation" the first publication of any future public letters.'[172] Besides providing kudos to boost sales, it was hoped that Smith O'Brien would also endorse *The Irishman*'s nationalist views.

One of the inner circle of the original Young Irelanders, in 1858 Pigot conveyed in letters to Smith O'Brien the impression of aspiring to make *The Irishman* a nationalist paper similar to the ideal he perceived in Thomas Davis's *Nation*: 'To be national without exaggeration or boasting, to be "separatist" without seditious rhetoric, to be energetic without being ungentlemanly in violence, to be pure, & free from mean personality.'[173] Something that Davis would have approved of was *The Irishman*'s original design of binding together Irish nationalists from north and south by publishing the paper in both Belfast and Dublin, an attempt to revive the elusive ideal of unity of creed. *The Irishman*'s intention was to supply a niche unfilled by other nationalist newspapers. Holland believed that Ulster was virtually unrepresented by an Irish nationalist newspaper, and intended to remedy this by 'knitting Ulster more closely to the rest of Ireland in that National Unity, which is all that is needed to establish the welfare and independence of our country.'[174]

Although at the end of 1858 Pigot seemed to think that *The Irishman*'s espousal of nationalist politics was mediocre, he believed that it would improve, occupying 'a very important place as an organ of national opinion throughout Ireland.'[175] However, even though unlike the earlier *Irishman*

[171] Letter from John Edward Pigot to Smith O'Brien, 21 Dec. 1858, Smith O'Brien Papers, NLI, MS 446/3078.

[172] Postscript in letter from J.E. Pigot to Smith O'Brien, 15 Dec. 1858, Smith O'Brien Papers, NLI, MS 446/3076.

[173] Letter from J.E. Pigot to Smith O'Brien, 17 Dec. 1858, Smith O'Brien Papers, NLI, MS 446/3077.

[174] 'Prospectus', *Irishman*, 17 July 1858.

[175] J.E. Pigot to Smith O'Brien, 21 Dec. 1858, Smith O'Brien Papers, NLI, MS 446/3078.

and *The Tribune* it was more of a challenge to *The Nation*, proved partly by its longevity, *The Irishman* never reached the popularity of its contemporary. And despite good intentions at the beginning, as it went on, *The Irishman* certainly did not reflect the early *Nation* as remembered by Pigot; it became less subtle and cruder in its tone when espousing Irish nationalism, particularly when battling with its newspaper rivals in Dublin.

Like the other advanced Dublin nationalist newspapers earlier in the decade, there was an ambiguity over the extent to which *The Irishman* should employ physical force rhetoric when trying to stand out from the other nationalist papers as a strong voice on behalf of the Irish people. For example, *The Irishman*'s prospectus, while certainly not supporting constitutional agitation, commented: 'the sword of the warrior has rusted: to-day we fight with the tongue of the teacher and the pen of the journalist; but, pen or sword, we still fight for the one cherished possession of our ancient race, the unconquerable and undying Nationality of the Irish people.'[176] By contrast, the following week, in a review of a military pamphlet, Holland wrote of the usefulness of the pike 'to turn out, at a moment's notice, in a volunteer force.'[177] To raise the profile of *The Irishman*, contributions to the paper from John Mitchel appeared periodically over the next few years. From October 1858, chapters from *The Last Conquest of Ireland (Perhaps)* were printed, originally a series of letters published in Mitchel's American newspaper, *The Southern Citizen*, narrating a history of Young Ireland and 1848, and later published as a book in 1861 by *The Irishman*'s office. This work presented a compelling argument that the Great Famine was deliberately created by the British government, an accusation that was immortalized by Mitchel: 'The Almighty, indeed, sent the potato blight, but the English created the famine.'[178] This moral indictment, since refuted by revisionist scholars in the twentieth century, became an enduring tenet in the Irish Republican tradition. Mitchel's contribution to *The Irishman* was an indication of the paper's political direction, which became more overtly revolutionary as time went on, coinciding with a growing conspiratorial movement from 1858.

There was in the latter part of the 1850s a more determined attempt to organize a revolutionary secret society. The Crimean War had presented circumstances conducive to a possible insurrection by the advanced nationalists, but no group at that time in Ireland had been equipped to take advantage of that opportunity. These nationalists now realized more than

176 'Prospectus', *Irishman*, 17 July 1858.
177 'Military. The Sword and the Pike', *Irishman*, 24 July 1858.
178 Mitchel, *Last Conquest of Ireland*, p. 219.

ever that an organization should be in place, ready to respond to any occasion that might offer hope for the future. When Philip Gray, a highly inspirational figure among these conspirators, ruptured a blood vessel in 1856 and died early the following year, he was eclipsed by James Stephens, who, at the request of the Emmet Monument Association in America, founded the oath-bound IRB on 17 March 1858. Although commonly entitled the Irish Republican Brotherhood, the new organization was initially known as the Irish Revolutionary Brotherhood, particularly by Irish nationalists in America. Among the leading members of the Emmet Monument Association were Young Ireland refugees John O'Mahony and Michael Doheny, who were still committed to freeing Ireland from British rule by force. In 1859 the Association changed its name to the Fenian Brotherhood, when the word 'Fenian' came to be applied to revolutionists both in America and Ireland.[179] These two organizations operated independently, a striking difference being that the IRB was a secret society and the Fenian Brotherhood was not.

The first priority of the IRB was recruitment and James Stephens was successful in persuading the majority of the members of the Phoenix National and Literary Society to join him; this thriving political society had been founded two years earlier by Jeremiah O'Donovan Rossa, who was to have an important role in the IRB's newspaper in the mid-1860s. A.M. Sullivan took the opportunity to make it clear that *The Nation* was not to be involved with the newly formed conspiratorial IRB. While travelling in the south around the late summer of 1858 he discovered not only that secret conspirators were actively using William Smith O'Brien's name as a recruiting ploy, but also that *The Nation* was believed to be linked with this new revolutionary group.[180] Sullivan responded by publishing a letter in *The Nation* written by Smith O'Brien, who distanced himself from the IRB, and accompanied it with an editorial advising people not to join secret societies. Sullivan's resistance to the IRB was not because it was revolutionary, but because the group was secret.[181] His opposition to these conspirators in *The Nation*, along with the priests' denunciations, had an effect as enrolment into the society ceased for the time being. But

[179] The IRB people were unhappy about this title. When accused of being Fenians they, most likely for practical reasons, denied it in their newspaper: 3rd LA, *The Irish People*, 9 April 1864. Of course, they were correct in that they were not members of the Fenian Brotherhood.

[180] Letter from Sullivan to Smith O'Brien, 25 Oct. 1858, Smith O'Brien Papers, NLI, MS 446/3074.

[181] Sullivan, *New Ireland, II*, pp. 14–16.

when O'Donovan Rossa and other Phoenix members were arrested that December, James Stephens blamed *The Nation*, and accused Sullivan of being an informer.[182] In the light of Stephens's failure to get *The Nation* onto the side of his newly formed IRB, this accusation, although false, was used in future attacks on Sullivan when the antagonism between constitutional and revolutionary nationalism was reignited with much bitterness in the next decade.[183] Shunned by *The Nation*, the Fenians looked to an alternative organ to express their views. Although not controlled by the Fenians, *The Irishman* came to provide them with a platform for their doctrine in a new era of Irish nationalism.

An important theme in the 1850s was the revival of physical force nationalism. In 1848 it was an emotional response to the Great Famine and to the ease of the success of the French Revolution in February 1848. In the 1850s, rather than being a rash policy, the concept of physical force had time to ferment. Although the 1849–50 *Irishman* did not directly promote physical force, there was a sense that it was not out of the question as a future strategy. The failure of constitutional nationalism to make any meaningful progress throughout much of this decade left the way open for the advancement of physical force nationalism. This policy was revived through *The Tribune* with its warlike rhetoric, and although this paper was short-lived it suggested that revolutionary nationalism was still considered a viable way of achieving Irish independence. *The Nation*, too, while not sanctioning a policy of physical force, began casting off its moderate tone in the latter part of the 1850s under the proprietorship of A.M. Sullivan. Although the 1858 *Irishman* did not directly advocate revolution, it became more daring than its earlier namesake, and for the next few years it was to become a medium for the conspiratorial activists now beginning to emerge as a force in Ireland.

---

[182] Sullivan, *New Ireland, II*, pp. 79–80. O'Donovan Rossa spent eight months in prison for conspiracy, but the charge was dropped.

[183] A defining moment in the IRB's early history came in 1861 with a conflict over the funeral of Terence Bellew MacManus, an exile in America whose body was transported to Ireland for burial where he was to be honoured as an 1848 hero. An acrimonious wrangle arose between IRB members and the constitutional nationalists, one of whom was A.M. Sullivan, over who was to control the funeral arrangements. It ended with triumph for James Stephens when many thousands of people participated in an impressive funeral procession through Dublin on 10 November 1861. This event, another episode in the battle between the revolutionists and constitutionalists, was a resounding success for IRB morale and recruitment.

Conclusion

What was striking about the period 1849 to 1859 was that, amidst the sense of anguish and loss, the Irish nationalist cause was not only able to survive, but at times even to thrive. The private thoughts of three significant figures in Irish nationalism involved with *The Nation* reflected a sense of despair during the earlier years of this period: John Blake Dillon's belief in 1849 that the Irish nation had 'perished irrecoverably,' Lalor's analogy of a 'coffin-lid' when writing to Duffy that September, and Duffy's letter to Smith O'Brien in November 1852 lamenting that 'the very memory of our National hopes has died out of all but a few hearts.'[184] And of course, ultimately, Duffy's 'corpse' and departure from *The Nation* and Ireland seemed to symbolize an utter lack of hope in any progress for the Irish nationalist cause.[185] Yet despite all this pessimism Irish nationalism did survive, and it was the Dublin nationalist press that had taken a foremost role in this, which eventually led to the emergence of potentially resolute constitutional and physical force movements.

Following the collapse of the Irish nationalist movement in the summer of 1848 and the devastation of the Great Famine, while not forgetting the positive role of the moderate *Freeman* papers, Irish nationalism was revitalized in 1849 when the political thinking and cultural sentiments of *The Nation* and *The United Irishman* were recycled in *The Irishman* of 1849–50. Reminiscent of '48, at the end of 1849 and in the early part of 1850 there were three warring nationalist groups, Conciliation Hall followers, the IDA and the Irish Alliance, each represented by their respective newspapers. The emergence of the IDA and the Irish Alliance demonstrated the power of newspapers to inaugurate and represent new nationalist organizations, despite the failures of Irish nationalism in 1848. The 1850s also presented four innovative features: the initial development of socialism in association with the Irish nationalist agenda, an experiment in a strong land organization, a brief social and economic union of Catholics and Protestants of north and south, and the formation of an independent Irish parliamentary party. Members of the Dublin nationalist press were at the heart of these innovations, both as political activists and journalists.

Consistent in its concern to improve the economic and social conditions of those living in rural areas, a characteristic of the Dublin nationalist

[184] Duffy, *Two Hemispheres, vol. II*, pp. 3–4; Letter from Lalor to Duffy, 28 Sept. 1849, Duffy Papers, NLI, MS 5757/215–6; Letter from Duffy to Smith O'Brien, 7 Nov. 1852, Duffy Papers, NLI, MS 5758/109.

[185] 'Mr. Duffy's Address', *Nation*, 18 Aug. 1855.

press from 1849 to the mid-1850s was its orientation more towards social than political matters, championing the issues of the lower classes. With the idea of socialism the Dublin nationalist press was widening its scope and bequeathing the notion that the welfare of the lower classes in terms of socialist ideology was an essential part of Irish nationalism, and this thinking was to have a future role in the republican nationalist agenda. Although the press both north and south had much responsibility for the growth of the tenant right societies and its personnel had direct responsibility for the running of the tenant right organization in the early 1850s, the Dublin nationalist press had a much higher profile in this movement; for example, Duffy and *The Nation* were central to the founding of the Irish Tenant League. The Independent Opposition Party and the Tenant League, promoted in particular by the Dublin nationalist press, Duffy's *Nation*, Gray's *Freeman*, Lucas's *Tablet*, but not forgetting Maguire's *Cork Examiner*, were to be revived later by Parnell, who formed the Irish Parliamentary Party and led the highly successful Land League.

What the 1850s lacked was a strong charismatic leader, one of the same ilk as Daniel O'Connell or Parnell. And although at times the Dublin nationalist newspapers in the 1850s took on an almost quasi-leadership role, there is no substitute for a flesh-and-blood leader who can have an impact visually and orally to express ideas and rouse the people intellectually and emotionally into supporting the nationalist cause or, importantly, for having that leader's words and actions reported in newspapers. Smith O'Brien came closest to that position when he returned to Ireland from exile in the late 1850s, but he was unwilling to lead another nationalist organization and essentially acted in an advisory role.

The tenuous link between Irish nationalists in Ireland and America in the 1840s developed into a much stronger relationship in the 1850s. Despite the political failures experienced by Dillon and other rebel journalists, determined not to give up the Irish nationalist cause, they now campaigned in America, the more extreme of them emerging to dictate events in Ireland. A notable role of *The Irishman* of 1849–50, the later 1858 *Irishman* and *The Tribune* lay in keeping alive the rhetoric of extreme Irish nationalism. Refusing to allow Irish nationalism to lie fallow after 1848, there was an almost palpable sense in the Dublin nationalist press, especially in the advanced papers, that despite the 1848 failed rebellion and the Great Famine, the Irish nation was not extinguishable.

CHAPTER 4

The Irish People and the Fenian movement

'We cannot repeat too often that for us there is but one road to liberty. We must look this fact steadily in the face, and prepare, as best we may, for a life and death struggle to save our race from extinction,' *The Irish People*, April 1864.[1]

IN THE 1880S, James Stephens, former head of the IRB, claimed retrospectively that Fenianism 'saved the cause of Irish nationalism from irremediable destruction.'[2] How far this statement is true is a matter of debate. What is important, though, is that the IRB, despite the *débâcle* of 1867, was destined to have a decisive influence upon the events leading to the 1916 Rising and the eventual Anglo-Irish settlement.

The IRB, whose members were known as Fenians, argued that the survival of the Irish nation was dependent on complete separation from Great Britain, to be achieved only by a militant revolution. Although as an organization it continued until 1924, the IRB was at its zenith in the mid-1860s coinciding with the publication of its own weekly newspaper of politics and literature, *The Irish People*, founded in November 1863 and suppressed by the government in less than two years.

Unlike the Irish nationalist movements led by Daniel O'Connell in the early part of the nineteenth century or Charles Stewart Parnell later in the century, there were no high-profile charismatic leaders, and no monster meetings with their visual and aural stimuli to arouse active support for the Fenian cause. Notwithstanding Stephens' adept marketing skills, as the IRB was a conspiratorial society, it was somewhat limited in the effective

[1] 4th LA, *Irish People*, 16 April 1864.

[2] 'Stephens on Fenianism' in Desmond Ryan, *The Fenian Chief: A biography of James Stephens*, Patrick Lynch (intro.) (Dublin: M.H. Gill & Son Ltd., 1967), pp. 325–6.

propagation of its doctrine compared with other main nationalist organizations of the mid-nineteenth century. This changed with the founding of the IRB's own Dublin-based newspaper to transmit its teachings via the medium of the printed word. As a mouthpiece of the IRB *The Irish People* greatly furthered the Fenian cause, and thus created an enduring impact on the development of Irish nationalism.

The Irish People was critical for the survival of the IRB. John O'Mahony, head of the Fenian Brotherhood and a Gaelic scholar, who gave this organization its name in 1859, believed that the word 'Fenian' captured the ethos and spirit of the movement at this time.[3] Gaelic legend depicted the Fenians as gallant 'military defenders of the island; their leader was Fionn Mac Cumhail, and the legions were, after his name Fionn, called Fiana-h-Erionn.'[4] Importantly, *The Irish People* revealed that the IRB's ideology embraced far more than just the concept of physical force. The land question, for instance, was a key theme in *The Irish People*, not least for its value as one of the arguments for the case against British rule. Although cultural nationalism was not uppermost in the IRB's battle-plan for Irish independence, many columns in *The Irish People* were filled with literary items, and while providing the paper with a broad appeal, like other Dublin nationalist papers, they also often complemented the political messages in the leading articles. Highly evident in its pages was *The Irish People*'s marked censure of the British government, whose intention, the Fenians claimed, was to destroy the Irish nation. The IRB's two main opponents, apart from the British government, were the constitutional nationalists and the Catholic Church, and *The Irish People* effectively challenged both of them. It particularly focused on the continuity of ideas from the 1840s *Nation* and the Wolfe Tone tradition, especially the concepts of physical force and republicanism. Although *The Irish People* emulated patterns of rhetoric that commonly appeared in the mid-nineteenth-century Dublin nationalist press – apart from the unique circumstances of the Irish Confederates in 1848 – its militant intentions posed a far greater threat to peace than any other nationalist newspaper during that period in Ireland.

---

[3] O'Mahony, an exile from 1848, lived in Paris with James Stephens until 1852, when he travelled to New York, later becoming Head Centre of the Fenian Brotherhood in 1859.

[4] 2nd LA, *Irish People*, 17 Sept. 1864.

The founding of *The Irish People*

It was in an atmosphere of disillusionment with the constitutional politics of the 1850s, coinciding with both the founding of *The Irishman* and the IRB in 1858 and a downturn in agricultural fortunes the following year, that the writings of the nationalist press in Ireland began to take on an increasingly more intimidating edge. By the early 1860s, the Chief Secretary's office noted that 'The Nation, The Irishman, Dundalk Democrat, Tipperary Vindicator, Connaught Patriot, and others openly taught disloyalty to the British Crown.'[5] *The Freeman*, however, continued to support moderate constitutional nationalism, while the tone of *The Nation* was more radical in comparison. At this time *The Irishman* was the most advanced of the Dublin nationalist papers; having been denied access to *The Nation*, it was in *The Irishman* that the Fenians could express some of their views. While his brother T.D. Sullivan edited *The Nation*, A.M. Sullivan took control of three other Dublin newspapers, *The Morning News* (1859–64), the first daily morning penny paper in Dublin, *The Evening News* (1859–64) and *The Weekly News* (1860–87). These three papers were more concerned with Catholic issues than with Irish nationalism, with the exception of the weekly paper from the end of 1865, when it profited financially from the coverage of the Fenian trials. Under the Sullivans' influence *The Nation* itself veered more towards Catholic issues. In September 1860, for example, when the Papal States were attacked by the Piedmontese, *The Nation* was in the vanguard of producing an abundance of heroic rhetoric on the Irish volunteer group, the Battalion of St Patrick, despite its defeat in battle. R.V. Comerford believed that 'support of the papacy had demonstrated most convincingly the strength and depth of Irish catholic identity.'[6] There is no doubt that *The Nation* was both promoting and reflecting Irish public opinion. Furthermore, the past had shown that in the mid-1840s it did not benefit *The Nation* to have an uneasy relationship with the Catholic Church. The Sullivans may also have been mindful of the commercial success of the 1852 *Weekly Telegraph* with its marked pro-Catholic editorials. While reviving the old spirit of *The Nation* by reasserting the importance of cultural nationalism and bringing a more radical tone to its pages, the

---

[5] A report based on 'Official correspondence, Feb. 1855–Aug. 1869, on Fenianism in Ireland and America', Sir Thomas Larcom Papers, NLI, MS 7517/103. This report may have been written by Samuel Lee Anderson, a solicitor who helped to compile a case for the Fenian trials in 1865.

[6] R.V. Comerford, *The Fenians in Context: Irish Politics and Society, 1848–82* (Dublin: Wolfhound Press, 1985), p. 62.

Sullivans now departed from the non-sectarianism of the 1840s. *The Irish People*, on the other hand, was firm in its belief that unity of creed was essential for the advancement of the Irish nationalist cause.

Since its inception in 1858 the IRB had become embroiled in a bitter conflict with the constitutional nationalists of *The Nation*. Originating in claims by James Stephens that A.M. Sullivan had been an informer (denied by Sullivan), this increasingly acrimonious conflict lasted several years. The IRB had no print medium of its own with which to respond to the attacks by *The Nation*, or indeed to the press generally in Ireland, which was also hostile towards Fenianism. After a recruitment boost in 1861, the following year saw the Fenian movement entering a period of despondency, much of it due to the growing attacks in the press. Thomas Clarke Luby, who was to become a leading writer for *The Irish People*, described it almost as if Fenianism was under siege: apart from *The Irishman* newspaper,

> the storm of calumnies and denunciations now showered down on our heads, as thick and fast as hailstones big and hard as bullets. All the so-called *patriotic* papers … were doing their best or worst against us. *The Freeman* & *Nation* were conspicuous in the fight, especially the last-named degenerate organ.[7]

Up to 1863 the Fenians could, to a limited extent, defend themselves against the constitutional nationalists in *The Irishman* newspaper, but only while Denis Holland was the proprietor and editor. This paper became the unofficial representative of the Brotherhood of St Patrick, founded in 1861, and although an open nationalist organization, it also included some Fenian members.[8] However, when Holland fell into financial troubles, he relinquished the proprietorship of *The Irishman* to former Young Irelander P.J. Smyth in April 1863. The new owner made it known that his paper was to be independent of political pressure, which meant that the IRB was left without any representation in the Dublin nationalist press.

This development in the Dublin press prompted James Stephens to seriously consider the advantages of a new newspaper, exclusively under IRB control. At the start of 1863 the Fenian organization remained in

---

[7] Luby to John O'Leary, 1891, Thomas Clarke Luby Papers, NLI, MS 331.

[8] For further information on the Brotherhood of St Patrick and the press in England see: Anthony McNicholas, 'Rebels at Heart: The National Brotherhood of Saint Patrick and the *Irish Liberator*', *Media History*, vol. 13 (1), 2007, pp. 25–41; 'Co-operation, compromise and confrontation: The *Universal News*, 1860–69', *IHS*, vol. 35 (139), May 2007, pp. 311–26; *Politics, Religion and the Press: Irish Journalism in Mid-Victorian England* (Oxford: Peter Lang AG, 2007).

a dispirited state; morale was low and there was little money available. Although Stephens had hitherto denounced newspapers by arguing that he could shape public opinion far more effectively through his secret society, with his enthusiasm for the cause waning and the future of the IRB in jeopardy, in the summer of 1863 he unexpectedly announced the practical necessity of starting a newspaper to 'recruit our finances and propagate our principles.'[9] He now acknowledged the value of a newspaper as an effective means of promoting Fenianism and combating constitutional nationalism. Although it seemed incongruous to publish a newspaper that represented a secret political society, its intention, apart from encouraging recruitment to the organization, was to provide a focus for current members, while the leadership also hoped the IRB's views could be embraced by a wider public; ironically, as we shall see, the eventual suppression of its newspaper and the arrest and trial of its leaders brought far more publicity than the Fenians could ever have hoped for. Encouraged by much enthusiastic support from IRB members during the setting-up of *The Irish People*, Stephens wrote to John O'Mahony eight weeks prior to its first issue saying that without this new newspaper 'the cause would have been lost.'[10] Stephens later believed that he had indeed made the right decision, for the following year he told O'Mahony that *The Irish People* had 'become a *necessity – a matter of life and death to the organisation*.'[11]

The three leading figures involved in the publication of *The Irish People* were neo-Young Irelanders, inheritors of the romantic nationalism evoked by the 1840s *Nation*. The group of writers who initially founded *The Nation* came from the middle class; *The Irish People*'s leading journalists, Thomas Clarke Luby, John O'Leary and Charles Joseph Kickham, were, by comparison, from the lower middle class. A.M. Sullivan of *The Nation*, despite opposing Fenianism, believed them to be among the 'few men whose rare abilities and invincible courage and fidelity rendered them of priceless value' to the IRB.[12] During the 1850s and early 1860s Luby, O'Leary and Kickham had served their apprenticeships in nationalist journalism. Luby, second in importance to Stephens in the IRB, was nominated by him as the proprietor of *The Irish*

[9] Luby to O'Leary, 1891, Luby Papers, NLI, MS 331.

[10] Letter from James Stephens to John O'Mahony, 4 Oct. 1863, O'Mahony Papers, in W. D'Arcy, *The Fenian Movement in the United States: 1858–1886*, 2nd ed. (New York: Russell & Russell, 1971), p. 31.

[11] Letter from J. Hamilton [James Stephens] to J. O'Mahony, 11 Dec. 1864, Fenian Brotherhood Collection, Catholic University of America (CUA), Box 1, Folder 6. http://www.aladino.wrlc.org/gsdl/collect/fenian/fenian.shtml Accessed 6 April 2005. See also: Bourke, *John O'Leary*, p. 47.

[12] Sullivan, *New Ireland, vol. II*, p. 81.

People. Previously a contributor to the 1849–50 *Irishman* and an associate editor of the 1855–6 *Tribune*, Luby became one of *The Irish People*'s main writers. John O'Leary, another key member of *The Irish People*'s team, had already gained some experience in journalism during his stay in New York on IRB business in 1859 when he contributed to *The Phoenix*, a newspaper espousing Fenianism that had been founded by John O'Mahony. After a few years' absence from the Fenian cause, Stephens invited O'Leary to join *The Irish People*'s staff when he became its editor. Charles Joseph Kickham, a contributor of poetry and prose to nationalist publications, and a valiant defender of Fenianism in *The Irishman* during 1862, was also appointed by Stephens as one of the paper's chief writers. A.M. Sullivan observed that Kickham wrote for the literary periodical *Celt* (1857–59) 'some really exquisite poetry of the simple ballad class, as well as some stories of Irish peasant life exhibiting considerable dramatic power.'[13] Another leading figure of *The Irish People* was Jeremiah O'Donovan Rossa from the Phoenix National and Literary Society, which, as we saw, had been amalgamated into the IRB in 1858. A key figure in IRB recruitment, O'Donovan Rossa now became the new paper's business manager. Stephens himself was only involved in writing one leading article in each of *The Irish People*'s first three issues; editorial control thereafter was in the hands of O'Leary, Luby and Kickham.

Although modelled on the early 1840s *Nation*, the IRB's paper assumed a far more consistently combative approach. Priced 2d unstamped, and 3d stamped, *The Irish People* was issued every Saturday from 28 November 1863 until 16 September 1865 when it was suppressed by the government. Published from Parliament Street, almost on the doorstep of Dublin Castle, *The Irish People* was distributed throughout Ireland and Great Britain; copies of the paper were also despatched to the Fenian Brotherhood in America. The premises of *The Irish People* were, in fact, the headquarters and hub of IRB activity, a distinctive example of the indivisible line between a political organization and its print medium.[14]

The leading IRB journalists, O'Leary, Luby and Kickham, were familiar, both in theoretical and practical terms, with the physical force tradition. Their admiration for the militant rhetoric of the Young Irelander

---

[13] Sullivan, *New Ireland, vol. II*, p. 82. Numerous editions have been published of Charles J. Kickham's famous novel about rural life in Ireland: *Knocknagow: or, The homes of Tipperary* (Dublin: James Duffy, Sons & Co., 1879).

[14] Luby to O'Leary, 1892, Thomas Clarke Luby Papers, NLI, MS 333. Luby, O'Leary and Kickham's importance to the IRB can be seen in a document by Stephens appointing them as a provisional 'Executive' in his absence, subsequently used as evidence in their indictments during the Fenian trials.

John Mitchel, the most outspoken advocate of physical force in the 1840s, combined with their involvement in the rebel activities of 1848–49, influenced them in advancing revolutionary doctrine in *The Irish People*.[15] For example, in an oration for Mitchel's funeral in 1875, Luby declared: 'In my devotion to his principles, I sacrificed brilliant prospects and broke with influential relatives and friends. Principles, not dissimilar to John Mitchel's, I have ever since endeavoured, to the utmost of my feeble ability, to propagate by pen and word and deed.'[16] While it was Mitchel in his *United Irishman* who had inspired them with the idea of achieving Irish independence through physical force, it was the writings of Thomas Davis in *The Nation* that had imbued them with a spiritual sense of Irish nationalism. In his old age, for instance, O'Leary wrote 'for all that is Irish in me, and, above all, for the inspiration that made me Irish, the fountain and the origin must always be sought in Davis.'[17] Although *The Irish People* had a variety of contributors to its pages, O'Leary, Luby and Kickham were the foremost messengers of Fenian philosophy, crafting the paper's contents to promote the cause of Irish revolutionary nationalism.

The Irish People and the ideology of Fenianism

The essential aim of *The Irish People* was to persuade people to support the idea of revolutionary nationalism, in particular as military recruits to the IRB, and to maintain contact with existing members. As John O'Leary stated in his memoirs, *The Irish People* 'served as a sort of recruiting agency for the organization, was a natural channel of communication between its members, and kindled enthusiasm inside and outside the Fenian body.'[18] It was not just

[15] While Luby, O'Leary and Kickham had some peripheral involvement in the attempted rebellion of 1848, Stephens can be singled out for his presence on the barricades in the town of Killenaule, Co. Tipperary, with John Blake Dillon. Already noted in the previous chapter of this book, Luby and O'Leary were revolutionary conspirators in 1849, but there is no apparent evidence suggesting Kickham's involvement; Stephens was an exile in Paris at this time.

[16] 'Funeral Oration over John Mitchel delivered in Madison Square Garden, New York, 1875', Thomas Clarke Luby Papers, NLI, MS 330.

[17] O'Leary, *Fenians and Fenianism, I*, p. 3.

[18] O'Leary, *Fenians and Fenianism, II*, p. 2. It could be argued that the IRB's use of *The Irish People* was a forerunner of later revolutionary political movements; Lenin, when drawing up plans for his new socialist organization, claimed: 'But this work *cannot possibly be carried on* in contemporary Russia without an All-Russian newspaper, issued very frequently. An organisation that is built up around this newspaper, an organisation of *collaborators* of this paper (collaborators in the broad sense of the word, *i.e.*, all those

important for the IRB to recruit prospective soldiers into its organization, but to elicit backing from non-combatant members of society who could also support the Fenian cause. This thinking indicates the hope that many people would be influenced by Fenian doctrine, and when the intended revolution occurred it would meet minimal resistance. It was expected that those purchasing *The Irish People* would be actively contributing to the funds of the IRB; John O'Mahony advised local leaders in America of

> the necessity of supporting The Irish People, our Irish organ, and making up clubs of subscribers for it wherever possible. A subscriber to this paper is pecuniarily as good as an actual member of the Fenian Brotherhood, for the profits derived from it go to support the organization at home. Men unwilling to be initiated, may be thus got to help us indirectly, but efficiently.[19]

However, as far as the intention of raising money for the IRB in Ireland was concerned, *The Irish People* failed, having begun, according to O'Leary, on an 'incredibly small sum of money'; it soon had to rely on funds from its American counterpart.[20] But when the newspaper project got under way a new spirit was injected into the Fenian movement, and the paper achieved much success enticing new membership into the conspiratorial IRB. While it fell short of yielding finance, *The Irish People* compensated by increasing awareness and enthusiasm for the Fenian cause.

In terms of circulation, *The Irish People* could be deemed to have had some success. A.M. Sullivan claimed that *The Irish People*

> swept all before it amongst the Irish in England and Scotland, almost annihilating the circulation of the *Nation* in many places north and south of the Tweed. On the other hand, in Ireland it

working for it) will be ready *for everything*, from protecting the honour, the prestige, and continuity of the party in periods of acute revolutionary "depression" to preparing for, commencing and carrying out the *national armed insurrection*.' V.I. Lenin, 'The "Plan" for an all-Russian political newspaper', in *What Is To Be Done?* (Connecticut, USA: Martino Publishing, 2013), p. 163. As *The Irish People* was crucial to the existence of the IRB, so Lenin believed that a newspaper was essential to the success of his political organization.

19 'Copy of Circular to the Centres of the Fenian Brotherhood', 15 Jan. 1864, in *Report of The Proceedings at the First Sitting of the Special Commission for the County of the City of Dublin, held at Green-street, Dublin, for the Trial of Thomas Clarke Luby, and Others, for Treason-Felony, "The Fenian Conspiracy," commencing on November 27, 1865* (Dublin: Alex Thom, 1866), p. 226.

20 O'Leary, *Fenians and Fenianism, II*, p. 1.

was never able to approach our journals in circulation; and in many places we drove it totally from the field.[21]

The overall average weekly circulation of *The Irish People* is unknown as there is no evidence to show how many unstamped copies were sold. Official figures indicate that from October 1864 to September 1865 *The Irish People* bought far fewer stamps than the other Dublin nationalist weeklies.[22] However, stamps had to be purchased in advance and *The Irish People* had very little money; in fact, initially no stamps were bought by the paper for several months, suggesting that *The Irish People* relied solely on unstamped copies at this time.[23] A police report claimed a circulation figure of 10,000, and Marcus Bourke, O'Leary's biographer, believes that it never went beyond this number.[24] Evidence suggests though that the Fenian newspaper did indeed thrive; for example, a letter from a Limerick news agent to *The Irish People*'s office stated, 'I received 7 Doz of your last issue in good time on Friday evening last all of which I sold, and there were persons I had to dissapoint [*sic*] from the Country.'[25]

Like other nationalist newspapers, circulation in terms of access to *The Irish People*'s contents was certainly not restricted to its purchasers. There was much passing around, and the tradition of communal reading was still widespread; for instance, a correspondent from Myshall, Co. Carlow, informed the editor of *The Irish People* in July 1864 that he recently 'saw a group of men and boys listening to a young man reading the IRISH PEOPLE' outside a chapel.[26] *The Irish People* could also be shared among members of the local IRB groups, or 'Circles.'

Agents in the United States reported ninety-four named subscribers to *The Irish People* in early 1864.[27] Within a year this number had apparently peaked at 600 in April 1865.[28] According to a British government report

[21] Sullivan, *New Ireland, II*, p. 112.

[22] Based on 'Return of Registered Newspapers and Publications in United Kingdom, and Number of Stamps issued 1864–66', HCP, 1866 (491) XL.113.

[23] 'Return of Registered Newspapers and Publications in United Kingdom, and Number of Stamps issued, 1863–4', HCP, 1865 (471) XXXI.65.

[24] Fenian Papers, The National Archives of Ireland (NAI), F Series, 8919R, in Owen McGee, *The IRB: The Irish Republican Brotherhood, from the Land League to Sinn Féin*, 2nd ed. (Dublin: Four Courts Press, 2007), p. 34; Bourke, *O'Leary*, p. 71.

[25] Darby L. O'Grady, Newcastle West, 23 Aug. 1865, Fenian Briefs 1865–9, NAI, Box 3, Envelope 9.

[26] 'Original Correspondence', 11 July 1864, *Irish People*, 23 July 1864.

[27] *The Irish People*, 20 Feb. and 26 March 1864.

[28] K.J. Quigley, 'American financing of Fenianism in Ireland 1858–1867' (MA thesis, St Patrick's College, Maynooth, 1983), p. 40, in Ramón, *A Provisional Dictator*, pp. 158–9.

on Fenianism, 'The Irish People obtained a very extensive circulation' in America.[29]

Included in *The Irish People*'s surviving business papers is a list, albeit undated, of ninety-nine news agents spread over Ireland and Great Britain, from diverse areas such as Cork, Londonderry, Sheffield and Glasgow. Also amongst its business papers, lists reveal subscribers to *The Irish People* in New York, Massachusetts, Kansas and Quebec.[30] The IRB newspaper, it seems, had a wide geographical circulation on both sides of the Atlantic.

There were, however, obstacles to the sale of *The Irish People*. On the one hand, there were those who could not afford to buy the paper, while priests actively discouraged anyone selling or reading *The Irish People*. As O'Leary explained, priests 'certainly succeeded in hindering or hampering the circulation of the paper in many places, and so imposed a financial loss upon us, as well as much worry, odium, and business injury upon many people.'[31] Free copies of *The Irish People* were given to teachers for tactical reasons; they were literate and in a position in their community to pass on information. Despite government threats, teachers continued to read the paper and, because of that, many lost their jobs.[32] John Devoy, at that time an *Irish People* agent in Naas, Co. Kildare, gave away fifty copies each week, essentially to those who could not afford the price, stating that this practice was not uncommon.[33] Although not good business sense, this custom was sanctioned by O'Donovan Rossa, who deemed it more important to spread the Fenian message than to increase the finances of the IRB.

Following in the tradition of Wolfe Tone and the press of the United Irishmen, *The Irish People* emulated the 1840s *Nation* by calling for all classes and creeds in Irish society to work for the nationalist cause. An editorial stated, for example, that 'We do not contemplate Ireland Catholic or Protestant; we contemplate her free and independent; and we extend the hand of love and fellowship to every man of every class and creed who would earnestly labour to make her so.'[34] However, while embracing a

[29] Larcom Papers, NLI, MS 7517/109.

[30] 'Business Papers', Fenian Briefs, 1865–9, NAI, Box 5, Envelope 18.

[31] O'Leary, *Fenians and Fenianism, II*, p. 174.

[32] O'Leary, *Fenians and Fenianism, II*, p. 120.

[33] John Devoy, *Recollections of an Irish Rebel*, Seán Ó Lúing, (intro.) (Shannon: Irish University Press, 1969), pp. 42–3; 1st ed. (New York: 1929). See also: Ryan, *The Fenian Chief*, p. 187.

[34] 3rd LA, *Irish People*, 11 June 1864. This ideal, promoted by *The Irish People*, was later promulgated in the IRB's Constitution of 1873: Bulmer Hobson, *The Irish Times*, 6 May 1961, in Leon Ó Broin, *Revolutionary Underground: The Story of the Irish Republican Brotherhood 1858–1924* (Dublin: Gill and Macmillan Ltd., 1976), p. 7.

small number from the middle classes, membership of the IRB was mainly Catholic lower-class, and this was varied in terms of occupation, social status and location. O'Leary observed that the IRB included 'shopmen' of varying grades, many from the large city establishments, artisans, small farmers, shopkeepers, servant boys and labourers.[35] T.W. Moody found that members included 'schoolmasters, commercial travellers, business and professional men.'[36] While there were far fewer members in the countryside, IRB supporters predominated in urban areas that were more conducive to the spread of newspapers and the exchange of ideas. This was particularly relevant to Great Britain with its industrial conurbations, where the working classes were more dynamically politicized than in Ireland with their agitation for political reforms and trade union activity. Furthermore, urban people had greater opportunity to be better educated and to be more politically aware than those in rural areas. It is not surprising, overall, that the urban working classes were receptive to *The Irish People*.

As *The Irish People* was intended to appeal to a wide variety of classes in Irish society, it needed to be well written. The journalism in this paper was, in fact, of an impressive standard. For example, in 1865 Lord Wodehouse, the Lord Lieutenant of Ireland, who was a regular reader of *The Irish People*, believed that it was 'very superior to the *Nation* which is a poor sneaking rebel, and indeed is better written than most of the Irish papers: of course it preaches open rebellion.'[37] R.V. Comerford, in his biography of Charles J. Kickham, remarked that *The Irish People* had 'acquired a high reputation in the history of Irish political journalism.'[38] While the IRB was largely a movement of the lower classes, there are indications that a number of people of a higher social status also read the paper. John Devoy noted, for example, that 'several prominent people' were subscribers to *The Irish People*, among them the Irish Liberal-Conservative MP and barrister Isaac Butt, and Parnell's mother, Delia, who was 'a strong sympathizer with the movement.'[39] Another clue that the better off read the paper is reflected in the type of advertisements appearing frequently in *The Irish People*: they included such items as restaurants and chandeliers. However, despite its intentions and its good journalistic quality, *The Irish People*'s appeal for

---

[35] O'Leary, *Fenians and Fenianism, II*, pp. 237–9.

[36] T.W. Moody, *Davitt and the Irish Revolution 1846–82* (Oxford: Oxford University Press, 1981), pp. 40–1.

[37] Wodehouse to Foreign Secretary, Lord Clarendon, Clarendon Deposit, c.99, 26.2.1865 in Leon Ó Broin, *Fenian Fever. An Anglo-American Dilemma* (London: Chatto and Windus, 1971), p. 9.

[38] Comerford, *Charles J. Kickham*, p. 68.

[39] Devoy, *Recollections*, p. 43.

inclusiveness was somewhat undermined by the paper's criticism of the upper and middle classes.

The Irish People deplored what it perceived to be the lack of commitment by the middle classes to the nationalist cause, but realized their potential usefulness for its success. Viewed from a practical perspective, the middle classes could provide financial assistance, particularly necessary for procuring arms, and social leadership; their support could also be indicative of the credibility of the movement and so help to make Fenianism seem more respectable. At times it appeared that the Fenian journalists wanted to shame the middle classes into joining their cause; they were often portrayed as traitors, particularly their part in the failure of constitutional political activities of the 1850s. However, according to *The Irish People*, their offences could be redeemed if they now joined the revolutionary movement.[40] The middle classes, though, generally distrusted the conspiratorial IRB.

While *The Irish People* held out some small hope of persuading some of the middle classes to join them, they knew that the upper classes would definitely remain aloof from the IRB. Perceived by the IRB as foes of Ireland, *The Irish People* wrote that, 'The higher classes, with a very few exceptions, are not Irish but English' and 'our enemies.'[41] This presented a problem for the IRB: by associating themselves with the doctrine of inclusivity, originating with the heroic rebels of the past, *The Irish People*'s journalists could gain more credibility, but the Fenians were, at the same time, realistic in thinking that the landed aristocracy could never be reconciled to their cause. Apart from the physical force issue, the IRB's policy of land redistribution following separation from Great Britain would never have been acceptable to them. For *The Irish People*, the ideal of unity of class meant, in reality, the exclusion of the upper classes.

In relation to unity of creed, although membership of the IRB was, understandably, overwhelmingly Catholic, there were some non-Catholic members in Ulster. Frank Roney, who was appointed by Stephens as a 'Centre' in Ulster (a senior organizer, the IRB equivalent to the rank of colonel) observed that the IRB thrived in Co. Down, where Protestants were particularly supportive.[42] Through its rhetoric *The Irish People* encouraged Protestant support for the IRB, and vigorously opposed sectarianism. Like other Irish nationalists, sectarianism was seen by the Fenians as harmful to the separatist cause. Fighting against religious bigotry, *The Irish People* argued that if the Protestants could be 'calmly reasoned with, they would

[40] 1st LA, *Irish People*, 26 March 1864.

[41] 1st LA, *Irish People*, 26 March 1864.

[42] Frank Roney, *Irish Rebel and Californian Labor Leader*, p. 57.

soon see that the present National movement involves no question of religion or race, but has been set on foot solely with the view of saving from utter ruin an entire nation.'[43] The IRB's non-sectarian image mirrored the philosophy of Theobald Wolfe Tone and Thomas Davis. In trying to maintain this tradition, *The Irish People* stated, for example: 'An Irish nation, according to DAVIS's broad idea, should include all races and sects of Irishmen.'[44] Ideologically, this line of thinking stressed that the nature of an Irish nation should be inclusive. In practical terms, like other past nationalists, the IRB's journalists thought that if Catholics and Protestants could unite it would greatly increase the strength of their organization. *The Irish People* believed that, 'when we see the all-damning blight of religious intolerance surely and steadily stealing away like night mists before the rising sun, we know we are in the true path, and that sooner or later, it must lead us to liberty.'[45] The Fenians, however, could not undo the legacy of religious strife, and despite its non-sectarian appeal, *The Irish People*, like the 1840s *Nation* before it, failed to attract as many Protestants as it had hoped.

A potential barrier to the recruitment of IRB members was the Catholic Church, which had traditionally condemned secret societies. A determined offensive against Fenianism by the Catholic Church began before the start of *The Irish People* when the IRB appeared to undermine the social and spiritual control of clerical dominance over the people. The relationship between priests and their parishioners originated, claimed *The Irish People*, when the people were subjugated by England and reduced to 'ignorant slaves'; in this state 'the people naturally looked for guidance to the only educated class that cared for or sympathised with them.'[46] Allegiance to the IRB meant being influenced by another authority other than the parish priest and the Church believed that its power over people's lives was being threatened. Important for encouraging cohesiveness, inspiring confidence and disseminating its political beliefs, the IRB provided social and political activities for its mainly lower-class members that were independent of the Church and, indeed, of middle-class control. As the middle classes were affiliated to the Catholic Church it was in the latter's interest to challenge the IRB.

The opposition of the Catholic Church to Fenianism was intensified with the advent of *The Irish People*, which provided the IRB with a platform to defend itself and challenge attacks by the Church. Catholics were

---

43 2nd LA, *Irish People*, 25 June 1864.
44 1st LA, *Irish People*, 16 April 1864.
45 2nd LA, *Irish People*, 25 June 1864.
46 1st LA, *Irish People*, 9 April 1864.

confronted by Pastorals, the confessional and ultimately the withdrawal of sacraments. Letters from those experiencing the wrath of local priests provide evidence of the hostility of the Catholic Church towards Fenianism, where spiritual censure included tirades from the pulpit. Near the end of March 1864, for example, a correspondent from Co. Antrim informed *The Irish People* that, following Sunday Mass, his parish priest read out some of Archbishop Paul Cullen's recent Pastoral Address, which had condemned the Fenians and their press, and afterwards 'he told the people that it was most damnable to entertain such notions as Nationality in Ireland, that they were no patriots who did so, and as for Fenians, they were monsters too horrible to be tolerated in a Christian land.'[47] Concerned about the power of Fenianism, later that year Cullen was prominent in founding the National Association of Ireland in alliance with John Gray of *The Freeman's Journal*.[48] It was a moderate nationalist group which Cullen hoped would draw support away from the Fenians, but failed. *The Irish People* railed against this new group and was joined by *The Nation*, which had not forgotten what it deemed as Cullen's betrayal of the independent Irish party in the previous decade. Opposition of the Catholic Church to Fenianism, however, did not prevent thousands from joining the IRB, or reading its newspaper, even though most of the priests decreed it a mortal sin. Despite the Catholic Church's censure, membership continued to increase during *The Irish People*'s existence, suggesting that the IRB, through the medium of its newspaper, appeared to be a successful opponent of the Catholic Church's offensive on Fenianism.

Most of the articles on the topic of religion and politics were written by Charles Kickham, who proved a valiant defender against clerical attacks on the IRB and *The Irish People*. Like many other Fenians, he reconciled his Catholic faith with his political beliefs. *The Irish People* claimed that politics and religion were separate spheres of society, and believed that the participation of the Church in politics was of no value to the Irish nationalist cause; for example, *The Irish People* cited what it believed to be the priests' 'hostility' towards the insurgents in the attempted 1848 rebellion and the Catholic Church's harmful involvement in the 1850s tenant league movement.[49] The Catholic Church was criticized by the IRB for making

[47] 'Original Correspondence', 28 March 1864, *Irish People*, 9 April 1864.

[48] Focusing on issues that included religious education, disestablishment of the Church of Ireland and land reform, this organization, one of whose members was John Blake Dillon, did not have much success, in part due to internal strife and opposition from other nationalists.

[49] 2nd LA, *Irish People*, 4 June 1864.

'no distinction between purely spiritual and mere temporal matters,' which clouded its judgement in political affairs.[50] Aware of the influence priests could have, *The Irish People* was concerned that there should be a separation between religion and politics: 'We distinctly declared that it was our wish that the Catholics of Ireland should revere their clergy as ministers of religion. But we deny the right of the clergy to dictate to the people in politics.'[51]

By keeping Catholic priests out of politics the IRB was not only protecting its own recruitment drive but also attempting to create a non-sectarian persona for the organization with the potential to attract Protestants into its ranks. Had support been forthcoming from the Catholic Church this would have been problematic for the IRB, for the alignment of the Catholic religion and nationality as one cause worth dying for was contrary to the organization's image of Fenianism as a non-sectarian movement; although this was to change with Patrick Pearse and the extreme nationalist of the twentieth century, when Catholicism and revolutionary nationalism became indivisible.

While *The Irish People* adopted a defensive position in relation to the Catholic priesthood in furthering the Fenian cause, its writers found it essential to apply an offensive approach against the constitutionalists, and the nature of their discourse was sometimes laced with humour, sarcasm and ridicule. Constitutional nationalism was something *The Irish People* passionately opposed. A thriving constitutional movement could have hindered the progress of a revolutionary organization. The IRB, through *The Irish People*, was therefore unrelenting in attacking its critics, particularly its arch enemy, *The Nation*. When *The Irish People* was founded, not only did it immediately articulate in print the existing bitter conflict between revolutionary and constitutional nationalism, it intensified the rivalry between these two opposing forces. The division between constitutional and extreme nationalists during the nineteenth century was especially marked during the early to mid-1860s, particularly coinciding with the lifespan of the IRB newspaper, during which the battle between *The Nation* and *The Irish People* fuelled much antagonism that went beyond the confines of newsprint.

One of the bitterest clashes between constitutionalists and revolutionists occurred over Dublin Corporation's decision to erect a statue of Prince Albert rather than one of Henry Grattan in College Green. On Monday 22 February 1864 a protest meeting was held at the Rotunda, arranged by A.M. Sullivan and others with similar political views. As Grattan was seen

[50] 1st LA, *Irish People*, 9 April 1864.

[51] 'Pulpit denunciations – priests in Politics', *Irish People*, 24 Sept. 1864.

traditionally to represent the constitutional nationalists, they believed this to be an opportunity to stir up public feeling for their cause. However, while Grattan was far less odious to the Fenians than Prince Albert, a symbol of British rule, the IRB was determined to prevent the constitutionalists gaining from this protest meeting. Under the guise of ridding the meeting of the presence of Sullivan for being a 'felon-setter' (informer), the Fenians caused disruption by hurling invective at him, which erupted into violence. The Dublin newspapers' reports on this incident caught the intensity of the passions felt by the opposing groups of Irish nationalists. *The Freeman's Journal* observed that 'For a considerable time the Round Room of the Rotunda was the scene of a carnival of uproar and disorder; the like of which, it is no exaggeration to say, was never witnessed within the walls of that or any other building.'[52] In a leading article, *The Irish People* hailed the collapse of this meeting as a great success: 'The people of Dublin gained a glorious moral triumph. They consummated a noble act of public justice. They made manifest to the world that there is one thing above all which Irishmen will never tolerate, and that is a felon-setter acting the part of a patriot.'[53] Ironically, despite the Fenians being the initiators of the violence, through its impassioned rhetoric *The Irish People* gave the impression of assuming the moral high ground. But although the IRB had won this round, in a subsequent meeting relating to the statue they were outwitted by the constitutionalists who had provided special entry tickets and guards at the door. This whole event, much of it indirectly caused by the battle-lines drawn between *The Nation* and *The Irish People*, is a notable example of the Dublin nationalist press operating in a highly divisive and negative manner.

An incident like this shows the dual nature of Fenianism. IRB members sometimes conducted themselves in an aggressive manner, the above meeting being one of the most outrageous examples, whose 'violence, disorder, and ruffianism, has rarely, if ever, been equalled in the city of Dublin,' according to *Saunder's Weekly*.[54] However, producing a quality newspaper could be seen to elevate the IRB's image, and it could be further argued that *The Irish People* gave Fenianism a sense of respectability. For example, the journalists argued intelligently, eloquently and compassionately about the state of the Irish nation, which demonstrated that they were not just a bunch of roughnecks on hand to sabotage nationalist meetings organized

52 'The monster meeting in the Rotundo [*sic*] – extraordinary scenes', *Freeman's Journal*, 23 Feb. 1864.

53 1st LA, *Irish People*, 27 Feb. 1864.

54 'The Prince Consort testimonial – meeting at the Rotundo', [*sic*] *Saunder's Weekly*, Feb. 1864, reprinted in *Irish People*, 27 Feb. 1864.

by the constitutionalists. It must be said, though, that physical force was essentially their milieu both rhetorically and in practice.

Although conflict between constitutional and revolutionary nationalists stimulated political debate, energies directed at each other rather than at the government may have inhibited progress in persuading public opinion to support the nationalist cause. It gave Dublin Castle much satisfaction to see *The Irish People* 'at war with its brothers in treason, the "Nation," "Morning News," and "Irishman."'[55] Conversely, the government would have been far more concerned if the nationalist movement, rather than being composed of competing groups, had been united in one body as it was in 1843, enabling it to make convincing strides in the development of the Irish nationalist cause. The bitter newspaper conflict between *The Irishman* and *The Nation* in 1849–50 had been another example of wasted energy. Only when co-operation occurred between individual Fenians and the constitutionalists in the 1879–82 Land War did the nationalist movement achieve impressive gains. In 1881 Parnell's *United Ireland* newspaper, edited by William O'Brien, had a central role in appealing to both moderate and extreme nationalists, thus providing cohesion to the nationalist cause at that time. *The Irish People*, on the other hand, had no wish to accommodate the constitutional nationalists.

According to *The Irish People*, the constitutionalists were deceiving the Irish people by trying to persuade them that peaceful methods could win justice for Ireland. Considering this policy to be flawed, and in a tone reminiscent of John Mitchel's mocking *United Irishman* editorials, *The Irish People* was determined to expose the constitutionalists. As Belfast Fenian Frank Roney stated in his memoirs, one of the main objectives of *The Irish People* was 'to make manifest those who were the covert enemies of Irish liberty while claiming to be its sincere friends.'[56] Believing that revolution was the only way forward for the nationalist movement, *The Irish People* reminded its readers that, historically, peaceful methods of furthering the Irish nationalist cause had proved ineffective and were discredited. Sometimes the Fenians would write in general terms of the powerlessness of peaceful agitation:

> But neither parliamentary nor non-parliamentary agitators – nor a happy combination of both – can any longer deceive the

---

[55] 'Opinion of Solicitor General', J.A. Lawson, 22 Feb. 1864, NAI, Chief Secretary's Office Registered Papers (CSORP) 1864/12151; see also: Sir Thomas Larcom Papers, NLI, MS 7586.

[56] Roney, *Autobiography*, p. 69.

> Irish people. The people know they cannot be saved by either declamation or begging petitions ... We trust and believe that it is clear as noonday to the Irish people, that Ireland must be saved by deeds and not by words.[57]

Another strategy of the IRB was to target specific people and events. *The Irish People* especially alluded to the failure of the Tenant League and the betrayal by Keogh and Sadleir in the early 1850s. The IRB also reproached present-day constitutionalists, using their own words against them in an attempt to discredit their moral force stand. For example, *The Irish People* attacked Irish MPs, most notably sarcastically singling out Daniel O'Donoghue, the Independent Opposition MP for Co. Tipperary:

> The O'DONOGHUE declared that he 'found the English House of Commons to be an assembly over which the Irish people exercise *no control whatever.*' But with that consistency for which he has always been so remarkable, the 'gallant young Chieftan' [*sic*] follows up this declaration with another, to wit – that he had no notion of abandoning the English House of Commons![58]

Overall, the constitutional nationalists were portrayed as impotent, illogical, selfish and betrayers of the people. While A.M. Sullivan was particularly targeted by the Fenians, John Gray of *The Freeman's Journal* was also attacked. Sneering at his recent knighthood, *The Irish People* declared: 'If Ireland be miserable to-day, it is because, listening to the counsels of political humbugs like SIR JOHN, she failed to adopt a war-policy.'[59] Criticism of the constitutionalists in *The Irish People* was relentless: 'They injure, rather than serve, the national cause, by deluding people who can't at once see through them, into putting a faith in their patriotism, which they are sure to disappoint.'[60] The Irish National League, a new constitutional nationalist group, founded in early 1864 by Young Irelander John Martin (who was back in Ireland after an unconditional pardon in 1856) was attacked and ridiculed by *The Irish People*; this organization made little headway and it is likely that the Fenians' newspaper rhetoric was a factor in its failure.[61]

57 4th LA, *Irish People*, 16 April 1864.

58 4th LA, *Irish People*, 10 Sept. 1864.

59 4th LA, *Irish People*, 20 Feb. 1864. Gray's knighthood was conferred on him in June 1863 for chairing a committee that improved Dublin's water supply.

60 3rd LA, *Irish People*, 9 Jan. 1864.

61 See, for example: 3rd LA, *Irish People*, 20 Aug. 1864.

The Irish People's journalists projected a compelling argument for militancy by presenting the Irish nation as a long-suffering victim of English rule desperately in need of rejuvenation. Readers were continually reminded that

> the history of Ireland has been little more than a series of horrors which, whether in lands savage or civilized, the world has never seen surpassed, if ever equalled – the butcheries of the Eighth Henry, of Elizabeth, of the iron-handed Cromwell, the indescribable atrocities of the penal laws, down to the famine graves of 1847, and the wholesale flight of the Irish race which we now witness over the waves of the Atlantic.[62]

The Fenians perceived their cause to be noble, and articulated this idea through a romantic discourse. It was their belief that 'They [prostrate nations] must be purified by a long course of heroic sacrifice. ... The true aim of man's life is the elevation of his being. We should each and all endeavour to "make our lives sublime," by ever pursuing the path of duty careless of consequences.'[63] *The Irish People* referred to the Irish struggle against England in terms of its longevity and its nature; the longer the struggle the more purified the nation would become because of the duration of the suffering and the resistance to tyranny. The idea of the link between suffering and regeneration was not just the preserve of the Fenians in Irish nationalism. At a Repeal banquet in August 1843, John Blake Dillon had spoken of the relationship between the sufferings of the Irish people and its regenerative force as one that was 'purifying the people for the trial through which they have to pass.'[64] However, at this time the Young Irelanders were not actively pursuing a physical force policy, and language like this and its accompanying bellicose literature in the early 1840s *Nation* was more to do with sabre-rattling and certainly not a directive to its readers to take up arms. The Fenian journalists, on the other hand, believed that it was their destiny to tread the noble path of militant resistance to their perception of invasion and subjugation, stating:

> The struggle of a people against oppression must always involve danger and much sacrifice ... To all who live and look around them in the island, its wretched condition must be palpable. The

62 3rd LA, *Irish People*, 9 July 1864.
63 3rd LA, *Irish People*, 22 Oct. 1864.
64 'The Banquet', Castlebar, Co. Mayo, 30 July 1843, *Nation*, 5 Aug. 1843.

> only means of remedying that wretched condition is palpable, too, and whenever our time for revolution comes we must not be afraid of death ... The fate of Ireland is in the hands of her people ... if they UNITE, ORGANISE, and PREPARE for a struggle that the future is likely to bring, they may have the satisfaction of seeing Ireland free, and their names shall be blest.[65]

The Irish People conveyed an impression of pursuing a just and sacred crusade, and whoever joined this cause would not only be keeping alive the traditional resistance to English rule but would also be saviours of the Irish nation. Apart from recruiting soldiers, convincing public opinion was an essential part of the preparation for combating the opposition when rebellion began, thus helping the IRB to achieve success. Articulating the nobility of the Fenian cause in *The Irish People* was a way of rallying both combatant and non-combatant support, which included convincing those in influential positions in society.

In harmony with the noble quality of the Fenian cause, *The Irish People* stressed the nature of the practical reality of preparation required for military action where, during this pre-revolutionary stage, members of the IRB were to be trained as superior soldiers. In May 1864 *The Irish People* stated:

> that the sort of preparation we contemplate would, in the first instance, act beneficially upon the morals of the people. It would tend to raise our young men above all low habits and degrading vices. It would make them respect themselves, and fire them with the ennobling ambition of the soldier of liberty. The consciousness of having run some risk, and of being ready to run all risks for poor old Ireland, would fill them with an honest pride, and make them sober, manly, industrious, and tolerant. In a word, organization would make the young men of Ireland, morally and physically, better men.[66]

According to the IRB's newspaper, by joining its organization the young men would be lifted to a higher personal status, becoming superior human beings in thought and deed. Rhetoric such as this was intended to persuade people that they could be a part of an elite group whose mission was to save the Irish nation from destruction. But to what extent these theoretical

[65] 4th LA, *Irish People*, 5 Nov. 1864.
[66] 1st LA, *Irish People*, 28 May 1864.

intentions filtered down in practical terms to the lower ranks of the IRB is difficult to say. What is known is that a year later *The Irish People* observed that while some newspapers had seen Fenians as disreputable, their image of them had now changed, adding: 'Our young men are becoming more intelligent and manly, and, consequently, more moral every day; and this change is most apparent precisely in those places where the *Irish People* is most read.'[67] This article suggests that *The Irish People* had made a positive impression on those who had contact with its rhetoric. In his memoirs O'Leary claimed that from around the start of *The Irish People* those now joining the IRB were a 'better class of young men' who possessed improved social and educational skills, implying that his paper may have had some responsibility for this new trend of membership.[68] Isaac Butt's defence of the Fenian prisoners in 1865–68 and his work for their release as president of the Amnesty Association suggests a mark of the Fenians' positive character.[69] Whether or not it could be related to *The Irish People*, the qualitative nature of the Fenians could also be observed, for example, by 'a virulent enemy of Fenianism who had first-rate opportunities of knowing the Irish masses in Great Britain, [who] testified that "Fenianism tended to sobriety, to solid reading, to self-respect and general improvement of conduct and appearance."'[70] Importantly, if the quality of the IRB's membership was high this would accord with the Fenians' adoption of the concept of self-reliance.

Arguing the case for militancy, *The Irish People* appropriated the idea of self-reliance that had originated in *The Nation*. In an *Irish People* article entitled 'National self-reliance,' referring to 'ourselves alone,' the IRB campaigned that it was essential for the people of Ireland to prepare themselves for armed rebellion.[71] Sufficient preparation would enable the revolution to be successful, and this was a much-discussed prerequisite in *The Irish People*: 'we should be preparing – silently, actively preparing.'[72] The Irish people could not rely on other nations to free them. Even if help were forthcoming from abroad, a home force was essential not only

[67] 1st LA, *Irish People*, 17 June 1865.

[68] O'Leary, *Fenians and Fenianism, II*, p. 236.

[69] Isaac Butt had previously defended Young Irelanders William Smith O'Brien, Thomas Francis Meagher and Charles Gavan Duffy in 1848–49.

[70] This unnamed person was a follower of Isaac Butt: Emile Strauss, *Irish Nationalism and British Democracy* (London: Methuen & Co., 1951), p. 150; F. Hugh O'Donnell, *A History of the Irish Parliamentary Party, vol. I*, (London: Longmans, Green & Co., 1910), p. 317, in Strauss, *Irish Nationalism and British Democracy*, p. 150.

[71] 2nd LA, *Irish People*, 2 Jan. 1864.

[72] 3rd LA, *Irish People*, 16 April 1864.

to ensure military success, but also to prevent any foreign country that was assisting from pursuing its own designs on Ireland. *The Irish People* declared that, 'They must first make themselves able to rely, if need be, on their own hearts and arms.' It would arouse the support of other nations, for when 'they have self-reliance they will also be able to win the sympathy, and probably the recognition and aid of other nations.'[73] The Fenians were also following the United Irishmen's tradition: in the 1790s they organized a home army and persuaded the French government to supply them with military assistance in the coming rebellion. But this tradition was also intertwined with another, taking advantage of any difficulty in which Britain might find itself embroiled. The IRB was conscious, therefore, that it should be ready to seize any moment that may present itself when Britain would become militarily vulnerable; as a leading article in *The Irish People* declared: 'Nations that never relax preparations for the overthrow of their tyrants, are always able to seize on favourable opportunities.'[74] *The Irish People* further stressed the IRB's intention to pursue this strategy in line with the concept of self-reliance.

For the IRB's journalists, however, the idea of self-reliance extended beyond just having a revolutionary army to rid Ireland of British rule and to achieve independence; it would protect the people, keeping them safe and allowing time for the Irish nation *by itself* to regenerate the country politically, economically and culturally. The concept of self-reliance had a revival in 1905 when Arthur Griffith, one of the founders of Sinn Féin, advocated a dual monarchy under a British crown with a particular stress on economic and cultural independence. While Griffith did not advocate physical force, in the next decade after the 1916 Rising, a reconstructed Sinn Féin became associated with republicanism and militancy, echoing *The Irish People*'s policies. *The Irish People* believed that once Ireland was independent of Great Britain she would have proved her strength, by herself, through war and could begin to regenerate the nation, and self-reliance in war would give way to self-reliance in peace.

It was not, however, just the strength to achieve political autonomy that was important to *The Irish People*, but to stand proudly among the world's nations. Even though empowerment was a concept remote from the psyche of the Irish nation still suffering from the devastation of the Great Famine, the IRB's newspaper nevertheless suggested that it was attainable by insurrection. In one of its more impassioned articles *The Irish People* wrote:

---

[73] 2nd LA, *Irish People*, 2 Jan. 1864.

[74] 2nd LA, *Irish People*, 2 Jan. 1864.

> The day Irishmen humble the haughty crest of England, they chain the glory of Ireland for ever to the Stars; they strike a blow that resounds through eternity. On that day, prayers of gratitude and blessings shall mount to heaven from trampled regions in every corner of the globe, and Irishmen shall be hailed by the world, not merely as the deliverers of the sacred Isle, but as the redeemers of enthralled mankind![75]

By providing a scenario of what it would be like if the Fenians were to be successful, *The Irish People* alluded to the universal prestige that would be heaped on the Irish people once victory was secured. The IRB's journalists used this line of rhetoric as part of an appeal to the pride and self-esteem of a nation believed by Irish nationalists to have been greatly downtrodden by its neighbour, and the glory that would accrue if successful in a war against this allegedly powerful and despised tyrant.

One of the most important ways to encourage membership of the IRB was to convince people that they would succeed in combat against the armed forces of the British government. They needed to be persuaded that they were capable of effective militarism and to be imbued with confidence. In explaining the failure of the attempted '48 rebellion, the Fenians blamed insufficient preparation. The Young Irelanders, *The Irish People* believed, were '*amateur* revolutionists.'[76] Learning from failures of the past, the IRB was adamant that it should be fully prepared and not blunder into any premature action. People had to be assured of the viability of success in physical combat. The Fenian journalists, therefore, informed them that they were powerful, strong and noble and, given the opportunity, could prove it. Toby Joyce, in his study of Fenianism in the mid-1860s, identified a link between the IRB and the cult of manhood that had developed alongside nationalism in Europe during the nineteenth century.[77] From its first issue *The Irish People* presented a psychological discourse with an emotional appeal to people's self-esteem, dignity, pride and nobility: 'never have the youth of this country been moved and pervaded by a nobler spirit of patriotism – never been more compact of the stuff of martyrs and heroes.'[78] This was a challenge to

[75] 1st LA, *Irish People*, 13 Feb. 1864.

[76] 1st LA, *Irish People*, 30 April 1864.

[77] Toby Joyce, '"Ireland's trained and marshalled manhood": The Fenians in the mid-1860s' in Margaret Kelleher, James M. Murphy (eds.), *Gender Perspectives in Nineteenth-Century Ireland. Public and Private Spheres* (Dublin: Irish Academic Press, 1997), p. 71.

[78] 1st LA, *Irish People*, 28 Nov. 1863.

an individual's manhood and in turn to the manhood of the Irish nation, sentiments later to be echoed by Patrick Pearse. O'Donovan Rossa claimed in his memoirs that 'The I.R.B. movement generated a spirit of manhood in the land that the enemy could not crush.'[79] *The Irish People*'s editorials were often written in the form of a charismatic leader rallying the troops:

> Youth of Ireland! You are our vanguard. Be prepared to meet the foe in an ordered phalanx, and your measured tramp shall hush the voice of denunciation – you will inspire the waverer with courage – the doubter with confidence – the selfish with devotion – the despairing with hope – the apathetic with life, and UNITED Ireland leaping to her feet, shall, with one sweep of her unfettered arm hurl the invader into the sea.[80]

Such language was intended to stir the emotions of young men and entice them into the IRB, as well as to retain the loyalty of existing members.

The motif of manliness frequently appeared in *The Irish People*, especially in the context of the ongoing American Civil War (1861–65) where many Irish-Americans participated both in the Union and Confederate armies.[81] *The Irish People* emphasized the positive military qualities of the Irish in the Civil War. For example, they reported that, 'in the present American war regimental officers, born in Ireland under lowly roofs and trained to roughest toil, (some even beginning life as mere rude labourers) lead their men through dread battles with prompt intelligence, with a nobleness and devotion.'[82] Irish rebels living in America also became involved in the war; Thomas Francis Meagher, for instance, was a general in the Union Army.[83]

---

79 Diarmuid O'Donovan Rossa, *Rossa's Recollections 1838 to 1898: Memoirs of an Irish Revolutionary*, Seán Ó Lúing (intro.), (Shannon: Irish University Press, 1972), p. 250; originally in *United Irishman*, New York, 11.1.1896 to 7.5.1898; 1st ed. (New York: 1898).

80 1st LA, *Irish People*, 23 Jan. 1864.

81 *The Irish People* maintained a neutral stance towards the American Civil War. When an American correspondent began to make contributions from 9 July 1864 it was made clear by the editor that the correspondent's views were entirely his own, and stated that: 'We know there are many good Irishmen in the North and South, of every possible shade of political opinion, and it would pain us extremely to wound the feelings of any man (in America or out of it) who is willing to *serve* Ireland. Of course we, like all the world, feel an intense interest (for are not the lives of but too many of our brothers at stake) in the great quarrel which is now being fought out in America; but after all, our one object in life is not to save or sunder the Union, but to free Ireland.'

82 3rd LA, *Irish People*, 26 Dec. 1863.

83 'America. General Meagher in Boston', *Boston Pilot*, [n.d.], reprinted in *Irish People*, 12 March 1864.

The American Civil War more than anything else was used by *The Irish People* to raise the prestige of the military qualities of the Irishman:

> It has restored the Irish people's weakened confidence in the courage of their hearts and the might of their arms ... What wonder, that they [foreign nations] began to look on the distinct nationality of Ireland as dead ... this American war has given us back our military reputation in its pristine lustre.[84]

Many Irishmen, in fact, joined the Civil War armies in America to learn a soldier's skill in preparation for the expected fight for the revolutionary cause in Ireland.[85] With the intention of boosting morale in Ireland, much space was devoted in *The Irish People* to chronicling the events of the American Civil War, keeping before the people the military prowess and bravery of Irish soldiers.

While *The Irish People* could discuss Fenian principles, it could not openly associate itself with the affairs of the secret organization that it represented. On the other hand, as the Fenian Brotherhood was allowed to operate legally in America, *The Irish People* often chronicled its activities, which was very useful for boosting the morale of IRB members in Ireland.[86] Frequent reports and promises from the Fenian Brotherhood were reprinted from American newspapers in *The Irish People*. A message was delivered from the Chicago Congress of the Fenian Brotherhood to the people of Ireland, for example, stating, 'We are solemnly pledged to labour earnestly and continuously for the regeneration of our beloved Ireland ... And when the wished-for hour will have arrived, we shall be prepared with you to meet the implacable persecutors of our race in battle array.'[87] With its distribution in America, *The Irish People* had an impact on the Fenian Brotherhood. Irish immigrants in America, either escapees from the Great Famine or from the British authorities, could empathize with those in the home country through their membership of the Fenian Brotherhood. As Luby recollects, 'the real strength of American "*Fenianism*" ... dates from

[84] 3rd LA, *Irish People*, 26 Dec. 1863.

[85] See, for example: O'Donovan Rossa, *Rossa's Recollections*, p. 258.

[86] There was also an open political organization called the Fenian Sisterhood, founded to support the Fenian Brotherhood. Members of the Fenian Sisterhood were well respected; for example, a letter from Illinois to the editor of *The Irish People* states: 'The ladies in America are with this cause, heart and hand. In many places they have organised, held regular meetings, sent contributions to the cause, and done all in their power to advance the interests of the Fenian Brotherhood!': *Irish People*, 4 June 1864.

[87] *New York Sunday Mercury*, [n.d.], reprinted in *Irish People*, 5 Dec. 1863.

the "*Irish People*" period.'[88] In its writings the Fenian Brotherhood often mirrored the content and style of the IRB journalists, particularly their fiery language. More significantly, the rhetoric of the Fenian Brotherhood, reprinted in *The Irish People*, implied that a dedicated and powerful organization in America was ready to assist the IRB in Ireland. It must have been an important psychological boost for members to have what appeared to be this greater community across the Atlantic willing to help them, and to believe that success was more attainable with this additional support from a seemingly formidable ally.

A significant event that required direct co-operation between *The Irish People* and the Fenian Brotherhood was the week-long Chicago Fair. An 'Address of national Irishmen in America to their country-people in Ireland' on 1 January 1864 stated that its purpose 'during Fair time, [was] to appeal to the minds and hearts of the Irish in America to fall into the Irish national ranks.'[89] The people in Ireland were asked for contributions to be forwarded to America via *The Irish People*'s offices, and sold at the Chicago Fair. O'Donovan Rossa assumed control of the administration of all manner of Irish nationalist memorabilia (whether genuine or not) that arrived at *The Irish People*'s offices to be despatched abroad. Contributors' receipts printed in the paper show an array of items that included: 'a splendid portrait of John Mitchel,' 'A sword taken from the English at the battle of New Ross, in '98,' 'An old griddle that baked bread for the rebels in '98,' and 'an old edition of the ancient poetry of Munster, in English and Irish.'[90] Although primarily intended to raise money, according to *The Irish People*, the Chicago Fair was a highly successful project demonstrating effective collaboration between the IRB's paper and the Fenian Brotherhood. The Fair also involved those who were not active members of the IRB or the Fenian Brotherhood who knew that the proceeds of the Fair were likely to be used for revolutionary purposes.

The Irish People was not just focused on a military revolution. Although it was once thought by historians that the Fenians had little or no interest in the land, this was an important theme in the IRB's newspaper. Michael Davitt, a member of the IRB and the founder of the Irish National Land League in 1879, had originally complained that, 'The [Fenian] movement had one negative virtue … it was not an agrarian association.'[91] This is a

[88] Luby to O'Leary, 1891, Luby Papers, NLI, MS 331.

[89] 'Chicago Fair', *Irish People*, 20 Feb. 1864.

[90] 'Chicago Fair', *Irish People*, 26 March 1864.

[91] Michael Davitt, *The Fall of Feudalism in Ireland or the Story of the Land League Revolution*, Seán Ó Lúing (intro.) (Shannon: Irish University Press, 1970), p. 77; 1st ed. (London & New York: Harper and Bros., 1904).

distorted image of the IRB for *The Irish People* was deeply passionate about the question of land. Rural deprivation was a strong motif in *The Irish People* and was particularly valuable for the IRB's critique of the government and the landed aristocracy. Thomas Frost, a Chartist journalist, believed that

> It was a social as well as a political revolution which they [the Fenians] meditated, and "Ireland for the Irish," as interpreted by them, meant the dispossession of every landowner who could not prove his descent from the old Milesian stock, and the partition of his estate among those who could.[92]

In his memoirs James Stephens stated that separation from England was to be the first task; once settled, the land question would be addressed.[93] In other words, the IRB initially contemplated a political revolution, to be followed immediately by a social revolution. The Fenians' land policy differed from the original theories of James Fintan Lalor that were adopted by the 1879–82 Land War strategists who believed that a campaign for land reform should precede political changes. However, the political goal of complete separation from Britain was far stronger for the Fenians than for these Land War nationalists. As argued in *The Irish People*, the IRB earnestly believed that it was only by adopting a political physical force policy that the land question could ever be settled.

As a solution for the land issue *The Irish People* promoted the idea of peasant proprietorship, initiated into Irish nationalist thinking as a major policy by Lalor in the 1840s *Nation* and *The Irish Felon* (notwithstanding Thomas Davis's 'Udalism and Feudalism' in the March 1841 issue of *The Citizen*). In 1846 during the Great Famine, both *The Nation* and political economist John Stuart Mill had suggested a reclamation of waste lands and the creation of a peasant proprietorship on them; Mill believed that

> By this plan one-fourth or one-third of the Irish peasantry would, in two or three years, be not only in a state of present ease, but under the influence of the strongest attainable motives to industry, prudence, and economy, and with their interests all ranged on the side of tranquillity and the law, because the law would have ceased to be their oppressor, and becomes their benefactor.[94]

---

[92] Thomas Frost, *The Secret Societies of the European Revolution 1776–1876, vol. II* (London: Tinsley Bros., 1876), p. 279.

[93] Ryan, *Fenian Chief*, p. 65.

[94] 1st LAs, *Nation*, 24 Oct. and 14 Nov. 1846; 1st LA, *Morning Chronicle*, 15 Oct. 1846.

This idea surfaced again in *The Irish People*: 'There are millions of acres of reclaimable waste land in Ireland. Why is that source of wealth and of employment for the people neglected? Because England rules us.'[95] With the establishment of a peasant proprietorship, a correspondent argued, people would have power over their own resources and destiny; the peasant proprietor would be 'Landlord, tenant, and labourer: more – he knows no master, pays no rent, dreads neither ejectment or bailiff. He improves his lands, toils for himself, and enjoys the produce. His manhood is changed, he stands erect in the face of God, proud and independent.'[96] *The Irish People* gave the idea of a peasant proprietary much publicity, an objective that was resumed again in earnest during the 1879–82 Land War.

The Fenian journalists claimed that the land system was destroying the Irish nation: 'No *rights* of property are so sacred or indefeasible, that the lives of a nation are to be sacrificed to them. Any system, that exterminates a nation, is unlawful and condemned!'[97] Influenced by Lalor's ideas, *The Irish People* proclaimed that English rule and its land system in Ireland were responsible for the Great Famine. In his private letter of 25 January 1847, intended for circulation among the Council members of the Irish Confederation, Lalor had written that the English land system, combined with the devastating effects of the Famine, 'will leave Ireland *without a people*, unless it be met and conquered by a revolution which will leave it without landlords.' Lalor had envisaged a social revolution at this time, but nearly a year and a half on, with no progress in this direction, this private letter was printed in *The Irish Felon* accompanied by an article calling the people to 'arm at once' in the name of self-defence against the annihilation of the people.[98] The concern for the defence and survival of the Irish nation and the sense of urgency that Lalor evoked was echoed in *The Irish People.*

The IRB's newspaper also alluded to what it portrayed as the illegality of English aristocratic ownership of Irish land. It was a common perception

---

95 4th LA, *Irish People*, 13 Feb. 1864.

96 'Original Correspondence', 'M', 'To the small farmers of Ireland. Letter III', *Irish People*, 26 March 1864. This was the third in a series of letters that resemble J.S. Mill's arguments and theories on the land issue in Ireland. These letters may have been written by David Bell, who had been a prominent activist in the 1852 tenant right movement; he was also an editor of the radical London *National Liberator* until his resignation in June 1864. A letter to T.C. Luby indicates that he had submitted items on landlordism for inclusion in *The Irish People*: Bell to Luby, 10 July 1864, Fenian Briefs, NAI, Box 3, Envelope 9. [Bell may also have written one or more of *The Irish People*'s leading articles on the land problem.]

97 1st LA, *Irish People*, 25 June 1864.

98 3rd and 6th LAs, *Irish Felon*, 1 July 1848.

of the Irish people at that time that, according to tradition, the land rightly belonged to them and *The Irish People* reflected this view. In trying to make sense of the 1867 Fenian rebellion, J.S. Mill was to issue a pamphlet the following February, *England and Ireland*, in which he wrote: 'The traditions and recollections of native Irish society are wholly the contrary [to Britain's notion of land ownership] ... In the moral feelings of the Irish people the right to hold the land goes, as it did in the beginning, with the right to till it.'[99] What was important to the Fenians was their conception of freeing Ireland from the 'conquerors,' English rulers and English landlords, of undoing the political and social framework of the country; and in this they promoted an inextricable link between land and politics that would underpin late nineteenth-century Irish nationalism. *The Irish People* stated:

> By force of arms Ireland was wrested from her rightful owners, the Irish people. By no other means will she ever be restored ... Every man has one simple object to accomplish. It is to rid the land of robbers, and to render every cultivator of the soil his own landlord, the proprietor, in fee simple, of the house and land of his father.[100]

Lalor had maintained that the land of Ireland belonged to the entire nation and not a specific class, an argument which James Connolly, inspired by Lalor's newspaper writings, adopted as part of his political creed in the next century. This argument had also been developed by Mill in his *Principles of Political Economy* (first published in 1848), wherein he stated that land was a common heritage: 'It is the original inheritance of the whole species.'[101] What all this meant in simple terms was that, in theory, the land of Ireland belonged to everyone, but in practice more particularly to the Irish as they had inhabited the land prior to the English. As *The Irish People* declared:

> Land is the great raw material out of which everything valuable, to supply man's necessities, and to minister to his enjoyments, is originally extracted. It is the inheritance of no privileged class, but of the entire community; and should be parcelled out by the State

---

[99] J.S. Mill, *Essays on England, Ireland, and the Empire*, John M. Robson (ed.), Joseph Hamburger (intro.), *The Collected Works of John Stuart Mill, vol. VI* (Toronto: University of Toronto Press; London: Routledge & Kegan Paul, 1982), p. 513.

[100] 1st LA, *Irish People*, 17 Sept. 1864.

[101] J.S. Mill, *Principles of Political Economy With Some of Their Applications to Social Philosophy*, John M. Robson (ed.), V.W. Bladen (intro.), *Collected Works, vol. II* (Toronto: University of Toronto Press, 1965), p. 230.

> on such terms as are most conducive to protect and to promote the interests of all.[102]

The Irish People argued on three counts: their theoretical reasoning over land ownership, the fact of a perceived invasion by another country, and the imposition of that country's law (i.e. the English landlord system).

Of all the past events that were exploited by *The Irish People* to criticize the Union, it was the Great Famine that had most potential to command a response from readers. It was believed by many people in Ireland, particularly those involved with the advanced nationalist press in 1848–50, that the Famine had been made much worse – or possibly was even created – by the British government; for example, in January 1850 *The Irishman* referred to the 'English-made starvation ... the hundreds of thousands that died like dogs within those four dismal years, by the aid, and through the power and influence, of English rule.'[103] *The Irish People* capitalized on that belief, for the Famine was still fresh in the memory of its survivors:

> The horrors of war, have seldom equalled, and certainly never exceeded, those of the Irish famine of '47. The babe suckling at the dead mother's breast, whole families living on putrid carrion, hundreds dying and dead by the wayside ... There is no instance on record of 2,000,000 of human beings perishing by the sword of revolution, or the consequences of revolt, and yet Ireland in one famine lost at the very least that number of her population.[104]

Rekindling images like these of the recent past was potentially a strong argument for Ireland's separation from Britain, especially when Ireland was currently suffering an agricultural depression (1859–64). One of the consequences of the Famine was a hastening of the increase in pasture land over arable land. *The Irish People* railed against what they deemed the unpatriotic greed of the large graziers who supplied food for English tables.[105] A critique of the large graziers was to surface later with influential Irish nationalists, such as William O'Brien in January 1898 with his United Irish League (UIL), for, in the long-term, the Famine's effects were still being felt in the West.

The land question easily lent itself to Fenian doctrine. *The Irish People*

---

[102] 1st LA, *Irish People*, 30 July 1864.
[103] 3rd LA, *Irishman*, 26 Jan. 1850.
[104] 4th LA, *Irish People*, 11 June 1864.
[105] 2nd LA, *Irish People*, 30 July 1864.

did much to propagate what it believed was the oppressive and predatory nature of the landlord system in Ireland, an interpretation of Irish history that remained unchallenged until late in the twentieth century. This traditional perception of the landlord system was a major grievance at the heart of Irish nationalism and was exploited by *The Irish People* as justification for the dispossession of the landocracy in Ireland, and the need for separation from Great Britain. The idea that the Irish existed in bondage under British rule was a powerful motif in *The Irish People*, and was a grievance alluded to in the Fenian trials following the suppression of *The Irish People*. To discredit English landlordism in Ireland, *The Irish People* used the system of American slavery as an analogy to illustrate the plight of Irish land workers. By comparing the lifestyle of an American slave with an Irish peasant, the latter was shown to be subjected to a much harsher and more inhumane existence. *The Irish People* argued that, in reality, the English landlord system in Ireland not only produced slavery, but this was a much more undignified and humiliating way of life than the system of plantation slavery as practiced in the antebellum South.[106]

Leslie Williams has suggested that a comment on colonialism by philosopher Jean-Paul Sartre has a relevance for Ireland of the mid-nineteenth century: 'How can an elite of usurpers … establish their privileges? By one means only: debasing the colonized to exalt themselves, denying the title of humanity to the natives.'[107] Williams implied that, despite the Act of Union, the British press remained locked in a colonial discourse in relation to how it perceived Ireland, and to maintain power over Ireland the British establishment press portrayed the Irish as something less than human. Michael de Nie's study of the British press's negative perception of the Irish people shows that they were identified by their ethnic Celtic inheritance, their Catholic religion and their peasant class; these elements in the construction of the Irish identity were, according to the British press, the reasons for their inferiority.[108] The IRB found this viewpoint highly useful, reflected by *The Irish People* printing extracts from British establishment newspapers and journals that ridiculed and belittled the Irish who, from

[106] 2nd LA, *Irish People*, 11 June 1864.

[107] This quotation is from Richard Ned Lebow, *White Britain and Black Ireland: The Influence of Stereotypes on Colonial Policy* (Philadelphia: Institute for the Study of Human Issues, 1976), p. 13, in Williams, *Daniel O'Connell, The British Press and The Irish Famine*, p. 45. Leslie Williams believed that the negativity of the British press towards Ireland influenced the British response to the Great Famine, especially in relation to what was written about O'Connell and Repeal: Williams, *Daniel O'Connell, The British Press and the Irish Famine*, p. xiii.

[108] de Nie, *The Eternal Paddy*, see in particular pp. 3–35.

peasant to politician, were described as sub-human and abnormal. *The Irish People* drew readers' attention to items like these as evidence for their argument that the British press wished to humiliate the Irish, thereby hoping to stir up passions against Britain and deepen the divisions between the two nations. Showing how the British ruling class, through the medium of its own press, perceived the Irish people had been a feature of Mitchel's *United Irishman* with a short series entitled 'The Enemy's Press,' which, for instance, reprinted an extract from *The Spectator* demonstrating 'How to Roast an Irish Patriot.'[109] Capitalizing on this practice, John O'Leary commented 'that one of the best ways of inflaming the Irish mind against England is to let it know what England, at the bottom of her heart and soul, ever thinks and feels about Ireland. Instead, then, of raging against the Saxon, I let the Saxon rage against us.'[110] Extracts were also taken from *The Saturday Review*, a newspaper read by the British elite and notable for its attacks on the Irish people. One of its articles near the end of 1863 stated:

> We believe that certain natural laws are at work which are likely enough to produce a great physical as well as moral change in the animal of Ireland. Just as the Red Man and the Bush-man and the Maori melt away before the sure and certain advance of the superior race, so will the worse elements of Irish humanity yield to the nobler and civilising elements now at work in Ireland.[111]

This article could reinforce Michael de Nie's study in which he has found that the British press hoped that an inferior Irish race would behave more like the superior Anglo-Saxon race, and despaired of it when it failed to do so, thus, the British press claimed, justifying British political rule in Ireland. From *The Irish People*'s perspective, *The Saturday Review* article appeared not only to denigrate the Irish race, but to demonstrate the seeming intention of the British ruling elite; with British superiority the Anglo-Saxon race would crush and destroy the identity of the Celts. While such articles extracted from the British press were deemed by *The Irish People* another way of influencing the IRB's cause, they may perhaps give a certain credence to Leslie Williams' theory about the colonial relationship between Britain and Ireland.

Britain's behaviour as an imperial power also provided the Fenians with what they considered another approach to persuading people to join their

---

109 *United Irishman*, 1 April 1848.

110 O'Leary, *Fenians and Fenianism, vol. I*, p. 255.

111 Reprinted in 4th LA, *Irish People*, 12 Dec. 1863.

cause. *The Irish People* addressed what it believed to be the incongruity of what the British viewed as their own civilized superiority, and the reality of their base and uncivilized behaviour towards primitive races. Having portrayed an image of what it judged as Britain's brutal and immoral conduct towards the Irish people, the IRB's newspaper argued that the British government acted in a similar way towards other countries. A poignant case was that of British imperialism in New Zealand where *The Irish People*, in creating a positive image of the Maoris so that their rhetoric would have maximum effect, described them as 'a noble-looking race, high-spirited and freedom-loving' who were being destroyed

> by another race, a race of grasping white men, one of the most rapacious races (perhaps the most rapacious) the world has ever seen, [who] began to look on the fertile soil of the Maories' [*sic*] island home with a covetous eye. The race we speak of is that which nicknames itself Anglo-Saxon![112]

The Irish People's intention was to juxtapose images of the two races with positive and negative characteristics, contrasting the seemingly wicked nature of the English race with the pleasant nature of the Maoris. As we saw in Chapter 1 of this book, language that portrayed the nature of British imperialism as evil and destructive was used by the Dublin nationalist press as an argument to depict the British as morally unfit rulers of Ireland.

In its columns *The Irish People* presented an image of a dying Irish nation locked in conflict with an increasingly powerful military and economic British nation to affirm the idea of Britain as Ireland's enemy. Reminiscent of the 1840s Repealers and reiterating John Mitchel's despair of English capitalism, blame was directed at English legislation, which

> proved destructive to our manufacture of paper, our manufacture of flour, and, indeed, every other manufacture which Irish enterprise has endeavoured to cultivate. These are the melancholy consequences of our subjugation to a nation of shopkeepers whose god is gold; whose desk is their alter [*sic*]; whose ledger is their bible; and whose exchange is their church.[113]

From the IRB's perspective, not only was English law blamed for the lack of Irish economic advancement, but an indirect comparison was drawn

---

[112] 2nd LA, *Irish People*, 23 July 1864.
[113] 1st LA, *Irish People*, 22 Oct. 1864.

between two opposing ideologies. While the English were depicted as wicked capitalists, harming the wellbeing of the Irish people, the IRB, with its policy of peasant proprietorship, could be seen as veering towards a social state that benefited its lower-class members. By making the people of Ireland feel that they were under siege from a heartless enemy, *The Irish People* portrayed images of a large, fierce, predatory empire destroying a small, ancient country, again echoing Mitchel, who had likened the British Empire to a 'carnivorous old monster' that 'drank the blood and sucked the marrow from the bones of Ireland.'[114] *The Irish People* believed that the Irish race was in peril, stating that 'if the conspiracy of the government and the landlords against the Celts of Ireland should continue … The counties of Ireland shall then, indeed, be as much English counties as Yorkshire; Scotch herdsmen and English churls shall usurp the place of the Irish peasant.'[115] While Britain was gaining internationally in strength and power in the mid-nineteenth century, especially with its expanding industrialization and its imperialism, the Irish nation, according to *The Irish People*, was becoming increasingly weaker, and would eventually be displaced by the British nation.

What particularly concerned the IRB journalists was the continuing emigration from Ireland. Following several years of decline, emigration rose from 70,117 in 1862 to 117,229 in 1863; but these returns, produced by the Registrar General, were believed by economic historian C. Ó Gráda to be highly underestimated.[116] In a paper delivered to the Statistical Society in May 1864, the political economist Denis Caulfield Heron, QC claimed that from January 1862 the population was 'diminishing at the rate of 100,000 per annum' with 'emigration rapidly increasing.'[117] During the lifespan of *The Irish People* emigration appeared to be especially high, and the image presented to readers to convey this was the draining of Irish blood from its soil: 'Day after day the island is drained of its best and dearest blood. In countless masses the people [are] flying from the woe-stricken land … England strikes at the very existence of our race.'[118] The threat of extinction to the Irish nation was made to seem not only very real, but imminent:

114 'To his Excellency The Earl of Clarendon, Her Majesty's Detective-General, High Commissioner of Spies, and General Suborner in Ireland', 1st LA col., *United Irishman*, 8 April 1848.

115 2nd LA, *Irish People*, 12 Dec. 1863.

116 C. Ó Gráda, 'A Note on Nineteenth-Century Irish Emigration Statistics', *Population Studies*, vol. 29 (1), March 1975, pp. 144–5.

117 'The State of Ireland', Report of mtg., Statistical Society, 19 May 1864, *Irish People* 28 May 1864. See also: 2nd LA, *Irish People*, 18 June 1864.

118 2nd LA, *Irish People*, 12 Dec. 1863.

> The Englishman ... hopes ... either to see the Irish race altogether rooted out from their own soil, or else so outworn in strength and numbers, that perforce, however reluctantly, they must 'give in' and consent at last to lose their individuality in what is nicknamed 'the Anglo-Saxon' population of the Empire ... Considering the enormous proportions of the exodus, we do not conceal or deny the fact, that danger now menaces the existence of our race, greater than any that ever struck at it before.[119]

The Irish People exploited the loss of population caused by emigration and argued that while it continued at this accelerated rate, the chances of the Irish nation surviving were bleak.

The concept of sacrifice was an important theme in *The Irish People*. The Fenians believed that independence had to be won 'by heroic sacrifice, in the face of perils and death.'[120] For the IRB, sacrifice for Ireland was like a necessary rite of passage to the freedom and rebirth of the Irish nation. *The Irish People* saw sacrifice in spiritual terms as something to which the Irish people should aspire. Patrick Pearse had similar thoughts about revolution and sacrifice. He stated in 1913: 'bloodshed is a cleansing and a sanctifying thing, and the nation which regards it as the final horror has lost its manhood. There are many things more horrible than bloodshed; and slavery is one of them.'[121] Although there are echoes from the earlier Fenian philosophy in Pearse's writing, such as the references to manhood and slavery, unlike the 1860s Fenians, Pearse articulated the revolutionary cause through Messianic imagery, rooted in Roman Catholic teaching.[122] It must be emphasized that while 1860s Fenian rhetoric could be expressed in spiritual terms, it was not linked to Roman Catholicism, as this would not have been in harmony with *The Irish People*'s ethos of unity of creed.

The Irish People and nationalist literature

Fenian doctrine could also be communicated by *The Irish People*'s views on culture. Apart from the physical loss of people from Ireland, the Fenians lamented the waning of Irish culture, which they believed would, along

[119] 2nd LA, *Irish People*, 9 April 1864.

[120] 4th LA, *Irish People*, 30 Jan. 1864.

[121] Pearse, 'The Coming Revolution', Nov. 1913, *Political Writings and Speeches*, p. 99.

[122] See, for example, Sean Farrell Moran, 'Patrick Pearse and the European Revolt against Reason', *Journal of the History of Ideas*, vol. 50 (4), Oct.–Dec. 1989, pp. 625–43.

with emigration, eventually lead to the decline of the Irish nation. Although they did not actively use their energies to pursue or augment a cultural movement, the very presence of Irish literary contributions in *The Irish People* indicated the importance they attached to Irish culture. Like many of their Young Ireland forebears in *The Nation*, the Fenians thought that in order to prevent the continuing loss of an Irish identity it was necessary not just to keep safe, but to nurture and recreate an Irish cultural society in opposition to an imported English culture. They strove to achieve this in *The Irish People*. For instance, in a literary review of *Little Star, and other Poems. Original and translated* by 'A.M.W.,' much encouragement was given to the author not only for the quality of her verse, but its content: 'We are anxious to see our old songs and ballads, especially those written in Irish, disseminated among all classes of the Irish people.'[123] Acknowledging the influence of women in family life, *The Irish People* urged that they 'be national in word and deed, as well as in thought. The books they read, and the songs they sing should be Irish.'[124] Like the Young Irelanders before them, the Fenians concern was not just for maintaining an Irish way of life, but also involved a defensive reaction to what they saw as the destructive and demoralizing influences of English rule on Irish society. This disquiet was revived again by many Irish nationalists towards the end of the nineteenth century, coinciding with the formation of the Gaelic Revival, which was to be subject to IRB infiltration.

The Fenians were influenced by Thomas Davis, who believed, like many who followed him, that if the Irish people were shown to possess a distinct cultural identity that was separate from Britain, they were justified in seeking a political severance from the Union. Popular literature was one way in which this could be achieved, a tool to promote a sense of nationalism amongst the people. In its literary columns *The Irish People* continued this policy by printing stories and poems of an Irish nationalist nature. But, more importantly, like past newspapers that supported nationalist organizations, *The Irish People* was also instrumental in using its literary items to persuade people to support the Fenian cause.

Although *The Irish People* was conscious of the interdependent nature of the relationship between literature and nationalism, its journalists believed that literature could not ultimately be used to achieve separation from Britain. This view contrasts with the Young Irelanders, especially Davis, who saw a cultural movement, of which literature was an important component, as an essential means by which its aims could be achieved. On the other hand,

123 'Literature. Reviews', *Irish People*, 2 July 1864.

124 1st LA, *Irish People*, 5 Nov. 1864.

the Fenians thought that, while it was necessary to imbue its followers with a nationalist spirit through literature, in the end only a political revolution achieved by physical force could free Ireland from the Union with Great Britain. As for the journalists' leading articles, alluding to the 1848 *débâcle*, *The Irish People* believed that defiant editorial rhetoric alone would not gain independence from the British government: 'Strong words are undoubtedly powerful engines to sway the souls of men, but they never can, at any time or in any country, supply the place of silent action.'[125] And by 'silent action' the IRB meant conspiratorial preparation for an insurrection. Nonetheless, literature still had a valuable role in *The Irish People*.

The literary side of *The Irish People*, which overall seemed to be of a good standard, complemented the editorial and letter sections of the paper, and featured poetry and stories, many of which tended to promote an Irish nationalist spirit. In his speech for the defence in O'Leary's trial, Isaac Butt provided an evaluation of *The Irish People*:

> I have been for some months in the habit of constantly reading it; and I confess I was astonished to find that it contained literature of a very high character. You will find history, antiquities, and a number of other literary matters dealt with in it in a most admirable manner.[126]

The literary columns often recounted legendary or historical events and characters from the distant past to the more recent past that both reflected and reinforced the political views of the journalists in *The Irish People*'s leading articles. A common theme in the paper was that of traditional Irish resistance to foreign rule. The militant ideology of the IRB was particularly emphasized by the literary side of *The Irish People*. There was, for instance, a poetical tale in early 1864 of the 'Legend of Tiernan; or The Blue Knight' by 'Merulan' (Robert Dwyer Joyce), recounting brave deeds against the English.[127] During the first four months of 1864 *The Irish People* printed a serialization of the biography of 'Michael Dwyer, the insurgent Captain of the Wicklow mountains'; this work was written by John Thomas Campion, a nationalist poet who had contributed to several newspapers, including the 1840s *Nation* and *United Irishman*.[128] Michael Dwyer was the leader

---

125 1st LA, *Irish People*, 26 Dec. 1863.

126 *Proceedings at the First Sitting of the Special Commission … for the Trial of Thomas Clarke Luby*, p. 506.

127 'Literature', *Irish People*, 16 Jan. 1864.

128 Later published in book form: John Thomas Campion, *Michael Dwyer, or The*

of a group of Irish rebels who after the '98 insurrection eluded arrest and sought refuge in the mountains of Wicklow; he surrendered in 1803. One of the most effective devices of *The Irish People,* and one used by Thomas Davis in *The Nation,* was to recall the revolutionary heroes of the past. The '98 rebellion was still in the memories of the people who could relate to the United Irishmen and their heroic exploits. More poignant, however, was the current conflict of the American Civil War, which involved the military participation of Irishmen who fought in both the Unionist and Confederate armies. This was the focus of the poem 'The Fairies' Return' by 'Spes' (John Thomas Campion), the following extract from which extols the military prowess of Irishmen in the midst of battle:

> There – where the fray was furiest –
> The two mighty hosts between –
> In either army – floated –
> An unswerving flag of Green –
> In the van – they ever fluttered –
> Ever met – and ever clashed,
> And we *felt* the shock of battle
> When that radiant colour flashed –
>
> Oh! we saw our Irish fighting
> In a glorious warrior band,
> And their 'Sunburst' grandly lighting
> The broad war-paths of the land – [129]

The presence of the Irish soldiers is represented by the Sunburst Flag of the IRB and the Fenian Brotherhood; a green background with a sunburst, this was adapted from the mythical Fianna's flag, which had a blue background.[130] The images portrayed by Campion's verse reinforced the rhetoric in *The Irish People*'s editorials and also the messages conveyed by the American Fenians that were reprinted from their press; the Irish would be just as brave and powerful in battle against their English oppressors as

Insurgent Captain of the Wicklow Mountains (Glasgow: Cameron, Ferguson & Co. [1869]); (New York: P.J. Kenedy, 1875, 1882); (Dublin: M.H. Gill & Son, 1910, 1940).

[129] 'Original Poetry', *Irish People*, 9 Jan. 1864.

[130] Variations of the Fenian flag included one with four green stripes that represented Ireland's provinces, with a green corner on which sat thirty-two stars signifying the counties; this design is similar to one of the flags of the Union Army of the American Civil War.

they were in this Civil War, where Irish soldiers could be seen as role models for current IRB members and prospective recruits.

The appeal of the IRB's newspaper was intended to be broad, and this was reflected in the varied selection of literary contributions. Items of a more intellectual nature were included in *The Irish People*. There appeared, for example, a sketch called 'A sunbeam peep through a lattice,' a discussion by young people of classical poetry, in particular Dante and Petrarch.[131] The author was 'T.I.' (Thomas Caulfield Irwin), a poet of quality who was a regular contributor to *The Irish People*. For others, the opportunity to express support for the Fenian cause came in another form, writing letters to the editor that appeared in the 'Original Correspondence' columns of the paper. There is no apparent evidence to suggest that these letters were not genuine, and in his old age O'Leary commented on some of the authors; nor does his biographer challenge the authenticity of these letters.[132]

Much of the strength of a nationalist organization lies in its grass-roots support and it was the 'Original Correspondence' section of *The Irish People* that, as time progressed, indicated a rising level of local support attested by an increase in the number of letters and their positive comments. O'Leary himself noted that 'as the paper went on, our correspondents increased vastly in number.'[133] As for their content, there was much praise for *The Irish People*, for example in a letter written in May 1864 from Mitchelstown, Co. Cork, stating:

> it is a pleasing task to congratulate you on the extraordinary success of your journal. Sorely, indeed, since '48, have the persecuted Irish race felt the want of a truly national organ, that will never shrink from exposing the doings of the despot, always take part with the oppressed, and shelter them from the machinations of their merciless masters.[134]

A year later a correspondent named 'Heber' wrote: 'Our glorious movement is spreading abroad with a rapidity and an *intensity* that nothing can *now* arrest. Your teachings are gaining converts everywhere.'[135] Letters similar to these seemed to provide evidence of the value of *The Irish People* to the

[131] 'Literature', *Irish People*, 5 Nov. 1864.
[132] O'Leary, *Fenians and Fenianism, II*, pp. 3–5, 63–65 and 71.
[133] O'Leary, *Fenians and Fenianism, II*, p. 63.
[134] 'Original Correspondence', *Irish People*, 4 June 1864.
[135] 'Correspondence' [by now the term 'Original' was omitted], Letter, [n.d.], *Irish People*, 24 June 1865.

IRB. Importantly, letter writing gave Fenian supporters a voice, allowing them to express their open allegiance (albeit often using pseudonyms) to the militant nationalist cause. While the 'Original Correspondence' section of *The Irish People* may have helped to raise morale amongst IRB followers by printing their views, it also suggested the existence of enthusiastic local support throughout much of Ireland, as well as in England and Scotland, giving the impression of a united, widespread movement. This image may have boosted morale and promoted solidarity especially since, in theory, the IRB's rules meant that only those belonging to a specific military Circle knew each other to maintain secrecy. But now their own paper provided, in effect, not only a direct link with the Fenian leadership, but a shared purpose with other IRB members.

The 'Original Correspondence' section of the paper was highly important. It was a backcloth to the editorials and provided grass-roots evidence to substantiate the knowledge and concepts that formed part of *The Irish People*'s doctrine. Several letters were submitted on the ongoing theme of priests in politics. Especially prevalent in the correspondence section was the topic of eviction and emigration, from a woeful account of an individual incident to a general observation. A letter from 'A Queen's County Man' reported an incident in which an absentee landlord evicted his tenants, not for owing rent, but to extend a hunting area.[136] From Clonakilty, Co. Cork, Ellen Eliza Callanan wrote:

> Travel through the country, and in every village, town, and hamlet you will see the people flying from the land. You will see strong men crying bitterly – yes, so bitterly as to make you wish you had not eyes to see, ears to hear, nor sense to understand what all this meant … It is the operation of the law … despatching our people either to the emigrant ship or to the workhouse … Yes, the Irish People *will* be exterminated unless they themselves resolve otherwise, and unite for self-preservation.[137]

According to *The Irish People*'s editorials, letters such as these that focused on the suffering of the people could be linked to the landlord system, and they provided the Fenians, like the Repealers before them, evidence that could be used for their attack on British rule.

Another letter writer from Co. Cork was local IRB leader James F.X. O'Brien, who used the pseudonym 'De l'Abbaye'; on 30 October 1864

136 'Original Correspondence', Letter, 24 April 1864, *Irish People*, 30 April 1864.

137 'Original Correspondence', Letter, [n.d.], *Irish People*, 9 Jan. 1864.

he wrote that for nearly every trade in Cork 'the struggle for bare existence is a desperate one' and the remedy was to 'let Ireland be an independent nation … and our country will soon be happy and prosperous.'[138] O'Brien's rhetoric was meaningful and sincere for he was to go on to participate in the 1867 rebellion; he was arrested and convicted for high treason, but the death penalty was commuted to penal servitude.[139] As one of the insurgents at Cappoquin, O'Brien is another important link that demonstrates the continuity between the 1849 conspiracy and the IRB in personnel, strategy and ideology.

The Irish People and its influence on the rise of the IRB

The effectiveness of *The Irish People* can be measured by the achievement of its main aim of improving recruitment into the conspiratorial IRB. Correlating the expansion of the IRB with the presence of its newspaper, Luby says: ''twas *after* the founding of the "*Irish People*," that the movement became really strong in Connaught & in Ulster; and, indeed, got considerably increased strength elsewhere in Ireland. But, above all … we had no movement in England and Scotland until after the "*Irish People*" had appeared.'[140] John O'Leary agreed with Luby that the IRB was limited in numbers and localities until the start of *The Irish People*, after which the 'organization grew rapidly.'[141] Recruitment into the IRB was at its highest from 1863 to 1866, corresponding to the lifespan of *The Irish People* and the aftermath of its suppression. As an Irish republican newspaper observed in 1911, 'the two years of its existence marked the most flourishing period in the history of the Organisation.'[142] Official government sources had reached a similar conclusion; in 1864, 'From the exertions of the traveling agents and the influence of the "Irish People" the conspiracy in this country gained considerably in strength before the end of the year.'[143] While there are various contemporary numerical estimates of those belonging to the IRB during the mid-nineteenth century, there is no reliable evidence in terms of definitive membership numbers. Philip Coyne, an envoy from the

138 'Original Correspondence', *Irish People*, 5 Nov. 1864.

139 Devoy, *Recollections*, p. 44. O'Brien later turned to constitutional nationalism as an MP for the Irish Parliamentary Party.

140 Luby to O'Leary, 1892, Luby Papers, NLI, MS 333.

141 O'Leary, *Fenians and Fenianism, II*, pp. 234–5.

142 'Lucan', 'The Fenian Movement, 1858–1867', *Irish Freedom*, May 1911.

143 Larcom Papers, NLI, MS 7517/127.

Fenian Brotherhood during the latter part of 1864, conducted a survey of the IRB and estimated a membership of at least 54,000, although Stephens claimed his report was incomplete and the figure was much higher.[144] John Devoy, who had been appointed by Stephens as Chief Organizer of Fenian disaffection among the British Army's soldiers in Ireland from October 1865, stated that both he and Stephens believed that IRB membership in 1864 had reached around 80,000 strong in Ireland and Great Britain.[145] This figure was exclusive of IRB members in the British Army; an official report on Fenian activity concluded in early 1866: 'there need be no doubt disaffection prevails among Her Majesty's soldiers to a very considerable extent.'[146] Early in 1865, a police constable was told by an informer who had belonged to the IRB's 'Committee of Safety,' that he had been present 'at the making up of the Fenian return for Ireland, and that the number of organized and drilled Fenians in this country was 129,000 men.'[147] While this amount may well have been exaggerated, certainly by the summer of 1865 the police reported from all over Ireland that

> Fenianism was spreading rapidly, that the Fenians were constantly holding meetings and drilling, and that a rising was generally talked of and expected to take place soon after harvest time. In Kilkenny, Cork, Waterford and some other places … half the male population were Fenians, and fully bent on having a rising.[148]

During 1865 the spirit of Fenianism abounded, captured, for example, by *The Nation*'s report in mid-September on 'Fenianism in Waterford':

> at half-past five o'clock in the morning, and in the very centre of the city, in an unoccupied house, we saw two squads of ten men each being drilled by two drill instructors … All the regular ballad-singers of the city have been subsidised by them [Fenians]. These commence operations every evening with nightfall, and,

---

144 Letter from Stephens to O'Mahony, 11 Dec. 1864, Fenian Brotherhood, CUA, Box 1, Folder 6; see also: D'Arcy, *Fenian Movement in the United States*, p. 45.

145 Devoy, *Recollections*, p. 33.

146 Summary of recent reports on Fenianism by Superintendent Daniel Ryan, Dublin Metropolitan Police, 26 Feb. 1866, The National Archives (TNA), HO45/7799/87, Box 1, Pouch 2.

147 Fenian Richard Hoare to Thomas Talbot, reported to The Inspector General, Carrick-on-Suir, Co. Tipperary, 23 Feb. 1865, Fenian Papers 1857–83, NAI, Police and Crime Records, Fenian Police Reports, Box 2.

148 Larcom Papers, NLI, MS 7517/139.

> surrounded by large crowds, sometimes as many as 200 persons ... continue to sing seditious songs until past eleven o'clock ... These productions are of the most treasonable and seditious character.[149]

According to Devoy, 'Had the Rising taken place in 1865,' which was the original intention, 'while this spirit prevailed and the organization was still intact, instead of in 1867, when only a broken remnant of it remained and many of the best men were either in prison or refugees in England or America, the history of Fenianism would have been very different.'[150] The prominent Irish nationalist William O'Brien also believed that

> It was in 1865, and not in 1867, that Fenianism had the capacity to strike a formidable military blow at England ... the civilian organisation was, to all intents and purposes, the enrolment of three-fourths of the able-bodied population of the country ... For the province of Munster, at least, I can say with certainty that any young man of spirit who was not a sworn or unsworn item in the ranks, would have felt as much ashamed of himself as a young Englishman who should refuse to volunteer if a foreign army were landed in Kent.[151]

It does appear that the suppression of *The Irish People* and the arrests that followed impacted on the decision of Stephens to postpone the rising in 1865.[152] That year, when *The Irish People*, the 'important organ of the conspiracy' according to the authorities, was suppressed, although lacking in arms and without strong and competent military leadership, Fenianism in Ireland appeared to be at its most powerful, both numerically and in terms of possessing the willpower and passion to fight. This coincided with what the authorities considered an increasing militant tone in *The Irish People* during 1865, indicating that it had a key role in promoting physical force nationalism at that time.[153]

The Irish People's influence may be linked, to a certain extent, to the military action that was taken within eighteen months of the paper's

---

149 *Nation*, 3rd ed., 16 Sept. 1865.

150 Devoy, *Recollections*, pp. 55–6.

151 'Was Fenianism ever formidable?' *The Contemporary Review*, 71, Jan.–June 1897, p. 681.

152 Stephens' decision to postpone the 1865 IRB rising was a subject of debate among his contemporaries. For a recent summary of this controversy see: Ramón, *A Provisional Dictator*, pp. 190–2.

153 Larcom Papers, MS 7517/142.

suppression in September 1865. Fenianism was strong among the Irish in Britain, especially the northern industrial areas. Arthur Forrester, for instance, a teenager from Lancashire, who wrote prose and poetry for *The Irish People*, was to become involved in an IRB raid on Chester Castle.[154] Irish-American Captain (later Colonel) Thomas J. Kelly, on a mission from the Fenian Brotherhood in 1865 to investigate IRB strength, noted the 'immense organization lately done in England.'[155] An official report concluded in early 1866 that 'In London, Sheffield, Manchester, Birkenhead and Liverpool, the Fenians are stated to be very numerous.'[156] Marxist historian Emile Strauss claimed that 'Fenianism developed on something approaching a mass scale … in the larger Irish colonies of British industrial towns.'[157] It is no coincidence, especially in the light of the comparative popularity of *The Irish People* in Britain, that on 11 February 1867 it was from these large northern towns that some 1,200 IRB members had begun to descend on Chester Castle to steal its store of arms, a well-orchestrated prelude to a planned insurrection in Ireland. According to the Chief Constable of Cheshire, save for a last-minute informant, the IRB's raid on Chester would have been successful.[158] From the autumn of 1865 there were still IRB members poised and ready to fight for the Fenian cause despite a lack of arms. The planned attack on Chester Castle and the rising in early March 1867 suggest that IRB members, whether in Ireland or England, may have been influenced by *The Irish People*'s physical force doctrine, and later by *The Irishman*, the Fenians' representative in the press following the suppression of *The Irish People*.

Apart from increased recruitment into the IRB there were other signs suggesting the effectiveness of *The Irish People*'s militant rhetoric. For example, a letter to the editor from a regular Tipperary correspondent, 'Harvey Birch' (Thomas Dougherty Brohan), claimed: 'Nothing in life is troubling the young men in the country now but longing for the fight to come.'[159] Amongst documents seized by the police were letters written to *The Irish People* illustrating the impact of its revolutionary message. For

154 Moody, *Davitt and the Irish Revolution*, p. 48. From January 1869, Forrester was to become a regular correspondent of the Fenian paper, *The Irishman*.

155 Letter from Kelly to O'Mahony, 21 June 1865, O'Mahony Papers, D'Arcy, *Fenian Movement in the United States*, p. 57.

156 Summary of recent reports on Fenianism, 26 Feb. 1866, TNA, HO45/7799/87, Box 1, Pouch 2.

157 Strauss, *Irish Nationalism*, p. 149.

158 Letter from Chief Constable, Cheshire, to Major Greig, Head Constable of Liverpool, 14 Feb. 1867, TNA, HO45/OS7799/209, Box 1, Pouch 4.

159 'Original Correspondence', *Irish People*, 16 Jan. 1864.

instance, as one young man wrote in April 1865, 'would it not be a glorious and noble sight for to see youths fighting and dying for their deeply wronged Country.'[160] Another correspondent wrote: 'The young men of this parish had no thoughts of uniting together to assist in the regeneration of their Country until of late when some young men introduced among them your patriotic and honest journal and its teachings.'[161]

During the 1860s an organized Fenian movement on both sides of the Atlantic, publicized and promoted by *The Irish People*, edged republicanism towards the centre-stage of Irish nationalist ideology. As a British government report observed: 'above all, the constant communication with America had the effect of rendering the movement intensely republican.'[162] Republicanism meant complete separation from a British government, and the necessity of achieving this was a major theme in *The Irish People*. While there were similarities between American and Fenian republicanism, such as the influence of Thomas Paine's ideology, and the belief in a democratic society with the separation of church and state, there was a noticeable difference. Whereas American republicanism, espoused by Thomas Jefferson, had at its heart the concept of civic virtue, Fenian republicanism, as expressed in *The Irish People*, was far more concerned with the survival of the Irish national identity. The IRB urged, for example, that 'The people for whom God created it must get this island into their own hands. If they do not the Irish nation must disappear from the face of the earth.'[163] *The Irish People* wanted to protect the Irish national identity which, the Fenians believed, had been eroded by the British connection especially since the Great Famine, and the only way to save it was to completely sever ties with Britain and establish a republican government.

It was not just the IRB's belief that Ireland had a right to control its own destiny as a separate nation from Britain. Apart from safeguarding the Irish nation, there were other major themes in *The Irish People* that related to the need to seek an Irish republic, which harked back to Wolfe Tone's wish 'To subvert the tyranny of our execrable government': a perceived long struggle of subjugation by a foreign power and the nature of the rule by the British government, both of which took on a new meaning with the government's response to the Famine.[164] Railing against the British

---

[160] Chas Ryan, 25 Apr. 1865, Fenian Briefs, 1865–9, NAI, Box 2, Envelope No.3.

[161] 'A friend of freedom (in confidence, Mr. Michael Walsh)', 10 July 1865, Fenian Briefs, NAI, Box 2, Envelope No. 3.

[162] Larcom Papers, NLI, MS 7517/81.

[163] 1st LA, *Irish People*, 16 Sept. 1865.

[164] Extract from Theobald Wolfe Tone's declaration written in August 1796, Marianne

government's 'murderous destruction' of the Irish people from the Famine to the present time of 1864, and echoing John Mitchel's writings, *The Irish People* seemed convinced that the British government was deliberately trying to destroy the Irish nation.[165] Unsurprisingly, *The Irish People* shared Mitchel's intense hostility towards British rule. Following in the tradition of the United Irishmen, the Fenians believed that a republican government could only be sought through a militant revolution. Citing the achievement of America and France in winning freedom from what was seen as tyranny and founding republican states, *The Irish People* declared: 'in the streets of Paris, and upon the rich soil of America, blood was shed before freedom came; and so must it be in Ireland.'[166] For the Fenians, republicanism and physical force revolution were inextricably linked.[167]

Intended to coincide with the Fenian rebellion in Ireland on 4–5 March 1867, the IRB issued a Proclamation that reflected much of the ideology and rhetoric that had been printed in *The Irish People*.[168] Echoing *The Irish People*, the Proclamation claimed that the land of Ireland, currently possessed by an aristocratic few, belonged to the people of Ireland, and demanded its restoration. Another issue in the Proclamation that had received attention in *The Irish People* was the 'complete separation of Church and State.' Probably the most poignant theme in the Proclamation was the concept of romantic revolution, 'manfully deeming it better to die in the struggle for freedom than to continue an existence of utter serfdom.' Leading articles in *The Irish People* had, indeed, urged the young men to be manly, martyrs willing to die for a noble cause.

An overarching theme in the 1867 Proclamation and one shared by *The Irish People* was the perceived injustice of British rule over the Irish people. The beginning of the Fenian Proclamation stated: 'We have suffered centuries of outrage, enforced poverty, and bitter misery. Our rights and liberties have been trampled on by an alien aristocracy.' Although the Fenians were making a statement about the relationship between Ireland and Britain, there were also resonances in the 1867 Proclamation of political, social and economic injustices that were in tune with contemporary

Elliott, *Wolfe Tone: Prophet of Irish Independence* (New Haven & London: Yale University Press, 1989), p. 411; 2nd ed. (Liverpool: Liverpool University Press, 2012).

165 1st LA, *Irish People*, 20 Aug. 1864.

166 1st LA, *Irish People*, 18 June 1864.

167 For a history of the relationship between republicanism and Roman Catholicism see Andrew Boyd, 'Catholicism and republicanism in Ireland', *Contemporary Review*, vol. 266 (1,549), Feb. 1995, pp. 57–64.

168 Newspapers that carried the 1867 Proclamation included *The Times*, 8 March, *The Irishman*, 9 March and *The Tablet*, 9 March.

Victorian radical thinking. Reflecting the issue of class conflict, an emerging European theme of this era, the lower orders in Ireland wanted a fairer share of the country's wealth and a voice in the running of government. In other words, Irish nationalism became inextricably linked with the Victorian radicals' critique of society's unjust attitude towards the lower classes and their demand for more social, economic and political equality. As already noted in the previous chapter, several meetings between Fenian leaders and prominent members of the English Reform League occurred in 1866 and 1867 to discuss possible co-operation between the two organizations. Fenian leaders General Gustave Cluseret and Colonel Thomas Kelly, in fact, sought advice from the British radical Charles Bradlaugh in drawing up the IRB's Proclamation.[169] *The Irish People* was a forerunner of the 1867 Proclamation that wished to see a restructuring of society with the Irish nation governed as a democracy: in a future Irish state the political power that was currently in the hands of the few should be transferred to the many. In June 1864 the IRB's paper stated: 'The liberty we shall win must, in the first instance at least, be democratic liberty.'[170] The right to throw off an oppressive and unjust government, and the need for equality and freedom in a democratic society that reflected the political thinking of the age, was an integral part of the rhetoric of *The Irish People* and later informed the thinking behind the 1867 Proclamation that was to accompany the Fenian rebellion.

Fearing that a revolution was imminent in late 1865, the British government went on the offensive and decided to take action against *The Irish People*. When the paper first made its appearance in November 1863 Dublin Castle was not overly concerned. *The Irish People*'s seditious rhetoric was similar to that of other newspapers then in circulation in Ireland and these had not prompted any real concern about the threat to peace, one reason being that they did not speak on behalf of a unified nationalist movement, as in the early 1840s Repeal days. The government initially

[169] As a young soldier sent on duty to Ireland, Charles Bradlaugh witnessed first-hand the suffering endured by the Irish people. Henceforth, he became a passionate advocate of the Irish cause; he wrote many articles on Irish issues in his newspaper *The National Reformer*. However, although a republican himself, he did not believe that either Ireland or England was ready for a republication government at this time; he was against violence and also did not think that the IRB should engage in revolution owing to the overwhelming military odds against them. Nonetheless, Bradlaugh was willing to give the Fenians some support, as his daughter's book shows: Hypatia Bradlaugh Bonner, *Charles Bradlaugh*, 7th ed. (London: T. Fisher Unwin, 1908), pp. 252–62. Bradlaugh was also against separation between Ireland and England, but thought that the Irish people should govern themselves in a federal arrangement like the United States.

[170] 1st LA, *Irish People*, 11 June 1864. See also another example: 4th LA in the same issue.

suspected that *The Irish People* was solely the organ of the American Fenians, intent on invading Ireland and establishing a republic.[171] The authorities, however, began to associate *The Irish People* with secret society activists in Ireland. The February 1864 Rotunda protest meeting over Prince Albert's statue, which had received much press coverage, may have been an occasion that brought specific attention to the IRB and its connection with *The Irish People*.[172] By siding in its editorials in such a triumphant manner with the opponents of the constitutional nationalists, *The Irish People* had clearly demonstrated an allegiance with conspirators in Ireland. Furthermore, *The Irish People*'s office, which was the headquarters of the IRB, came under surveillance by the police who increasingly began to suspect a connection between the revolutionary conspiracy that was gaining strength in numbers and *The Irish People*, a paper that was becoming bolder in its rhetoric and, indeed, was advocating revolution. Following the end of the American Civil War in April 1865, not only were Irish soldiers returning to Ireland to fight for the nationalist cause, but Irish-American officers were being enlisted by the IRB for training purposes. Finally, the police acted when they believed that they had found incriminating documents, in particular a letter discovered by Pierce Nagle, a spy who worked part-time in *The Irish People*'s publishing office. Dated 8 September 1865, the letter was written by James Stephens and indicated the imminence of a rising: '*This year – and let* [*sic*] there be no mistake about it – must be the year of action … the flag of Ireland – of the Irish Republic – must this year be raised.'[173] The police raided *The Irish People*'s premises on 15 September 1865 (the day before its last issue), its purpose twofold: to suppress *The Irish People* while at the same time felling the insurrectionary conspiracy that it represented.

But this government action, and the arrests and trials of those associated with the production of *The Irish People* that followed, did not mean an end to Fenianism. On the contrary, publicity from the press, particularly in Dublin, brought much notoriety to the Fenians. Coverage of their trials mostly came from *The Irishman*, *The Nation* and *The Weekly News*, which gave the prisoners – individuals who appeared to behave sincerely, dedicated

---

171 Report from Daniel Ryan, Superintendent, Dublin Metropolitan Police, 23 Dec. 1863, NAI, CSORP 1864/11941.

172 Letter (writer's name withheld) to O'Donovan Rossa, 15 April 1903, in Joseph Denieffe, *A Personal Narrative of the Irish Revolutionary Brotherhood*, Seán Ó Lúing (intro.) (Shannon: Irish University Press, 1969), pp. 292–3; (New York: serially in *The Gael*, 1904); 1st ed. (New York: 1906).

173 *Proceedings at the First Sitting of the Special Commission … for the Trial of Thomas Clarke Luby*, p. 121.

to Ireland – a voice with which to express their nationalist views, thus further disseminating Fenian philosophy. These journalists were shown in their closing speeches in particular to be eloquent and dignified; at the end of his trial Luby stated:

> I think when the proceedings of this trial go forth through the Press to the world, people will say the cause of Ireland is not to be despaired of, that Ireland is not a lost country. – As long as there are men in any country prepared to expose themselves to every difficulty and every danger, and who are prepared to brave captivity and even death itself, if need be – that country cannot be lost.[174]

During the trial O'Donovan Rossa conducted his own defence and insisted that it was his legal right to read to the court all of *The Irish People*'s issues, but through sheer exhaustion he was forced to stop after eight and a half hours.[175] The four leading Fenian prisoners were originally charged with high treason but this was reduced to treason-felony, a charge easier to prove and which did not carry the death penalty. Luby and O'Leary were sentenced to twenty years' penal servitude, Kickham fourteen, and O'Donovan Rossa, having had a similar charge against him in 1859, received life. During the trials, rather than being severely damaged, the Fenian movement thrived. This was reflected in the necessity to pass the Habeas Corpus Suspension Act on 17 February 1866, which demonstrated that the IRB had definitely not been crushed.

After their arrests the IRB's writers, and others associated with the production of their paper, achieved far more publicity for their cause than they ever did during *The Irish People*'s existence, as widespread press reporting of the trials reached a larger, more diverse public. John Devoy claimed that the trials provided enormous publicity for Fenianism and stimulated recruitment into the IRB, maintaining that many of the new members came from the commercial and professional classes who had previously remained aloof from the organization.[176] However, with the suspension of habeas corpus in February 1866 the IRB as a military organization became considerably more vulnerable. What had been printed in *The Irish People* and what was reported of its staff in the trials, though, may have had an enduring impression on IRB members, for many remained

[174] *Proceedings at the First Sitting of the Special Commission ... for the Trial of Thomas Clarke Luby*, p. 321.

[175] Sullivan, *New Ireland, vol. II*, pp. 159–60.

[176] Devoy, *Recollections*, p. 88.

resolutely loyal and risked their lives for the nationalist cause in March of the following year.[177]

The press publicity surrounding the trials of *The Irish People* and of those involved in the failed 1867 March rebellion when the Fenians took to the field were to have a far-reaching effect on the development of Irish nationalism. The spirit of romantic nationalism conveyed by *The Irish People* became inextricably linked with the revolutionary past of those sacrificing their freedom and risking death to save the Irish nation. The most publicized case was that of Thomas Francis Bourke, an Irish-American who had participated in the 1867 rebellion. His speech from the dock at the end of his trial received much acclaim from the nationalists. He declared:

> if it is the will of the Almighty and Omnipotent God that my devotion for the land of my birth shall be tested on the scaffold, I am willing there to die in defence of the right of men to free government – the right of an oppressed people to throw off the yoke of thraldom. I am an Irishman by birth, an American by adoption; by nature a lover of freedom – an enemy to the power that holds my native land in the bonds of tyranny.[178]

The sentiments expressed by Bourke chimed with those preached constantly in *The Irish People*; for example, Bourke's reference to throwing 'off the yoke of thraldom.' The Fenian newspaper had also made many claims about the prospective support of those Irish immigrants in America who were willing to help the cause in Ireland. Bourke is an example of one of the numerous Irish-Americans who travelled across the Atlantic to assist the IRB in its rebellion, illustrating the significance of the American connection.

Following the suppression of *The Irish People*, subscribers turned to *The Irishman*. Fenian and nationalist journalist James O'Connor noted that in June 1865 Richard Pigott became the proprietor of *The Irishman* and seemingly raised its circulation 'from a few thousand to fifty thousand a week.'[179] Bearing in mind that it accounted for only a part of newspaper

177 The March 1867 rebellion was thwarted for several reasons, including a lack of arms, spies, the overwhelming number of British troops and a failure to carry out the order that guerrilla tactics should precede full-scale warfare.

178 'The Speech from the Dock', *Nation*, 4 May 1867.

179 James O'Connor, *Recollections of Richard Pigott* (pamphlet) (Dublin: M.H. Gill & Son, 1889), p. 9. O'Connor also observes in his *Recollections* that 'Pigott never exhibited any but a business interest in politics', p. 33. Richard Pigott was a highly disreputable character who was notorious for the forged letters that incorrectly linked Parnell with the violence of extreme nationalists.

sales, the average weekly stamp return of *The Irishman* was 269 from October 1864 to September 1865, and rose to 433 between 30 June 1865 and 30 June 1867, but thereafter the number subsided.[180] When considering these figures it has to be taken into account that *The Irishman* would not have seen a commercial advantage until after *The Irish People*'s suppression, when the unstamped sales would have followed a similar pattern. The upturn in *The Irishman*'s circulation suggested the need of IRB members, in the vacuum left by *The Irish People*, to have their own newspaper. Much of the reportage in *The Irishman* concentrated on the amnesty appeal that followed the trials to free imprisoned IRB members. O'Connor stated that 'From '65 to '69, the *Irishman* was crammed with Fenian news and its leading articles were vigorously and boldly written … in defence of the prisoners and of the revolutionary movement.'[181]

The story of the Fenians made sensational reading from which nationalist papers benefited commercially, and this continued well beyond the suppression of *The Irish People* and the trials of the prisoners; dramatic events that followed included the planned Chester raid, the 1867 rebellion, and the trial and executions of the Manchester Martyrs, the latter involving three Fenians who were convicted of an unlawful killing and hanged. Newspaper reportage, particularly in the Dublin nationalist press, meant that Fenianism certainly had a high profile in public life in the 1860s.

Those working on the advanced nationalist press, despite the risk to their freedom, kept alive the nationalist message and spirit. James O'Connor, for instance, who worked in *The Irish People*'s office as a book keeper, also contributed articles to the paper; he was arrested and sentenced to seven years' penal servitude. Following an amnesty in 1869, he later became an editor of Pigott's *Irishman*, and worked for other nationalist newspapers, notably William O'Brien's *United Ireland*.[182] This sense of commitment and loyalty to the nationalist movement was typical of the journalists who worked for the Dublin nationalist press in the mid-nineteenth century.

The Irish People played an important role in the development of Irish nationalism, not only for supporting a revolutionary movement in the mid-nineteenth century, but also for the inspiration it bequeathed to later generations of Irish nationalists. In showing that a physical force doctrine

---

[180] Based on 'Return of Registered Newspapers and Publications in United Kingdom, and Number of Stamps issued 1864–66', HCP, 1866 (491) XL.113; 'Return … 1865–68', HCP, 1867–68 (461) LV.539.

[181] O'Connor, *Recollections*, pp. 9–10.

[182] Cormac F. Lowth, 'James O'Connor, Fenian, and the Tragedy of 1890', *Dublin Historical Record*, vol. 55 (2), Autumn 2002, pp. 132–53.

was accompanied by other concerns, *The Irish People* expounded a broad portrayal of Fenian ideology, while at the same time articulating the Fenian spirit admired by later Irish nationalists, a spirit that was described by John O'Leary as a willingness to 'sacrifice, if needs be, liberty or life for Ireland.'[183] This legacy was especially relevant around the turn of the century with the appearance of (often short-lived) newspapers that were inspired by Fenianism. One such paper beginning in September 1899 had the same title of *The Irish People*. Founded by William O'Brien, who, like many nationalists of his generation, had been influenced by the 1860s Fenian spirit, this newspaper supported the UIL, an organization that was trying to reconcile a fragmented nationalist movement.[184] O'Brien was pursuing home rule, and although not advocating physical force, the UIL assumed a militant tone, championing the cause of rural distress in the West, which had been a major concern of the IRB's *Irish People*.

One of the most advanced of the early twentieth-century newspapers was the IRB's monthly *Irish Freedom*, which in July 1911 voiced its impression of early Fenianism:

> It has been said of the Young Ireland Movement that it brought a new soul into Ireland, though it might, with more accuracy, be said that it gave that soul an expression in Irish literature. But Fenianism brought that soul into the Irish people, and raised in them a spirit which has never since died out of Ireland. It pulled the country clear out of the trammels of constitutional agitation and moral force into the complete Nationalism of Tone and Mitchel … Fenianism brought back into Ireland faith and determination: faith in Ireland's ability to win her freedom, and determination to win it; and courage to fight every influence that stood in the way.[185]

The Irish People had helped to instil this militant nationalist spirit into a substantial section of the population of Ireland and Great Britain in the mid-nineteenth century. More than anything else, the IRB's 1860s newspaper evoked a powerful, uncompromising will to win freedom for Ireland. During its existence *The Irish People* fought against those that tried to obstruct the progress of the Fenian cause: the advocates of constitutional nationalism, the Catholic Church, the landed aristocracy and the British

183 O'Leary, *Fenians and Fenianism, II*, p. 243.

184 Sally Warwick-Haller, *William O'Brien and the Irish Land War* (Dublin: Irish Academic Press, 1990), pp. 18 and 200.

185 'Lucan', 'The Fenian Movement', *Irish Freedom*, July 1911.

government. All this the militant Irish nationalists in the early part of the twentieth century recognized. When *Irish Freedom* first began in November 1910, its mission statement announced: 'We stand, not for an Irish Party, but for National tradition – the tradition of Wolfe Tone and Robert Emmet, of John Mitchel and John O'Leary.'[186] The inclusion of O'Leary in this revolutionary lineage recognized his promotion of the physical force tradition as an IRB leader in the years before his death in 1907 and his editorship of *The Irish People*.

An advocate of revolutionary nationalism in the early twentieth century was James Connolly, whose perception of the advanced nationalists and their newspapers of the mid-nineteenth century may have helped to shape his socialist doctrine; he thus acknowledged them as 'Irish Pioneers of the Socialist Movement.'[187] It has already been mentioned in the previous chapter of this book that Connolly believed there was an indissoluble relationship between nationalism and socialism. Connolly certainly believed that he had identified this link in the Fenian movement of the 1860s. For example, the following extract from a July 1864 issue of *The Irish People* was printed in large type inside a decorative box in *The Harp*, the socialist monthly newspaper edited by Connolly:

> Who are the rightful owners of the soil? The people! ... Throughout all we see one grand system of oppression constantly at work ... It is a system which in its least repulsive aspects, compels thousands and tens of thousands to fret and toil, to live and die in hunger and rags and wretchedness that a few useless drones may revel in indolence and luxury. Such a system is accursed alike of man and of God and our country never will possess an hour's prosperity or peace until it is swept away, root and branch.[188]

Although there seems to be no evidence to suggest that the IRB's journalists saw themselves or their organization as advocating socialism, Connolly interpreted their writings as a socialist discourse that explained and articulated the conflict between Ireland and Britain. However, there can be no ambivalence over the interpretation of another doctrine: Connolly and *The Irish People* both unequivocally believed in the concept of revolutionary nationalism.

---

186 1st LA, *Irish Freedom*, Nov. 1910.

187 'Labour in Irish history', *Harp*, May 1910.

188 3rd LA, *Irish People*, 9 July 1864, reprinted in *Harp*, July 1908 (where it differs very slightly from the original).

Another believer in revolutionary nationalism was Patrick Pearse, for whom the 1860s Fenians were an inspiration. Pearse's extensive study of the mythological Fianna enabled him, from a romantic perspective, to relate to the mid-nineteenth-century Fenians. Pearse paid tribute to them in the December 1913 issue of *Irish Freedom*, adding: 'surely it is a sin against national faith to expect national freedom without adopting the necessary means to win and keep it. And I know of no other way than the way of the sword.'[189] This was a major tenet of Fenianism expressed continuously in *The Irish People*, that the winning of freedom for Ireland could only be achieved by physical force. Indeed, *Irish Freedom*, suppressed in 1914, preached the creed of early Fenianism. On the first of August 1915 Pearse delivered his famous oration at the graveside of O'Donovan Rossa at Glasnevin Cemetery (the burial place of O'Leary, O'Mahony and Stephens) in which he cited a direct link between early Fenianism and prospective revolutionists:

> ... the seeds sown by the young men of '65 and '67 are coming to their miraculous ripening to-day ... Life springs from death; and from the graves of patriot men and women spring living nations. The Defenders of this Realm ... have left us our Fenian dead, and while Ireland holds these graves, Ireland unfree shall never be at peace.[190]

In the short term, after the IRB trials in the mid-1860s, an expression of nationalist sentiment manifested itself into the high-profile amnesty movement for the Fenian prisoners towards the end of the decade. In the long-term, the powerful concept of romantic nationalism, reaffirmed by *The Irish People*, lived on.

Conclusion

Although Fenian ideas were not original, being the legacies of past Irish nationalists, *The Irish People* helped to keep them alive. A tunnel vision approach was adopted by the IRB and reflected by its newspaper, whereby all energies and resources were directed to one goal and one means, separation from Great Britain by military force. There was a highly determined campaign by *The Irish People* to deter any attempts by the

[189] 'From a hermitage', *Irish Freedom*, Dec. 1913.

[190] Pearse, 'O'Donovan Rossa – Graveside Oration', Aug. 1915, *Political Writings and Speeches*, pp. 136–7.

constitutional nationalists to achieve political gains, and thus the newspaper helped prevent any meaningful advancement of constitutional nationalism during this period. However, *The Irish People* presented a broad range of interests, showing that its concerns were not only with physical force revolution but with a wider critique of the political and social framework of Ireland. Although the IRB was determined not to use its energies organizing land or cultural movements, which it believed would ultimately yield little towards achieving independence, this did not mean neglect of these areas of concern. In *The Irish People* the land and rural distress was one of the most discussed issues, and the importance of culture was evidenced by the presence of the literary columns, where much of the poetry and stories augmented the moral and political issues in the articles and editorials. The influence of the Catholic Church in its campaign to persuade its parishioners not to join the IRB was effectively discouraged by *The Irish People.* The paper also advocated the separation of church and state, an integral component of the republican ideal.

The impact of *The Irish People* in America in bringing Fenians together on both sides of the Atlantic in terms of ideology and strategy cannot be underestimated; importantly, republicanism became a permanent feature of Irish nationalist thinking. Funding from the Fenian Brotherhood meant the survival of *The Irish People*, while news in the paper of American Fenian support, which also showed Irish immigrants as models of bravery in the Civil War battlefields, was intended to be inspirational to those in the IRB. Although *The Irish People* was unsuccessful in raising finances, it drew numerous new members into the organization and preserved their loyalty to the Fenian cause.

In keeping with the Irish nationalist press of the mid-nineteenth century, *The Irish People* had a role in helping to raise political awareness among the people. For example, *The Irish People* particularly exploited what past Irish nationalists saw as the differences between the two nations of England and Ireland: the IRB depicted England as morally deficient and cruel in its behaviour towards the people of Ireland, whereas Ireland was portrayed as the small downtrodden victim of English rule. Presenting an image of what it perceived as the Saxon enemy in its newspaper was a metaphor through which the IRB recruited members for the separatist nationalist cause. Fenian rhetoric was intended to inculcate a revolutionary spirit into the people, reviving what it saw as the centuries-old tradition of England as the oppressor of the Irish people and the necessity of resisting its unjust political domination. The IRB's claim that all Ireland's problems emanated from English occupation, which could not be resolved until England relinquished rule over Ireland, was pursued relentlessly in *The Irish*

People. A poignant image presented in the paper was that of a dying nation desperately in need of regeneration by young soldiers, laced with compelling rhetoric coalescing qualities of nobleness, power, strength and courage from a mythical and historical past into the present.

Initially begun to raise finances and promote an organization that was heading for the abyss, *The Irish People* became a lifeline to the IRB. When Dublin Castle realized that those who published this newspaper had the means to carry out their rhetoric, both the paper and its creators were seized with the intention of destroying them. Ironically, the trials provided even greater publicity for the Fenian cause and, far from being defeated or silenced, the Fenians went on to stage a rebellion. Following the paper's suppression Fenian ideology reached an even wider public, and was an inspiration to later generations of Irish nationalists. While it cannot be claimed that the cause of Irish nationalism would have been lost without the advent of Fenianism, what is known is that Fenianism's physical force spirit, passionately conveyed in *The Irish People*, had a defining role in securing Ireland's independence from Great Britain.

Reflections

THERE IS LITTLE DOUBT that the Dublin nationalist press had a profound influence over the development of Irish nationalism during the mid-nineteenth century. The extent to which Irish nationalists used the press to further their cause is a striking indication that the Dublin nationalist press and Irish nationalism were inextricably linked. The press provided these political activists with a regular platform, where they sought to infuse a vision of Irish nationalism into Irish society. During the nineteenth century, newspapers became increasingly accessible, coinciding with the gradual removal of taxes and the presence of a growing literate population, which meant that newsprint became a crucial medium for the dissemination of Irish nationalism. The mid-nineteenth century was a defining period of Irish nationalist history, not least due to the contribution these newspapers made to the development of Irish nationalism during that time, but also the influences they would have later in the century and beyond.

The Nation, clearly the most influential Dublin nationalist newspaper in the mid-nineteenth century, acted as the model for other nationalist papers during this period. With Thomas Davis as the ideological leader of the Young Irelanders in *The Nation*'s early years, its emphasis on cultural nationalism and non-sectarianism was an inspiration to contemporaries and future Irish nationalists alike. Under the custodianship of Charles Gavan Duffy in 1842, *The Nation* began as a spirited constitutional nationalist newspaper; after six years it briefly turned to revolutionary nationalism in the political fervour of 1848, and was duly suppressed. On its reissue towards the end of 1849 *The Nation* reverted back to constitutional nationalism, but adopted a more measured tone. With the involvement of A.M. Sullivan from the mid-1850s, however, *The Nation* increasingly recovered the feisty journalism of its early years, although now it veered more towards Irish Catholic nationalism. Two papers that had less influence on the development of Irish constitutional nationalism, *The Pilot* and *The Dublin Weekly Register*, were both gone by 1850. *The Freeman* group, however, was the rock of the Dublin nationalist movement in the mid-nineteenth century, firmly supporting constitutional nationalism, and produced the only nationalist papers in Dublin that continually survived during this whole time.

In contrast to the comparative longevity and political orientation of John Gray's papers, *The United Irishman*, *The Irish Tribune*, *The Irish Felon*, *The Irishman* and the other rebel papers all represented revolutionary nationalism for a short spell in 1848. *The Irishman* of 1849–50, fiercely opposed to constitutional nationalism, was notable for its socialist rhetoric; with its antecedents located in the rebel press of 1848, it was the first Dublin newspaper that firmly placed working-class aspirations at the heart of Irish nationalism. In the early 1850s two innovations in Irish nationalist history occurred when *The Tablet* joined *The Nation* and *The Freeman* in, firstly, promoting a tenant right movement, an initiative that involved co-operation between Ireland's northern and southern counties, and, secondly, supporting the establishment of an independent Irish parliamentary party. However, the failure of these two experiments left a vacuum for the advanced nationalists to articulate some of their ideas in the 1855–56 *Tribune*. This paper can be identified for its defiance against the British government during the Crimean War and for its suggestion that physical force nationalism was still a viable option, provided circumstances were favourable for its success. From 1858 *The Irishman*, opposed to constitutional nationalism like its earlier namesakes, also assumed a defiant tone, especially when some of its contributions came from the Fenians. *The Irish People*, however, went much further in this direction, and is memorable for its espousal of revolutionary and republican nationalism. Even though the Fenian paper was suppressed near the end of 1865 its ideology became a long-term feature of Irish nationalism.

During the twenty-five years from 1842 to 1867 the number of papers that came and went, and their various affiliations to different ideas and organizations, reflect the uncertainty and turbulence that existed during this time. The Great Famine has a crucial impact on this period, when social and economic upheaval brought a dramatic acceleration to changes that were already taking place in Irish society. This phenomenon was combined with what appeared to Irish nationalists to be the British government's negative response to the consequences of the potato blight. Under these circumstances the Dublin nationalist press, more than ever, campaigned for an independent Ireland free from British rule, whether by peaceful means or by physical force. Ironically, when Irish society seemed at its most dysfunctional during the period of the Great Famine, it was building a collective memory that was necessary for the creation of a lasting national identity.

The Dublin nationalist press in the mid-nineteenth century is characterized by its success in drawing vast numbers of people into nationalist organizations. Newspapers gave a nationalist group credibility, and in publicizing its activities, provided a focus for its followers and information for current and prospective supporters. The presence of *The Irish People* newspaper from 1863 to 1865, for example, coincided with a large increase in membership of the IRB, and generated support for Irish revolutionary nationalism. The most positive effect arising from the link between newspapers and Irish nationalism came with the founding of *The Nation* in the autumn of 1842, when its support for the Loyal National Repeal Association was a major force that led to constitutional nationalism gaining an unprecedented popular following through to the autumn of 1843. This progress was evidenced not only by the greatly increased numbers joining the Repeal Association, but also by the impressive attendances at the monster meetings where the publicity in the Dublin nationalist press had a snowball effect; the more they were reported, the more extravagant these meetings became in their expression of Irish nationalism. The success of such gatherings, which were accompanied by pre- and post-publicity in the Dublin nationalist press, was to pave the way for the public demonstrations and newspaper reporting that promoted the 1879–82 Land War. Importantly, no political movement could properly exist without the support of a newspaper, reflected, for instance, by James Fintan Lalor's marked perseverance in attempting to link a conspiratorial nationalist organization with a new newspaper in 1849, while the defection of Irish Democratic Association members to the Irish Alliance, the latter represented by *The Nation*, suggests that its society could not survive following the termination of 1849–50 *Irishman*. As a newspaper could increase the support for the nationalist organization it represented, this organization could often, in turn, boost the sales of a newspaper – a two-way dependency indicating the reciprocal nature of the link between the nationalist newspapers and the organizations they represented.

While the presence of a nationalist newspaper could mean the advancement of the organization that it represented, another characteristic of the Dublin nationalist press was its destructive nature. This had a most profound effect on the development of Irish nationalism in the mid-nineteenth century when the Dublin nationalist press was at the heart of the dissensions within the nationalist movement. Newspapers were commercial concerns, and hence market share and financial solvency could sometimes be just as relevant as ideological perspectives, reflected in the battle between the 1849–50 *Irishman* and the reissued *Nation*. Newspapers empowered Irish nationalists and drove them into making decisions not necessarily conducive to the advantage of Irish political nationalism. Bitter conflicts arose between newspapers that represented contrasting shades of Irish nationalist opinion, ideologically and strategically, and these worked against the cohesion that was badly needed to assist the development of Irish nationalism. The acrimonious discord in the mid-1860s between the constitutional *Nation* and the revolutionary *Irish People* provides an important example of the polarization in the nationalist movement during this period. All these quarrels in the Dublin nationalist press, however, demonstrate the importance Irish nationalists attached to the power of their newspapers, enabling them to promote their views and engage in battle, not only with the British government but with each other. The dynamics of the relationship between the O'Connellites and *The Nation*'s associates brought much discord into the Repeal Association. *The Nation*'s success in its early years empowered the Young Irelanders to believe that they could seriously challenge Daniel O'Connell's authority over Irish nationalist policies. The opposition of O'Connell and his Old Ireland followers to this challenge led to the 1846 split in the Repeal Association. When Charles Gavan Duffy quarrelled with leader writer John Mitchel over what was to be preached in *The Nation*, it undermined the Irish Confederation and prompted Mitchel to produce *The United Irishman* as a rival to *The Nation* to publicize his newly acquired revolutionary ideas. The success of his paper in 1848 encouraged Mitchel to embark on a mission that goaded the British government into suppressing *The United Irishman* and ordering his arrest, prompting the other Dublin rebel papers to follow a path of self-destruction.

The Dublin nationalist newspapers of this period produced memorable nationalists, the most notable being Thomas Davis, James Fintan Lalor and John Mitchel; they not only inspired contemporaries, but had a profound influence on later Irish nationalists. Davis was particularly remembered for his all-inclusive vision of the Irish nation embracing political and cultural nationalism, Lalor mainly for his theory of the vital link between the land and nationalist politics, and Mitchel for his perspective on the Great Famine and his espousal of revolutionary and republican nationalism. What these nationalists wrote was preserved in newsprint to be used by later Irish nationalists to enhance or legitimize specific nationalist agendas. Important political activists and journalists in the early twentieth century such as Arthur Griffith, Patrick Pearse and James Connolly were especially inspired by the writers of the mid-nineteenth-century Dublin nationalist press.

The two main nationalist leaders of the mid-nineteenth century, Daniel

O'Connell and William Smith O'Brien, were closely associated with the Dublin nationalist press where they also produced occasional written contributions of their own. Speeches conducted not only by these two leading Irish nationalists, but also others, such as Young Irelander Thomas Francis Meagher who was a particularly effective speaker, could be printed in the newspapers to reach an audience that was far wider than just those present at meetings. These platform orations could also be discussed and analysed by the newspaper journalists, thus reinforcing and endorsing the speechmakers' political messages. But the Dublin nationalist papers themselves could also assume a quasi-leadership role in the absence of a prominent public figure; this was, by necessity, especially true of *The Irish People*, which represented the conspiratorial IRB.

Whether it was to lead to the progression or the regression of the Irish nationalist cause, the power of ideas and their political value in newspapers was crucial to the development of Irish nationalism in the mid-nineteenth century. The concept of the unity of class and creed, whose antecedents originated with Theobold Wolfe Tone and the United Irishmen, was preached in the Dublin nationalist press, particularly by Thomas Davis. However, whereas the idea of the unity of class may have worked to a certain extent in the heady monster meeting heyday of 1843, its practical reality had little chance of achieving success. Using persuasive language in the Dublin nationalist press mainly to target a specific audience was more productive in drawing certain groups of people into the movement, but this meant the exclusion of other sections of society. Two main issues that demonstrated the difficulties of appealing to all classes were tenant right and physical force. While the plight of the poor in rural areas was a genuine concern for the nationalist journalists, the use of the idea of tenant right, and ultimately peasant proprietorship, was a way of enticing the lower classes into the Irish nationalist movement, even if it was at the expense of alienating the upper classes. A more divisive issue than that of tenant right was the idea of physical force, which appealed to an even more restricted audience. Although rhetoric of this nature in the Dublin nationalist press could be effective at times, fearful of a threat to the established order, the upper classes and most of the middle classes were unwilling to embrace any notion of physical force.

Promoting the idea of the unity of creed was also problematic for the development of the Irish nationalist cause. While the Dublin nationalist newspapers did attempt to draw Protestants into their political campaigns – with some success in 1843 – their organizations remained overwhelmingly Catholic even though some Protestants, the most notable being Thomas Davis, were leading advocates of Irish nationalism. Attempting to persuade

Protestants to join them by advocating unity of creed, Irish nationalists sometimes articulated their ideology through a class divide. *The Irishman* of 1849–50, for example, sought to exploit the division between the upper and lower classes of Irish society, where British rule was equated with the landlord class, both perceived as enemies of the lower classes. However, the force of sectarian strife worked against this policy.[1] The minority Protestant communities in Ireland were undermined in the mid-nineteenth century by the force of Irish nationalism and this trend continued throughout the rest of the century. Ironically often led by Protestants, the voice of the majority Catholic population was seen to express political ambitions, particularly in the mass meetings of Repeal and, of course, not least, through its press, which became more daring in its rhetoric during this period. The Dublin nationalist press became a powerful medium for articulating and asserting Catholic rights in the mid-nineteenth century and this had an adverse effect on Protestant mentality. The Protestant population, who mainly resided in the north, naturally resisted the call for independence from Britain fearing an alteration of the balance of power. There was 'a deep rooted dread of Roman Catholic ascendancy' among Protestants, even though the Dublin nationalist press tried to reassure the Protestant minority in Ireland that its values would be protected if independence from Britain was accomplished.[2] Despite reassurances in the Dublin nationalist press, the Protestant minority was mostly unwilling to support movements that seemed to have the potential to create a Catholic ascendancy. This was not helped when, from the mid-1840s, arguments over religion arose and the future of Repeal entered a period of uncertainty with friction brewing between the O'Connells and *The Nation*, particularly when John O'Connell assumed leadership duties from his father and drew the Repeal Association ever closer to the Catholic Church. From the mid-1850s, *The Nation* itself, the erstwhile champion of unity of creed, veered towards commenting and reporting on Catholic issues, while the advanced nationalist papers who continued to advocate unity of creed were less influential in Irish society during this time.

When the Dublin nationalist newspapers in the mid-nineteenth century spoke on behalf of Catholic Ireland and the injustices inflicted during centuries of English rule, especially in light of the Reformation, they

[1] For example, the Dolly's Brae riots, when clashes between Orangemen and Catholics caused injuries and fatalities on 12 July 1849; see for instance: 2nd LA, *Freeman's Journal*, 16 July 1849.

[2] Protestant Ulsterman John Martin speaking at a Repeal Association mtg., 23 Feb. 1846, *Nation*, 28 Feb. 1846.

firmly established the notion of the majority Irish Catholic population as the legitimate and rightful owners and rulers of Ireland. Evoking a shared memory of the experiences of the Catholic community in its perceived long, heroic struggle against the English was a popular theme in the leading articles and literary columns of the Dublin nationalist press. Rhetoric of this nature would certainly have had an impact on who should belong to the Irish national community, thus making it difficult for both Protestants and Catholics to become part of an inclusive Irish Christian nation. Despite a call for the unity of creed, the Dublin nationalist press in the mid-nineteenth century tended to work overall against the integration of Catholics and Protestants, consequences that would affect the future political settlement of Ireland.

Many other Irish nationalist ideas were articulated in the Dublin nationalist newspapers that were either developed or introduced in the mid-nineteenth century and would make a distinct impression on Ireland's future. The idea of some form of independence from Britain took a resolute hold over Irish nationalist hopes during this time and was eventually achieved in the 1921 Anglo-Irish Treaty. Once the idea of Repeal was on the nationalist agenda, despite the British government's resistance, it would not go away. While the campaign for Repeal was introduced by O'Connell in the 1830s, with the emphatic support of the Dublin nationalist press, this idea developed in the next decade from an aspiration into something that Repealers convinced themselves was attainable. Despite a reality check at Clontarf, the idea of Repeal remained strong among Irish nationalists. Striving for Irish independence became a spectacle of advance and retreat; rhetoric in their press often made Irish nationalists believe that they could achieve far more than what was practicable. Given the strength of opposition from the British government and its superior military forces, which could crush, and did crush, attempted Irish insurgency, seeking Irish independence in the mid-nineteenth century appeared too ambitious. Even so, during this time the idea of Irish independence was firmly established and debated with passion and courage by the Dublin nationalist journalists.

Following the failure of constitutional and revolutionary political movements in the two decades after the late 1840s, Isaac Butt's conception of Federalism in the 1870s, in essence similar to that proposed in 1844, was a compromise accepted by both constitutionalists and some extreme nationalists in the Home Rule movement. Federalism was later discussed in the early twentieth century as a solution to the Ulster crisis and the third Home Rule Bill. By this time, though, compared with the 1840s, Federalism had become more limited in its scope and was apt to be seen as allowing Ireland little more than the rights of a province. Another form of Irish independence was the idea of a republic. Originally a concept from 1798, this was promoted by the advanced nationalist papers in the mid-nineteenth century, most emphatically *The Irish People*, and except for much of Ulster, republicanism became fixed in Irish nationalist thinking to become a reality in 1949.

Unlike physical force nationalism, the idea of constitutional nationalism was supported by most of the Dublin nationalist papers during the mid-nineteenth century. For a short period in the 1850s, the notion of an independent Irish parliamentary party took root; its fleeting success suggested a path to political advantage in the British House of Commons. This concept failed to grow to any significance until Parnell's day, when circumstances were more favourable and his parliamentary party became an important feature of Irish politics in the latter part of the nineteenth century.

Although a minority concept, physical force, the ideological rival of constitutional nationalism, was adopted and promoted by some Irish nationalist newspapers in the mid-nineteenth century, becoming firmly established as a long-term characteristic of the Irish nationalist cause. Furthermore, a resurgence of the idea of secret conspiracy in 1849 gradually evolved into an impressive movement in the 1860s, surviving to take a key role in the nationalist political activities of the early twentieth century. Associated with physical force revolution was the idea of sacrifice for the regeneration of Ireland; a powerful image in the more advanced Dublin nationalist newspapers, noticeably the 1855–56 *Tribune* and *The Irish People*, this was mostly aimed at impressionable young men who would be the main participants in an armed struggle and, importantly, was a concept that would have a special significance in the 1916 Rising.

Though physical force was not particularly desired by Irish nationalists in the mid-nineteenth century, it was adopted as a desperate measure during the Great Famine when John Mitchel and others believed that it was the only way to save the Irish population from starvation, disease and death. Mitchel, like other Irish nationalists, thought that only an Irish government could properly address the effects of the potato blight. Constitutional nationalism was clearly the first choice for agitation to secure political gains, but when that seemed to fail, for others, physical force became an alternative strategy. But attempts at rebellion in 1848, 1849 and 1867 revealed that Irish nationalists were no match for both the powerful military force and law-making process (such as coercion bills) of the British state.

Many other factors worked against the physical force activists in their organizations during the middle decades of the nineteenth century: internal strife, the presence of spies, a lack of effective military leadership, to name a few, and, importantly, the demoralization of the Irish nation from the effects of the Famine. When physical force alone was seen not to work in the face of overwhelming odds some revolutionists realized the practicality of working with the constitutionalists. After the failure of 1867 some individual IRB members believed in the usefulness of compromise and flexibility. And it was only when working with the Land Leaguers and Home Rulers, and later around the turn of the century with the Gaelic cultural revivalists, that the Fenians made realistic progress towards achieving Irish independence from Britain.

The IRB's use of leisure-time activities as a means of communication and political networking to promote their cause in the 1860s was revived by the later revolutionists, but to a much greater extent, when they infiltrated organizations associated with the Gaelic Revival, such as Cumann na nGaedheal.[3] *The Irish People* was not just successful in recruitment but also in fostering a sense of community within the IRB membership. Ironically, the IRB, which had advocated unity of creed, particularly in the mid-nineteenth century, distanced itself from this concept as it became increasingly involved with the Gaelic Revival's activities, when Irish nationalism and Catholicism became even more tightly linked as one cause.

Although socialist groups would later emerge from around the end of the nineteenth century, in particular with James Connolly and the founding of the Irish Socialist Republican Party in 1896, elements of the socialist dogma were espoused in the mid-nineteenth-century Dublin nationalist press. Connolly developed the idea of fusing socialism and nationalism as a dual goal, the one dependant on the other for the good of the Irish people. Many socialists believed that change in society could not be accomplished through constitutional methods. This mirrored the socialist rhetoric espoused by the 1849–50 *Irishman*, which had been inspired by Mitchel's *United Irishman*. The 1849–50 *Irishman*, when it represented the Irish Democratic Association, firmly established the idea of the lower classes having their own socio-political nationalist aspirations; its separatist and militant ideology and socialist rhetoric resonated in the following century with a growing politicized working class.

One of the most enduring concepts of the mid-nineteenth century was self-reliance. Originating with *The Nation* and expressed as 'ourselves alone,' this idea, echoed by other nationalist papers, advocated a cultural, economic and political regeneration of Ireland by the Irish people themselves; this was later developed by Arthur Griffith in the early twentieth century to

[3] Cumann na nGaedheal (Party of the Irish) was an umbrella nationalist organization founded in 1900, which became an official political party in 1923.

form the theoretical basis of the Sinn Féin movement. Politically, it was similar to Repeal's advocacy of complete Irish independence under a dual monarchy with Britain. Reminiscent of James Fintan Lalor's writings, while militancy was not to be ruled out by Sinn Féin, political self-reliance was to be accomplished through the strategy of passive resistance. Irish MPs would withdraw from the British parliament and form their own political assembly in Ireland, an action that had its antecedents in the Council of Three Hundred suggested by Daniel O'Connell, and later advocated with more conviction by the Irish Confederates. As for economic proposals, the mid-nineteenth-century nationalist newspapers called for the development of Ireland's natural resources, her industries to be protected by tariffs, and a concentration on home markets, policies that were also later preached by the Sinn Féiners. While Griffith had developed his thoughts and presented them to the public, basing his models of self-reliance and passive resistance on Hungary and Germany as they had, in his view, already been proven to work, he had also been greatly influenced by the mid-nineteenth-century Dublin nationalist writers, especially Thomas Davis, John Mitchel and James Fintan Lalor.[4] Although the British government held too tight a grip on Ireland in the mid-nineteenth century for much progress in the way of self-reliance, this concept captured the imagination of the numerous moderate and advanced Irish nationalists who later joined the Sinn Féin movement in an atmosphere of hope and belief encouraged by the Gaelic Revival.

Campaigning for land reform was a major feature of the Irish nationalist cause in the mid-nineteenth century. The idea of landlordism, and what it stood for, was attacked in the Dublin nationalist press from different perspectives, from theoretical arguments over the legal and moral ownership of land down to the practical realities of the legal arrangements between landlord and tenant. Land was on the agenda of most nationalist groups in the mid-nineteenth century and while political power lay with the landowners, there was little nationalists could effectively do to seek a change in the land law. Peasant proprietorship was suggested by some Irish nationalists, especially the more advanced activists, who demanded the return of the land to the Irish people from the 'English conquerors.' A policy that James Fintan Lalor preached, the notion of the land question as a way of advancing the Irish nationalist cause, was taken up by the Land League and it achieved a degree of success in the 1879–82 Land War.

[4] For an analysis of Arthur Griffith's Sinn Féin's theories see, for example: Donal McCartney, 'The Political use of History in the work of Arthur Griffith', *Journal of Contemporary History*, vol. 8 (1), Jan. 1973, pp. 3–19.

Lalor saw the conquest of land synonymous with the political conquest over Ireland's indigenous population, and it was his idea to use the land problem to reverse 'the conquest of Ireland.' Lalor's rhetoric, particularly the concept of solving the land issue before any other nationalist issue, assumed a high profile in some of the Dublin nationalist newspapers, where the effects of the Great Famine convinced nationalists even more that land reform was essential for the well-being and stability of Ireland's rural inhabitants. It was not until the advent of an Irish parliamentary party in the early 1850s, combined with a stronger rural base of tenant farmers, that concerted action was attempted, but this had only a fleeting success; it proved, however, that the attainment of land reform was possible. Led by Michael Davitt and Parnell, the formidable Land League, composed of constitutional nationalists and some IRB members, and supported by an impressive campaign in the press, achieved a modicum of success with the Land Act of 1881 granting the 3 fs (fair rent, free sale, and fixity of tenure). Land reform would eventually help to change the social composition of rural communities where farmers would be politicized and emerge as a strong group in Irish society. In mid-nineteenth-century Dublin nationalist newspapers the ideas were there; attempts were made to solve the land problem, lessons were learned and the press played a crucial role in helping the campaign for land reform to become firmly entrenched in Irish nationalist thinking. Others, like William O'Brien, would subsequently take up the torch and work to solve the land problem, culminating in the important Wyndham Land Act of 1903.

The power of the Dublin nationalist press also had an impact on the Catholic Church, fearful of losing its authority and control over the Irish Catholic community. The Church was suspicious of newspapers that had a distinct non-sectarian policy, such as the 1840s *Nation*. It was even more critical when this policy was combined with revolutionary politics, evidenced by its notable attacks on *The Irish People*. The Catholic Church was one of the IRB's most formidable opponents, but journalists working for *The Irish People* effectively defended Fenianism. Paralleled with its increasing power and status in Irish society in the mid-nineteenth century, the Catholic Church established a firm foothold in moderate nationalist politics. This relationship was reciprocal; while nationalists allied with the Catholic Church for pragmatic or strategic reasons, priests needed to become involved with nationalist politics so as to safeguard their influence over society. In O'Connell's times the 1840s Repeal Association was shown to have worked successfully with the co-operation of priests, particularly in their role as Repeal Wardens, whilst John O'Connell was especially determined to steer the Repeal Association even more towards Catholic issues in an attempt to isolate *The Nation*'s Young Irelanders, his nationalist rivals, and to protect his position within the Association. With so many priests actively involved in 1840s nationalist politics, it certainly gave the appearance that Irish nationalism was a Catholic movement. While the O'Connellites were supported by the moderate Dublin nationalist newspapers, the link between Catholicism and constitutional nationalism was strengthened further by the Sullivan brothers' newspapers, thereby indelibly fusing an Irish Catholic national identity. Furthermore, the Catholic Church gained in stature when the Church of Ireland was disestablished in 1869; this was essentially due to agitation by nationalists, a key example of reciprocity between the Catholic Church and Irish nationalists, although ironically this Act of Parliament was hastened by the Fenian threat in the mid-1860s. The Catholic Church continued its involvement in nationalist organizations beyond the mid-nineteenth century; for example, it supported the Gaelic League. But while the Catholic Church and its priests aided nationalists, Protestants became more alienated, which did not bode well for the future of the island's different religious communities. And as time was to tell, the Catholic Church's social and spiritual values were to have a significant influence in the future Irish Free State.

The receptivity of Irish people to the call of the nationalist cause owes much to the writing skills of the journalists. Based on the progress of the nationalist political organizations in the mid-nineteenth century, and official and anecdotal circulation figures of newspapers, it would appear that rhetoric disseminated by the Dublin nationalist press proved to be highly effective. The nature of the discourse applied by the Dublin nationalist press tended towards a balance between emotive language, intended to arouse feelings, and rational argument, appealing to the intellect. The government's steps to curtail the power of the Dublin nationalist press by the suppression of its newspapers and the numerous indictments against its creators was testimony to its powers of persuasion. Such action by the government against the nationalist press would be repeated in later decades and all this added to the image, as perceived by nationalists, of Ireland as a victim of British rule.

A key objective of the Dublin nationalist press was to provide knowledge of the historical relationship between England and Ireland, which proved to be a productive way of fostering anti-English feelings. The perceived negativity of the English connection was presented on a regular basis; questions of morality pervaded the rhetoric of the nationalist journalists with accusations that England's politics and English society were corrupt and debased, lending a backdrop to their overarching charge that for centuries Ireland had been a victim of England's misrule and injustice. From

O'Connell's tirades printed in the 1840s Repeal press to *The Irish People* in the 1860s, the anti-English rhetoric of the mid-nineteenth-century Dublin nationalist press was exploited as a way of unifying the people, and drawing them into the Irish nationalist cause. Later in the century, anti-English rhetoric developed into a phobia that gripped the Irish Catholic community, and found expression in the Gaelic Revival's activities.

The need to inculcate the idea of an Irish nation into the people was deemed essential for the development of Irish nationalism, and was much publicized by the Dublin nationalist press in the mid-nineteenth century. Nationalists saw Britain's relationship with Ireland in the context of the Act of Union as incongruous for they maintained that the Irish people had a different identity from the people of Great Britain. Now that Ireland was joined politically with Britain, many Irish nationalists believed that the Irish national identity, which had been eroded over time through Ireland's colonial connection with Britain, was being weakened even more, particularly with the acceleration of changes brought about by the Great Famine. But the more Anglicized Irish society became, the more the Dublin nationalist press resisted British rule. Ethnicity played a key part in the war of words between the Irish press and the British press, each deriding the other's ethnic characteristics. Led by *The Nation*, the nationalist press strove to promote a national Irish identity, evidenced by their leading articles and their support of cultural groups and reading rooms, and not least by the content of their literary columns. Language, however, as Thomas Davis recognized, is one of the most important characteristics of national identity and yet the nationalist newspapers, paradoxically, continued to address their public almost entirely through what they themselves sometimes termed the oppressor's language, rather than print in Gaelic. They were going with the flow of the decline of the Irish language in favour of English, the perceived language of progress at this time. Ideas for preserving Gaelic were suggested, however, even if they were used symbolically as a sign of defiance against British rule. Importantly, in fighting for the survival of the Irish nation, particularly in the context of a dying native language, the Dublin nationalist newspapers, and the organizations they represented, provided collective experiences for Irish people that promoted a sense of belonging, a national identity that was necessary for the creation of an independent nation state.

The minds of the Dublin nationalist newspaper writers were particularly focused on an issue that was to provide Irish nationalists with emotive and compelling argument for independence from the mid-1840s onwards: the British government's handling of the Great Famine. The response of Irish nationalists to Westminster's 1840s famine policy certainly changed the nature of Irish nationalism and the dynamics of nationalist rhetoric. While not all Irish nationalists were committed to this new political direction, in 1848 Irish nationalism evolved into a revolutionary movement, fuelled not only by the short-lived rebel newspapers but also by *The Nation* during the spring and summer of that year. Besides contributing to the proliferation of the Clubs in 1848 and persuading those belonging to them to become more belligerent, it seemed as if the newspaper writers of the Irish Confederation were indoctrinating each other with their own impassioned and seditious rhetoric, which not only led to the suppression of their newspapers, but also contributed to the downfall of the Irish nationalist movement that summer. Promoted by John Mitchel in 1848, Irish nationalism developed into a new form, evoking an intense feeling of disquiet and anger that was aimed at the British government for its response to the potato blight. Simmering in the 1850s, this new direction escalated in the next decade, articulated in particular by *The Irish People*, and became an enduring part of Irish nationalist rhetoric. The historical legacy of Ireland as a victim of British rule was developed by the Dublin nationalist press in the mid-nineteenth century, offering a perception of the past that was particularly propagated by republican nationalists until it was challenged by revisionist historians, such as Conor Cruise O'Brien and Roy Foster, who opposed what they deemed the extremes of Anglophobic Irish nationalism.

Nationalism had an important impact on Irish society in the mid-nineteenth century. Notwithstanding the political activities of the Ribbonmen, descendants of the conspiratorial Defenders who had been allied with the United Irishmen in the 1798 insurrection, it was in this period that Irish nationalism became more identified with the lower strata of society, who assumed a growing presence in the nationalist cause. There does seem to be a correlation between this manifestation and the expansion of the Dublin nationalist newspapers, when they were made available through the nationalist organizations themselves, reading rooms and, not least, improvement in the levels of literacy. Moreover, most of the Dublin nationalist papers in this period were weekly, which was more appropriate for the lifestyle of the lower classes since the ritual of reading aloud, for example, often took place after Sunday Mass. More than ever, with the growth of the Dublin nationalist press, the pursuit of Irish nationalism became a shared experience between leaders and followers. The Dublin nationalist newspapers provided a medium through which leaders could communicate with their supporters. Importantly, at a time when the political franchise was highly restricted, the Dublin nationalist press had a distinctive function: to speak on behalf of the people through their leading articles, to give them a voice by printing their letters, and to publicise their political activities. In a way, for the many who lacked political representatives of their own, the nationalist press became a source of political power and journalists their political leaders. The Dublin nationalist press did much to promote a political consciousness among the lower classes, especially with the post-Famine urban growth that created a favourable environment for the accessibility of newspapers and the communication of ideas.

Women were given an opportunity to express their support for the Irish nationalist cause in the mid-nineteenth century, not least in their writings for the Dublin nationalist press, where they produced some fine verse. Among the women involved in these papers was the respected poet 'Speranza' (Jane Francesca Elgee), who, along with Margaret Callan, an assistant in *The Nation*'s office, took charge of Duffy's paper while he was imprisoned in July 1848.[5] Apart from their notable contributions to the columns of the Dublin nationalist press, these women tended mostly to be involved in supporting roles in the Irish nationalist movement during the mid-nineteenth century, although this was beginning to change. Fenian John Devoy claimed that women 'were the chief agents in keeping the [IRB] organization alive in Ireland from the time that Stephens left for America early in 1866 until the Rising of March 5, 1867.'[6] The women writers of the mid-nineteenth-century Dublin press who had shown their worth in the Irish nationalist cause were an inspiration for others. By the early twentieth century, women had become increasingly involved in the Irish nationalist movement; in 1896 poets Anna Johnston and Alice Milligan founded the advanced nationalist newspaper the *Shan Van Vocht* ('poor old woman').[7] Women were especially praised by the militant nationalist paper *The Spark*:

> In the Gaelic League, in the Industrial Associations, in Sinn Fein, the G.A.A., and, latest of all, in the Volunteer movement, they have given vivid evidence of their ability and capacity for genuine constructive work. Their judgment and their instinct have been rarely at fault, and most aggravating of all to the compromising male mind, they have been aggressively logical.[8]

Showing their ultimate commitment to Ireland, some women fought in the 1916 Rebellion. While the more extreme element of the Irish nationalist movement gave women the opportunity to express their loyalty to Ireland,

---

[5] Duffy, *Four Years of Irish History*, pp. 680–1

[6] Devoy, *Recollections*, p. 113.

[7] A monograph of Milligan's work has recently been published: Catherine Morris, *Alice Milligan and the Irish Cultural Revival* (Dublin: Four Courts Press, 2012).

[8] *The Spark*, 14 Feb. 1915.

it also provided a way for them to become politically involved in a growing modern society.

Modernity and Irish nationalism were complementary. In politics the extension of the franchise for a wider participation in the running of society was an aspiration for many Irish nationalists and was also a characteristic of modern times. An important concept that cut across opposing Irish nationalist policies, and one that resonated with radical Victorian thinking, held that when Ireland achieved independence, its government should be based on democratic principles. Developed from the days of the United Irishmen, universal male suffrage was firmly placed on the nationalist agenda in the mid-nineteenth century by many moderates and revolutionists alike. As George Boyce observed, 'nationalism and democracy walked hand in hand in Ireland.'[9] Thomas Davis's dictum 'Educate, that you may be free' was practised by the Dublin nationalist press.[10] These newspapers helped to create a modern society while aiding the dissemination of nationalist doctrine. The expansion of education, a potential gateway to opportunities and advancement in society, was promoted by the nationalist newspapers, where reading was greatly encouraged among the lower classes. Importantly, modernity is about communication and gaining knowledge. Nationalist newspapers imparted information to the people not just on local political, social and economic issues, but also made them aware of happenings in Great Britain and the wider world, helping to make Ireland less insular. Crucially for the development of Irish nationalism, they reminded the people of Ireland that they had a worthy and distinct cultural heritage, and were justified in seeking an improved quality of life in a land free from British rule.

A key aspect of the Dublin nationalist press was the link with America, which hosted many escapees from the effects of the Great Famine and from punishment by the British government for rebel activities. Irish nationalist newspapers were sent to North America, inspiring the creation of groups that mirrored those in the British Isles. Apart from providing volunteers willing to join those in Ireland in engaging in military combat against the British, most of their activities were centred around fund-raising for their mother country. The Dublin nationalist press did much to promote and publicize the Irish nationalist movement in America during the mid-nineteenth century, a link that was to become increasingly important for the realization of Irish nationalist aspirations.

---

[9] D. George Boyce, *Nineteenth-Century Ireland: The search for stability* (Dublin: Gill and Macmillan Ltd, 1990, 2005), p. 278.

[10] *Nation*, 5 Oct. 1844.

Irish nationalism was communicated not only through the usual prose columns of news and analysis in the Dublin nationalist press, but also through literature. While stories and verse could be enjoyed in their own right, they played a vital role in drawing people into the nationalist cause through different modes of expression; of particular value were verses composed to Irish airs. Literature was also a way of showing that the Irish still possessed their own cultural identity, and thus much encouragement was given to Irish writers. One favoured tactic of these newspapers was to familiarize readers with their heroic past through historical verse. Literary contributions, often based on research conducted by antiquarians, complemented and reinforced the political messages in the leading articles. In the 1858 *Irishman* William Smith O'Brien, writing to a newly formed Irish language association, praised the research conducted by antiquarians that provided insight into Ireland's historical and cultural past:

> Honour to the men – whether of Saxon, Norman, or Gaelic descent – whether Protestant or Catholic – whether rich or poor – who have laboured with a fond enthusiasm, to preserve and make known these memorials. Let us hope that amongst the members of your society will be found some who will emulate the zeal and continue the labours of those antiquarians to whom we are indebted for the little that is known by the public respecting the remains of Irish literature.[11]

Knowledge of the past was deemed essential for the development of Irish nationalism; rendering it accessible to the people through the medium of literature was highly useful, something the United Irishmen's press had done hitherto with much success.

The mid-nineteenth-century Dublin nationalist press was characterized not only by an emphatic attack on the 1800 Act of Union, but also, arguably by default, on the Protestant Ascendancy. The religion, political leadership and ownership of land by the Anglo-Irish were all resolutely challenged from this time, when campaigns by the Dublin nationalist press had the effect of undermining the Protestant Ascendancy. The democratization of the political system began with changes to the franchise from the 1850 Reform Act, followed by others later in the century that included the secret ballot in 1872 which meant that farmers could vote independently of their landlords. The economic and social powers of landlords were challenged in the mid-nineteenth century, which led to the Land Acts from 1870 onwards;

---

[11] 'The Irish Language', *Irishman*, 21 Aug. 1858.

crucially, the 1898 Local Government Act signalled an end to the control of local government by landlords. Furthermore, as noted earlier, church reform was accomplished in 1869 with the disestablishment of the Church of Ireland. At the turn of the century, the Protestant Ascendancy seemed to be in meltdown. By then the social, economic and political landscapes of Ireland had dramatically changed since the mid-nineteenth century. The hegemony of the Anglo-Irish over Irish society was now slipping away and it was only a matter of time before the majority Irish Catholic population achieved some form of independence from Great Britain. Through their increasing ascendancy the Catholic rural and urban middle classes seemed poised to take over the privileged place of the Anglo-Irish in society. Adding to this disquiet was the growing industrialization with its attendant factories, machines and slums, and an expanding proletariat, which also appeared to threaten the quality of life of the Anglo-Irish in this new modern age.

While the Anglo-Irish had an important role in the cultural leadership of mid-nineteenth-century Ireland, this was considerably overshadowed by the presence of *The Nation*. As the twilight years of the nineteenth century testified, although the Anglo-Irish experienced a diminishing social status, some of them sought refuge in a new dawn of creative energy found in what they perceived as an idyllic Gaelic past. The Anglo-Irish now achieved due recognition for their literary achievements in a revival that was based on antiquarian research and writings that their predecessors, notably Samuel Ferguson, had undertaken earlier in the century; these, combined with inspiration drawn from the archives of the cultural columns of the 1840s *Nation*, became the focus of a new and successful cultural identity.

Like the Anglo-Irish in the mid-nineteenth century, the Young Irelanders and the Fenians had sought an Irish cultural identity, but while appreciating culture for its own sake, what culture could do for Irish nationalism was far more important to them. Initially inspired by his friendship with an elderly John O'Leary, who introduced him to the romantic nationalism of the mid-nineteenth century, Yeats was in the vanguard of those Anglo-Irish writers who believed that literature should not be used for political ends. Another cultural group that emerged around the turn of the century that also wished to keep politics out of its activities was the Gaelic League.

The initial intention of the Gaelic League leadership, and in particular Douglas Hyde, who was President of the League, was that it should be non-political and non-sectarian, and in its early days it drew support from both Catholics and Protestants. The essential aim of the League was to preserve Gaelic culture and, in particular, the Irish language. The passing of a traditional rural society was seen by some Leaguers as a cultural tragedy and they wished to recreate what was deemed to have been lost over the years in the coming of a modern age. Douglas Hyde and other members hoped, furthermore, that a mission to save and promote the Irish language would unite creeds and rise above politics in an appreciation of a shared cultural past, echoing the early *Nation*. An emerging lower middle class that was well educated, and had more leisure time at its disposal, embraced the cultural activities of the Gaelic League. As improvements in social and economic conditions and the widening of the democratic political process gave Catholics a new confidence in society, the time seemed auspicious for a new national identity. Having acquired a political identity through their parliamentary party, though by this time somewhat tarnished following the fall-out from Parnell's political demise, it seemed natural for Catholics to assert their cultural identity in justifying their claim that they ought to become an independent nation state. This is what the mid-nineteenth-century Dublin nationalist press was saying; for example, the 1849 *Irishman* argued that qualification as a nation required both political independence and a unique culture. Perhaps it could be suggested that, by around the turn of the nineteenth century, the Irish Catholics did not have a strong enough claim to become a politically independent nation state as they had absorbed too much English culture, especially with the English language. The Dublin nationalist press of the mid-nineteenth century had emphasized, then, that although Ireland still had a unique cultural identity, it was slipping away. Nevertheless, there was now a *need* to carve out a distinct cultural identity, motivated in part by the disillusionment with politics and political leaders following the fall of Parnell. The people needed something to imbue them with belief and pride in their country.

The Gaelic Revival, also known as the Irish-Ireland movement, came to the rescue and, like the Anglo-Irish literary revival, it was based on the studies previously undertaken by scholars and antiquarians earlier in the century, many of whose works had been made popular by *The Nation*. It was not until the irrecoverable loss of the Irish language became an imminent reality that serious action was taken to preserve it in the late nineteenth century, although there remained a few isolated areas mainly in the west where Irish was still spoken. Like the changes in land ownership, this could be seen as moving towards a reversal of the conquest of Ireland, set in motion in the mid-nineteenth century, when the Dublin nationalist press, and *The Nation* in particular, made certain that the Irish language would not die out. Today, in the twenty-first century, the Irish language remains an identifiable part of the Irish nation.

Another movement that challenged the hegemony of English culture was the Gaelic Athletic Association (GAA), founded in 1884 by Michael Cusack. The GAA was much broader than the Gaelic League; besides the middle classes it also appealed to and involved the lower classes. Its main objective was to revive and promote Irish sports and other leisure activities. Although it was infiltrated by the IRB from the start, after 1901 the GAA was reformed as an open organization with wide appeal that included priests. While Eric Hobsbawm's concept of the 'invention of tradition' may have had some relevance to the nationalist writings of the mid-nineteenth century where there could sometimes have been a fine line between historical fact and myth, his theory appears far more applicable to the Gaelic Revival that began in the late nineteenth century, when there was much more of a contrived redefinition of the past and a far more self-conscious determination to resist Anglicization.[12] When the GAA was established, for example, the game of hurling was reinvented from a childhood memory with new rules and given a particular Irish nationalist persona to distinguish it from English games. Both the Anglo-Irish literary movement and the Gaelic League, like the Dublin nationalist press in the mid-nineteenth century, also looked to the past to regenerate the present.

The Gaelic League and the GAA gave the people a belief in their own cultural identity and later inspired them to engage in political activities to achieve independence. Of the two organizations associated with the Gaelic Revival, the GAA was probably the most effective, although the Gaelic League had an influence on future Irish nationalist leaders, for most of the signatories of the 1916 Proclamation had been members of the League. The 1840s *Nation*'s insistence on the importance of cultural nationalism could now be seen as a significant factor in the campaign to free Ireland from British rule. The League helped to politicize many Catholics, especially around 1911–12 with the prospect of Home Rule in sight. The eager response of those who participated in the activities of the Gaelic League and the GAA suggested that they were ready for a revived cultural identity. Despite initially being an inclusive movement, however, the Gaelic League failed to maintain unity of creed, and while it wished to keep politics out of its organization, ironically, it was from the Irish-Ireland movement that an advanced political force progressed to dominate Irish politics in the early twentieth century and led to a much troubled and divided Ireland.

In the mid-nineteenth century, while the proprietors, editors and writers of the Dublin nationalist press were responsible for recording current events, their participation in nationalist movements which influenced what they wrote in their newspapers greatly impacted on the development of Irish

---

[12] Eric Hobsbawm, 'Introduction: Inventing Traditions', in Eric Hobsbawm and Terence Ranger (eds), *The Invention of Tradition* (Cambridge: Cambridge University Press, 1983), pp. 1–14.

nationalism. Although these newspapers had an inspiring and primary role in the success of Irish nationalism in 1842–43, their central part in the Repeal secession of 1846 and that of the Irish Confederation in 1848 was highly damaging to the progress of the Irish nationalist cause. The Dublin nationalist press was linked with the 1848, 1849 and 1867 uprisings, both through personnel and ideology. In promoting the revival of Irish nationalism in the 1850s, the Dublin nationalist press supported important movements that were to come to fruition later: the cause of tenant right, the suggestion of a nationalist socialist agenda and the experimental formation of an independent Irish parliamentary party. Besides resolutely pursuing the advancement of constitutional nationalism, by the 1860s the Dublin nationalist press had established a firm commitment to revolutionary nationalism. These newspapers were also dedicated to the development of Irish cultural nationalism, particularly evident in their literary columns. The Dublin nationalist press was, undoubtedly, a key contributor to the formation and promotion of an Irish national identity, although, despite the aspirations of the 1840s *Nation*, it was an identity in which the union of class and creed essentially remained an elusive ideal. Clearly, the mid-nineteenth-century Dublin nationalist newspapers were not only important for the creation and dissemination of Irish nationalist ideology for their contemporaries, but also for laying down ideological pathways for future generations of Irish nationalists.

Select Bibliography

Primary Sources

Manuscripts

CATHOLIC UNIVERSITY OF AMERICA

Fenian Brotherhood Collection

NATIONAL ARCHIVES OF IRELAND

Chief Secretary's Office Registered Papers, 1864
Fenian Briefs, 1865–9
Police and Crime Records, Fenian Papers 1857–83

THE NATIONAL ARCHIVES, KEW

Home Office Fenian Papers

NATIONAL LIBRARY OF IRELAND

Thomas Davis Papers
Charles Gavan Duffy Papers
James Fintan Lalor Papers
Thomas A. Larcom Papers
Thomas Clarke Luby Papers
John Mitchel Correspondence 1852–55
William Smith O'Brien Papers
Young Ireland Papers

TRINITY COLLEGE DUBLIN, MANUSCRIPT ROOM

John Blake Dillon Papers
Police reports on political activities in Ireland, 1848

ROYAL IRISH ACADEMY, DUBLIN

Thomas Davis Papers
Charles Gavan Duffy Papers
Minutes of the Council of the Irish Confederation

Reference/Official documents

The Newspaper Press Directory and Advertisers' Guide (London: C. Mitchell, 1846, 1851 and 1864–65).

House of Commons Parliamentary Sessional Papers, 19th Century Newspaper Stamp Returns 1842–67.

Report of The Proceedings at the First Sitting of the Special Commission for the County of the City of Dublin, held at Green-street, Dublin, for the Trial of Thomas Clarke Luby, and Others, for Treason-Felony, "The Fenian Conspiracy," commencing on November 27, 1865 (Dublin: Alex Thom, 1866).

Newspapers

The Commonwealth, 1866–67 (London).
The Dublin Weekly Register, 1818–50.
The Evening Freeman, 1831–71.
The Freeman's Journal, 1763–1924.
The Harp, 1908–09 (New York); 1910 (Dublin).
The Irish Felon, 1848.
Irish Freedom, 1910–14.
The Irishman, 1848.
The Irishman, 1849–50.
The Irishman, 1858–85
The Irish People, 1863–65.
The Irish Tribune, 1848.
The Limerick and Clare Examiner, 1846–55.
The Morning Chronicle, 1769–1865 (London).
The Morning Register, 1824–43.
The Nation, 1842–97.
The Pilot, 1828–49.
Scissors and Paste, 1914–15.
The Spark, 1915–16.
The Tablet, 1840–49 (London); 1850–58 (Dublin); 1858–present (London).
The Times, 1785–present (London).
The Tribune, 1855–56.
United Ireland, 1881–98.
The United Irishman, 1848.
The Weekly Freeman's Journal, 1818–71.

Contemporary publications

Bradlaugh Bonner, H. *Charles Bradlaugh*, 7th ed. (London: T. Fisher Unwin, 1908).

Campion, J.T. *Michael Dwyer, or The Insurgent Captain of the Wicklow Mountains* (Glasgow: Cameron, Ferguson & Co. [1869]); (New York: P.J. Kenedy, 1875, 1882); (Dublin: M.H. Gill & Son, 1910, 1940).

Connolly, J. *Labour in Irish History* (Dublin: Maunsel & Co., 1910). Many editions have since followed.

Davitt, M. *The Fall of Feudalism in Ireland or the Story of the Land League Revolution*, Ó Lúing, S. (intro.) (Shannon: Irish University Press, 1970); 1st ed. (London & New York: Harper and Bros., 1904).

Denieffe, J. *A Personal Narrative of the Irish Revolutionary Brotherhood*, Ó Lúing, S. (intro.) (Shannon: Irish University Press, 1969); (New York: serially in *The Gael*, 1904); 1st ed. (New York: 1906).

Denvir, J. *The Life Story of an Old Rebel*, Ó Broin, L. (intro.) (Shannon: Irish University Press, 1972); 1st ed. (Dublin: Sealy, Bryers & Walker, 1910).

Devoy, J. *Recollections of an Irish Rebel*, Ó Lúing, S. (intro.) (Shannon: Irish University Press, 1969); 1st ed. (New York: 1929).

Dillon, W. *Life of John Mitchel, vols. I/II*, Dillon, J. (intro.) (London: Kegan Paul, Trench & Co., 1888).

Doheny, M. *The Felon's Track or History of the Attempted Outbreak in Ireland Embracing the Leading Events in the Irish Struggle from the year 1843 to the close of 1848*, Griffith, A. (pref.) (Dublin: M.H. Gill & Son Ltd., 1914); 1st ed. (New York: W.H. Holbrooke, 1849).

Duffy, C.G. *Young Ireland: A Fragment of Irish History, 1840–1850* (New York: D. Appleton, 1881).

— *Four Years of Irish History, 1845–49: A Sequel to "Young Ireland"* (London & New York: Cassell, Petter, Galpin & Co., 1883).

— *The League of North and South: An Episode in Irish History, 1850–1854* (London: Chapman & Hall Ltd., 1886).

— *Thomas Davis. The Memoirs of an Irish Patriot 1840–1846* (London: Kegan Paul, Trench, Trübner & Co. Ltd., 1890).

— *Short Life of Thomas Davis 1840–1846* (London: T. Fisher Unwin, 1895).

— *My Life in Two Hemispheres, vols. I/II* (London: T. Fisher Unwin, 1898).

Fox Bourne, H.R. *English Newspapers: Chapters in the History of Journalism, vol. II* (London: Chatto & Windus, 1887).

Frost, T. *The Secret Societies of the European Revolution 1776–1876, vol. II* (London: Tinsley Bros., 1876).

Healy, T.M. *Letters and leaders of my day 1855–1931, vols. I/II* (London: Thornton Butterworth, 1928).

Hepburn, A.C. *The Conflict of Nationality in Modern Ireland: Documents of Modern History* (London: Edward Arnold, 1980).

Kickham, C.J. *Knocknagow: or, The homes of Tipperary* (Dublin: James Duffy, Sons & Co., 1879). Numerous editions have followed.

Killen, J. (ed.), *The Decade of the United Irishmen: Contemporary Accounts 1791–1801* (Belfast: Blackstaff Press, 1997.

Lalor, J.F. *James Fintan Lalor: Patriot and Political Essayist 1807–1849*, Fogarty, L. (ed.), Griffith, A. (pref.) (Dublin: Talbot Press; London: T. Fisher Unwin, 1918); 2nd ed. (Dublin: Talbot Press, 1947).

— *The Writings of James Fintan Lalor*, O'Leary, J. (intro.) (Dublin: T.G. O'Donoghue, 1895).

Leno, J. Bedford. *The Aftermath: With Autobiography of the Author* (London: Reeves & Turner, 1892).

Madden, D.O. *Ireland and its Rulers; since 1829* (London: T.C. Newby, 1843–44).

Mill, J.S. *Principles of Political Economy With Some of Their Applications to Social Philosophy*, Robson, J.M. (ed.), Bladen, V.W., (intro.), *Collected Works, vols. II/III* (Toronto: University of Toronto Press, 1965).

— *Essays on England, Ireland, and the Empire*, Robson, J.M. (ed.), Hamburger, J. (intro.), *Collected Works, vol. VI* (Toronto: University of Toronto Press, 1982).

— *Newspaper Writings*, Robson, A.P. & Robson, J.M. (eds and intro.), *Collected Works, vols. XXII–XXV* (Toronto: University of Toronto Press, 1986).

Mitchel, J. *The Last Conquest of Ireland (Perhaps)* (Glasgow: Cameron, Ferguson & Co., [1876]); 1st pub. in book form by (Dublin: *The Irishman*'s office, 1861); latest printing, Maume, P. (ed.) (Dublin: University College Dublin Press, 2005).

— *Jail Journal*, Griffith, A. (pref.), 2nd ed. (Dublin: M.H. Gill & Son Ltd., [1913]).

Moran, D.P. 'The Gaelic Revival', *The New Ireland Review*, vol. 12, Jan. 1900, pp. 257–72.

O'Brien, W. 'Was Fenianism ever formidable?', *The Contemporary Review*, vol. 71, Jan.–June 1897, pp. 680–93.

O'Connell, M.R. (ed.), *The Correspondence of Daniel O'Connell 1846–7, vols. VII/VIII* (Dublin: The Blackwater Press, 1980).

O'Connor, J. *Recollections of Richard Pigott* (pamphlet) (Dublin: M.H. Gill & Son, 1889).

O'Donovan Rossa, D. *Rossa's Recollections 1838 to 1898: Memoirs of an Irish Revoutionary*, Ó Lúing, S. (intro.) (Shannon: Irish University Press, 1972); originally *United Irishman*, New York, 11 January 1896 to 7 May 1898, 1st ed. (New York: 1898).

O'Leary, J. *Recollections of Fenians and Fenianism, vols. I/II* (London: Downey & Co., 1896); reprinted Bourke, M., (intro.) (Shannon: Irish University Press, 1969).

O'Neill Daunt, W.J. *Ireland and her Agitators* (Dublin: John Browne, 1845).

— *Personal Recollections of the late Daniel O'Connell, M.P., vol. II* (London: Chapman & Hall, 1848).

Pearse, P. H. *Collected Works of Pádraic H. Pearse: The Story of a Success. The Man called Pearse, vol. IV/Political Writings and Speeches, vol. V*, Ryan, D. (ed.) (Dublin/Cork/Belfast: The Phoenix Publishing Co. Ltd., [1920–25]).

Pigott, R. *Personal Recollections of an Irish National Journalist*, 2nd ed. (Dublin: Hodges, Figgis & Co.; London: Simpkin, Marshall & Co., 1883).

Pope-Hennessy, J. 'What Do the Irish Read?', *The Nineteenth Century*, vol. 15, June 1884, pp. 920–30.

Rutherford, J. *The Secret History of the Fenian Conspiracy: Its Origin, Objects, and Ramifications, vols.I/II* (London: C. Keegan Paul & Co., 1877).

Roney, F. *Frank Roney, Irish Rebel and California Labor Leader: An Autobiography*, Cross, I.B. (ed.) (Berkeley: University of California Press, 1931).

Savage, J. *'98 and '48: The Modern Revolutionary History and Literature of Ireland*, 3rd ed. (New York: Redfield, 1856).
— *Fenian Heroes and Martyrs: Edited, with an historical introduction on "The Struggle for Irish Nationality"* (Boston: Patrick Donahoe, 1868).
Sullivan, A.M. *New Ireland: Political Sketches and Personal Reminiscences, vol. I*, 4th ed. (London: Sampson Low, Marston, Searle & Rivington, 1878); *vol. II*, 2nd ed. (1877).
Tone, T.W. *Life of Theobald Wolfe Tone Written by Himself and Continued by his Son, vols. I/II*, Tone, W.T.W. (ed.) (Washington: Gales & Seaton, 1826).

Secondary Sources

Books

Allen, J. & Ashton, O.R. (eds) *Papers for the People: A study of the Chartist press* (London: The Merlin Press Ltd, 2005).
Anderson, B. *Imagined Communities: Reflections on the Origin and Spread of Nationalism*, 3rd ed. (London & New York: Verso, 2006).
Anderson, W.K. *James Connolly and the Irish Left* (Dublin: Irish Academic Press Ltd., 1994).
Aspinall, A. *Politics and the Press 1780–1850* (London: Home & Val Thal, 1949).
Black, J. *The English Press 1621–1861* (Stroud: Sutton Publishing Ltd., 2001).
Bourke, M. *John O'Leary. A Study in Irish Separatism* (Tralee: Anvil Books, 1967).
Boyce, D.G. *Ireland 1828–1923: From Ascendancy to Democracy* (Oxford: Blackwell Publishers, 1992).
— *Nationalism in Ireland*, 3rd ed. (London & New York: Routledge, 1995).
— *Nineteenth-century Ireland: The search for stability*, 2nd ed. (Dublin: Gill & Macmillan, 2005).
Boyce, D.G., Curran, J. & Wingate, P. (eds) *Newspaper history from the seventeenth century to the present day* (London: Constable, 1978).
Boyce, D.G., Eccleshall, R. & Geoghegan, V. (eds) *Political Thought in Ireland since the Seventeenth Century* (London & New York: Routledge, 1993).
Boyce, D.G. & O'Day, A. (eds) *Parnell in Perspective* (London: Routledge, 1991).
— *The Making of Modern Irish History: Revisionism and the revisionist controversy* (London & New York: Routledge, 1996).
— *The Ulster Crisis 1885–1921* (Basingstoke, Hampshire: Palgrave Macmillan, 2006.
Boyle, J.W. (ed.) *Leaders and Workers*, 2nd ed. (Dublin & Cork: The Mercier Press, 1978).
Brown, M. *The Politics of Irish Literature: From Thomas Davis to W.B. Yeats* (London: Allen & Unwin, 1972).
Buckley, D.N. *James Fintan Lalor: Radical* (Cork: Cork University Press, 1990).
Callanan, F. *The Parnell Split 1890–91* (Cork: Cork University Press, 1992).
Comerford, R.V. *Charles J. Kickham: A Study in Irish nationalism and literature* (Dublin: Wolfhound Press, 1979).

— *The Fenians in Context: Irish Politics and Society, 1848–82* (Dublin: Wolfhound Press, 1985).

Cullen, L.M. *An Economic History of Ireland since 1600*, 2nd ed. (London: Batsford, 1987).

Cullen, L.M. (ed.) *Formation of the Irish Economy* (Cork: Mercier Press, 1969).

D'Arcy, W. *The Fenian Movement in the United States: 1858–1886*, 2nd ed. (New York: Russell & Russell, 1971).

Davis, R. *The Young Ireland Movement* (Dublin: Gill & Macmillan Ltd., 1987).

de Nie, M. *The Eternal Paddy: Irish Identity and the British Press, 1798–1882* (Madison: The University of Wisconsin Press, 2004).

de Paor, L. *On the Easter Proclamation and Other Declarations* (Dublin: Four Courts Press, 1997).

Dudley Edwards, R. *Patrick Pearse: The Triumph of Failure* (London: Victor Gollancz Ltd., 1977).

Eagleton, T. *Scholars and Rebels in Nineteenth-Century Ireland* (Oxford: Blackwell Publishers Ltd., 1999).

Elliott, M. *Wolfe Tone: Prophet of Irish Independence* (New Haven & London: Yale University Press, 1989); 2nd ed. (Liverpool: Liverpool University Press, 2012).

English, R. *Irish Freedom: The History of Nationalism in Ireland* (London: Pan Macmillan Ltd., 2006).

Foster, R.F. *Modern Ireland 1600–1972* (London: Penguin Books, 1989).

— *Paddy & Mr Punch: Connections in Irish and English History* (London: Penguin Books Ltd., 1995).

Geary, L.M. (ed.) *Rebellion and remembrance in modern Ireland* (Dublin: Four Courts Press Ltd., 2001).

Glandon, V.E. *Arthur Griffith and the Advanced-Nationalist Press: Ireland, 1900–1922* (New York: Peter Lang Publishing Inc., 1985).

Gray, P. *Famine, Land and Politics: British Government and Irish Society 1843–1850* (Dublin: Irish Academic Press, 1999).

Gwynn, D. *Young Ireland and 1848* (Cork: Cork University Press, 1949).

Healy, J.J. *Life and Times of Charles J. Kickham* (Dublin: J. Duffy & Co., 1915).

Hearn, J. *Rethinking Nationalism: A Critical Introduction* (Basingstoke & New York: Palgrave Macmillan: 2006).

Hobsbawm, E. & Ranger, T. (eds) *The Invention of Tradition* (Cambridge: Cambridge University Press, 1983).

Hobsbawm, E.J. *Nations and Nationalism since 1780: Programme, myth, reality*, 2nd ed. (Cambridge & New York: Cambridge University Press, 1992).

Inglis, B. *The Freedom of the Press in Ireland 1784–1841* (London: Faber & Faber, 1954).

Jenkins, B. *Irish Nationalism and the British State: From Repeal to Revolutionary Nationalism* (Montreal & London: McGill-Queen's University Press, 2006).

Jones, A. *Powers of the Press: Newspapers, Power and the Public in Nineteenth-Century England* (Aldershot: Scolar Press, 1996).

Kee. R. *The Green Flag: A History of Irish Nationalism* (London: Penguin Books Ltd., 2000).
— *The Laurel and the Ivy: The story of Charles Steward Parnell and Irish Nationalism* (London: Penguin Books, 1994).
Kinealy, C. *This great calamity, 1845–52*, 2nd ed. (Dublin: Gill & Macmillan, 2006).
— *Repeal and revolution: 1848 in Ireland* (Manchester: Manchester University Press, 2009).
Knowlton, S.R. *Popular Politics and the Irish Catholic Church: The rise and fall of the Independent Party 1850–1859* (New York & London: Garland, 1991).
Legg, M.L. *Newspapers and Nationalism: The Irish Provincial Press 1850–9* (Dublin: Four Courts, 1999).
Lyons, F.S.L. *Ireland since the Famine*, 2nd ed. (London: Fontana Press, 1985).
Macintyre, A. *The Liberator: Daniel O'Connell and the Irish Party 1830–1847* (London: Hamish Hamilton, 1965).
McConville, S. *Irish Political Prisoners, 1848–1922: Theatres of War* (London & New York: Routledge, 2003).
McDowell, R.B. (ed.) *Social Life in Ireland, 1800–1845* (Dublin: Colm O'Lochlainn, The Sign of the Three Candles Press, 1957).
McGee, O. *The IRB. The Irish Republican Brotherhood, from the Land League to Sinn Féin*, 2nd ed. (Dublin: Four Courts Press, 2007).
McNicholas, A. *Politics, Religion and the Press: Irish Journalism in Mid-Victorian England* (Oxford: Peter Lang AG, 2007).
Mokyr, J. *Why Ireland starved: A quantitative and analytical history of the Irish economy, 1800–1850*, 2nd ed. (London: Allen & Unwin, 1985).
Molony, J.N. *A soul came into Ireland: Thomas Davis 1814–1845* (Dublin: Geography Publications, 1995).
Moody, T.W. *Davitt and Irish Revolution 1846–82* (Oxford: Oxford University Press, 1981).
Moody, T.W. (ed.) *The Fenian Movement*, 2nd ed. (Cork & Dublin: The Mercier Press, 1978).
Morris, C. *Alice Milligan and the Irish Cultural Revival* (Dublin: Four Courts, 2012).
Morash, C. *Writing the Irish Famine* (Oxford: Clarendon Press, 1995).
Morris, C. *Alice Milligan and the Irish Cultural Revival* (Dublin: Four Courts, 2012).
Mulvey, H.F. *Thomas Davis and Ireland: A Biographical Study* (Washington, D.C.: The Catholic University of America Press, 2003).
Munter, R. *History of the Irish Newspaper, 1685–1760* (Cambridge: Cambridge University Press, 1967).
Newsinger, J. *Fenianism in Mid-Victorian Britain* (London & Boulder, Colorado: Pluto Press, 1994)
Norman, E.R. *The Catholic Church and Ireland in the Age of Rebellion, 1859–1873* (London: Longmans, 1965).

Nowlan, K.B. *The Politics of Repeal: A Study in the Relations between Great Britain and Ireland, 1841–50* (London: Routledge & Kegan Paul, 1965).

Ó Broin, L. *Fenian Fever: An Anglo-American Dilemma* (London: Chatto and Windus, 1971).

— *Revolutionary Underground. The Story of the Irish Republican Brotherhood 1858–1924* (Dublin: Gill and Macmillan Ltd., 1976).

Ó Cathaoir, B. *John Blake Dillon, Young Irelander* (Dublin: Irish Academic Press Ltd., 1990).

Ó Ciosáin, N. *Print and Popular Culture in Ireland, 1750–1850* (Basingstoke: Macmillan; New York: St Martin's Press, 1997).

O'Connell, M.R. *Daniel O'Connell: The Man and his Politics*, foreword by C.C. O'Brien (Dublin: Irish Academic Press, 1990).

Ó Gráda, C. *Black '47 and Beyond: The Great Irish Famine in History, Economy, and Memory* (Princeton, New Jersey & Chichester, West Sussex: Princeton University Press, 1999).

O'Hegarty, P.S. *John Mitchel: An Appreciation, with some Account of Young Ireland* (Dublin & London: Maunsel & Co. Ltd., 1917).

O'Mahony, P. & Delanty, G. *Rethinking Irish History: Nationalism, Identity and Ideology* (Basingstoke: Macmillan Press Ltd., 1998).

Oram, H. *The Newspaper Book: A History of Newspapers in Ireland, 1649–1983, vol. I* (Dublin: MO Books, 1983).

Ó Tuathaig, G. *Ireland before the famine 1798–1848* 2nd ed. (Dublin: Gill & Macmillan, 1990).

Price, R. (ed.) *1848 in France* (London: Thames and Hudson Ltd., 1975).

Rafferty, O.P. *The Church, the State and the Fenian Threat, 1861–75* (Basingstoke: Macmillan; New York: St Martin's Press, 1999).

Ramón, M. *A Provisional Dictator: James Stephens and the Fenian Movement* (Dublin: University College Dublin Press, 2007).

Ryan, D. *The Fenian Chief: A biography of James Stephens*, Lynch, P. (intro.) (Dublin: M.H. Gill & Son Ltd., 1967).

Shipkey, R.C. *Robert Peel's Irish Policy: 1812–1846* (New York & London: Garland Publishing Inc., 1987).

Sloan, R. *William Smith O'Brien and the Young Ireland Rebellion of 1848: The road to Ballingary* (Dublin: Four Courts, 2000).

Spencer, P. & Wollman, H. *Nationalism: A Critical Introduction* (London: Sage Publications, 2002).

Strauss, E. *Irish Nationalism and British Democracy* (London: Methuen & Co., 1951).

Thornley, D. *Isaac Butt and Home Rule* (London: MacGibbon & Kee, 1964.)

Thuente, M.H. *The Harp Re-strung: The United Irishman and the Rise of Literary Nationalism* (Syracuse: Syracuse University Press, 1994).

Vaughan, W.E. (ed.) *A New History of Ireland: Ireland under the Union, 1801–1870, vol. V* (Oxford: Oxford University Press, 1989).

Warwick-Haller, S. *William O'Brien and the Irish Land War* (Dublin: Irish Academic Press, 1990).

Whyte, J.H. *The Independent Irish Party: 1850–9* (London: Oxford University Press, 1958).
Williams, L.A. *Daniel O'Connell, The British Press and The Irish Famine: Killing Remarks* (Hampshire & Vermont: Ashgate Publishing Ltd., 2003).
Winstanley, M.J. *Ireland and the Land Question 1800–1922* (London: Methuen, 1984).

Articles and chapters

Anton, B. 'Women of *The Nation*', *History Ireland*, vol. 1 (3), Autumn 1993, pp. 34–7.
Aspinall, A. 'The Circulation of Newspapers in the Early Nineteenth Century', *The Review of English Studies*, vol. 22 (85), Jan. 1946, pp. 29–43.
Beames, M.R. 'The Ribbon Societies: Lower-Class Nationalism in Pre-Famine Ireland', *Past and Present*, vol. 97 (1), Nov. 1982, pp. 128–43.
Bew, P. & Maume, P. 'The Great Advocate', *Dublin Review of Books*, (8) Winter 2008–09, http://www.drb.ie, accessed 27 June 2009.
Boyd, A. 'Catholicism and republicanism in Ireland', *Contemporary Review*, vol. 266 (1,549), Feb. 1995, pp. 57–64.
Brillman, M.L. 'Loyalty and Repeal: The *Nation*, 1842–46', in Rafter, K. (ed.), *Irish journalism before independence: More a disease than a profession* (Manchester: Manchester University Press, 2011), pp. 36–48.
Buckley, M. 'John Mitchel, Ulster and Irish Nationality (1842–1848)', *Studies. An Irish Quarterly Review*, vol. 65, Spring 1976, pp. 30–44.
Cannavan, J. 'Romantic Revolutionary Irishwomen: Women, Young Ireland and 1848', in Kelleher, M. & Murphy, J.M. (eds), *Gender Perspectives in Nineteenth-Century Ireland. Public and Private Spheres* (Dublin: Irish Academic Press, 1997), pp. 212–20.
Clarke, R. 'The Relations between O'Connell and the Young Irelanders', *Irish Historical Studies*, vol. 3 (9), March 1942, pp. 18–30.
Comerford, R.V. 'Patriotism as pastime: The appeal of fenianism in the mid-1860s', *Irish Historical Studies*, vol. 22 (87), March 1981, pp. 239–50.
Curtis, Jr., L.P. 'Moral and Physical Force: The Language of Violence in Irish Nationalism', *Journal of British Studies*, vol. 27 (2), April 1988, pp. 150–89.
Delanty, G. 'Negotiating the Peace in Northern Ireland', *Journal of Peace Research*, vol. 32, (3) 1995, pp. 257–64.
de Nie, M. '"A Medley Mob of Irish–American Plotters and Irish Dupes": The British Press and Transatlantic Fenianism', *Journal of British Studies*, vol. 40 (2), April 2001, pp. 213–40.
Dudley Edwards, R. 'The contribution of Young Ireland to the national idea', in Pender, S. (ed.), *Essays and Studies Presented to Professor Tadhg Ua Donnchadha (Torna) on the occasion of his seventieth birthday September 4th 1944* (Cork: Cork University Press, 1947), pp. 115–33.
English, R. 'Reflections on Republican Socialism in Ireland: Marxian Roots and Irish Historical Dynamics', *History of Political Thought*, vol. 17 (4), Winter 1996, pp. 555–70.

Escott, T.H.S. 'The Journalist in Ireland', in *Masters of English Journalism. A Study of Personal Forces* (London: T. Fisher-Unwin, 1911), pp. 305–21.

Farrell Moran, S. 'Patrick Pearse and the European Revolt against Reason', *Journal of the History of Ideas*, vol. 50 (4), Oct.–Dec. 1989, pp. 625–43.

Foley, M. 'Colonialism and Journalism in Ireland', *Journalism Studies*, vol. 5 (3), Aug. 2004, pp. 373–85.

Foy, M. 'Ulster Unionist Propaganda against Home Rule 1912–14', *History Ireland* vol. 4 (1), Spring 1996, pp. 49–53.

Garvin, T. 'Defenders, Ribbonmen and Others: Underground Political Networks in Pre-Famine Ireland', *Past & Present*, vol. 96 (1), Aug. 1982, pp. 133–55.

Glandon, V.E. 'The Irish Press and Revolutionary Irish Nationalism', *Éire-Ireland*, vol. 16 (1), 1981, pp. 21–33.

Hammond, J.W. '"The Dublin Gazette", 1705–1922', *Dublin Historical Record*, vol. 13 (3/4), 1953, pp. 108–17.

Higgins, R. 'The *Nation* Reading Rooms', in James H. Murphy (ed.), *The Oxford History of the Irish Book, vol. IV: The Irish Book in English, 1800–1891* (Oxford: Oxford University Press, 2011), pp. 262–73.

Hill, J.R. 'The Intelligentsia and Irish Nationalism in the 1840s', *Studia Hibernica* (20), 1980, pp. 73–109.

Inglis, B. 'Review of Aspinall, A. *Politics and the Press*', *Irish Historical Studies*, vol. 6 (24), Sept. 1949, pp. 301–3.

— 'O'Connell and the Irish press 1800–42', *Irish Historical Studies*, vol. 8 (29), March 1952, pp. 1–27.

Joyce, T. '"Ireland's trained and marshalled manhood": The Fenians in the mid-1860s', in Kelleher, M. & Murphy, J.M. (eds), *Gender Perspectives in Nineteenth-Century Ireland: Public and Private Spheres* (Dublin: Irish Academic Press, 1997), pp. 70–80.

Kane, A. 'Narratives of Nationalism: Constructing Irish National Identity during the Land War, 1879–82', *National Identities*, vol. 2 (3), 2000, pp. 245–64.

— 'The ritualization of newspaper reading and political consciousness: The role of newspapers in the Irish land war', in McBride, L.W. (ed.), *Reading Irish Histories: Texts, contexts, and memory in modern Ireland* (Dublin: Four Courts Press, 2003), pp. 40–61.

Kelly, M. 'Dublin Fenianism in the 1880s: "The Irish Culture of the Future"?', *The Historical Journal*, vol. 43 (3) 2000, pp. 729–50.

Knowlton, S.R. 'The Politics of John Mitchel: A Reappraisal', *Eire-Ireland* vol. 22 (2) Summer 1987, pp. 38–55.

Knowlton, S.R. 'The Quarrel between Gavan Duffy and John Mitchel: Implications for Ireland', *Albion: A Quarterly Journal Concerned with British Studies*, vol. 21 (4), Winter 1989, pp. 581–90.

Lanier, S.C. '"It is new-strung and shan't be heard": Nationalism and memory in the Irish harp tradition', *British Journal of Ethnomusicology*, vol. 8, 1999, pp. 1–26.

Larkin, F.M. '"A Great Daily Organ": The *Freeman's Journal*, 1763–1924', *History Ireland*, vol. 14 (2), March/April 2006, pp. 44–9.
— 'Parnell, politics and the press in Ireland, 1875–1924' in McCartney, D. and Travers, P. (eds), *Parnell Reconsidered* (Dublin: University College Dublin Press, 2013), pp. 76–91.
Lenin, V.I. 'The "Plan" for an All-Russian Political Newspaper', in *What Is To Be Done?* (Connecticut, USA: Martino Publishing, 2013), pp. 143–65.
Lowth, C.F. 'James O'Connor, Fenian, and the Tragedy of 1890', *Dublin Historical Record*, vol. 55 (2), Autumn 2002, pp. 132–53.
Lynch, N. 'Defining Irish Nationalist Anti-imperialism: Thomas Davis and John Mitchel', *Éire-Ireland*, vol. 42 (1/2), Spring/Summer 2007, pp. 82–107.
Mac Giolla C. 'Fenian documents in the State Paper Office', *Irish Historical Studies*, vol. 16 (63), March 1969, pp. 258–84.
McCaffrey, L.J. 'Isaac Butt and the Home Rule Movement: A Study in Conservative Nationalism', *The Review of Politics*, vol. 22 (1), Jan. 1960, pp. 72–95.
— 'Irish Nationalism and Irish Catholicism: A Study in Cultural Identity', *Church History*, vol. 42 (4), Dec. 1973, pp. 524–34.
McCartney, D. 'The Political Use of History in the Work of Arthur Griffith', *Journal of Contemporary History*, vol. 8 (1), Jan. 1973, pp. 3–19.
McDowell, R.B. 'Irish Newspapers in the Eighteenth Century', *The Crane Bag*, vol. 8 (2), 1984, pp. 40–3.
McNicholas, A. 'REBELS AT HEART: The National Brotherhood of Saint Patrick and the *Irish Liberator*', *Media History*, vol. 13 (1), 2007, pp. 25–41.
— 'Co-operation, compromise and confrontation: The *Universal News*, 1860–69', *Irish Historical Studies*, vol. 35 (139), May 2007, pp. 311–26.
Mercier, V. 'Irish Writers and English Readers: Literature and Politics, 1798–1845', in Dillon, E. (ed.), *Modern Irish Literature: Sources and Founders* (Oxford: Clarendon Press, 1994), pp. 35–63.
Moody, T.W. 'Thomas Davis and the Irish nation', *Hermathena. A Dublin University Review*, 103, Autumn 1966, pp. 5–31.
Newsinger, J. 'Old Chartists, Fenians, and New Socialists', *Éire-Ireland*, vol. 17 (2), Summer 1982, pp. 19–45.
Ó Cathaoir, B. 'The Rising of 1848', *History Ireland*, vol. 6 (3), Autumn 1998, pp. 26–8.
O'Connell, Maurice R. 'Young Ireland and the Catholic Clergy in 1844: Contemporary Deceit and Historical Falsehood', *The Catholic Historical Review*, vol. 74 (2), April 1988, pp. 199–225.
Ó Gráda, C. 'A Note on Nineteenth-Century Irish Emigration Statistics', *Population Studies*, vol. 29 (1), March 1975, pp. 143–9.
O'Higgins, R. 'The Irish Influence in the Chartist Movement', *Past and Present*, vol. 20 (1), Nov. 1961, pp. 83–96.
O'Neill, T.P. 'Fintan Lalor and the 1849 movement', *An Cosantoir: The Irish defence journal*, vol. 10 (4), April 1950, p. 174–9.

Owens, G. 'Popular mobilisation and the rising of 1848: The clubs of the Irish Confederation', in Geary, L.M. (ed.), *Rebellion and remembrance in modern Ireland* (Dublin: Four Courts Press, 2001), pp. 51–63.

Pender, S. 'Fenian Papers in the Catholic University of America', *Journal of the Cork Historical and Archaeological Society*, vol. 75 (221), Jan.–June 1970, pp. 36–53.

Pickering, P.A. '"Irish First": Daniel O'Connell, the Native Manufacture Campaign, and Economic Nationalism, 1840–44', *Albion: A Quarterly Journal Concerned with British Studies*, vol. 32 (4), Winter 2000, pp. 598–616.

Quigley, K. 'Daniel O'Connell and the Leadership Crisis within the Irish Repeal Party, 1843–1845', *Albion: A Quarterly Journal Concerned with British Studies*, vol. 2 (2), 1970, pp. 99–107.

Quinn, J. 'John Mitchel and the rejection of the nineteenth century', *Éire-Ireland*, vol. 38 (3/4), Fall/Winter 2003, pp. 90–108.

Rafroidi, P., 'Principal Irish Periodicals from 1789 to 1850', in *Irish Literature in English. The Romantic Period (1789–1850), vol. II*, translated from 1972 French ed. (Gerrards Cross, Bucks.: Colin Smythe Ltd., 1980), pp. 379–92.

Rynne, F. 'Focus on the Fenians: The *Irish People* trials, November 1865–January 1866', *History Ireland*, vol. 13 (6), Nov./Dec. 2005, pp. 41–6.

Sloan, B. 'The autobiographies of John Mitchel and Charles Gavan Duffy: A study in contrasts', *Eire-Ireland*, vol. 22 (2), Summer 1987, pp. 27–37.

Sloan, R. 'O'Connell's liberal rivals in 1843', *Irish Historical Studies*, vol. 30 (117), May 1996, pp. 47–65.

Wheatley, M. 'John Redmond and federalism in 1910', *Irish Historical Studies*, vol. 32 (127), May 2001, pp. 343–64.

Conferences

Benatti, F. 'Reading Networks in Ireland: *The Nation*, 1842–6', Trading Books – Trading Ideas Conference, Koninklijke Bibliotheek, The Hague, Netherlands, 14 July 2006.

Theses

Cullen, P.M. 'James Stephens and the *Irish People* in the evolution of Irish nationalist politics in the nineteenth century', (MPhil, University College Cork, 1997).

Leo, M. 'The influence of the Fenians and their press on public opinion in Ireland, 1863–70' (MLit., Trinity College Dublin, 1976).

O'Brien, W.G. 'Imagining Catholic Ireland: The nationalist press and the creation of national identity, 1843–1870' (PhD, University of Limerick, 2007).

Tally, P.F. 'The Growth of the Dublin Weekly Press and the Development of Irish Nationalism, 1810–79', (PhD, University of Wisconsin-Madison, 2003).

Reference

Boylan, H. *A Dictionary of Irish Biography* 3rd ed. (Dubin: Gill & Macmillan, 1998).

Connolly, S.J. (ed.) *The Oxford Companion to Irish History*, 2nd ed. (Oxford: Oxford University Press, 2002).

Matthew, H.C.G. & Harrison, B. (eds) *Oxford Dictionary of National Biography* (Oxford: Oxford University Press, 2004–present).

North, J.S. *The Waterloo Directory of Irish newspapers and periodicals, 1800–1900* Phase II, (Waterloo, Ontario: North Waterloo Academic Press, 1986).

Index

Printed and bound by CPI Group (UK) Ltd, Croydon, CR0 4YY

23/04/2025

14660988-0005